D1337281

INDEPENDENT SECTOR

INDEPENDENT SECTOR is a coalition of 650 corporations, foundations, and voluntary organizations with national interests in and impact on philanthropy, voluntary action, and other activities related to the educational, scientific, cultural, and religious life, as well as the health and welfare, of the nation.

INDEPENDENT SECTOR is a meeting ground where diverse elements in and related to the sector can come together and learn how to improve their performance and effectiveness.

INDEPENDENT SECTOR is serving the sector through
- education, to improve the public's understanding of the independent sector
- research, to develop a comprehensive store of knowledge about the sector
- government relations, to coordinate the multitude of interconnections between the sector and the various levels of government
- encouragement of effective sector leadership and management, to maximize service to individuals and society, by promoting educational programs for managers and practitioners
- communication within the sector to identify shared problems and opportunities

The impact of INDEPENDENT SECTOR's effort can be measured by the growth in support of the sector, as manifested by increased giving and volunteering.

For additional information, please contact

INDEPENDENT
SECTOR

1828 L Street, N.W.
Washington, DC 20036
(202) 223-8100

THE FUTURE OF THE NONPROFIT SECTOR

Virginia A. Hodgkinson
Richard W. Lyman
and Associates

△ △ △ △ △ △ △ △ △ △ △ △ △ △ △

THE FUTURE OF THE NONPROFIT SECTOR

△ △ △ △ △ △ △ △ △ △ △ △ △ △ △

Challenges, Changes, and Policy Considerations

 Jossey-Bass Publishers

San Francisco • London • 1989

THE FUTURE OF THE NONPROFIT SECTOR
Challenges, Changes, and Policy Considerations
by Virginia A. Hodgkinson, Richard W. Lyman, and Associates

Copyright © 1989 by: Jossey-Bass Inc., Publishers
350 Sansome Street
San Francisco, California 94104
&
Jossey-Bass Limited
28 Banner Street
London EC1Y 8QE

Copyright under International, Pan American, and
Universal Copyright Conventions. All rights
reserved. No part of this book may be reproduced
in any form—except for brief quotation (not to
exceed 1,000 words) in a review or professional
work—without permission in writing from the publishers.

Library of Congress Cataloging-in-Publication Data

Hodgkinson, Virginia Ann.
    The future of the nonprofit sector : challenges, changes, and
policy considerations / Virginia A. Hodgkinson, Richard W. Lyman,
and associates.
        p.   cm. — (The Jossey-Bass nonprofit sector series)
    ISBN 1-55542-179-2
    1. Corporations, Nonprofit—United States.   I. Lyman, Richard W.
II. Title.   III. Series.
HD2769.2.U6H64   1989
338.7'4—dc20   89-45596
                                                                 CIP

Manufactured in the United States of America

The paper in this book meets the guidelines for
permanence and durability of the Committee on
Production Guidelines for Book Longevity of
the Council on Library Resources.

JACKET DESIGN BY WILLI BAUM

FIRST EDITION

Code 8952

INDEPENDENT
SECTOR   A Publication of INDEPENDENT SECTOR

The
Jossey-Bass
Nonprofit
Sector
Series

Contents

△ △ △ △ △ △ △ △ △ △ △ △ △ △ △

ix

Foreword

△ △ △ △ △ △ △ △ △ △ △ △ △ △ △ △

The publication of *The Future of the Nonprofit Sector* is a heartening demonstration of the rapid growth of serious research on nonprofit organizations, philanthropy, and voluntary action.

When, in 1978, we formed an organizing committee to determine whether a national organization representing the independent sector in all its diversity was feasible, it was immediately clear that we needed research to provide us with a better understanding of the sector. This was among the primary reasons why INDEPENDENT SECTOR was established. Since this organization's founding in 1980, it has become increasingly evident that building a knowledge base about the sector, including its roles and accomplishments, is our best means of strengthening the sector and dealing with governmental challenges that would limit its service to the public.

The contributors to this volume do not provide simple answers to questions about the role and functions of the nonprofit sector. Many of them note the increasing complexity of defining both the sector and its responsibilities, and several contributors identify major policy problems, including increasing governmental regulation, that will continue to challenge leaders of nonprofit organizations. Some question the criteria for tax-exempt status and suggest that certain nonprofit organizations should no longer be tax-exempt, while others remind us that charitable organizations need to pay more attention to the growing problems of low-income people and of the fundamentally moral purposes that these organizations serve. Many of the chapters reveal the appalling lack of recorded history and good information available to study the various issues. But taken together the chapters do provide a far clearer picture of the terrain than we had a decade ago. They also remind us that in trying to define this sector we must not forget that it functions in a wider society of government and business and that it is at the blurred boundaries of these sectors that many public policy issues emerge.

One of the objectives of the INDEPENDENT SECTOR research program is to encourage the development of a bookshelf on philanthropy that will build a new tradition of scholarship on and about this sector. This volume is an important part of that effort. It marks a major advance in providing current and future scholars with an analysis of what the sector was, is, and can become. The resolution of many of the challenges facing the nonprofit sector will be determined by informed people who lead nonprofit organizations and take heed of what we are learning about improving our effectiveness and better educating the public about this sector and about the trends that may damage the sector's potential to serve the public in the future.

Virginia Hodgkinson and Richard Lyman deserve great credit for preparing this volume. It provides scholars and practitioners with clear guidelines for building a stronger voluntary sector.

July 1989   Brian O'Connell
                                     President
                                     INDEPENDENT SECTOR

Preface

△ △ △ △ △ △ △ △ △ △ △ △ △ △ △ △

The rapid restructuring of the U.S. economy has led to changing perceptions about the respective roles of the nonprofit sector, government, and business in providing the kinds of services the public wants or needs on an organized basis. A variety of public policy issues and challenges to the nonprofit sector reflect these changes, such as proposals to alter the determination of tax-exempt status of nonprofit organizations, which were caused by competition between nonprofits and small business; proposals to tax nonprofits on portions of their income or to limit or eliminate property tax exemptions; attempts to limit the advocacy rights of organizations receiving government funds; and increasing limitations on the traditional resources of nonprofit organizations through cutbacks in federal funding for a variety of human services and the elimination of the charitable deduction for nonitemizers. These major economic and public policy shifts have led to a blurring of distinctions on the respective roles and responsibilities of nonprofits, government, and business and, accordingly, some confusion in public understanding of the roles that each of the sectors play in our society. The authors of *The Future of the Nonprofit Sector* analyze these and other issues from the perspective of the nonprofit sector and contribute to the public debate.

The purposes of this volume are to identify, review, and define the major issues affecting the nonprofit sector; to review current trends in the sector and their implications for public policy; and to identify major problems that need further study and resolution. This volume is needed because research on the nonprofit sector was neglected until a decade ago. Recent research about this sector has led to a variety of perspectives on the role and functions of the nonprofit sector, and many of the contributors to this volume are engaged in research that could have a major impact on the policy debates that relate to the future of nonprofit organizations. If this volume helps to identify the issues more clearly, to delineate areas of confusion or contradiction, and to offer a more orderly agenda for research and action, then it will have served its purpose.

After reviewing the chapters in this book, one can only conclude that we have come a considerable distance in stimulating research. The variety of both the subjects dealt with and the scholars dealing with them is impressive, as is the degree of sophistication with which much of the research and analysis was carried out and presented. It is surely cause for celebration that research on the nonprofit sector is characterized more than it used to be by critical scholarly approaches rather than by a polarization between thinly disguised advocacy and crude quasi-Marxist polemic. One of the very real virtues of bringing these various perspectives together is that it causes the authors—law professors, economists, philosophers, experts in public administration, historians, statisticians, psychologists, sociologists, marketing people, geographers, and educationists—to meet and encounter firsthand one another's various thought processes. The structure of American higher education tends to keep them apart, and so does the nature of specialized learning; scholarly disciplines advance along narrow trails, developing languages peculiar to themselves and understandable only to devotees of the same specialty.

That is why the gathering of the academic disciplines represented by this volume is so important. Although much of the work is narrow, disciplinary inquiry and some of it is important but limited nuts-and-bolts advice from the factory floor of philanthropy, the fact of its being brought together in this way offers hope for improved understanding of the not-for-profit sector as a whole: what it has been; what it is today; and what its possibilities are for the future, which we can only dimly discern but in many ways is already upon us.

Because of the interdisciplinary nature of this volume, the authors have multiple, seemingly contradictory, views and conclusions about the significance of public policy changes and the current and future roles of the nonprofit sector. The variety of these points of view should provide the reader with a sense of how large, complex, and integral to the basic functioning of our nation the sector is. This volume clearly shows that there is not a consensus among scholars and practitioners about the role, scope, and responsibilities of the nonprofit sector, nor is there one even about what kinds of organizations ought to be included within the sector. Some of the controversy clearly emerges from scholars becoming acquainted with the nonprofit sector, but it emerges as well from the growing intrasectoral shifts and restructuring taking place within the larger society.

Who Should Read This Book

Although this volume should be of interest particularly to researchers in social science disciplines, it should also be read by executives of voluntary organizations, foundation and corporate grantmakers, and public policy decision makers. It includes an examination of many of the policy issues that are facing and will continue to face both policy makers at the national and local levels and leaders of voluntary organizations. Some of these public policy challenges and the recommendations for their resolution, particularly those that deal with the commercialization of nonprofit organizations and public accountability, could lead to profound changes in the structure of the nonprofit sector and in the criteria for tax exemption. Because of this, this book ought to be studied by all those in leadership positions in nonprofit organizations. This volume is intended to both stimulate further research and enhance public discussion of important public policy issues concerning the role of the nonprofit sector in a rapidly changing economy and society.

Organization and Overview of the Contents

The volume is divided into seven parts that elucidate the practice and key areas of inquiry as well as the public policy debate that could have a major impact on the future of the nonprofit sector.

Part One gives a broad overview of the changing roles

and responsibilities of the nonprofit sector. Chapter One introduces the major challenges facing the nonprofit sector. The authors of the following chapters examine past and current trends and suggest what functions nonprofit organizations may fulfill in the future as a result of major changes occurring in federal public policy, political ideology, and the U.S. economy.

In Chapter Two, "How the Legitimacy of the Sector Has Eroded," Carroll L. Estes, Elizabeth A. Binney, and Linda A. Bergthold analyze a series of disturbing trends that have led to the erosion of the importance of the nonprofit sector in American society. These trends include declining public support and understanding about the sector and its functions; declining federal support for nonprofits; state governments' questioning of the tax-exempt status of nonprofits; and a tendency within nonprofit organizations to sacrifice "end" goals of service, charity, and democratic participation for the "means" goals of management for survival.

In Chapter Three, "The Changing Partnership Between the Voluntary Sector and the Welfare State," Lester M. Salamon reviews the research conducted on the nonprofit sector by the Urban Institute over the past five years and suggests that nonprofit organizations engaged in social welfare are moving from a partnership with government to a more active role in the private economy. He notes that such a trend could lead to nonprofit organizations serving only clients who can afford to pay for their services and abrogating their responsibilities to serve populations in need. This change in role could affect the tax-exempt status of many organizations and the long-term health of the nonprofit sector.

In Chapter Four, "The Evolving Role of Foundations," James Allen Smith provides a historical analysis of the role that private foundations have played in supporting various social science research institutions, or "think tanks," and the impact of such research on public policy.

In Chapter Five, "Trends in Accountability and Regulation of Nonprofits," Marion R. Fremont-Smith presents an overview of nonprofit organizations' accountability to the public beginning with English common law in the sixteenth century and going through current efforts at the state and federal levels to regulate nonprofit organizations. She also predicts the areas in which the regulation of nonprofit organizations is likely to continue.

Part Two provides a major discussion of the specific trend in the nonprofit sector toward earned income and commercialism. While some authors seem to contradict one another, these chapters reveal the scope and importance of this issue both in public policy and in the mission and practice of organizations.

Henry Hansmann leads off the policy debate in Chapter Six, ''The Two Nonprofit Sectors,'' by arguing that there are not one, but two nonprofit sectors. One sector is primarily commercial; that is, its organizations, such as hospitals, rely primarily on fees for services for much of their income. The other sector is primarily donative—its organizations, such as human service agencies or advocacy organizations, rely on private contributions for a large proportion of their income. Hansmann argues that only donative nonprofit organizations should receive tax preference under the law.

In Chapter Seven, ''The Complexities of Income Generation for Nonprofits,'' Burton A. Weisbrod reviews the complex economic issues that were brought about by a decline in government funding to nonprofits. He discusses various public policy choices and their impact on both nonprofits and small business and suggests that many nonprofits have a fundamental public purpose regardless of the fact that their income is derived primarily from fees.

James M. Ferris and Elizabeth Graddy, in Chapter Eight, ''Fading Distinctions Among the Nonprofit, Government, and For-Profit Sectors,'' discuss the trend toward commercialism in nonprofits and the entry of business into traditional nonprofit service areas as contributing factors to the fading distinctions among the sectors. They also discuss the public policy implications of these trends.

In Chapter Nine, ''Cash Cows or Sacred Cows: The Politics of the Commercialization Movement,'' Reid Lifset focuses on the political implications of the competition between small business and nonprofit organizations and discerns that nonprofits and small business are bearing the burden given to them by the state, which is abdicating some of its fundamental responsibilities through fiscal retrenchment.

In Chapter Ten, "The Use of For-Profit Subsidiary Corporations by Nonprofits," James J. McGovern provides a historical analysis of the use of for-profit subsidiary corporations by nonprofits and then describes the public policy ramifications of their increasing use. He suggests that more detailed information is needed to determine the scope and reasons for such commercial activities before making major changes in public policy.

Finally, in "Beyond Tax Exemption: A Focus on Organizational Performance Versus Legal Status" (Chapter Eleven), Dennis R. Young proposes that public policy should consider the services actually performed rather than the legal structure of the organization. Accepting that nonprofit organizations usually identify and initiate services that are later provided by government and for-profit organizations, the basis for special government status ought to be exemplary service or process.

Part Three addresses the traditional role and responsibility of the nonprofit sector, which was to serve constituencies in need. Organizations have served both as advocates of underserved or underrepresented groups and as providers of services. Modern scholars are reexamining the role and level of responsibility that nonprofit organizations and government have to serve these groups. Since the federal government has significantly reduced funding in social welfare programs during the last decade, this question has become more pertinent. The chapters in this section address these issues by looking at specific constituencies.

In Chapter Twelve, "Encouraging Advocacy for the Underserved: The Case of Children," Robert H. Bremner traces the role and functions of advocacy organizations that support children, a group unable to represent itself. He traces the problems and complex issues that relate to children in America, including poverty, abuse, foster care, and children's rights. He also analyzes the role, functions, relationship, and impact of nonprofit advocacy organizations regarding government.

In Chapter Thirteen, "The Problem of Poverty and Why Philanthropy Neglects It," Susan A. Ostrander examines the traditional philanthropic and charitable conceptions of people in poverty as well as the public perception of governmental responsibility. She argues that the current perceptions that government programs lead to continued dependency and that private philanthropy helps people become "independent" create dichotomies that prevent solutions to the problem of poverty. She also argues for new conceptions of philanthropy that dispense with the donor's control over the recipient and move toward reciprocal relationships between donors and donees.

In Chapter Fourteen, "The Future of Hispanics and Philanthropy," Janice Petrovich summarizes the findings of a major survey of Hispanics in the northeast United States that was to determine both their needs and an agenda for action. Part of this agenda includes the recommendation that Hispanics increase their active leadership and participation in nonprofit service, community development, and advocacy organizations in order to meet their objectives of fuller participation in society.

In Chapter Fifteen, "Helping the Underserved Abroad: The Case of Famine Relief," Robert L. Payton uses the outpouring of philanthropy triggered by the Ethiopian famine in 1984–1985 as a case study to explore individual philanthropy's ability to provide emergency relief and its inability to provide sustained support to long-term resolutions of crisis situations.

Financing nonprofit organizations is both a public policy issue and a management concern. The authors in Part Four address the twin issues of finance and management from a variety of points of view.

In Chapter Sixteen, "Responsible Management in the Nonprofit Sector," Michael O'Neill argues that responsible management is moral and entails carrying out the specific goals of an organization, no matter which sector the group belongs to. However, the fact that nonprofit managers work with morality and ethics as part of their organizational missions gives them added managerial responsibility as well as a "moral dimension" to their leadership.

In Chapter Seventeen, "Increasing Government Support for Nonprofits: Is It Worth the Cost?," Jack Moskowitz reviews the traditional partnership of government and nonprofits that delivers human services and argues that current federal policy designed to reduce federal funding and privatize human service provision is erroneous. He provides case studies of exemplary private nonprofit–governmental partnerships that demonstrate the efficiency and cost effectiveness of these arrangements in dealing with such critical issues as providing services to the homeless.

In Chapter Eighteen, ''New Approaches to Financing Nonprofit Organizations: The Role of Lending,'' Steven A. Waldhorn, James O. Gollub, and Joyce A. Klein propose that designating loan funds for innovative human service agencies can provide an important new mechanism for financing nonprofit organizations. The authors also provide options that might attract investors interested in financing the sector through loans.

In Chapter Nineteen, ''Charitable Giving Options That Do Not Affect Government Revenue,'' Lawrence B. Lindsey proposes some options that would allow a charitable deduction for all itemizers without costing the federal government any revenues. One reason that the charitable deduction was not made law in the 1986 tax revisions is because the Treasury Department estimated that it would lead to a loss of revenue to the federal government. Lindsey's options would allow for an increase in a traditional source of funds, individual giving, without adding additional cost to government.

Part Five is devoted to evaluating the future of corporate giving in light of the major changes that are taking place in the economy. Corporate giving, which grew faster than other forms of giving in the 1970s, has recently declined. Concurrent with this decline, the administration has been calling on the private sector to take more responsibility for funding human services in areas in which the federal government was cutting back its funding. The authors in this section examine the significance of these trends.

In Chapter Twenty, ''Corporate Contributions to the Year 2000: Growth or Decline?,'' Hayden W. Smith reviews trends in corporate giving over the past fifty years. He suggests that although corporate giving tripled during the last decade, there are some indications that the growth rate will decline in the foreseeable future.

In Chapter Twenty-One, "Corporate Social Responsibility and Public-Private Partnerships," Peter Goldberg analyzes what corporate leaders have learned about public-private partnerships and examines the responsibility and limitations of corporations in alleviating poverty.

In Chapter Twenty-Two, "Trends in Corporate Reporting on Philanthropic Efforts," Robert O. Bothwell and Elizabeth Wiener present the results of a survey on the information corporations provide about the grants they make. The authors defend the need for openness in grant reporting and discuss how the lack of such information impedes some nonprofit organizations when they are seeking access to corporate funding programs.

In Chapter Twenty-Three, "Cause-Related Marketing: Advantages and Pitfalls for Nonprofits," Kathleen A. Krentler reviews a new movement among corporations to support certain nonprofit organizations in order to increase their business. She compares such marketing-related programs with corporate giving programs and discusses the potential advantages and pitfalls for nonprofit organizations involved in such partnerships.

The health of the nonprofit sector depends on individuals giving their time and money. The authors in Part Six examine trends in volunteering, community generosity, giving by the wealthy, and the education of future generations in these democratic traditions.

In Chapter Twenty-Four, "Key Indicators of Generosity in Communities," Julian Wolpert presents the results of an analysis of eighty-five metropolitan areas to determine the major indicators of community generosity. He provides a profile of generous communities compared with not-so-generous communities and demonstrates that generous communities are those in which there is a partnership between private and public support for community activities and services.

In Chapter Twenty-Five, "Volunteer Demographics and Future Prospects for Volunteering," Robert J. O'Connor and Rebecca S. Johnson analyze the demographics of volunteers. The authors discern that although the pool of volunteers will increase slightly over the next five years, there could be a decline beyond that.

In Chapter Twenty-Six, "Charitable Giving Patterns by Elites in the United States," Teresa J. Odendahl concludes from a study of the motivations for giving among wealthy individuals that very few wealthy individuals are interested in supporting social service activities. She states that even in an era of federal cutbacks to social welfare, wealthy individuals cannot be depended on to change their giving patterns.

In Chapter Twenty-Seven, "Fostering Philanthropic Values in a Modern Democracy," Margot Stern Strom and Alan L. Stoskopf discuss the role of the nonprofit sector in preserving and maintaining democratic values and the current lack of attention given by educational institutions to teaching and fostering those values. They conclude that if the relationship of giving, volunteering, and not-for-profit association to democratic values is not taught again in the schools, the whole tradition could decline.

Part Seven contains three concluding chapters.

In Chapter Twenty-Eight, "Alternative Futures for the Sector," Forrest P. Chisman describes the various scenarios for the future of the independent sector based on his analysis of the historical relationships among the three sectors and the effect on these sectors of weak and strong economic conditions. He proposes that even under a negative scenario the independent or nonprofit sector has the capacity to provide leadership for progressive change.

In Chapter Twenty-Nine, "Agendas for Nonprofit Sector Research: A Personal Account," John G. Simon reflects on research done at the Program on Non-Profit Organizations at Yale University, the oldest national research effort on this sector. He also provides his list of research needs for the future.

Finally, in Chapter Thirty, we present "Meeting the Challenges of the Future," an agenda for action.

Acknowledgments

This volume grew out of the research program of INDEPENDENT SECTOR, a national coalition of foundations, corporations, and voluntary organizations founded in 1980 as a forum to encourage the giving, volunteering, and not-for-profit initiative that helps all of us better serve people, communities, and causes. One of the purposes of this research program is to encourage and stimulate research on this sector at colleges and universities. The contributors to this volume are part of this effort. Therefore, we are indebted to INDEPENDENT SECTOR and to the many foundations and corporations that are supporting such research. In addition, we recognize the unflagging dedication of the INDEPENDENT SECTOR research staff, especially Mindy Berry and David Stuligross, in the preparation of this book.

Much of the success of the INDEPENDENT SECTOR research program is the result of the research committee, chaired by Robert L. Payton. Because of his leadership and indefatigable efforts, enormous progress has been made to increase scholarly interest in this area of inquiry.

We are also indebted to John Simon and Paul DiMaggio, who provide the leadership for the Program on Non-Profit Organizations at Yale University. Their program, established in 1977, has sponsored over two hundred scholars from the United States and abroad in studying many aspects of the nonprofit sector, and they have provided all of us with new understanding and questions. Several of those scholars are contributors to this volume.

Finally, we must acknowledge the enormous support of Russy D. Sumariwalla, senior fellow at the United Way Institute, who has been an active colleague and cosponsor of the annual research forums that provide a meeting ground for scholars and practitioners. This meeting ground has improved and expanded the research effort over the years and has led to the development of a research community in which common issues are discussed. Through these forums, all of us have had the opportunity to meet many talented young scholars, some of whom are contributors to this volume, who will provide leadership to this sector in the future.

July 1989   Virginia A. Hodgkinson
                                              Washington, D.C.

                                              Richard W. Lyman
                                              Stanford, California

The Authors

△ △ △ △ △ △ △ △ △ △ △ △ △ △ △

Linda A. Bergthold is a consultant to National Medical Audit. Prior to taking on this position, she was an adjunct professor of sociology and project director at the Institute for Health and Aging at the University of California, San Francisco. Bergthold has published several articles on business and health politics and is the author of a forthcoming book, *Purchasing Power in Health: Business, the State, and Health Care Politics* (1990).

Elizabeth A. Binney is a research associate in the Institute for Health and Aging and a graduate student in the Department of Social and Behavioral Sciences at the University of California, San Francisco.

Robert O. Bothwell has been executive director of the National Committee for Responsive Philanthropy in Washington, D.C., since its founding in 1976. He helped to create a national movement of alternative organizations to United Way, assisted these organizations in raising over $100 million in 1985–1986, and was the leader of successful efforts to open up the federal government's charity drive to advocacy and nontraditional nonprofits. He is coauthor, with E. Bruce and T. Saasta, of the 1980 study *Foundations and Public Information: Sunshine or Shadow?* and coauthor, with E. Wiener, of a similar study of corporate philanthropy, which is soon to be released. He is also principal author of *New Approaches to Increase Private Funds for Neighborhood Organization Development,* a report published by the National Commission on Neighborhoods in 1978.

Robert H. Bremner is professor emeritus at the Ohio State University, where he taught courses on the history of American philanthropy, social welfare, and social thought. His publications include *American Philanthropy* (2nd ed., 1988), *The Public Good* (1980), and *Children and Youth in America: A Documentary History* (with others, 1974).

Forrest P. Chisman is director of the Project on the Federal Social Role. Prior to taking on this position, he was an official with the Department of Commerce during the Carter administration. Chisman is coauthor, with A. Pifer, of *Government for the People* (1987) and *Attitudes, Psychology and the Study of Public Opinion* (1977).

Carroll L. Estes is professor of sociology, chairperson of the Department of Social and Behavioral Sciences, and director of the Institute for Health and Aging at the University of California, San Francisco. Estes conducts research and writes about policy issues in long-term care for the elderly and the effects of fiscal crises and new federalism policies on both the private nonprofit sector and the aging. She is the author of *The Aging Enterprise* (1979) and *The Decision Makers: The Power Structure of Dallas* (1963) and coauthor of several volumes, including *Long-term Care of the Elderly: Public Policy Issues* (with C. Harrington, R. S. Newcomer, and Associates, 1985). Estes is past president of the Western Gerontological Society (now called the American Society on Aging) and the Association for Gerontology in Higher Education.

James M. Ferris is associate professor of public administration at the University of Southern California. His research has focused on the economics of local government service delivery, which includes contracting and the use of volunteers by local governments. He has recently developed a course on the political economy of the nonprofit sector under a grant from the Association of American Colleges.

Marion R. Fremont-Smith is a partner in the Boston law firm of Choate, Hall & Stewart. She is a director of INDE-PENDENT SECTOR, chairperson of the Exempt Organization Committee of the American Bar Association, Tax Section; and a member of the Internal Revenue Service Commissioner's Advisory Group on Exempt Organizations. She is the author of *Philanthropy and the Business Corporation* (1972), *Foundations and Government: State and Federal Law Supervision* (1965), and numerous articles on philanthropy and the law.

Peter Goldberg is an independent consultant to both nonprofit and for-profit executives throughout the Northeast. Formerly vice-president for public responsibility at the Primerica Corporation, he has advocated extensively for increased social awareness within the business community.

James O. Gollub is program manager of socioeconomic studies for the Center for Economic Competitiveness and director of the Life Span Program at SRI International. His work with the Life Span program focuses on the analysis of older adult markets.

Elizabeth Graddy is assistant professor in the School of Public Administration at the University of Southern California. She has conducted research on contracts governments have with nonprofits for the delivery of local health services and is interested in the evolution of industrial structures, including the nonprofit sector.

Henry Hansmann is professor of law at Yale University. He is the author of a number of articles on the law and economics of nonprofit organizations and currently is at work on a book entitled *The Ownership of Enterprise.*

Virginia A. Hodgkinson is vice-president of research at INDEPENDENT SECTOR and executive director of the National Center for Charitable Statistics. Formerly, she was executive director of the National Institute of Independent Colleges and Universities. Her most recent publications include *Giving and Volunteering in the United States* (with M. S. Weitzman, 1988), *From Belief to Commitment: The Activities and Finances of Religious Congregations in the United States* (with M. S. Weitzman and A. D. Kirsch, 1988), *Dimensions of the Independent Sector: A Statistical Profile* (with M. S. Weitzman, 1986), and *Americans Volunteer 1985* (with M. S. Weitzman, 1985).

Rebecca S. Johnson is manager of program and product development at United Way of America.

Joyce A. Klein is a policy analyst at the Center for Economic Competitiveness at SRI International. She was formerly the project manager for the feasibility study of the Corporation for Social Investment.

Kathleen A. Krentler is associate professor of marketing at San Diego State University. Her academic research, teaching, and service activities have focused on the marketing problems of nonprofit organizations. With support from the Institute for Nonprofit Management and the Ford Foundation, she recently completed a study investigating the effects of AIDS awareness on blood donation behavior.

Reid Lifset has worked for National Public Radio's for-profit subsidiary, NPR Ventures, in strategic planning. During the summer of 1988, he was a John D. Rockefeller III fellow at the Program on Non-Profit Organizations at Yale University. His primary area of research has been in the history, politics, and commercial activities of nonprofit organizations.

Lawrence B. Lindsey is assistant professor of economics at Harvard University and faculty research fellow at the National Bureau of Economic Research. He served three years on the President's Council of Economic Advisers, where he was senior staff economist for tax policy. He is the author of numerous articles on tax policy and charitable giving.

Richard W. Lyman is director of the Institute of International Studies at Stanford University. From 1980 to 1988, Lyman was president of the Rockefeller Foundation. He has served on the board of directors and as chairperson of INDEPENDENT SECTOR. He has also served on the board of directors of the Council on Foundations. He taught modern British history for twelve years before becoming provost of Stanford University in 1967. He was president of Stanford from 1970 to 1980. Lyman is the author of *The First Labour Government, 1924* (1957) and a number of articles on historical topics and contemporary philanthropy. He is a fellow of the Royal Historical Society and of the American Academy of Arts and Sciences.

James J. McGovern is assistant chief counsel, Employee Benefits and Exempt Organizations, Office of the Chief Counsel, at the Internal Revenue Service. The opinions expressed in Chapter Ten are his own and do not necessarily represent the views of the Internal Revenue Service. He has written and lectured extensively on the law of tax-exempt organizations.

Jack Moskowitz is vice-president for federal government relations at United Way of America. He monitors legislation and day-to-day government activities that could affect the United Way movement. He is known in Congressional circles as a leading authority on tax reform. Before joining United Way of America in 1977, he was Common Cause's principal lobbyist for energy and tax matters. He has also served as executive director of the National Committee on Tax Justice.

Robert J. O'Connor is director of key markets information at United Way of America. He is responsible for directing market research for donor, volunteer, and corporate markets. Previous professional pursuits include consumer research for the Life Insurance Marketing and Research Association and public opinion research as a senior research associate for the American Council of Life Insurance.

Teresa J. Odendahl is an anthropologist, consultant, and writer on nonprofit matters. She was project manager of the "Foundation Study," which was sponsored jointly by the Yale University Program on Non-Profit Organizations and the Council on Foundations. She contributed to and edited *America's Wealthy and the Future of Foundations* (1987) and is coauthor of *Working in Foundations: Career Patterns of Women and Men* (with E. Boris and A. K. Daniels, 1985).

Michael O'Neill is professor and director of the Institute for Nonprofit Organizations Management at the University of San Francisco (USF) and former dean of USF's School of Education. He founded USF's Master of Nonprofit Administration degree program in 1983. He wrote *The Third America: The Emergence of the Nonprofit Sector in the United States* (1989) and coedited *Educating Managers of Nonprofit Organizations* (with D. R. Young, 1988).

Susan A. Ostrander is associate professor of sociology and American studies at Tufts University. She is the author of several articles on voluntary social welfare agencies, which were collected in a book entitled *Women of the Upper Class* (1984). She is also a senior editor of *Shifting the Debate: Public-Private Relations in the Modern Welfare State* (1987). She was a visiting scholar at Radcliffe College for the Spring 1988 semester.

Robert L. Payton is director of the Center on Philanthropy and professor of philanthropy at Indiana University, Indianapolis. Formerly, he was a scholar-in-residence in philanthropic studies at the University of Virginia. Prior to that, he was president of the Exxon Education Foundation, Hofstra University, and C. W. Post College. He is presently a member of the INDEPENDENT SECTOR research committee, and from 1983 to 1988 he was chairperson of that committee. His most recent book is *Philanthropy: Voluntary Action for the Public Good* (1988).

Janice Petrovich is deputy national executive director of the ASPIRA Association and director of the ASPIRA Institute for Policy Research. As an educational researcher and policy analyst, she has recently written a book entitled *Northeast Hispanic Needs: A Guide for Action* (1987), which includes the results of a conference and a survey of Latino leaders with recommendations to foundations, corporations, and nonprofit organizations on how to effectively address Latino needs.

Lester M. Salamon is director of the Institute for Policy Studies at Johns Hopkins University. He directed the Urban Institute's Nonprofit Sector Project from 1981 to 1986 and served as deputy associate director of the U.S. Office of Management and Budget between 1977 and 1980. He is author or coauthor of numerous articles on the nonprofit sector, a series of studies on the nonprofit sector in communities across the country, and a book entitled *The Federal Budget and the Nonprofit Sector* (with A. J. Abramson, 1982). Salamon is a member of the National Center for Charitable Statistics Committee, the Government Relations Committee of the United Way of America, and the editorial board of the *Journal of Voluntary Action Scholars.*

John G. Simon is Augustus Lines Professor of Law, deputy dean of the Yale Law School, and cochair of the Program on Non-Profit Organizations at Yale University. He has engaged in teaching and research on philanthropy and the nonprofit sector since the early 1960s and has also served as officer or trustee of a number of nonprofit groups. He is coauthor of the *Ethical Investor* (with C. Powers and J. Gunnemann, 1972) and has written many articles and chapters on various topics in law, philanthropy, and education. He is a member of INDE-PENDENT SECTOR's research committee and of the commissioner of Internal Revenue Service's advisory committee on tax-exempt organizations.

Hayden W. Smith is senior vice-president of the Council for Aid to Education (CFAE) in New York City. Prior to 1968, when he joined the council as director of research, he was senior economic advisor at the Exxon Corporation. He is the author of several papers on the economics of higher education, the role of voluntary support in financing colleges and universities, corporate contributions and corporate aid to education, and the impact of tax policies and utility regulation on charitable giving. His best-known report is *A Profile of Corporate Contributions,* an analysis of the 1977 corporate income tax file that was published by CFAE in 1983.

James Allen Smith is a member of the adjunct faculty of the New School for Social Research, where he teaches in the program on nonprofit management. He served as resident scholar at the Rockefeller Archives Center for the 1988–89 academic year. He has worked on the staff of the Twentieth Century Fund and has written a book, *The Policy Elite* (1989), on the role of policy research organizations in the United States.

Alan L. Stoskopf is program associate at Facing History and Ourselves National Foundation, Inc. He has taught extensively on the secondary and adult education levels in West Africa, the United Kingdom, and the United States. He has developed curriculum and trained teachers as the project coordinator for the foundation's World of Difference project, which was cosponsored with Massachusetts World of Difference Program, and as director of the legal studies program in Brookline Public Schools. Currently, he is contributing author and educator of the foundation's Choosing to Participate project.

Margot Stern Strom is executive director of Facing History and Ourselves National Foundation, Inc., which was certified by the U.S. Department of Education in 1980 as an "exemplary" model teacher-training program in the National Diffusion Network. She is also research associate and cofounder of the Harvard Graduate School of Education's Center for the Study of Gender, Education, and Human Development. She coauthored the student/teacher resource book *Facing History and Ourselves: Holocaust and Human Behavior* (with W. S. Parsons, 1982), and she has written numerous articles for educational journals exploring the impact of the foundation's programs on students' thinking and teachers' professional development.

Steven A. Waldhorn is director of the Center for Economic Competitiveness at SRI International. At the center he has worked on national research programs on innovative approaches to community development and human service problems.

Burton A. Weisbrod is Evjue-Bascom Professor of Economics at the University of Wisconsin, Madison, where he is also the director for health economics and law. His research has been in the economics of education, health, and cost-benefit analysis and the role of the private nonprofit sector. His book *The Nonprofit Economy* was published in 1988.

Elizabeth Wiener is a journalist and has worked most recently for the National Committee for Responsive Philanthropy (NCRP). While at NCRP she was editor of *Responsive Philanthropy* and assistant director of study on corporate philanthropy and public information.

Julian Wolpert is Henry G. Bryant Professor of Geography, Public Affairs and Urban Planning at Princeton University's Woodrow Wilson School. He was elected to the National Academy of Sciences in 1977 and is the author of numerous articles on regional philanthropy and nonprofit organizations.

Dennis R. Young is Mandel Professor of Nonprofit Management and director of the Mandel Center for Nonprofit Management at Case Western Reserve University. He is a visiting faculty of the Program on Non-Profit Organizations at Yale University and was formerly director of the Nonprofit Studies Program in the W. Averell Harriman College at the State University of New York, Stony Brook. His books include *Educating Managers of Nonprofit Organizations* (coedited with M. O'Neill, 1988), *Casebook of Management for Nonprofit Organizations* (1984), and *If Not for Profit, For What?* (1983).

THE
FUTURE
OF THE
NONPROFIT
SECTOR

△ △ △ △ △ △ △ △ △ △ △ △ △ △

PART ONE

△ △ △ △ △ △ △ △ △ △ △ △ △ △ △

Changing Roles
and Responsibilities
of the Nonprofit Sector

The purpose of Part One is to provide a broad overview and analysis of the impact of public policy changes that took place primarily during the Reagan administration. After a long period of growth in federal funding for human service programs, the decade of the 1980s was characterized by major cutbacks in federal funding in a variety of human service areas, from education to the arts. These cutbacks were predicated on the assumption that the private sector ought to take more responsibility for supporting such activities. The private sector was defined as business as well as nonprofit organizations.

The ensuing events of major corporate restructuring, a major recession, and the growing dismantlement of long-standing but little understood public-private partnerships between the government at all levels and nonprofit organizations stimulated some substantial research efforts to chart and analyze these major changes in public policy. Furthermore, the movement of business corporations into areas such as hospitals and other health and human services led to challenges to nonprofits in the form of competition from for-profit organizations. Some nonprofits, in order to offset federal budget cuts, have moved toward more commercial practices, raising questions about their accountability to the public as well as their fundamental mission under law.

1

The contributors in this part provide an overview of the broad changes that occurred over this decade and their impact on the structure and functions of the nonprofit sector. The authors analyze the impact on nonprofits of the federal funding cutbacks, the changes in nonprofit operations and services to offset the loss of these funds, the changing role of foundations in funding public-policy research, and the increasing regulation of the sector by government. It is clear from these chapters that nonprofits function in the public realm and are deeply affected by governmental policies.

1

VIRGINIA A. HODGKINSON

△ △ △ △ △ △ △ △ △ △ △ △ △ △ △

Key Challenges Facing the Nonprofit Sector

Although the third sector, or voluntarism, was the focus of considerable attention by researchers during the nineteenth and early twentieth centuries, scholars since the Depression have been more interested in government and its relation to social programs than in the development, roles and functions, and changing institutions of the nonprofit sector. Since the mid-1970s, however, the efforts of the Commission on Private Philanthropy and Public Needs (the Filer Commission, 1972–1974), the establishment of the Program on Nonprofit Organizations at Yale (1977), the founding of INDEPENDENT SECTOR (1980), and the establishment of several academic centers focused on the study of the nonprofit sector and philanthropy have assisted in addressing major gaps in our knowledge about what this sector is and how it functions within the U.S. social and economic structures.

This emerging interest in the study of nonprofit institutions comes at the same time that our nation is going through a major economic and social transition, from an industrial state to an information and service society. The questions that the authors of this volume were asked to address, particularly in relation to the changing roles and responsibilities of business, government, and nonprofit organizations, generally concern the fundamental issues of institutional forms and relationships among the sectors in the midst of this major restructuring of

3

our economy and society. Thus, new public-policy challenges are arising and the social history of this nation is being rewritten concurrently with this growth in scholarly interest. The authors of this volume reveal the complexities inherent in analyzing social change while attempting to extract or reconstruct a historical tradition of this sector, to pose theories of its current and changing roles, and to identify trends that may lead to major new conceptions and structures in society beyond the year 2000. In the midst of such change, several challenges lie ahead that need to be addressed with vigor and foresight.

The Problem of Identification: A Sector with Many Names

Among the major obstacles preventing the development of an analytical framework for studying the roles and functions of this sector are the length of its tradition, the transformation over centuries of its roles and responsibilities to society, and the diversity of the kinds of institutions it encompasses. Some of the public-policy challenges can be attributed to the changing typology and functions of these institutions and how they are or ought to be defined. There is also the problem of determining what criteria ought to be used in granting nonprofit organizations tax-exempt status. Responses to these questions could enormously enlarge or diminish the scope of nonprofit activity in the United States.

The tradition of this sector is revealed in the inability of scholars to agree on what to call it. The Commission on Private Philanthropy and Public Needs (1975) wrestled with the question of a name for this sector in *Giving in America*. Members of the commission decided against negative names, such as *nongovernmental, nonprofit,* or *noncommercial. Voluntary* sector seemed to exclude philanthropic institutions. *Third* sector seemed to imply that it came after the government and business sectors, when historically it actually preceded them as a form of organization and action (Boorstin, 1963). Finally, however, the commission, like many of the authors of this volume, agreed that they could not come up with a better name and used all these names interchangeably. When the umbrella organization INDE-PENDENT SECTOR was founded in 1980, it, too, wrestled with a variety of names and decided through compromise to adopt one that is both inclusive and positive, although some scholars argue that using *independent* as a name for this sector belies its interdependent nature (Hall, 1987). More recently, Robert L. Payton argued that the term *philanthropy* or *philan-thropic* should be used as the umbrella term (Payton, 1984).

The inability to agree on a name leads to various analytical conceptions of the sector as well as difficulty in responding to public-policy issues dealing with definitions. A working defini-tion of *nonprofit* includes all organizations given tax-exempt status under the Internal Revenue Code (IRC) or established as nonprofits under state codes. Not all nonprofits that are tax-exempt can receive tax-deductible contributions. Those that can—the organizations defined as "charitable" under IRC Section 501(c)(3)—include educational, religious, scientific, and other charitable causes. These institutions must work in the "public interest" rather than to advance the interests of a private group. Although such language differentiates types of nonprofit organizations, "public interest" is not used as a legal test. Thus, defining what is a nonprofit organization or which nonprofit organizations should be tax-exempt can lead to much ambiguity. In addition, the language defining nonprofits under the federal tax code leaves a wide latitude for interpretation in determin-ing boundaries of the sector, shifting from "public interest" to "public needs" as society changes over time.

Henry Hansmann predicts in Chapter Six that by the year 2000 there will be two independent sectors—the "philanthropic," or "charitable," nonprofits and the "commercial" nonprofits. Many nonprofit institutions that once played primarily a philan-thropic role, such as most nonprofit hospitals, no longer do so. With the advent of private medical insurance and the Medicaid and Medicare programs, hospitals no longer serve as philan-thropic or charitable institutions that provide health care primar-ily to those who cannot afford it but rather serve as "commercial" institutions that derive their revenues from fees. Hansmann suggests that tax-exempt status for nonprofits should be limited, and that the fundamental criteria for tax-exempt status—as opposed to mere incorporation as a nonprofit organization—should be economic and regulatory. Charitable organizations should be donative—that is, derive their support from contributions—and should serve the poor or fill education and research needs. Once other major revenue sources, such as payment from insurance, become available, so that organizations receive the bulk of their income from sales of services, they should become commercial.

Hansmann further argues that commercial nonprofits should be permitted only in areas where there are no for-profit substitutes or where government regulation does not afford adequate protection to ensure quality service to consumers, as was the case with savings banks and is still commonly the case with day-care centers and nursing homes. By Hansmann's criteria, approximately two-thirds of the current nonprofit-sector revenues would fail to qualify for tax exemption.

Dennis Young suggests in Chapter Eleven that government should provide tax exemptions and other privileges not on the basis of an organization's structural form but rather on the basis of the quality of services that it provides, regardless of its nonprofit or for-profit status. Organizations ought to be judged on "process," not structural form.

In Chapter Nine, Reid Lifset identifies a distinguishing feature of institutional nonprofits as cross-subsidization—that is, those who can pay partially subsidize those who cannot in order to provide service to all members of the community. In his terms, efficiency of service includes equality of access as well as ability to provide quality service at the lowest possible cost. According to this definition, voluntary institutions are obligated to a primary mission of service and finding the resources to provide that service, whereas for-profit organizations are primarily concerned with providing a profitable service.

Adherence to a mission of service rather than profit also adds a moral dimension. Although business must carry out its operations in an honest and ethical fashion, Michael O'Neill points out in Chapter Sixteen that nonprofits have an added moral responsibility because they are "people" organizations and because they serve a higher proportion of clients who are at risk. Nonprofits add a dimension of advocacy and public education to empower the disenfranchised, to improve services to the underserved, and to improve the quality of life of all people.

The crisis of institutional identification has clearly become acute as a result of the federal policies of the Reagan era that encouraged the privatization of public services. Such privatization has led many nonprofits to cut back services, to seek to attract paying clientele, and to be more concerned with survival than with service. Such trends are documented by Carroll S. Estes, Elizabeth A. Binney, and Linda A. Bergthold in Chapter Two and Lester M. Salamon in Chapter Three and referred to by many of the other authors in this volume. This crisis in mission could lead to a change in public policy, public subsidies, and tax laws to ensure the distinction among institutional forms. Alternatively, as the functions and roles of for-profit and nonprofit become more alike, whole new criteria for evaluating and supporting public services may emerge.

In order to offset continued erosion of the nonprofit sector, nonprofit organizations, including hospitals, schools and colleges, and comprehensive social service agencies, will have to distinguish themselves from their for-profit and governmental counterparts on the basis of mission and type of service provided. Although a balance in the tripartite system of providing services in the public interest is certainly the best solution, nonprofits will have to take responsibility for public leadership. This will mean that nonprofits must judge and evaluate their own practices. Organizations that limit services to those with an ability to pay may need community censure. Organizations suffering from a resource crisis may have to increase their ability to attract public support through donations and volunteer service. Putting an emphasis on distinguishing mission, improving public education, and increasing community support could result in changing the focus of the public debate from increased privatization back to institutional purpose. The debate ought to address the level and kinds of services that should be provided to all citizens. Once this question is reviewed, the types of institutions providing the mix and delivery of these services and the kinds of public and private subsidies needed to provide them can be debated in the context of national goals. Unless nonprofit organizations enlarge the public debate to include these fundamental issues, the gradual diminution of the sector through legal and regulatory means will continue.

Clientele: A Crisis in Mission and Accountability

The crisis in identity arises from conceptions about the traditional roles of charitable organizations and the changes in their roles and functions. The recent attention given to research on the nonprofit sector has helped to identify both traditional and current missions and practices of the nonprofit sector and its relationship with government. The results of this research have led to the framing of issues for public discussion and public policy deliberation.

Nonprofit activity in the United States emerged from the Judeo-Christian heritage (Bremner, 1988). A majority of institutions, such as schools and hospitals, were founded by religious institutions with missions to serve the poor and underserved as well as to maintain the community. These values also have become part of the secular philosophy of the nation and provide the impetus for many social welfare programs. In addition to providing charity and relief to distressed individuals, this religious tradition advocates that the highest form of charity is to provide individuals with the means to help themselves or to become independent. The tradition of helping others to become independent has led in modern times to the creation of both publicly and privately supported programs to provide people with the means to participate more productively in society. These programs include publicly and privately supported social insurance programs for retirement, health, unemployment, and education, as well as aid to people in poverty. Such social programs have increased the health and productivity of American citizens during the past century. Very few of them have been limited to the poor; rather, most are available to all Americans.

The distinction between charity and philanthropy has caused tension in both private nonprofit and government-supported programs. It is this dichotomy between social insurance based on mutual obligation and charity based on support for women and children in distress that has led to a form of gridlock in public policy (Reich, 1987). This tension between charity (relief) and philanthropy (long-term problem solving) is evident in the attempts of the authors of this volume to define the role and responsibilities of the third sector. It also has been very evident in public-policy discussions for the past decade. Some of the discussion in this volume focuses on the sector's responsibility to the poor and underserved, with many authors raising the question about the primary clientele of nonprofit organizations and their responsibility and accountability to the public. In reality, the goals, practices, and missions of organizations in the nonprofit sector incorporate programs representative of the traditions of both charity and philanthropy, as evidenced in soup kitchens for the hungry and universities to transmit and advance knowledge.

The movement toward privatizing federal social welfare programs and the accompanying cutbacks in federal funding have led to a concern about defining the clientele of the nonprofit sector. The underlying assumption of several authors of this volume is that the primary clientele of the nonprofit sector is the poor. Even though service to the poor has traditionally been a major goal of religious, nonprofit, and governmental organizations, it has been but one of several major goals. From colonial times, self-help movements, community services, and the building and support of educational and health institutions, as well as support of the arts, have been among the major functions of the sector (Hall, 1982; McCarthy, 1982; Bremner, 1988). The nonprofit sector has been far more characterized by mutual obligation than by charitable relief (Curti, 1958).

When governmental programs were established to provide support for people in poverty, the public partnership between government and the nonprofit sector worked very well. Salamon has shown that nonprofits grew as service providers in conjunction with increases in government funding (Salamon, 1987). He points out that the growing partnership of the nonprofit sector with government grew out of "voluntary failure," or the inability of nonprofit organizations to find adequate resources to meet societal needs. Thus, government became a major funder of social welfare services and used nonprofits to provide a large share of service delivery.

The changing nature of service delivery and the methods of funding services have caused the change from a collaborative model between nonprofits and government to a competitive model among all three sectors. The changing paradigm and current decrease in government funding of social services, particularly for the poor, have led to the delegitimation of the nonprofit sector during the 1980s, as described in Chapter Two. It also has led to a shift from governmental funding of the poor to funding for middle-class programs, particularly in the areas of education, Social Security, and health. Chapter Three documents this process by noting the declining role of government as a producer of services and its increasing use of a voucher system. Such trends in support tend to emphasize services for those who can pay rather than to those who cannot. Vouchers are paid for through the tax system rather than directly funded by government agencies, and deductions for child care through the tax system provide more aid to higher-income families.

Shifting of responsibility from government to the market has been a major cause of competition between nonprofit and for-profit service providers. Thus, nonprofits have moved increasingly to charging fees to derive more revenues, and this shift to fees for services has led nonprofits to behave more like their for-profit counterparts. In the estimate of several authors, the movement of nonprofits toward commercial practices is leading to a reexamination of criteria for tax exemption.

The potential impact of the movement of nonprofit services toward a market orientation is even farther reaching. It is causing a crisis in public confidence in service provision by government and the nonprofit sector; it is eroding our faith in mutual obligation to serve those suffering from poverty, hunger, lack of education, and lack of skills; and it is leading to the basic abrogation of social responsibility by government and by the nonprofit sector, particularly in its advocacy functions. The process of reducing funds to government programs and shifting the burden to the private for-profit and nonprofit sectors to fill in the gaps may lead to an increasing lack of attention to the rights of children, to the rights of women in poverty, to discrimination, and to the equitable allocation of resources to all citizens. It makes all of the sectors more defensive and more competitive. It leads to a "we" versus "they" mentality, which creates a society of "haves" and "have-nots" (Reich, 1987). It also prevents a solution to common problems based on the participation of all the actors, including particularly those in poverty (the recipients), as discussed in Chapter Thirteen. It forces government and nonprofit organizations into a defensive posture regarding commerce and prevents a more global discussion of societal goals and needs and the resources to finance those needs. According to Salamon (Chapter Three) and Robert H. Bremner (Chapter Twelve), it leads nonprofits to reduce their fundamental role as advocates, diminishing the sector's ability to create the agenda for public debate.

In discussing the situation of people in poverty, health care, other social services, or the famine in Ethiopia, several authors have mentioned the inability of nonprofit organizations to serve needy clientele without government support. In Chapter Fifteen, Robert L. Payton uses a case study of the famine in Ethiopia to discuss the inability of individuals to sustain their support of repetitive famines. Such support emanates from the inherent values of Americans that, for example, people should not be allowed to starve. These values can have a profound impact in bringing a problem to world attention. Initial private giving can provide enormous relief, but sustained solutions require more than the generosity of private individuals; they require coherent planning and sustained support. Payton, as well as many of the other authors of this volume, would find that a reason for partnership with the government.

As Peter Goldberg points out in Chapter Twenty-One, corporations have also found that they cannot solve the problem of worker redundancy caused by a changing economy, nor can they provide adequate support for the poor. Goldberg concludes that corporate leaders can, however, exert leadership in public-policy debates by advocating public support for underserved populations.

Several authors of this volume acknowledge that there will be a continuing and growing need for the services of nonprofit organizations but that the growing problem of the national debt may prevent increasing public expenditures on such services. Forrest P. Chisman (Chapter Twenty-Eight) also reports a growing skepticism among the public that government is capable of solving the social problems that beset this nation. He argues that the independent sector should reactivate and renew its public leadership in creating the public-policy agenda as it did during the Progressive movement and the civil rights movement. Such movements led to social reform and action and resulted in the development of public support and national consensus. In Chapter Twelve, Bremner also argues that advocacy organizations are needed to provide education about societal problems, to seek public solutions and support, and to monitor government performance. He uses as a case study the importance of advocacy movements in improving the rights, defense, and support of children over the past two decades. Such efforts have been successful in bringing the issues of child development, public education, and public support of children in poverty back to the national agenda. He makes very clear, as does Chisman, that one of the fundamental responsibilities of nonprofit organizations is advocacy, whether for the rights of children, minorities, or people in poverty or for other public issues. Moreover, this function is as important as, if not more important than, the provision of direct services.

Nonprofit organizations that pay more attention to revenue generation and commercial practices than to their fundamental missions will be increasingly regulated by both the federal and local governments. It is not unlikely that such activities could result in a taxation on assets, as it did for foundations in 1969. Both James J. McGovern (Chapter Ten) and Marion R. Fremont-Smith (Chapter Five) suggest that the drift toward commercial practices will bring about such regulation, and they conclude that a change in tax exemption could mean a decline in the provision of social services.

Nonprofit organizations need to reexamine their fundamental missions and the clientele they serve. The trend toward providing services to clients who can pay without adequate provisions for the most vulnerable could lead to a reexamination of tax-exempt status for charitable organizations. Nonprofit organizations need to carefully document their programs and report to the public. Furthermore, they need to pay increasing attention to public education on important issues and on advocacy for social reform.

The Crisis in Financing

The reexamination of the role, functions, and mission of charitable organizations can be attributed in large part to (1) cutbacks in federal funding to nonprofit organizations during the 1980s; (2) the consequent action of many nonprofits to increase fees for service and to engage in commercial activities; (3) the growth of commercial service industries in a changing business economy; (4) the complaints by small businesses that nonprofits are engaging in direct competition with them; and (5) the increase in adversarial relations among all three sectors. It should not be surprising that distinctions among the sectors have blurred when for-profit corporations have moved aggressively into certain areas of health care and education. Nonprofits that traditionally have provided the largest proportion of these services have found themselves in competition with major corporate hospital chains, for-profit social services and counseling, and proprietary education. All of these industries are eligible for federal support or third-party insurance support, as are their nonprofit counterparts. In fact, these sources of funds have made possible the creation of profitable industries.

The representatives of several new commercial industries argue, as Hansmann does in Chapter Six, that once there is enough demand and enough resources to pay for services, maintaining the nonprofit form of organization is no longer necessary. Others would qualify this statement, as Burton A. Weisbrod does in Chapter Seven, to exclude services where the consumer lacks sufficient information to make an informed choice and such lack of information could be life threatening. In other words, choosing between different brands of chocolate chip cookies is very different from choosing an adequate nursing home or day-care center. Weisbrod argues that in these cases, consumers with little information will prefer or be more likely to trust the non-profit firm, where the service mission rather than the profit motive is primary.

The crisis of mission has occurred because of the downturn in governmental support, which some authors argue has provided the traditional source of financing for nonprofit services. As Salamon points out in Chapter Three, government has been the major partner in funding social services. Other types of non-profits, such as arts agencies, private nonprofit educational institutions, and religious organizations, are not as dependent on government. Hospitals have become reliant on third-party payment systems from government and private insurance companies as a major source of revenue, while for more than a decade donations have steadily declined as a proportion of their total income. Even though private contributions to social service agencies have increased since 1982, these have been able to replace only slightly more than 20 percent of the accumulated federal budget cuts from 1982 to 1986 (Salamon and Abramson, 1988). At the same time, nonprofit services have increased over this period, as reported in Chapters Two and Three. According to Chisman (Chapter Twenty-Eight), the lack of resources to respond to such increased demands has led to grave doubt about the ability of either government or the nonprofit sector to provide adequate services. This fiscal crunch has caused many nonprofits to increase their income from fees and to engage in commercial activities.

In addition to federal government program cutbacks, another major blow to the traditional financing of private non-profit and governmental agencies was the 1986 Tax Reform Act, which decreased taxpayers' incentive to make charitable contributions by excluding the charitable deduction for nonitemizers while decreasing the number of those eligible to itemize. As a result of these changes, economists predicted a decline in the rate of total giving by individuals. Lawrence B. Lindsey proposes in Chapter Nineteen that the government could increase incentives for charitable giving by individuals without a resultant loss in tax revenue either by imposing a limit on deductions for charitable giving or by extending the deduction to nonitemizers while lowering the standard deduction for nonitemizers. Either of these changes would increase individual giving for charitable purposes and provide more acceptable forms of financing for nonprofits than commercial ventures.

Another possible form of financing for larger nonprofit service agencies is low-interest loans to agencies that obtain revenues through client fees but still want to provide services to low-income clients on a sliding scale. In Chapter Eighteen, Steven A. Waldhorn, James A. Gollub, and Joyce A. Klein report that studies done at SRI International show that investment loans to nonprofits by foundations, corporations, and government can provide capital to develop human service programs; these are called program-related investments. Such loans can help to improve management, furnish venture capital to experiment with innovative programs, and provide a revolving fund for future investments. They have the further advantage of involving all sectors in a common investment to provide services for public purposes.

Both Burton A. Weisbrod (Chapter Seven) and Jack Moskowitz (Chapter Seventeen) would argue, although for different reasons, that if nonprofits serve identified public purposes, they should receive subsidies from public sources to carry out their mission. Weisbrod argues that lack of adequate support forces nonprofits to compete in the market and that such activity fundamentally affects their mission to provide a public good. Moskowitz demonstrates in a series of case studies that government-nonprofit partnerships can be very effective and cost efficient.

The financing of nonprofits is as much a public-policy issue as it is a private issue. Far more exploration needs to be done to identify private forms of financing that are not market driven. Furthermore, nonprofits need to lobby for more efficient forms of financing for their services through partnerships with government and/or the private sector, as well as for the provision of increased incentives for individual giving through the tax system. One solution suggested by Lifset's analysis of the fiscal crisis and the competitive environment with small business (Chapter Nine) is to move away from adversarial relationships where the public will be poorly served. Rather, nonprofit organizations should take the leadership in offering alternative solutions whereby the three sectors can work together to institute functional financing mechanisms that provide for the public good and, at the same time, create an environment in which business and nonprofits can coexist cooperatively.

Research and Education: A Crisis in Information

Policy makers need information in order to propose or to change public policy. The problem confronting the nonprofit sector has been a lack of research on its roles, functions, and distinctive contributions to American society. Some major strides have been made to address the gaps in our understanding about this sector over the past decade. Although some scholars have argued that singling out this sector for particular analysis may have been a cause of erosion in its support base and in public confidence (Hall, 1987), such attention has been very important to increasing our understanding of the nonprofit sector within the United States.

Research results are beginning to show that this sector is very complex. It includes a wide variety of institutions, organizations, and associations covering the span of human activities from hospices to self-help groups and from institutions of higher education to art museums. Salamon has shown that nonprofit organizations are the largest providers of social services in the nation. Scholars studying the theory of nonprofit organizations have found that there is no single theory that explains all of nonprofit activity, although John Simon, the founding director and current chair of the Program on Non-Profit Organizations at Yale University (Chapter 29), had fond hopes that they would develop such a theory. The assumptions concerning the roles and functions about this sector are as diverse as Hansmann's and Salamon's in this volume. Scholars, particularly Bremner and Salamon (Chapters Three and Twelve), have shown that partnerships between nonprofit organizations and local government have existed since colonial times. Partnership with the federal government grew exponentially with the rise of the welfare state after 1930. The authors also have shown that public-policy decisions since 1980 are dismantling these historical partnerships, leading to changes in service delivery and traditional forms of financial support. In turn, these changes have resulted in the trend toward commercial behavior by nonprofits. Other scholars have reiterated that nonprofits have received tax exemption because they perform public functions and that the fundamental distinction between nonprofits and for-profits is the moral dimension. Charitable organizations are established with a mission to provide services and advocacy.

Several authors identify the enormous gaps that still remain in our knowledge about this sector. Information about the commercial activities of nonprofits is very limited, although trends toward deriving revenues from increased fee income are documented among certain types of nonprofit organizations in Chapters Two and Three. The continuing need for nonprofit services is clearly demonstrated, both by demographic projections and by the survey research discussed in Chapters Two and Three, but there has been a lack of attention to what kinds of organizations can best serve these needs and how they should be financed. National goals for improving the quality of life and productivity of all Americans, particularly the growing proportion of women and children in poverty, have been neglected in recent years. Clearly, demographic trends and income statistics are showing that such issues must be addressed. If these authors are right, nonprofits have been neglecting their public leadership role.

The focus of much of the research in this volume is the major function of nonprofits to influence the national agenda on public policy relating to underserved populations. As a result of the effort of nonprofits to offset major federal funding cutbacks, the sector may have lost some of its ability to influence the public agenda. More research is needed on the advocacy functions of nonprofit organizations and their impact on public policy, such as James Allen Smith (Chapter Four) has conducted regarding the foundation funding of think tanks.

High on the priority list of a research agenda for the future should be a major effort to understand the complex interrelationships among the sectors and how changes in their roles can affect the mission of nonprofits to serve the public good. At present, there are many theories but little hard evidence about how competitive practices among sectors affect the equitable provision of services for various population groups.

Perhaps most important is the need for all Americans to understand how their society works. What are the roles of government, business, and nonprofit organizations in maintaining democratic values? The research reported in Chapter Twenty-Seven, by Margot Stern Strom and Alan L. Stoskopf, suggests that there is an appalling lack of education on the values, traditions, and institutions that provide citizens with an opportunity to participate in creating the public agenda. Nonprofit institutions traditionally have played an important role in this process, but this role is in danger of being forgotten if it is not part of the education of all Americans. The role of nonprofit institutions both in creating citizen leaders and in educating the public probably has much larger implications for the preservation of democratic traditions and values than is generally realized. In fact, citizen education may be this sector's most unique function. Not only do we need to know more about the importance of this role in preserving individual freedom and developing national consensus, but we need to know whether nonprofits are neglecting this responsibility (Mathews, 1987).

This volume demonstrates what is being learned about the role and functions of the independent, or third, sector in American society. It demonstrates even more the state of our ignorance. Unless more attention is paid to this sector, both in research and in public-policy deliberations, its capacity to serve the public good will continue to erode. This volume may provide the initial impetus to this effort.

References

Boorstin, D. J. *The Decline of Radicalism.* New York: Random House, 1963.

Bremner, R. *American Philanthropy.* (Rev. ed.). Chicago: University of Chicago Press, 1988.

Commission on Private Philanthropy and Public Needs. *Giving in America: Toward a Stronger Voluntary Sector.* Washington, D.C.: Commission on Private Philanthropy and Public Needs, 1975.

Curti, M. "American Philanthropy and the National Character." *American Quarterly,* 1958, *10,* 420–437.

Hall, P. D. *Organizations of American Culture, 1700–1900: Institutions, Elites, and the Origins of American Nationality.* New York: New York University Press, 1982.

Hall, P. D. "Abandoning the Rhetoric of Independence: Reflections on the Nonprofit Sector in the Post-Liberal Era." *Journal of Voluntary Action Research,* 1987, *16* (1–2), 11–28.

McCarthy, K. D. *Noblesse Oblige: Charity and Cultural Philanthropy in Chicago, 1849–1929.* Chicago: University of Chicago Press, 1982.

Mathews, D. "The Independent Sector and the Political Responsibilities of the Public." Keynote address presented at the INDEPENDENT SECTOR Spring Research Forum, New York, Mar. 19, 1987.

Payton, R. L. *Major Challenges to Philanthropy.* Discussion paper prepared for the INDEPENDENT SECTOR, Aug. 1984.

Reich, R. B. *Tales of a New America.* New York: Times Books, 1987.

Salamon, L. M. "Of Market Failure, Voluntary Failure, and Third Party Government: Toward a Theory of Government-Nonprofit Relations in the Modern Welfare State." *Journal of Voluntary Action Research,* 1987, *16* (1–2), 29–49.

Salamon, L. M, and Abramson, A. J. "Nonprofit Organizations and the FY 1989 Federal Budget." Report prepared for the INDEPENDENT SECTOR, May 1988.

2

CARROLL L. ESTES
ELIZABETH A. BINNEY
LINDA A. BERGTHOLD

△ △ △ △ △ △ △ △ △ △ △ △ △ △ △ △

How the Legitimacy of the Sector Has Eroded

The 1980s have been a time of crisis, turmoil, and change for the nonprofit sector, in terms of both the day-to-day operation of nonprofit organizations and the larger issues concerning the role of the sector in relation to other sectors of society—government, business, and the public. These changes reflect shifts in public policy as well as in public perceptions concerning the roles of government and the nonprofit sector with regard to the provision of certain services.

      This chapter examines the legitimacy of the nonprofit sector as a viable and significant entity in the context of its place as a distinctive "third sector" of the economy and polity. Legitimation and its opposite, delegitimation, are deceptively simple concepts, but ones that are crucial in denoting the strength and viability of any society and its social institutions. *Legitimacy* refers to the degree to which social systems or institutions are valued (Weber, 1958) and their underlying principles and legal authority accepted by members of society (Schaar, 1984). The stability of the nonprofit sector depends not only on its economic and organizational viability but also on its ability to generate and maintain support in the political system for its right to exist as a legitimate sector of society. Just as the legitimacy of the government depends on the effective performance of its functions (at least as defined by the most powerful groups in society) and the

21

preservation of the existing social order, the legitimacy of the nonprofit sector depends on the assessment of its performance by powerful forces, institutions, sectors, and individuals in society.

When the underlying beliefs, laws, or principles that support societies or institutions are questioned or challenged, their basic legitimacy is questioned or challenged. Such challenges to legitimacy, by definition, generate power struggles of enormous economic, political, and ideological moment. The processes of legitimation and delegitimation are, respectively, the attempts to bolster or undermine support for existing authority and modes of organization. Given that every social order, institution, and organizational entity requires legitimacy in order to exist and persist, powerful and successful legitimacy challenges are extremely serious. Legitimacy challenges may generate crisis tendencies (Habermas, 1975) and provoke periods of intense uncertainty as preexisting understandings are called into question and "new power centers confront existing [power] structures" (O'Connor, 1987, p. 145). A full-blown legitimation crisis occurs when there is a resulting breakdown in the supporting norms and institutional rationale for any sector of society (for example, the nonprofit sector), because its organization and activities can proceed only insofar as there is available legitimacy to support it.

According to recent thinking on the interpenetration of the nonprofit sector with government and business in the larger political economy (Van Til, 1982, 1987; Ostrander, Langton, and Van Til, 1987), legitimacy issues surrounding the nonprofit sector cannot be understood apart from considerations of the roles and problems of government and business sectors. Research that is addressed to the legitimacy of the nonprofit sector must fully specify the relationships between the conditions in the larger economy and business, the response of government (and the legitimacy questions that that may raise), and the issues and dilemmas confronting the nonprofit sector.

The primary sources of legitimacy of the nonprofit sector reside in its historical and contemporary role and character. In addition to serving as an alternative provider to government, nonprofit-sector institutions in U.S. society have enjoyed special legitimacy in terms of their traditional representation of pluralistic, participatory, and noneconomic motivations of charity and the spirit of giving, privatism, individualism, and the democratic impulse. Legitimacy questions inhere in the necessity for the nonprofit sector to straddle these values while simultaneously pursuing the newly imposed efficiency criteria in the context of an increasingly austere and competitive environment.

An important ideological aspect of the nonprofit sector, about which much has been written, is the notion that it is an "independent" sector—one that protects society from the threat of a vast, bureaucratic, and stifling government. The dilemma of this view of an independent nonprofit sector is that, while it has supported the notion of the nonprofit sector as a positive force against an overly powerful government (an antistatist notion), it has also supported the notion that the nonprofit sector does not need government or is somehow unrelated to it. This has left the nonprofit sector vulnerable to attacks on its base of support both in law and in government funding (Hall, 1987a; Salamon, 1987).

Dimensions of Crisis in the Nonprofit Sector

Recently, the situation of the nonprofit sector has been typified in terms of crisis and crisis tendencies (Hall, 1987a; Hall, 1987b; Estes and Alford, 1987). Hall (1987a) contends that three types of crises have occurred: (1) a crisis *of* the nonprofit sector arising from the shifting role of government in relation to society and the nonprofit sector within it; (2) a crisis *within* the nonprofit sector concerning problems of insufficient professionalism and managerialism; and (3) a crisis in "nonprofit scholarship." This chapter considers the legitimacy issues raised in regard to the first two types of crisis and to the authors' research on crisis tendencies and the nonprofit sector.

The crisis *of* the nonprofit sector consists of a number of dimensions, including government cutbacks and defunding and federal and state challenges to nonprofit organizational status, including legal, tax, and regulatory changes, that affect the organization, management, and revenues of nonprofit organizations (for example, treatment of related income; incentives for individual and corporate giving) and the activities that they are permitted to carry out, such as advocacy limitations (Skloot, 1987; Broaddus, 1987; Estes, Alford, and Binney, 1987). While these trends have been documented and discussed in many contexts elsewhere, they have not heretofore been examined as factors that collectively contribute to the legitimacy struggles of the nonprofit sector.

The crisis *within* the nonprofit sector consists of (1) responses by individual members (or subsectors) to pressures to embrace professionalism and managerialism, which emerged as early as the 1969 Tax Reform Act (Hall, 1987b) but which have been accentuated in the current climate of competition, and (2) the restructuring of the community service infrastructure, resulting from a combination of external and internal pressures on government and the nonprofit sector in the present era of austerity (Estes and Wood, 1986; Estes and Bergthold, 1989; Estes, Alford, and Binney, 1987).

Research at the Institute for Health and Aging of the University of California has identified multiple dimensions of this restructuring at the individual agency level in community organizations that deliver health and social services to the elderly. For example, important changes have been documented in the provision of home health care by nonprofits, including organizational and labor-force changes (increasing part-time and contract personnel); client and service changes based on ability to pay; a shifting ideological rationale for nonprofits, threatening goal displacement (a "means-ends" inversion in which the "process goals" of management, rationalization, and survival replace the "end goals" of service, charity, and democratic participation); and, in a limited number of cases, organizational death. Our contention is that such changes are reflective of crisis within elements of the sector that also contributes to legitimation crisis tendencies both of and within the nonprofit sector as a whole, and perhaps within the broader system (Estes and Alford, 1987).

Aspects of the Legitimation Crisis

For purposes of this analysis, the concepts of legitimation and its counterpart, delegitimation, must be disaggregated into conceptually and empirically measurable components. Friedrichs (1980) argues that legitimacy crisis may be expressed in terms of three dimensions: (1) subjective or perceptual, which includes ideological and attitudinal changes and challenges; (2) objective or behavioral, including actions taken by individuals, policy makers, groups, and others; and (3) structural, based on the characteristics of the state, economy, and society, such as dramatic demographic changes, tensions between world spheres, and the expanding role of mass communication.

While all three dimensions are relevant to a discussion of tendencies toward crises of legitimacy in the nonprofit sector, the first two can be further differentiated at two levels of analysis—"macro" and "micro"—to signify the different levels at which legitimacy challenges can be observed (see Table 2.1). Macrolevel perceptual and behavioral indicators of legitimation problems appear in the broad institutional relations and transactions between different sectors of society. Microlevel indicators reflect those changes occurring at the level of the individual nonprofit organization or subsector of nonprofits, such as health or social service agencies.

The Macrolevel: Perceptual and Behavioral Indicators

On the macrolevel, there are a series of perceptual indicators of legitimacy problems for the nonprofit sector in relation to other sectors of society. A number of these reflect struggles for the ideological center ground in the American value structure. The foresight of John Gardner in the founding of INDEPENDENT SECTOR (IS) in 1980 is an early manifestation of the acknowledgment of troubles on the horizon for the nonprofit sector. It is no coincidence that the efforts of INDEPENDENT SECTOR to claim (or possibly reclaim) the inherently social

Table 2.1. Indications of Legitimation Crisis Tendencies
in the Nonprofit Sector.

	Macro	*Micro*
Subjective/Perceptual	1. Formation of INDE-PENDENT SECTOR* 2. Small Business Administration report on nonprofits as unfair competition 3. House Ways and Means Hearings on nonprofit hospitals 4. United Hospital Fund "Mission Matters" program	1. Limited support for favored status for the nonprofit sector 2. Increased legitimacy for norms of efficiency 3. Increased legitimacy of health as "business" and for profits as service providers
Objective/Behavioral	**Political** 1. Legal issues regarding income and tax treatment 2. Regulatory changes to restrain advocacy activities of nonprofits and add special bidding requirements for nonprofits 3. Tax reform legislation disincentive for giving	1. Privatization of nonprofit services/activities; for example, changing tax status of nonprofits 2. Changing role of nonprofits: increased demand/need by uninsured as "pull" factor and financial issues as "push" factor 3. Organizational similarities in behavior of non-profits and for-profits
	Economic 1. Government funding cutbacks 2. Health care cost containment promoting competition between for-profits and nonprofits	

*The founding of INDEPENDENT SECTOR reflects both perceptual and behavioral dimensions of crisis tendencies facing the nonprofit sector.

Source: Institute for Health and Aging. University of California, San Francisco. DRG Impact Study, telephone surveys, 1987 instruments.

values of giving, volunteering, and the not-for-profit initiative have occurred in the context of the most conservative and politically organized antistate hostility in many decades. Moreover, both the necessity for IS and the response to its work reflect some of the contradictions arising in the interrelationships among the nonprofit sector, government, business, and the public.

In the last two decades, there has been increasing talk of "crisis" all across the societal spectrum, from the hypothesized breakdown of the moral order and loss of family to the deficit crisis. The politics of austerity, the profitability problems of businesses, and the attack on government (that is, on its legitimacy) all signal potential storm clouds over the nonprofit sector. The breadth and depth of the challenge presented to all sectors of society are illustrated in the wave of books on crisis and crisis tendencies that appeared in the 1970s, including *Legitimation Crisis* (Habermas, 1975), *The Limits of Legitimacy* (Wolfe, 1977), and *Fiscal Crisis of the State* (O'Connor, 1973), while public-opinion pollsters have documented a "crisis of moral leadership" and "resentment in America" (Yankelovich, 1972, 1975; Caddell, 1979) and social scientists worried about Watergate and a host of other social problems.

It is in this context that "serious inquiries into [the] future" of the nonprofit sector emerged (Hall, 1987b, p. 20), which resulted in the creation of the privately sponsored Filer Commission and its study (Commission on Private Philanthropy and Public Needs, 1975), as well as the Department of the Treasury's seven-volume publication on the nonprofit sector and the commission (Commission on Private Philanthropy and Public Needs, 1977). Simultaneously, a spate of articles and books on this subject began to appear, including *The Changing Position of Philanthropy in the American Economy* (Dickinson, 1970), "Federal Oversight of Private Philanthropy" (Ginsburg, Marks, and Wertheim, 1977), and *The Endangered Sector* (Nielsen, 1979). Thus, balancing the preservation of sectoral independence with increased demands for public accountability and a growing share of government funding claimed center stage of nonprofit concerns from the mid-1960s to the late 1970s.

For the 1980s, an opening salvo in the political and ideological struggle over nonprofit-sector legitimacy was delivered in the U.S. Small Business Administration's (1984) report *Unfair Competition,* which assailed nonprofits as unfair to small business and called for elimination of differential tax treatment for nonprofits and for-profits. Fallout from this report continues to be felt in the form of various policy remedies now being pressed in several states (Skloot, 1987), as well as on the federal level.

Additional indications of ideological battle lines drawn between norms of the market, efficiency, and competition versus those of charitable service and noneconomic motivations are found in the 1987 hearings of the U.S. House Ways and Means Oversight Subcommittee and proposals to decrease federal tax advantages for nonprofit hospitals and other health nonprofits ("Taxing Non-Profits," 1987). The recent counterattack of the nation's oldest federated charity, the United Hospital Fund of New York City, is another example (Seay and Vladeck, 1987). The fund's response has been to develop a campaign under the banner "Mission Matters," which "grew from a need to inform, and to balance what has evolved into a skewed public policy debate about the legitimacy of the not-for-profit organizational form as a result of a preoccupation with entrepreneurialism and competition, rather than social responsibility in health care" (B. Vladeck, personal communication, 1987).

The Mission Matters campaign seeks to raise public understanding of what is described as the distinctive character of nonprofit hospitals: their commitment to social values, to the community, and to their patients and services regardless of profit orientation; their governance and accountability to maintain a charitable organizational basis; and their institutional volunteerism. This "fight-back" strategy stakes a claim to the culture of caring by appealing to the historical norms and traditions of service of nonprofit hospitals and documenting their public contributions, such as medical research, education, and community services (more than $22 billion in charity care has been provided by nonprofit hospitals in the past five years). This is an overt although not unexpected example of the renewed interest in the "public presentation of self" by nonprofits under siege. Some segments of the leadership of the nonprofit sector are attempting to stem the tide of concern with appeals not only to government and business but also to the public.

In examining legitimacy on the behavioral or objective macrolevel, the political and economic dimensions are crucial. The 1981 Economic Recovery Act and the 1986 Tax Reform Act illustrate the importance and interrelationship of the political and economic dimensions. Both contain tax provisions that, it has been argued, would have a profound (and constraining) effect on economic incentives to give privately to nonprofits. While the 1981 Tax Equity and Fiscal Responsibility Act reduced taxes by $750 billion, theoretically providing more money for charitable giving by individual taxpayers, its substantial depreciation allowances and tax write-offs actually reduced incentives for corporate and individual giving. The 1986 Tax Reform Act abolished the charitable deduction for individuals who do not itemize their income taxes, a move that was anticipated to be a "blow" to individual incentives for giving, especially by those in lower income brackets, who actually contribute at higher rates than those in the higher income brackets (Clotfelter, 1985; Simon, 1987).

Political problems for the nonprofit sector also surfaced in forms such as legal challenges to the favored tax treatments of nonprofits in terms of unrelated business income; regulatory changes requiring nonprofits to incorporate the equivalent of for-profit taxes in bidding for government contracts (to make them less "unfair" to for-profit bidders) (Skloot, 1987); federal regulations restraining advocacy activities by nonprofits (Broaddus, 1987); regulatory provisions encouraging competition and the entry of proprietaries into many fields, most notably the health field (Marmor, Schlesinger, and Smithey, 1987); and multiple pressures for increased organizational rationality (that is, efficiency) of nonprofits.

Behavioral or objective macrolevel economic challenges appear largely in the form of budget cuts and defunding that have dramatically affected the nonprofit sector. Documentation reveals total cuts of 28 percent in federal support for nonprofits between 1980 and 1986, excluding health finance (Abramson and Salamon, 1986, p. 73). On the basis of current budget proposals, additional and significant cuts in federal support of nonprofit organizations (exceeding $22 billion) are projected for the 1987 to 1989 fiscal period. These cuts will bring overall federal reductions to more than 40 percent per year below 1980 funding levels (Abramson and Salamon, 1986, p. xvi). At the same time, major health cost containment policies have been introduced. With the economic stringency placed particularly on social services, community development, the arts, education, and health services (exclusive of health financing) in the 1980s (Salamon and Abramson, 1982, 1985), the viability and survival needs of nonprofit-sector organizations are key issues. These political and economic struggles have brought the legitimacy claims of the nonprofit sector into even sharper focus as we approach the 1990s.

The Microlevel: An Example
in Health and Social Services

To date, there has been no systematic documentation on the tendencies toward legitimation crisis in the nonprofit sector. Data from the Institute for Health and Aging regarding the impact of federal cost-containment policy on the delivery of health and social services for the elderly offer the only known empirical evidence on both the behavioral and perceptual (attitudinal) indicators of the changing roles of nonprofit, for-profit, and public service sectors. Researchers for the study (Estes and associates, 1988) interviewed representatives of community home health service agencies concerning their attitudes about whether public policy should guarantee legal protection or other advantages (via tax-exempt status, tax advantage, preference in contracts or grants, and so on) to any one of the three sectors over the others. Although the study was limited to only one sector of the community service infrastructure (home health), we believe that these data reflect a measure of the legitimacy struggles in which the nonprofit sector now finds itself engaged.

Interviews in 1987 with a random sample of 193 nonprofit and proprietary home health agencies in nine urban communities in five states (California, Florida, Pennsylvania, Texas, and Washington) document both the behavioral and the ideological dimensions of these struggles (Estes and associates, 1988). Home health agency directors were asked to assess the changes in the role of nonprofit, for-profit, and public agencies in the delivery of health and social services to the elderly between 1984 and 1987 and to indicate whether they believed that there were reasons for public policy to protect or provide special treatment to either the nonprofit, the public, or the for-profit sectors.

Data analysis indicates widespread environmental turbulence and uncertainty in the home health provider community, with all three sectors experiencing change. Also, it is apparent that behavioral indicators of role change often exist in contradiction to perceptual and attitudinal beliefs about what each sector's "proper" role is and the degree to which it is appropriate for government to support or favor one sector over another.

The Microlevel Behavioral Indicators. A substantial majority of home health respondents reported that all three sectors had undergone changes in their roles within the community delivery system. Approximately three-quarters of those interviewed described changed roles for both the nonprofit and for-profit sectors and two-thirds for the public sector (see Table 2.2). Analysis of survey questions about the nature of the change in these sectors yields interesting and provocative results. In describing the nature of changes in the nonprofit sector, almost half (48 percent) of the responses indicated that the nonprofit sector's role had increased, while one-third (33.5 percent) reported that in some way, the role of the nonprofit sector in the provision of health and social services for the elderly had decreased (see Table 2.3).

The most frequently cited reasons for an increased nonprofit-sector role included the increase in the demand for services and/or the demand for an expanded scope of services that nonprofit community agencies offer; increases in client pressures (including a dramatic increase in the need and/or expectation of the nonprofit sector to care for the indigent and those unable to pay); and changes in client patterns (including an increase in numbers of clients and an increase in the number of sicker clients). Two primary reasons were cited for the decreasing role

**Table 2.2. Percent of Home Health Agencies
Indicating Role Change in the Nonprofit, For-Profit, and Public Sectors.**

Role Change	Nonprofit	For-Profit	Public
Yes	74	77	67
No	25	23	33

Source: Institute for Health and Aging, University of California, San Francisco. DRG Impact Study, telephone surveys, 1987 instruments.

**Table 2.3. Percent of Home Health Agencies Indicating Type
and Direction of Role Change.**

Change	Change in Nonprofit	Change in For-Profit	Change in Public
Increased role	48.4	51.1	44.9
Decreased role	33.5	17.8	43.6
Other changes	18.1	32.2	11.5

Source: Institute for Health and Aging. University of California, San Francisco. DRG Impact Study, telephone surveys, 1987 instruments.

of the nonprofit sector: the inability or unwillingness of non-profit agencies to provide services and specific financial reasons, including reimbursement changes and increased fiscal constraint.

In general, those claiming a decreased role for the non-profit sector cited economic reasons (decreased funding, inability to provide services due to lack of funding, tightening eligibility due to reimbursement, and so on). On the other hand, those who cited an increased role for the nonprofit sector predominantly cited reasons of demand and "need." This apparently contradictory set of responses—the simultaneous "push" (in terms of financial limits) and "pull" (in terms of demand) on the non-profit sector—illustrates the fact that changes in the nonprofit sector's role are clearly tied to fundamental changes in the macro-level financing structures of health and social services. Nonprofit local providers currently face a crisis of growing demand concurrent with a relative decline in resources in a competitive and increasingly privatized environment of health care delivery (Estes and Wood, 1986; Bergthold, Estes, Alford, and Villanueva, 1987).

Interestingly, a majority of respondents cited similar changes in role for the public sector, with reasons supporting the cases for both an increased and a decreased role very similar to those given regarding the nonprofit sector. These data indicate that both the nonprofit and the public sectors are facing increased magnitude and scope of need and demand in an environment of high fiscal constraint. However, given the current dominant ideology, which discourages the public provision of services and encourages the privatization of welfare-state activities, the nonprofit sector faces a different dilemma from that of the public sector. While public-sector provision of such services has been attacked under the guise of cost containment, there is still considerable support for some system of public provision at the level of last resort (and to prevent the for-profit sector from having to directly absorb the costs of those who cannot pay).

Attacks on the traditional mission of the nonprofit sector and its right to tax advantages and other forms of state protection and the pressures of survival in a highly competitive and cost-containment-conscious environment pose a considerably different dilemma for the public sector. If one is to understand the significance of this dilemma and the effects of attempts to delegitimate the nonprofit sector, the data for the nonprofit sector must be contrasted with those for the proprietary sector.

The responses regarding the role of the proprietary sector differed in important ways from those concerning the nonprofit and public sectors. The primary for-profit change reported was toward an increased role (51.1 percent), while only 17.8 percent of the responses cited a generally decreased role for this sector. The increased role of for-profits was largely attributed to factors similar to those cited for the other two sectors: service factors, including increased demand, a more diversified and expanded scope of services, more home care and skilled home care, and more high-tech care. However, two differences were apparent between for-profits and both the public and nonprofit agencies. For-profits were much more likely to report attracting full-pay (fully insured or privately paying) patients to account for their increased role than were the other sectors, and there was virtually no indication that increases in either indigent or partial-pay care was responsible for the increased role of the for-profit sector.

While funding considerations were cited as a major factor in the declining role of nonprofit-sector agencies, only a small percentage of the responses cited funding considerations in the case of for-profits. The major reasons cited to explain the diminished role in community services for proprietaries are instructive: a narrowing scope of services; the ability to provide only profitable services; a tendency to decrease or drop Medicare patients entirely; and a "turning away from the elderly."

Issues of competition, marketing, and public relations are all strongly tied into the interrelationship and changing roles of the various sectors. In general, the changing roles of the three sectors can be differentiated on the basis of two factors: response to fiscal condition and response to demand. Overall, a dramatic increase in demand on the community health and social service delivery system has been documented (Goldberg and Estes, 1988). However, according to the data cited here, the nonprofit and proprietary sectors have responded differently to this demand. The home health agencies in the sample have described the successful targeting (that is, for paying clients) and efficiency practices that the proprietary sector has adopted in order to maintain solvency and profitability in a competitive environment. Study findings also show that nonprofit agencies are experiencing severe pressures to adopt similar practices of efficiency, solvency, and "profitability." Indeed, it appears that nonprofit home health agencies are being forced to adopt the practices of their proprietary counterparts. More important, the assumption by nonprofits of these practices may ultimately threaten not only the traditional role of the nonprofit sector in home health but also its ability to meet the increased demands being placed on it, particularly in the provision of care to indigent and partial-pay clients. Further, and most important, to the extent that the "bottom line" becomes the pervasive influence on the behavior of nonprofits, we would expect there to be legitimation problems (that is, attempts at delegitimation) in the nonprofit sector.

One of the bases of attack on the nonprofit sector has been the perception that, despite enjoying tax-exempt status and other advantages, nonprofits have begun to behave like proprietaries. A second is the relative efficiency of the sectors in providing for community need, especially in the current environment rife with cost-containment rhetoric. However, the home health data indicate that while the nonprofit sector is being forced to meet proprietary standards of efficiency (efficiency measured in terms of costs but not in terms of quality or access), nonprofit-sector agencies are simultaneously being asked to meet the increased demand caused in part by the federal Medicare cost-containment policies and by the ever-increasing ranks of the un- and underinsured (who, if served, will make nonprofit agencies "inefficient" by definition).

The Microlevel Perceptual Indicators. The microlevel behavioral indicators are of particular interest in light of data on attitudinal indicators of the legitimation problems of the nonprofit sector. In addition to being asked about actual role changes, home health agencies in the study were asked whether public policy should favor or protect any one of the sectors over another. The responses provided much insight into the ideological contradictions in the role of the nonprofit sector with respect to the other sectors, government and business.

The dominant perceptual and ideological view of the respondents interviewed is that the nonprofit sector should not receive special treatment such as tax advantages, despite the reported increase in demand and responsibility being placed on nonprofit services at the community level. Almost two-thirds of all responses (64 percent) indicated the belief that no sector should enjoy favor or protection through public policy. More significantly, only 18 percent of responses indicated support for protecting the nonprofit sector specifically. This finding suggests, we believe, that there is an extremely limited base of attitudinal support among home health care providers for the claims that the nonprofit sector justifies special treatment because of its unique attributes or responsibilities.

Respondents who felt that the nonprofit sector should be protected expressed two general positions: a belief that the nonprofit sector has better motives and a better interest in providing care than does the rest of the private sector and a belief that the care, services, and responsibility to the elderly and the maintenance of access for disadvantaged populations are better in the nonprofit sector. However, the majority, who felt that no sector deserved favor or protection, were split among a number of ideological rationales. The largest percentage of responses indicated that, on general principle, no sector should have an advantage over any other. Other categories of responses included the beliefs that principles of equality ("everyone should be treated equally," "no favoritism," "it is unfair to discriminate") should prohibit differential treatment and that principles of the free market (free enterprise, competition and competitive market, and so on) are most important and would be threatened by public policy that favored any one sector over the others. Yet other responses indicated the growing tensions between different types of providers as they try to exist in the current environment. These included the positions of many respondents who upheld the relative virtues of one sector as opposed to another ("proprietaries are as good as anyone else," "nonprofits are also profit oriented," and "nonprofits are favored at this time"), indicating that the current cost-containment and competitive environment has both sectors concerned with survivability and changes in their traditional roles.

Conclusion

The combination of macrolevel challenges to the nonprofit sector across perceptual (ideological), political, and economic lines and the microlevel empirical data reported here suggests that the nonprofit sector is experiencing a challenge to its legitimacy, a situation indicating real tendencies toward crisis. Crisis tendencies are manifested in significant efforts to erode public support for—that is, to delegitimate—the nonprofit sector as no longer deserving of special status in American society. These efforts appear to be particularly evident with regard to nonprofit health and social services.

The current structural-level conflicts and problems between the government and business are manifest in present struggles among the nonprofit sector, government, and the proprietary sector, and these struggles now reach into all major societal and institutional arenas: economic, political, and sociocultural. These conflicts help explain the process of attempted delegitimation of the nonprofit sector currently under way. The problems of the U.S. economy and the response of political conservatism have rendered government vulnerable to its own legitimacy crisis. Legitimation problems and public skepticism about government—a popular topic of pollsters and theorists since the mid-1970s—have been attributed to government's inability to fulfill the dual policy and fiscal functions necessary to promote favorable economic conditions and to meet the social needs of those who are displaced or made redundant by the economic system (O'Connor, 1973). For the nonprofit sector as for government, legitimacy challenges raise crucial questions of the integrity as well as the very raison d'être of these institutions. Such crisis tendencies result in historical moments when outcomes are uncertain, social struggles endemic, and potential consequences profound. In the present case, the future of the nonprofit sector hangs in the balance.

References

Abramson, A. J., and Salamon, L. M. *The Nonprofit Sector and the New Federal Budget.* Washington, D.C.: Urban Institute Press, 1986.

Bergthold, L., Estes, C. L., Alford, R., and Villanueva, T. "Public Light and Private Dark: The Privatization of Health and Social Services for the Elderly." Paper presented at meeting of the American Sociological Association, Chicago, Aug. 1987.

Broaddus, W. "Toe to Toe with IRS." *Foundation News,* Jan.-Feb. 1987, pp. 60-62.

Caddell, P. H. "Crisis of Confidence—Trapped in a Downward Spiral." *Public Opinion,* 1979, *2,* 2-8.

Clotfelter, C. *Federal Tax Policy and Charitable Giving.* Chicago: University of Chicago Press, 1985.

Commission on Private Philanthropy and Public Needs. *Giving in America: Toward a Stronger Voluntary Sector.* Washington, D.C.: Commission on Private Philanthropy and Public Needs, 1975.

Commission on Private Philanthropy and Public Needs. *Research Papers of the Commission on Private Philanthropy and Public Needs.* 7 vols. Washington, D.C.: U.S. Department of the Treasury, 1977.

Dickinson, F. G. *The Changing Position of Philanthropy in the American Economy.* Occasional Paper 110. New York: National Bureau of Economic Research, 1970.

Estes, C. L., and Alford, R. A. "Systemic Crisis and the Nonprofit Sector." Unpublished manuscript, University of California, San Francisco, 1987.

Estes, C. L., Alford, R. A., and Binney, E. A. "The Restructuring of the Nonprofit Sector." Unpublished manuscript, University of California, San Francisco, 1987.

Estes, C. L., and Bergthold, L. A. "Unravelling of the Nonprofit Sector in the U.S." *International Journal of Sociology and Social Policy,* 1989, *9,* (2–3), 18–33.

Estes, C. L., and Wood, J. B. "The Nonprofit Sector and Community-Based Care for the Elderly: A Disappearing Resource?" *Social Science and Medicine,* 1986, *23* (12), 1261–1266.

Estes, C. L., and Associates. *Organizational and Community Responses to Medicare Policy,* final report. San Francisco: Institute for Health and Aging, University of California, San Francisco, 1988.

Friedrichs, D. O. "The Legitimacy Crisis in the U.S.: A Conceptual Analysis." *Social Problems,* 1980, *27* (5), 540–555.

Ginsburg, D., Marks, L. R., and Wertheim, R. P. "Federal Oversight of Private Philanthropy." In Commission on Private Philanthropy and Public Needs, *Research Papers of the Commission on Private Philanthropy and Public Needs.* Vol 5. Washington, D.C.: U.S. Department of the Treasury, 1977.

Goldberg, S., and Estes, C. "Medicare DRGs and Post-Hospital Care for the Elderly: Does Out of the Hospital Mean Out of Luck?" Unpublished manuscript, Institute for Health and Aging, University of California, San Francisco, Apr. 1988.

Habermas, J. *Legitimation Crisis.* (T. McCarthy, trans.) Boston: Beacon Press, 1975.

Hall, P. D. "Abandoning the Rhetoric of Independence: Reflections on the Nonprofit Sector in the Post-Liberal Era." in S. A. Ostrander, S. Langton, and J. Van Til (eds.), *Shifting the Debate: Public/Private Sector Relations in the Modern Welfare State.* New Brunswick, N.J.: Transaction Books, 1987a.

Hall, P. D. "A Historical Overview of the Private Nonprofit Sector." In W. W. Powell (ed.), *The Nonprofit Sector: A Research Handbook.* New Haven, Conn.: Yale University Press, 1987b.

Marmor, T. R., Schlesinger, M., and Smithey, R. W. "Nonprofit Organizations and Health Care." In W. W. Powell (ed.), *The Nonprofit Sector: A Research Handbook.* New Haven, Conn.: Yale University Press, 1987.

Nielsen, W. A. *The Endangered Sector.* New York: Columbia University Press, 1979.

O'Connor, J. *Fiscal Crisis of the State.* New York: St. Martin's Press, 1973.

O'Connor, J. *The Meaning of Crisis.* New York and Oxford, England: Basil Blackwell, 1987.

Ostrander, S. A., Langton, S., Van Til, J. (eds.). *Shifting the Debate: Public/Private Sector Relations in the Modern Welfare State.* New Brunswick, N.J.: Transaction Books, 1987.

Salamon, L. M. "Of Market Failure and Third-Party Government: Toward a Theory of Government–Non-profit Relations." In S. A. Ostrander, S. Langton, and J. Van Til (eds.), *Shifting the Debate: Public/Private Sector Relations in the Modern Welfare State.* New Brunswick, N.J.: Transaction Books, 1987.

Salamon, L. M., and Abramson, A. J. *The Federal Budget and the Nonprofit Sector.* Washington, D.C.: Urban Institute Press, 1982.

Salamon, L. M., Abramson, A. J. "Nonprofits and the Federal Budget: Deeper Cuts Ahead." *Foundation News,* 1985, *26,* 45–54.

Schaar, J. H. "Legitimacy in the Modern State." In W. Connolly (ed.), *Legitimacy and the State.* New York: New York University Press, 1984.

Seay, J. D., and Vladeck, B. C. Mission Matters: A Report on the Future of Voluntary Health Care Institutions. New York: United Hospital Fund of New York, 1987.

Simon, J. G. "The Tax Treatment of Nonprofit Organizations: A Review of Federal and State Policies." in W. W. Powell (ed.), *The Nonprofit Sector: A Research Handbook.* New Haven, Conn.: Yale University Press, 1987.

Skloot, E. "Survival Time for Non-Profits." *Foundation News,* Jan.-Feb. 1987, pp. 38-42.

"Taxing Non-Profits: Still a Riddle." *Health Policy Week,* 1987, *16* (25), 1-2.

U.S. Small Business Administration. *Unfair Competition by Nonprofit Organizations with Small Business: An Issue for the 1980s.* (3rd ed.) Washington, D.C.: U.S. Small Business Administration, 1984.

Van Til, J. "Volunteering and Democratic Theory." In J. D. Hartman (ed.), *Volunteerism in the Eighties.* Washington, D.C.: University Press of America, 1982.

Van Til, J. "The Three Sectors: Voluntarism in a Changing Political Economy." In S. A. Ostrander, S. Langton, and J. Van Til (eds.), *Shifting the Debate: Public/Private Sector Relations in the Modern Welfare State.* New Brunswick, N.J.: Transaction Books, 1987.

Weber, M. "Legitimacy, Politics and the State." In H. Gerth and C. W. Mills (eds.), *From Max Weber: Essays in Sociology.* New York: Oxford University Press, 1958.

Wolfe, A. *The Limits of Legitimacy.* New York: Free Press, 1977.

Yankelovich, D. "A Crisis of Moral Leadership." *Dissent,* 1972, *21,* 523-526.

Yankelovich, D. "The Status of Resentment in America." *Social Research,* 1975, *42,* 760-777.

3

LESTER M. SALAMON

△ △ △ △ △ △ △ △ △ △ △ △ △ △ △

The Changing Partnership
Between the Voluntary Sector
and the Welfare State

> The future of the voluntary agency is indissolubly tied to
> the future of the welfare state, and both are increasingly
> perceived to be in crisis. (Kramer, 1981)

The past decade or more has witnessed a major assault on that
set of governmental social protections that has come to be known
as the modern "welfare state." Both in Europe and in the United
States, critics have argued that the welfare state has an inherent
tendency toward overexpansion, that it consequently overloads
the capacities of government, and that it makes excessive claims
on societal resources and therefore cuts too severely into the savings available to fuel further economic growth. In the face of
new demographic and social developments that promise to further expand the need for social welfare services, major efforts
have been launched to stabilize or reduce government expenditures and return a larger share of the responsibility for social
welfare services to private hands.

Unfortunately, Americans have attempted to come to
terms with this worldwide questioning of the welfare state with-

Note: This chapter appeared, in somewhat different form, in *Nonprofit and Voluntary Sector Quarterly,* 1989, *1* (1).

out taking sufficient account of the peculiar "institutional choices" (Ashford, 1986) that were made in the evolution of the American welfare state. Rather, our thinking and rhetoric have been dominated by a paradigm that has its roots more squarely in the European tradition. This "paradigm of conflict" posits an inherent conflict between the state and the private voluntary sector and views the rise of the welfare state as leading inevitably to the decline of the voluntary sector (see, for example, Nisbet, 1953; Berger and Neuhaus, 1977).

In previous work, I have argued that this "paradigm of conflict" seriously distorts the reality of the American welfare state as it had evolved through the early 1980s. Worse yet, it obscures the fact that America may already have developed a model for the future evolution of welfare provision that European critics of the traditional welfare state might find quite attractive. The central feature of this model is what might be called "the paradigm of partnership," an elaborate network of partnership arrangements between government and the voluntary sector for the financing and delivery of human services (Salamon, 1982, 1985, 1987a, 1987b; Salamon and Abramson, 1982). In many respects, these partnerships form the core of the American welfare state and constitute the principal financial fact of life of the American voluntary sector.

Recent developments have challenged this partnership in rather fundamental ways, however. In response, some (for example, Butler, 1985) have beckoned the nonprofit sector back to its essentially voluntary roots in line with the paradigm of conflict, while others (for example, Crimmins, 1985) have nudged it toward a more entrepreneurial future. Despite some significant starts (such as Gilbert, 1983), however, what has been lacking is an assessment that explicitly relates the future of the voluntary sector to recent trends in the modern welfare state, and that does so from a base of clear understanding about how the American welfare state actually operates. It is the purpose of this chapter to provide the basic components of such an assessment.

The central conclusion of the chapter is that powerful forces are leading the voluntary sector away from its recent role as a partner in public service. But rather than leading the sector toward a more charitable mode of operation, they are leading it instead toward greater integration into the private, market economy. To help the reader understand this development, the discussion here is divided into three parts. I begin by reviewing three major conclusions that flow from my earlier work on the recent pattern of government-nonprofit relations in the American welfare state. Next, I explore some of the salient trends in the operation of the American welfare state. Last, I examine the implications of these trends for the future character and role of the voluntary sector.

Prevailing Realities

The central fact of life of the American welfare state as it had evolved by the 1970s was a widespread pattern of partnership between government and the voluntary sector. Facing major new responsibilities in a context of continued public hostility to the bureaucratic state, government at all levels turned extensively to existing and newly created private nonprofit organizations to help it carry out expanded welfare-state functions. As a consequence, through direct and indirect grants and third-party payments, government support easily surpassed private charity as the major source of private nonprofit-sector income. For example, data we generated through the Urban Institute Nonprofit Sector Project revealed that in 1981, 40 percent of the income of a wide array of private nonprofit human service agencies, exclusive of hospitals and higher education institutions, came from government, as opposed to 30 percent from fees and 20 percent from private charity (Salamon, 1984, 1987b). No wonder the Commission on Private Philanthropy and Public needs (the Filer Commission) concluded that "government has emerged in the United States as a major 'philanthropist,' *the* major philanthropist in a number of the principal, traditional areas of philanthropy" (Commission on Private Philanthropy and Public Needs, 1975, p. 85).

This partnership between government and the nonprofit sector was not, moreover, simply a recent development, as some accounts of the sector suggest. Rather, its roots lay deep in American history. Summarizing the historical record, Waldemar Nielsen (1979, p. 47) points out that "collaboration, not separation or antagonism, between government and the Third Sector . . . has been the predominant characteristic" through much of our history.

Not only does this pattern of partnership have deep historical roots, it also has a strong theoretical rationale. Unfortunately, this rationale has been obscured by prevailing theories of the welfare state and of the voluntary sector, which emphasize, respectively, a hierarchically structured state and a voluntary sector filling in for "market failures" where government has yet to act (Weisbrod, 1977). In fact, however, the American state is highly fragmented and commonly relies on third parties to carry out public functions (Salamon, 1981). In addition, the notion of the voluntary sector as a last line of defense in cases of "market failure" and "government failure" takes too little account of the inherent strengths and weaknesses of the voluntary sector, particularly the sector's exceptional capabilities as a deliverer of human services and its difficulties in raising resources and ensuring uniformity of coverage and equity (Salamon, 1987a). Viewed from these perspectives, government-nonprofit cooperation appears not as an unfortunate aberration or "fall from grace" for the voluntary sector but as a productive adaptation of the traditional welfare state that takes advantage of government's peculiar strengths in raising resources and ensuring equity through a democratic political process and the voluntary sector's advantages as a deliverer of services in a more informal, smaller-scale fashion than large government bureaucracies frequently make possible.

This is not to say that this partnership has worked perfectly in practice. Relationships between government and the voluntary sector evolved in ad hoc fashion in the United States, with little opportunity to spell out clearly who was expected to do what and with what degree of oversight and control. What is more, the proliferation of programs in the 1960s created a managerial maze that would have been difficult to negotiate with even the best-constructed system. The government-nonprofit partnership was simply fragmented into too many individual parts for it to be likely that the whole would have the coherence that was needed. By the late 1960s and early 1970s, therefore, there was widespread agreement that a significant overhaul of this system was needed in order to permit it to achieve its real potential.

Recent Trends

Before such a rationalization of the existing system could occur, however, major policy changes were instituted that threaten to throw out the baby with the bathwater. Coupled with a number of other demographic and social developments, these changes seem likely to change the character of the voluntary sector in fundamental ways and remove the partnership between government and the nonprofit sector from its place as the central organizing principle of the American welfare state. This section examines five such changes that have important implications for the future of the voluntary sector in the American welfare state.

Resource Constraints

The most obvious change in the operation of the American welfare state in recent years has been the imposition of a significant restraint on its provision of resources. While the Reagan administration was far less successful than it had hoped to be in reducing budgetary outlays for human service programs, it did manage to halt a twenty-year pattern of rapid growth. Thus, after adjustment for inflation, federal spending on a wide array of human service programs as of fiscal year 1986 was still very near the level that it had reached in fiscal year 1980. And if we exclude the two major federal health programs, Medicare and Medicaid, spending on the remaining human service programs declined by 15 percent (Abramson and Salamon, 1986). Inevitably, this decline translated into fiscal constraints on the private, nonprofit sector. Overall, nonprofit organizations ended up in fiscal year 1986 with about the same level of federal support that they had received in fiscal year 1980, reversing a considerable period of rapid growth (Abramson and Salamon, 1986). Excluding Medicare and Medicaid, the real value of federal support to nonprofit organizations in the remaining fields actually declined 25–30 percent between 1980 and 1986. With rare exceptions, the states were not able to compensate for the federal cutbacks. On the contrary, in many areas federal contraction brought state contraction along with it (Nathan, Doolittle, and Associates, 1987; Salamon, Musselwhite, and De Vita, 1986).

Perhaps even more significant than the cuts in federal social welfare spending achieved during the Reagan era is the legacy of restraint imposed by the federal budget deficit created during this period. Although estimates of the size of the future deficit vary widely, there is little basis for optimism about the potential for major domestic spending increases in the foreseeable future.

From Categorical Aid to Universal Entitlements

In addition to the overall pattern of restraint, important changes have taken place in the composition of social welfare spending. In particular, the retrenchment hit hardest on the so-called discretionary spending programs and the means-tested welfare programs aimed at the poor and near poor. In contrast, the so-called entitlement programs, especially those targeted at the middle class, experienced considerable growth. In the process, a significant shift occurred in the structure of federal welfare spending—away from categorical programs aimed at the needy toward general entitlement programs available to significant portions of the middle class. (This shift is consistent with the "drift toward universalism" discussed by Gilbert, 1983.)

A comparison of federal spending for Social Security, Medicare, and other retirement programs—the major entitlement programs—to other domestic spending demonstrates this shift clearly (see Table 3.1). After adjustment for inflation, federal spending on the entitlement programs increased 38 percent between fiscal year 1980 and 1987, while spending on the

Table 3.1. Growth of Federal Entitlement and Other Domestic Programs, 1980–1987 (in Inflation-Adjusted Billions of Dollars).

Program	1980 Outlays	1987 Outlays (in 1980 Dollars)	Percentage of Change
Entitlements			
Social Security	$118.5	151.6	+ 28
Medicare	22.8	51.2	+ 124
Other retirement entitlements	31.7	35.8	+ 13
Total entitlements	173.0	238.6	+ 38
Other domestic programs	218.7	185.4	− 15
Total domestic programs	$391.7	$424.0	+ 8
Entitlements as a percentage of domestic programs	41.2	56.2	

Source: Computed from figures in U.S. Office of Management and Budget, 1987.

rest of the domestic budget *declined* by 15 percent. In this seven-year period, spending on these middle-class entitlement programs therefore increased from 41 percent of the domestic budget to 56 percent.

To be sure, the Reagan administration made efforts to cut back on entitlement payments to middle-income groups under a number of federal programs, including food stamps and college student aid. But some of these changes have been reversed, and coverage under other programs has been extended. For example, coverage under the federal government's Medicaid program, which originally was limited to welfare recipients, was recently expanded to allow states to cover the aged poor as well as pregnant women and children under five years of age in families whose income is 85 percent above the poverty line, whether the families are on welfare or not (Pear, 1988, p. 1). Reflecting these changes and other developments, Medicaid expenditures have continued to grow despite rather vigorous cost-control efforts. More generally, the recent reality has been one not of across-the-board restraint but of cutbacks falling most heavily on the most vulnerable, while support for the broad middle class has experienced considerable growth.

From Producer Subsidies to Consumer Subsidies

A third important trend in the structure of the American welfare state is a marked shift in emphasis away from aid delivered through producers of services to aid delivered through consumers. This trend is only the most recent manifestation of a broader pattern of government operation of which government reliance on nonprofit organizations is one part. This pattern involves the transformation of government from a direct producer of services into a financier or arranger of services provided by others (Salamon, 1981). Paying nongovernmental third parties, including nonprofit organizations, to deliver publicly financed services has been one way of accomplishing this transformation. Paying the consumer of services directly and letting him or her decide what provider to use is simply a more extreme version of the same idea.

While the shift from producer subsidies to consumer subsidies, or vouchers, is rooted in the broad movement toward third-party government, it has more proximate origins in the efforts by conservatives to "privatize" the public sector. As one advocate (Butler, 1985, p. 43) has observed, "From the privatizers' perspective, the voucher is a useful device to make private-sector alternatives financially available to low-income citizens." According to advocates of privatization, the great advantage of vouchers is that they rely on the market rather than on the government or the producer to determine the allocation of resources and thus they presumably increase efficiency and cut the important political link tying service providers, politicians, and bureaucrats together in support of public expenditures (Butler, 1985; Savas, 1987).

The extent of the shift toward voucher-type arrangements is quite striking. Looking only at federal assistance to the nonprofit sector, we find that the amount of federal aid that reached nonprofit organizations through voucher payments to individuals grew between fiscal year 1980 and fiscal year 1986 from 53 percent of all federal assistance to 70 percent. During this same period, producer subsidies that nonprofits received from the federal government—either directly or via state and local governments—fell from 47 percent of the total to 30 percent. In other words, while the total volume of federal support in constant 1980 dollars remained the same, consumer subsidies grew just about enough to offset the decline in producer subsidies (U.S. Office of Management and Budget, 1987).

In addition to the expansion of voucher-type programs and the contraction of direct-service programs, increased reliance is being put on so-called tax expenditures to subsidize human services. Like voucher payments to individuals, tax expenditures—that is, exemptions in the tax law for certain kinds of activities—channel government aid through the consumers of services. The main difference between tax expenditures and voucher payments is that the former operate through the tax system rather than the expenditure side of the budget. Not incidentally, they also tend to deliver their benefits disproportionately to the better-off, whose tax liabilities are more substantial to start with. Thus, in the field of day care, while the real value of federal spending for the Title XX social service program (the chief producer subsidy for day care as well as other social services) declined from $2.7 billion in fiscal year 1980 to the equivalent of $2.0 billion in fiscal year 1987, the federal tax credit for child- and dependent-care expenses increased more than 400 percent in inflation-adjusted terms, from $700 million in 1980 to $3.2 billion in 1987 (U.S. Office of Management and Budget, 1980). In other words, by 1987 the federal government was ''spending'' more on day care through consumer subsidies in the tax system than it was expending on day care and more than a dozen other social services through the producer payments provided by the Social Services Block Grant. Further shifts in the pattern of government support for day care are evident in state efforts to switch day-care funding for welfare recipients from the Social Services Block Grant, a producer-oriented discretionary program whose funding levels have been declining, to the Aid to Families with Dependent Children Program, an entitlement program whose funding levels have proved harder to cut. These and similar developments in other fields add up to a significant overall trend that, while relatively unheralded, has important implications for the evolution of government-nonprofit relations.

Demographic Developments

Beyond these programmatic shifts, important changes have also occurred in the basic demography of the welfare state and in the demands for its services. Some of these demographic changes are manifest in the trends noted earlier. Others have yet to make their full effects felt. Four of these changes seem particularly likely to have significant long-term consequences.

The Graying of the Population. One of the most dramatic changes confronting the American welfare state is the continued growth in the number and proportion of elderly people. Between 1960 and 1980, the number of people aged sixty-five and older increased by 50 percent, while the overall population grew by just over 25 percent. If this trend continues over the next forty to fifty years, the proportion of the population that is sixty-five and older will double. Moreover, among the elderly, the proportion that is over seventy-five is also projected to grow, so that it will reach 50 percent of the elderly over the next forty to fifty years. This demographic fact of life has already found expression in the growth of federal support to the elderly. Given the potent political power that the elderly can wield, there is every reason to expect continued pressures for expansion of the welfare-state benefits they receive.

The Changing Social and Economic Position of Women. Another recent change that has powerful implications for the character of the American welfare state is the transformation in the role of women. While this transformation has many dimensions, one of the most important is the surge in female labor-force participation. Between 1960 and 1980, the labor-force participation rate of women increased from 30.5 percent to 50.1 percent. Even more dramatic, the labor-force participation rate for married women with children under the age of six rose from

18.6 percent in 1960 to 45.1 percent in 1980. That same year, the labor-force participation rate for separated women with children under six reached 55.2 percent. For divorced women with children under six, it grew to 68.3 percent. Aside from its social and economic effects, this development signals a substantial increase in the need for day care.

Changes in Family Structure. Significant changes have also occurred in family structure. In 1960, there was one divorce for every four marriages. By 1980, there was one divorce for every two marriages. During this period, the number of children involved in divorces almost tripled, from 463,000 in 1960 to almost 1.2 million in 1980. Since divorce typically brings a significant loss in economic status, this development suggests increased demands on existing human services. What is more, a very significant increase also occurred in the proportion of births to unmarried women. Between 1960 and 1980, the proportion of such births jumped from 5.3 percent to over 18 percent. Among nonwhites, it rose from 22 percent to 48 percent. Although the proportion of births to unmarried women was lower among whites, the absolute number of such births to unmarried women was almost equal—320,000 whites and 346,000 nonwhites, for a total of 666,000 as of 1980, compared to 224,000 twenty years earlier (U.S. Bureau of the Census, 1986)

Emergence of an Urban Underclass. The fourth recent demographic development of great importance to the evolution of the American welfare state has been the emergence of a sizable cadre of hard-core inner-city poor people, which some scholars perceive as a veritable urban underclass. As University of Chicago sociologist William Julius Wilson (1987, pp. 7–8, 143) has put it:

> Regardless of which term is used, one cannot deny
> that there is a heterogeneous grouping of inner-city
> families and individuals whose behavior contrasts
> sharply with that of mainstream America. . . . To-
> day's ghetto neighborhoods are populated almost

exclusively by the most disadvantaged segments of the black urban community, that heterogeneous grouping of families and individuals who are outside the mainstream of the American occupational system. Included in this group are individuals who lack training and skills and either experience long-term unemployment or are not members of the labor force, individuals who are engaged in street crime and other forms of aberrant behavior, and families that experience long-term spells of poverty and/or welfare dependence. . . . The term ghetto underclass . . . suggests that a fundamental social transformation has taken place in ghetto neighborhoods, and the groups represented by this term are collectively different from and much more socially isolated than those that lived in these communities in earlier years.

From Cultural to Economic Explanations of Poverty

One further development in the evolution of the American welfare state worth mentioning involves a significant change in our thinking about the causes and solutions of poverty. The key aspect of this change is a loss of faith in the traditional dogma of professional social work, with its emphasis on casework and individualized services as a cure for poverty and distress. During the 1960s, this doctrine was translated into public policy through the 1962 amendments to the Social Security Act and, later, through portions of the Economic Opportunity Act. The central premise of this doctrine was that poverty was the product of a "culture of poverty" that could be broken only by the provision of a variety of supportive services. Attention consequently focused on the individual, whose maladjustment or aberrant behavior was perceived as being largely responsible for the persistence of poverty.

Whether this "services strategy" received a fair test or not, it now enjoys little sustained enthusiasm either from the left or from the right. Conservatives view the growth of supportive services during the 1960s as at best wasteful and at worst destructive of the work ethic and fundamental values of self-reliance. Liberals now question the tendency of the culture-of-poverty theory to degenerate into a new form of "blaming the victim," since it tended to focus on correcting the behavior of the poor, rather than the social and economic circumstances that were often responsible for their plight.

This latter critique has gained added force as awareness has grown of the impact of international economic changes on the availability of traditional manufacturing jobs in the United States. Now that unionized production workers—not just racially stereotyped ghetto dwellers—have found themselves exposed to structural unemployment and distress, attention has come increasingly to focus on the underlying economic causes of poverty. Even some presumably cultural phenomena, such as the rise in the numbers of households headed by females and out-of-wedlock births among blacks, have been reinterpreted in strongly economic terms that emphasize the negative impact of chronic joblessness on stable family life. According to this line of thought, what accounts for the deterioration of black family life in urban ghettos is not lax morals or a deteriorating sense of responsibility but a concrete decline in the pool of marriageable—that is, employed—black men (Wilson, 1987).

Implications for the Nonprofit Sector

The changes in the American welfare state just outlined have important implications for the evolution of the private nonprofit sector. Of course, how these implications play out depends on factors that are difficult to predict. But some of the main pressures in the system are already evident.

Overall Sector Growth. One of the obvious yet often overlooked implications of the trends just discussed is that the private nonprofit sector is not likely to wither away in the foreseeable future. The prevailing demographic trends alone suggest a significant increase in the demand for the kinds of services that nonprofit organizations traditionally provided, including day care, nursing-home care, family counseling, and hospital services. Moreover, the demand is growing not only among the poor— the traditional target group of charitable organizations—but also among the broad middle class. That is the meaning of the jump in labor-force participation rates among women with children under six, the growth in the numbers of elderly people, the continued rise in income support and medical assistance spending, and other, similar trends. Assuming a reasonable degree of responsiveness and efficiency on the part of nonprofit providers, there is every reason to expect that the nonprofit sector will capture a significant share of the expanded "business" that seems likely to result. At the same time, the growth seems likely to be concentrated in particular portions of the sector—the portions in which growing demand coincides with growing resources. Most likely, this coincidence will occur in the areas of services for the aged, health care, the arts and recreation, and day care for children.

Commercialization. If there is thus reason to expect considerable growth in the size and scale of the nonprofit sector in the foreseeable future, there is also reason to expect that this growth will lead to greater integration of the voluntary sector into the market economy. In part, this development reflects the expansion of the paying market for human services as a product of the demographic developments detailed earlier. In part, it also reflects the shift in government human service expenditures for the poor from producer subsidies to consumer subsidies. By explicit design, this shift moves the provision of human services even for the poor into a commercial-type market.

One important consequence of this development, which Neil Gilbert (1983, p. 23) has chronicled in *Capitalism and the Welfare State,* is the "penetration of profit-oriented agencies into the welfare state." Equally important, however, is the penetration of the mechanics of the market into the operation of nonprofit organizations. This penetration is evident in the growth of fee-for-service income in the funding structure of the nonprofit sector. Like the expansion of government support, such commercial income is by no means a new phenomenon for nonprofit organizations. For example, in the early 1900s, the Charities Aid Society of New York operated both a woodyard and a laundry that charged fees for their services and generated income for the organization (Gallagher, 1988, p. 35). Similar examples are evident in the settlement house movement of the Progressive Era. But it is clear that the scale of such support has grown substantially in recent years. For example, data we generated through the Urban Institute Nonprofit Sector Project reveal that as of 1981, private nonprofit human service agencies, exclusive of hospitals and higher education institutions, already received 30 percent of their income from service fees, more than from all sources of private giving combined (Salamon, 1984; De Vita and Salamon, 1987). This figure was even higher among some types of organizations, such as institutional care facilities and arts organizations. Perhaps even more significantly, a larger proportion of these nonprofit agencies received income from service fees than received it from any other single income source.

As government support declined in the early 1980s, moreover, nonprofit organizations turned increasingly to fees and service charges to finance their activities. In fact, such receipts accounted for 75 percent of the replacement income that the nonprofit sector generated in the early 1980s, enabling the sector to overcome its loss of government support and post an overall gain in income.

The developments discussed earlier suggest strongly that this trend is likely not only to continue but to accelerate. In the process, it seems likely that the same process of transformation that affected the nonprofit hospital between 1885 and 1915 is affecting a broad array of nonprofit human service agencies today. As historian David Rosner (1982, p. 6) has noted, that transformation involved a switch from small community institutions to large bureaucratic organizations staffed by professionals, supported by fees, oriented to paying customers, and "focused less on patients' overall social and moral well-being and more on their physical needs alone." Whether other segments of the nonprofit sector will join hospitals in becoming "once charitable enterprises" is hard to tell, but the pressures in that direction are unmistakable.

Reorganization of Assistance to the Needy. While it thus seems likely that a significant share of the activity of traditional human service agencies will assume an increasingly commercial cast, both subsidized and unsubsidized, it is also possible that other institutions will assume increased responsibility for the traditional charitable mission of the nonprofit sector. In other words, while nonprofit organizations move increasingly toward the higher end of the human service market, other institutions may be developing a sense of responsibility and a service rationale targeted on those left behind. These developments are even more speculative and uncertain than the ones just identified, but some of the main lines of potential evolution are beginning to be visible.

The key to this change is the growing realization that the traditional skills of the human service sector may be increasingly irrelevant to the problems facing the urban poor. As long as the prevailing conceptions attributed a significant share of the responsibility for poverty to the personal maladjustments of the poor, traditional social work practice and traditional social welfare agencies had a significant role to play in the alleviation of poverty. But as newer conceptions that attribute poverty more clearly to the maladjustments of the economy take hold, new solutions seem called for. In this emerging view, the solution to social distress is identical to the solution to economic distress—access to a decent job. Under these circumstances, the employer rather than the social worker becomes the pivot of social policy.

Fortunately, trends in the labor market are creating a powerful economic incentive for business to take an interest in the job situation of the urban poor. These trends suggest the real possibility of a significant shortage of trained labor in the years immediately ahead (U.S. Department of Labor, 1986). As one educator (Hornbeck, 1988) recently put it, "For the first time in our history, we are facing a situation where we can no longer afford the economic luxury of throwaway kids. We could never afford the moral luxury of throwaway kids, but only recently have the economic costs become prohibitive."

To the extent that these observations prove correct, they suggest a reorientation of antipoverty and charitable activity toward the preparation of skilled workers for the labor market. Private nonprofit organizations may play a role in this effort, but, except for the community-development corporations, these organizations have a limited track record in this area. More likely is an increase in partnership arrangements involving the business community and the public school system. Equally likely is increased reliance on penal institutions and the criminal justice system generally to ease the transition of the inner-city poor into the work force of the future. Finally, business enterprises themselves will play an increasing role, utilizing on-the-job training and employment guarantees to tighten the link between the inner-city poor and the world of work.

For-Profit–Nonprofit Competition and the Challenge to Tax Exemption. Taken together, the developments just cited will further intensify the competition between the for-profit and nonprofit sectors and weaken the traditional rationale for nonprofit tax-exempt status. Of course, increased competition between the sectors and loss of tax-exempt status do not necessarily go hand in hand. Competition between for-profit and nonprofit organizations does not need to provoke a challenge to the tax-exempt status of the nonprofit sector. While tax-exempt status gives nonprofit organizations certain advantages, it also exacts certain costs, such as limitations on the generation and distribution of profit. Thus, it is quite conceivable that the competition between nonprofit and for-profit organizations will increase without posing a serious challenge to the tax-exempt status of the sector. However, for this to occur, the sector will have to clarify the relative advantages and disadvantages of tax-exempt status and develop a rationale for tax exemption that takes account of the sector's changing role.

Conclusion

The "paradigm of competition" has long had a symbolic appeal for defenders of the voluntary sector, who see in it a clear explanation for why the sector should exist. However, this paradigm has never provided a very accurate picture of reality. Worse yet, by denigrating developments—such as the growth of government support—that gave the sector reasonable hope of perpetuating some of its central attributes, this paradigm has at times been self-defeating.

Now, new challenges confront the voluntary sector. Unlike prior challenges, which confronted the sector from the side of government, the new challenges confront it from the side of the private market. While this development may be more congenial to some of the sector's private supporters, it is by no means clearly more congenial to the sector's long-term health.

References

Abramson, A. J., and Salamon, L. M. *The Nonprofit Sector and the New Federal Budget.* Washington, D.C.: Urban Institute Press, 1986.

Ashford, D. "Welfare States as Institutional Choices." In N. Furniss (ed.), *Futures for the Welfare State.* Bloomington: Indiana University Press, 1986.

Berger, P. L., and Neuhaus, R. J. *To Empower People: The Role of Mediating Structures in Public Policy.* Washington, D.C.: American Enterprise Institute, 1977.

Butler, S. *Privatizing Federal Spending: A Strategy to Eliminate the Deficit.* New York: Universe Books, 1985.

Commission on Private Philanthropy and Public Needs. *Giving in America: Toward a Strong Voluntary Sector.* Washington, D.C.: Commission on Private Philanthropy and Public Needs, 1975.

Crimmins, L. *Enterprise in the Nonprofit Sector.* Washington, D.C.: Fund for Livable Places, 1985.

De Vita, C., and Salamon, L. M. "Commercial Activities in Nonprofit Human Service Organizations." Paper presented at the INDEPENDENT SECTOR Spring Research Forum, New York, Mar. 19–20, 1987.

Gallagher, J. G. *Unfair Competition? The Challenge to Charitable Tax Exemption.* Washington, D.C.: The National Assembly, 1988.

Gilbert, N. *Capitalism and the Welfare State: Dilemmas of Social Benevolence.* New Haven, Conn.: Yale University Press, 1983.

Hornbeck, D. Speech to Private Industry Council, Annapolis, Md., Mar. 1, 1988.

Kramer, R. M. *Voluntary Agencies in the Welfare State.* Berkeley: University of California Press, 1981.

Nathan, R. P., Doolittle, F. C., and Associates. *Reagan and the States.* Princeton, N.J.: Princeton University Press, 1987.

Nielsen, W. *The Endangered Sector.* New York: Columbia University Press, 1979.

Nisbet, R. *The Quest for Community: A Study in the Ethics of Order and Freedom.* New York: Oxford University Press, 1953.

Pear, R. "Expanded Right to Medicaid Shatters the Link to Welfare." *New York Times,* March 6, 1988, p. 1.

Rosner, D. *A Once Charitable Enterprise: Hospitals and Health Care in Brooklyn and New York, 1885–1915.* New York: Cambridge University Press, 1982.

Salamon, L. M. "Rethinking Public Management: Third-Party Government and the Changing Forms of Government Action." *Public Policy,* 1981, *29* (3), 255–275.

Salamon, L. M. "The Nonprofit Sector." In J. L. Palmer and I. Sawhill (eds.), *The Reagan Revolution.* Cambridge, Mass.: Ballinger, 1982.

Salamon, L. M. "Nonprofits: The Results Are Coming In." *Foundation News,* Aug. 1984, 16–23.

Salamon, L. M. "Government and the Voluntary Sector in an Era of Retrenchment: The American Experience." *Journal of Public Policy,* 1985, *6,* 1–20.

Salamon, L. M. "Of Market Failure, Voluntary Failure, and Third-Party Government: Toward a Theory of Government-Nonprofit Relations in the Modern Welfare State." *Journal of Voluntary Action Research,* 1987a, *16* (1–2), 29–49.

Salamon, L. M. "Partners in Public Service: The Scope and Theory of Government-Nonprofit Relations." In W. W. Powell (ed.), *The Nonprofit Sector: A Research Handbook.* New Haven, Conn.: Yale University Press, 1987b.

Salamon, L. M., and Abramson, A. J. *The Federal Budget and the Nonprofit Sector.* Washington, D.C.: Urban Institute Press, 1982.

Salamon, L. M., Musselwhite, J. G., and De Vita, C. J. "Partners in Public Service: Government and the Nonprofit Sector in the American Welfare State." Paper presented at the

INDEPENDENT SECTOR Spring Research Forum, New York, Mar. 1986.

Savas, E. S. *Privatization: The Key to Better Government.* Chatham, N.J.: Chatham House, 1987.

U.S. Bureau of the Census. *Statistical Abstract of the United States, 1986.* Washington, D.C.: U.S. Government Printing Office, 1986.

U.S. Department of Labor. *Workforce 2000.* Washington, D.C.: U.S. Department of Labor, 1986.

U.S. Office of Management and Budget. *Special Analyses, Budget of the United States Government, Fiscal Year 1980.* Washington, D.C.: U.S. Government Printing Office, 1980.

U.S. Office of Management and Budget. *Budget of the United States Government, Fiscal Year 1988.* Washington, D.C.: U.S. Government Printing Office, 1987.

Weisbrod, B. *The Voluntary Nonprofit Sector: An Economic Analysis.* Lexington, Mass.: Heath, 1977.

Wilson, W. J. *The Truly Disadvantaged: The Inner City, the Underclass, and Public Policy.* Chicago: University of Chicago Press, 1987.

△ △ △ △ △ △ △ △ △ △ △ △ △ △ △

The Evolving Role
of Foundations

It is always difficult to discern the who, what, and why in trying to explain how specific public decisions take shape in the policy-making labyrinth of Washington. It is more difficult still to look outside the processes of government decision making in order to comprehend the part played in American policy making by the tens of thousands of private nonprofit organizations—foundations, think tanks, and advocacy groups—that operate on the peripheries of our formal institutional structures.

Twenty years ago, Charles Lindblom described policy making as ''an extremely complex analytical and political process to which there is no beginning or end, and the boundaries of which are most uncertain.'' He saw policy making as a ''network of causes'' and the play of power as, among other things, ''a process of cooperation among specialists'' (Lindblom, 1968, pp. 4, 30).

Lindblom's insights are helpful in trying to understand the part American foundations have played in public policy making over the years. He reminds us that policy making during this century has increasingly become a matter for experts and professionals, although he tempers any inclination to bestow too much credit on any single agency or to attribute excessive influence to any one institution. Nonetheless, experts and specialists have become increasingly prominent in the ''network of

61

causes" shaping our public policy. In examining the role of foundations in policy making, scholars must ask how the framework of causal influences on policy, particularly the influence of policy experts, has evolved over the course of this century (see Aaron, 1978; Alchon, 1985; and Karl and Katz, 1987).

While it is occasionally possible to point to the policy impact of a particular foundation-sponsored report, to single out the research of a foundation-supported scholar, or to see how foundation-initiated demonstration projects have paved the way for specific governmental decisions, the impact of foundations is usually less direct and immediate. Precise lines of causation are difficult to connect even when we are trying to assess the role of those nonprofit organizations operating in close proximity to Congress and the executive branch. Kermit Gordon, president of the Brookings Institution during the late 1960s, an era when Brookings was unrivaled among Washington policy research institutes, said that "the path along which [research] affects decision making is so tortuous that the trail usually becomes difficult or impossible to follow." "In the end," he wrote, "the initiative may be decisive in inspiring an important policy decision, but it will have been strained through so many filters and combined with so many other ingredients that the causal chain may be untraceable" (Gordon, 1970).

Because the play of ideas and influences is so intricate, generalizations about the causes of policies must be offered cautiously. Policies have their own histories, narratives that are as individual and quirky as human biography. The accidents of historical timing, the tenor of personal relationships, misunderstandings, good fortune, and diligent individual effort are among the keys to comprehending how a particular policy is initiated, discussed and formulated, and then given shape within our formal institutional processes. As one moves back from a particular policy decision to seek its intellectual origins or to trace the contours of public discussion before ideas become bills, laws, or executive orders, the analytical tasks become even more problematic (see Polsby, 1984).

In a political system as open to diverse outside influences as ours, the making of public policy can begin at a great remove from legislative chambers and executive agencies. Understandably, the dynamics of policy initiation have attracted considerably less attention from political scientists and historians than have the formal political processes of enacting legislation, devising administrative regulations, and administering policies. Where do policy ideas originate? How do policy ideas with academic beginnings make their way from scholarly conferences, journals, and published studies into the formal policy-making process? How do ideas move from the inchoate, sometimes cacophonous realms of thought, talk, petition, or protest to be embodied in law, regulation, or executive order? This is the arena in which nonprofit institutions, especially foundations and research institutes, have tended to operate. It requires that the scholar look less to policy outcomes and results than to the ways in which the network of policy causes and the participation of experts and specialists in it have changed over the years.

Studying the role of foundations in policy making is not a matter of how a bill becomes a law but a matter of how ideas, knowledge, and expertise define the spectrum of public choices, shape the language of political debate, and establish authoritative criteria for making decisions. An appraisal of the role of foundations in public policy making should proceed on two planes. One level must examine the external play of ideas and expertise in the public arena, touching on foundations and their relationships to many other organizations, both nonprofit and governmental, engaged in policy research, planning, or advocacy. The other must explore the political consequences of decisions that have been made within foundations. These decisions are about the organization and aims of research, the support of particular academic disciplines, the means of communicating research results, and the routes of access to professional training; they are what Ellen Lagemann in her work on the Carnegie Corporation has described as ''the politics of knowledge'' (Lagemann, 1987).

In less than a century, American philanthropic foundations have done much to shape and reshape the framework for bringing knowledge to bear on public policy. Their influence has been felt in at least four ways: (1) They have been influential in instigating, organizing, or financing a variety of institutions, both public and private, that have sought to bring applied knowledge to bear on public problems. (2) They have brought about changes in the professional training and intellectual perspectives of many of those who are either employed in government or engaged in policy-relevant research in universities and think tanks. (3) They have played an important part in creating the framework—books, journals, conferences, educational endeavors—within which experts and citizens talk about public issues. (4) They have defined and propagated attitudes about the value and utility of the social sciences and particular disciplines within the social sciences as tools for public decision making.

The Changing Framework of Expertise

Since the early 1900s, foundations have helped alter the institutional framework by which expertise is brought to bear on public policy making. The changes are exemplified by two legislative acts separated by just over half a century: the Budget and Accounting Act of 1921 and the Congressional Budget and Impoundment Act of 1974.

The Institute for Government Research (IGR, the forerunner of the Brookings Institution) was established in 1916, with financial and organizational help from people clustered around the burgeoning Rockefeller philanthropic endeavors; its subsequent work in economics took shape in the 1920s thanks to a large Carnegie Corporation grant. The institute's founders, most of whom had been interested in reforming local and state governments, were keen on bringing sounder managerial techniques to the federal government. Their most eagerly pursued goal was to reform Washington's chaotic budget-making and accounting procedures by urging the president and Congress to establish a coherent executive budget procedure (Critchlow, 1985; Mosher, 1984).

With a gestation period of nearly two decades, the Budget and Accounting Act of 1921 owed its intellectual design and final passage to the work of IGR staff members. The institute, a privately funded body, played a decisive role, drafting both the House and Senate versions of the bills, arranging legislative hearings, and supplying technical help in setting up the Bureau of the Budget. No private group is ever likely to play such a prominent role again. With the creation of the Bureau of the Budget, the federal policy-making framework was altered in a way that also changed the role that outside agencies would be able to play in budget policy. Subsequent foundation initiatives have continued to change the network of causes that shape policy.

The changes that had taken place in the arena for budget decisions were apparent some fifty years later. If IGR's hand had been clearly visible in creating the Bureau of the Budget in the 1920s, Brookings was present but its role less clear-cut in the efforts to reform the budget process in the 1970s. Beginning in 1971 (with about $1 million from the Carnegie Corporation and the Richard King Mellon Foundation and another $1 million from its own operating budget), Brookings published a series of volumes, *Setting National Priorities,* that examined the president's yearly budget proposals. Brookings's analyses of competing budget choices and their long-term consequences were sought out by members of Congress and their staffs, government officials, journalists, and academics; circulation of the annual budget volumes peaked at more than 30,000 in the early 1970s. Through those studies and their earlier work on government finance, Brookings researchers earned a status as independent authorities on the budget and were called on throughout the budget cycle to testify before Congress, give seminars to congressional staff, and consult informally with federal executives.

The legislative debates that preceded the passage of the 1974 budget reforms show how much more complex the legislative process had become. At the height of the budget battles between President Nixon and Congress, there were more than 250 bills and resolutions introduced to reform the budget process. While a congressional joint study committee offered the leading proposal, the process was compounded by proposals emanating from partisan study groups, individual representatives, various subcommittees, and others outside of Congress (Schick, 1976, 1980; Ippolito, 1981).

Brookings and its foundation sponsors influenced the budget reforms in many intangible ways but not in ways that left a specific or unique imprint on the legislation. However, they had demonstrated with the *Setting National Priorities* volumes that congressional budget making could be improved if it were assisted by a professional research staff. The staffs of the Congressional Budget Office and the new budget committees would soon total about 350 employees. The changes in budget procedures and the professional staffs working within and for Congress once again altered the network of causes shaping budget policy.

The creation of Brookings, the Budget Bureau, the Congressional Budget Office, and other competing centers of public and private expertise in fiscal matters demonstrates how the institutional framework of American policy making changes. As a result, the role and influence of private institutions must constantly be redefined. Brookings stood virtually alone among research institutions in Washington in 1920; today there are approximately 100 private research centers and institutes concerned with policy issues in the capital and more than 1,000 across the country. Although it is often difficult to draw a sharp line between research and advocacy groups (many of which also contribute research to public debates), advocacy groups defending particular budgetary turf and advancing other causes have become even more numerous since the 1940s. The number of government agencies doing research and analysis has also increased; the U.S. Office of Management and Budget identified no fewer than 36 executive-branch offices engaged in policy analysis in the early 1970s (Meltsner, 1976). To take but one example, the Congressional Research Service, with a staff of about 900, is roughly ten times larger than the staffs of Washington's largest think tanks.

Training Experts, Applying Knowledge

Foundations and the research endeavors they have spawned exert a consistent pressure to make the federal goernment more expert in what it does. The emergence of policy-research institutions has necessarily gone hand in hand with the training of the researchers and analysts who populate them. It may be argued that the greatest long-term contribution that foundations have made to public policy making has been in supporting the infrastructure of American higher education, especially in social science and public administration. It is no coincidence that the American philanthropic foundation appeared at the turn of the century just when the now-familiar social science disciplines began to emerge from the older study of history and political theory. Foundations, especially the Laura Spelman Rockefeller Memorial in the 1920s, were central both in creating the disciplinary infrastructure of the social sciences within the leading graduate universities and in supporting applied research projects (Geiger, 1986; Bulmer, 1984; Bulmer and Bulmer, 1981; Sutton, 1988).

Two projects separated by four decades exemplify the contributions applied research has made to public policy. Research on business cycles initiated by Wesley Mitchell and his colleagues at the National Bureau of Economic Research (NBER) in the 1920s (with timely support from the Commonwealth Fund and the Carnegie Corporation) was conceived as a huge data-gathering effort. It was a project beyond the capacity of individual university economics departments (where graduate students were too few and the commitment to research indifferent), and it was not yet something that a government agency was willing or competent to undertake. While Mitchell exercised great caution in claiming that the growing understanding of business cycles had immediate policy uses, the work of the NBER would eventually usher in significant change. NBER staff members initially devised and then, in the late 1920s, helped the Department of Commerce to begin its long-running collections of economic indicators. Many of the statistical indicators of economic change that are issued by federal agencies have their origins in the NBER's early work (Mitchell, 1937).

Over the long term, the interest in measuring the performance of the economy (and the definition of the measures used) has had profound consequences for federal economic policy making. The acceptance of the social sciences, especially economics, as a useful tool for government administration and management is symbolized by the Employment Act of 1946. In creating the Council of Economic Advisers, the Employment Act gave formal policy advisory status to professional economists; in avowing a federal responsibility for the nation's economic well-being across the business cycle, the act also helped to institutionalize macroeconomic analysis. While the intellectual consensus upon which macroeconomic policy rested owed much to the American interpreters of John Maynard Keynes's work, many of the tools that were used in policy making had been designed and crafted in the "economics laboratory" of the NBER. Long-term foundation support for the discipline itself was instrumental in making economics the preeminent policy science in postwar America, with all the consequences that that discipline has had for the way we think about public policy.

During the 1970s and 1980s, deregulation has been one of the most consistent policy themes of both Democratic and Republican administrations. The ideological battles of the 1980s, however, have tended to obscure the origins of the movement to dismantle the framework of economic regulation that had evolved since the 1880s (McCraw, 1984; Derthick and Quirk, 1985). The self-consciously conservative philanthropy that has spurred the growth of conservative (and, to be more precise, libertarian or classical liberal) think tanks and that has endowed university chairs and research centers in the name of free enterprise has played a part. So, too, has corporate giving for policy research and the greater corporate involvement in public policy making through political action committees and corporate public affairs departments (Useem, 1983; Edsall, 1984).

However, the broad consensus that brought about deregulation in the 1970s had already begun to take shape within the economics profession during the 1960s. A Ford Foundation grant to the Brookings Institution in 1967 is exemplary of the ways in which changes within a field of study precede the coalescence of academic research and political opinion into policy. In the mid-1960s, staff members at both Ford and Brookings lamented the dearth of economists (and other social scientists and policy analysts) interested in microeconomic questions, especially in studies of productivity in regulated industries. With grants eventually totaling $1.8 million, Ford supported a Brookings project on government regulation.

The Brookings project proved administratively cumbersome but managed to involve junior faculty and graduate students in research projects and workshops at some of the nation's leading universities. While Brookings produced thirteen books and many more articles on the regulation of energy, transportation, communications, and other industries, the major consequence of the research program was to direct many young economists toward theoretical questions about regulation and into the analysis of specific industries. If "policy is people," as some in Washington suggest, the redeployment of economists into the field of regulation was a necessary first step for the policies that followed in the 1970s. It was less dramatic and less visible than the conferences, seminars, and media-oriented projects emanating from the American Enterprise Institute and other organizations committed to popularizing deregulation, but it was a necessary prior step for the policies that followed.

The Public Forum

Questions about the tone and tenor of our public discourse are amorphous, not the sort of questions with which scholars have often wrestled. Yet over the years foundations have played a central part in shaping the framework for this nation's discussion of public affairs. At their creation, some of the oldest foundations saw their mission as improving discussion of public issues among both professional researchers and the citizenry.

In 1906, when Margaret Olivia Sage, widow of the wealthy railroad investor Russell Sage, was searching for a way to use her late husband's wealth for some beneficent social purpose, her advisers solicited suggestions from charity workers and scholars about how best to use the money. The consensus was striking. Virtually all agreed that there were too few journals and books and no major libraries or research collections on social and economic issues and too few opportunities for communication among social researchers and policy activists. A program of research and publication was a novel and valuable idea in the early 1900s.

At the turn of the century, only some 6,000 books, fiction and nonfiction taken together, were published each year. Academic journals had only recently been started by the scholars who, beginning in the 1880s, banded together discipline by discipline to form professional associations; a handful of university departments sponsored regular journals and publications series. A few reform associations and settlement houses issued publications, while "muckraking" journalism gave a certain vitality to social and economic reporting in popular magazines. The basic infrastructure for communicating research findings and fostering public discussion was only in the most rudimentary stage of development. The Russell Sage Foundation, the prototypical think tank, devoted most of its resources in its early years to the tasks of research, publishing books and pamphlets, preparing exhibits, and supporting popular educational campaigns (Glenn, Brandt, and Andrews, 1947).

The framework for both professional and popular communication on matters of public consequence owes much to foundation-supported initiatives. Though commercial and technological factors drive much of publishing and journalism, foundations have played an important role in shaping the machinery for discussing serious public questions, whether through commission or task-force reports, research published by scholarly journals and university presses, or events reported and discussed on public radio and television. In the mid 1980s, my survey of twenty-five prominent public-policy research organizations in the United States found that they have annually issued approximately 250 books and more than 1,000 reports, conference proceedings, lecture series, and papers, not to mention countless op-ed pieces and newspaper articles (some of the larger think tanks distribute more than 200 op-ed pieces per year that find their way into the commercial press).

There are no simple conclusions to be drawn in trying to evaluate the consequence of this flood of publications. It is easy to lament the fragmentation of knowledge and the inconsequentiality of greatly overspecialized research, but there is also much of value that has emerged. It is also worrisome to see the fissure that seems to have widened between what the experts have learned and what the citizen knows or believes. It does seem that those who met in Margaret Olivia Sage's Fifth Avenue mansion in 1906 and planned a program of research and publishing, as well as the Russell Sage Foundation staff members who over the next two decades worked in the Department of Surveys and Exhibits to make research findings accessible to a broad citizenry, were better attuned to the public uses of social science research than are policy researchers today.

Democratic Politics and the Scientific Ethos

Questions about expertise and advocacy in a democratic society, the place of social science and political ideology in America, will never be confronted adequately in a chapter of this brief scope. It is nevertheless worthwhile in reflecting upon the policy-making role of foundations to consider the scientific metaphors (and illusions) that have animated foundations and their beneficiaries as they sought to develop the social sciences, build policy-research institutions, and apply research and expert knowledge to our social, economic, and political affairs.

When the oldest general-purpose foundations began their work after the turn of the century, they were driven by the optimistic conviction that they could create a science of society that would somehow deliver the nation from the divisiveness and corruption of politics. Foundation trustees and staff and the academic experts they funded were perpetually worried about the ideological divisions that tore the fabric of American politics. Social science and philanthropy were closely intertwined public endeavors that seemed to promise a deliverance from endless and fractious political controversy (Haskell, 1977, 1984; Furner, 1975). Foundation staff were more than a little fearful of the turmoil of democratic politics, seeing science and expertise as the antidote to chaos and the source of political consensus.

The central scientific metaphor for those engaged in philanthropy and social science research in the early 1900s was drawn from the field of medicine. Whether it was Frederick T. Gates sermonizing about the importance of scientific philanthropy to the Rockefellers or researchers from Russell Sage looking at urban tenements, they believed they could identify the root causes of social ills and that there were cures to the disorders of the social and economic system. The medical metaphor was succeeded by other scientific metaphors as social scientists looked for guidance to the quantifying physical sciences in the 1920s, rediscovered biological metaphors of adjustment in the 1930s, and embraced engineering and systems analysis in the 1950s and 1960s.

Viewed from a century-long perspective, the role that foundations have played in shaping public policy in the United States has been part and parcel of our attitudes and expectations about social science research and expertise. Several times in the course of the twentieth century, we have swung from high optimism about what we can learn about social and economic conditions and a concomitant faith in our abilities to act on that knowledge to the depth of national despair about problems that seemed beyond our intelligence to grasp and our capacity to devise solutions to. Foundation trustees and officers have not been immune to these oscillations of historical mood.

When foundation executives and scholarly observers ask themselves how a foundation's efforts can affect public policy, they might begin by reflecting on the scientific metaphors that their predecessors embraced and tried to translate into research and action in the social and economic arena. Those metaphors have had profound consequences for the way American philanthropy has conducted itself—searching for social cures and remedies in the 1910s, seeking mechanisms of social and economic adjustment in the 1920s and 1930s, fostering experimentation in the 1930s and 1940s, analyzing society as an engineering system in the 1950s and 1960s.

While the rational scientific faith that propelled philanthropy and social science along their parallel courses throughout most of this century has diminished since the late 1960s, the enduring questions about foundations and public policy making will continue to concern the ways in which social research ought to be organized and the means of recruiting, educating, and training those who will study public issues and administer both our public institutions and our private social agencies.

At the same time, we must also recall old questions, asked when foundations were still new but often overlooked as mature foundations came to concern themselves with training experts and advancing knowledge about society. How can foundations better use their resources to enhance a genuinely public debate? How can we ensure that our democratic citizenry is better informed and more engaged in public matters?

References

Aaron, H. *Politics and the Professors.* Washington, D.C.: Brookings Institution, 1978.

Alchon, G. *The Invisible Hand of Planning: Capitalism, Social Science, and the State in the 1920s.* Princeton, N.J.: Princeton University Press, 1985.

Bulmer, M. *The Chicago School of Sociology: Institutionalization, Diversity and the Rise of Sociological Research.* Chicago: University of Chicago Press, 1984.

Bulmer, M., and Bulmer, J. "Philanthropy and Social Science in the 1920s: Beardsley Ruml and the Laura Spelman Rockefeller Memorial, 1922–29." *Minerva,* 1981, *19,* 347–407.

Critchlow, D. T. *The Brookings Institution, 1916–52: Expertise and the Public Interest in a Democratic Society.* DeKalb: Northern Illinois University Press, 1985.

Derthick, M., and Quirk, P. *The Politics of Deregulation.* Washington, D.C.: Brookings Institution, 1985.

Edsall, T. B. *The New Politics of Inequality.* New York: Norton, 1984.

Furner, M. O. *Advocacy and Objectivity: A Crisis in the Professionalization of American Social Science, 1865–1905.* Lexington: University of Kentucky Press, 1975.

Geiger, R. *To Advance Knowledge: The Growth of American Research Universities, 1900–40.* New York: Oxford University Press, 1986.

Glenn, J. M., Brandt, L., and Andrews, F. E. *Russell Sage Foundation, 1907–46.* New York: Russell Sage Foundation, 1947.

Gordon, K. *Annual Report: 1968–69.* Washington, D.C.: Brookings Institution, 1970.

Haskell, T. *The Emergence of Professional Social Science: The American Social Science Association and the Nineteenth Century Crisis of Authority.* Urbana: University of Illinois Press, 1977.

Haskell, T. (ed.). *The Authority of Experts: Studies in History and Theory.* Bloomington: Indiana University Press, 1984.

Ippolito, D. *Congressional Spending.* Ithaca, N.Y.: Cornell University Press, 1981.

Karl, B. D., and Katz, S. N. "Foundations and Ruling Class Elites." *Daedalus,* 1987, *116,* 1–40.

Lagemann, E. C. "The Politics of Knowledge: The Carnegie Corporation and the Formulation of Public Policy." *History of Education Quarterly,* 1987, *27,* 205–220.

Lindblom, C. E. *The Policy-Making Process.* Englewood Cliffs, N.J.: Prentice-Hall, 1968.

McCraw, T. *Prophets of Regulation.* Cambridge, Mass.: Harvard University Press, 1984.

Meltsner, A. J. *Policy Analysts in the Bureaucracy.* Berkeley: University of California Press, 1976.

Mitchell, W. *The Backward Art of Spending Money.* New York: McGraw-Hill, 1937.

Mosher, F. *A Tale of Two Agencies: A Comparative Analysis of the General Accounting Office and the Office of Management and Budget.* Baton Rouge: Louisiana State University Press, 1984.

Polsby, N. *Political Innovation in America: The Politics of Policy Initiation.* New Haven, Conn.: Yale University Press, 1984.

Schick, A. *The First Years of the Congressional Budget Process.* Washington, D.C.: Congressional Research Service, 1976.

Schick, A. *Congress and Money: Budgeting, Spending and Taxing.* Washington, D.C.: Urban Institute Press, 1980.

Sutton, F. X. "Foundations and Higher Education at Home and Abroad." In *Working Papers.* New York: Center for the Study of Philanthropy, 1988.

Useem, M. *The Inner Circle: Large Corporations and the Rise of Business Political Activity in the United States and the United Kingdom.* New York: Oxford University Press, 1983.

MARION R. FREMONT-SMITH

△ △ △ △ △ △ △ △ △ △ △ △ △ △ △

Trends in Accountability and Regulation of Nonprofits

The continued existence of the independent sector requires general confidence that it is serving the public. In that sense, the term *independent sector* is a misnomer. In fact, the sector is accountable at all times to both the private sector and government. The result, as with many forms of regulation, is a constant tension between the demands of the public for ensurance of proper behavior and the demands of the sector for freedom to operate to achieve its charitable goals. (The terms *charitable* and *charities* are used in this chapter as they were used in the common law, encompassing the entire range of educational, scientific, religious, and charitable purposes that are also described by the term *philanthropic*.)

The purpose of this chapter is to review the current methods for ensuring accountability of the independent sector, to appraise their adequacy, and to explore how they are likely to change and the effect of these changes on the ability of the sector to maintain its independence.

Accountability Under the Common Law

The basic methods for ensuring accountability of the nonprofit organizations that constitute the independent sector were devised

Note: The author wishes to thank Christopher M. Jedrey for his helpful comments on this chapter.

as long ago as the sixteenth century, when the common law dealing with charitable trusts was developed and a pattern for government supervision was devised to ensure responsible behavior by the managers of these trusts. This law articulated a set of duties governing trustees. It also assigned the attorney general, representing the sovereign as parens patriae, the exclusive right to represent the indefinite class of individuals that these entities were designed to benefit. The concept of exclusive jurisdiction reflected the pragmatic view that no one would serve as a fiduciary of a charitable trust if he could be called to account by any member of the general public.

The nature of the duties set forth in the common law reflected the expectations of society: specifically, that there should be a singular and enveloping duty to carry out the charitable purposes of the trust; that it was necessary to keep the trust property productive; and that trustees should be prohibited from diverting charitable funds by improper investments or self-dealing. Regulatory power was ultimately lodged in the courts of equity, which could remove trustees, impose surcharges, and enjoin inappropriate actions.

These duties continue to form the basic law—in England and in the United States—governing the behavior of fiduciaries. Similarly, reliance on the attorney general as enforcement officer became the pattern in the United States and continues to this day in virtually all jurisdictions. Freedom was ensured under this system in that, so long as the trustees acted prudently and observed any restrictions imposed by donors, neither the court nor any government official was allowed to question the methods chosen to achieve the trust's purposes.

In the nineteenth century, the preferred legal form used to establish entities to conduct charitable activities began to shift from the charitable trust to the nonprofit, nonstock corporation, but, with a few exceptions, the laws designed to ensure accountability of charitable trustees were also applied to the directors of charitable corporations (who were and still are often called "trustees"). There were no major changes in the laws governing fiduciary duties or the methods used to ensure their accountability until the middle of the twentieth century. Charities could be called to account in court by a state attorney general, but, in actuality, there was little perceived need to resort to remedies of this nature. This situation changed in the mid-twentieth century with a vast expansion in the number of charitable organizations, traceable primarily to the increased importance of tax incentives for their establishment, particularly the ability of donors to make tax-deductible gifts to them.

Regulation Through Tax Laws

Both federal and state tax laws have consistently contained exemptions for the income of charities and permitted deductions for contributions to them. The earliest of federal statutes established the basic pattern for federal regulation. The purposes that were described as "charitable," "educational," and "religious" were specifically to be determined under common-law precedents, and the duty of loyalty to these purposes was articulated in the requirements that such an organization be "operated exclusively" for its exempt purposes and that "no part of its net earnings enure" to the benefit of any individual. In addition, beginning in 1943, certain charities were required to file annual information returns with the Internal Revenue Service, and these reports were made available to the general public. Until recent years, however, the view of Congress was that accountability in the first instance was concomitant with dependence on contributions from the general public. Thus, until 1969, annual reports were required only from what we now call private foundations; after that time, all organizations except churches were subject to the reporting requirement, and private foundations were required to file more information than other charities. In addition, in 1950, private foundations were subjected to restraints against the accumulation of income and self-dealing. It was also in 1950 that taxes were imposed on the unrelated business income of exempt organizations in a measure designed to prevent what was perceived as unfair competition with privately owned businesses. In 1954, the percentage limit for deductions was increased for gifts to religious orders, educational institutions, hospitals, churches, and conventions of churches; and in 1964, it was extended to all publicly supported organizations.

The Tax Reform Act of 1969, in addition to expanding reporting requirements, contained more pervasive federal regulation than any previously enacted laws. The new private foundation rules, imposing excise taxes not only on the charity but also on its managers, reflected a recognition that the enforcement tools available in state courts of equity were more effective for ensuring compliance than was loss of exemption. Under these rules, it was also possible to preserve charitable funds for the continued benefit of the general public. However, federal tax rules are of necessity designed to protect the integrity of the tax system. Accordingly, prohibitions against accumulation and rules limiting the holding of interests in business entities reflected the desire to obtain immediate benefit for society in exchange for the tax benefit given to the entity and its contributors, a concept with no counterpart in fiduciary law.

State Regulation of Charities Since 1950

Since 1950, twelve states have enacted legislation requiring certain charitable trusts and corporations to register and file reports with the state attorney general. The purpose of this legislation was to ensure that the attorney general would have sufficient information to permit him or her to enforce proper administration of charities. In addition, although Congress continued to believe that reliance on contributions from the general public would ensure accountability of publicly supported charities, the enforcement authorities in some states became concerned with the high cost of fund raising and instances of deceptive solicitations. The result was legislation requiring, in most instances, registration with a state authority, the filing of annual returns, and the licensing and bonding of solicitors. Some of these statutes placed limits on the amounts that could be spent on fund raising. However, in cases decided in 1980 and 1984, the United States Supreme Court held that state regulation of this sort violated constitutional rights of free speech and equal protection. Another method for regulating solicitation embodied in several of these statutes is to require disclosure at the time of solicitation of the cost of fund raising, expressed as a percentage of total funds raised. The provisions of this nature contained in the laws of North Carolina were held unconstitutional in the case of *Riley* v. *National Federation of the Blind of North Carolina,* which was decided by the U.S. Supreme Court in 1988.

Research papers sponsored by the Commission on Private Philanthropy and Public Needs (the Filer Commission) contain summaries of the status of federal and state regulations in the early 1970s and an analysis of the effectiveness of fund-raising percentage limits (Commission on Private Philanthropy and Public Needs, 1977). They also include important discussions of the need for uniform accounting standards and the benefits and limits of self-regulation. Overall, they emphasize the lack of information on the extent of abuse and the effectiveness of existing remedies.

In those states with active enforcement programs, the offices of the attorneys general have been able to correct a number of abuses involving self-dealing and improper diversion of funds. Of equal importance, they were instrumental in ensuring that provisions governing charities with obsolete purposes or impracticable provisions were revised by the courts to make them more responsive to current needs. However, as the size and nature of charitable activities expanded, conflicts relating to the appropriate nature of charitable enterprise emerged. The restructuring of hospitals into several component entities, following the pattern of parent and subsidiary corporations found in the business world, was a pervasive development, but there were also a number of attempts by the trustees of exempt organizations such as health maintenance organizations to convert them into private corporations, attempts that were blocked in states with active enforcement programs but that were apparently successful elsewhere. The response in the states to these developments was confused. For example, the duty of loyalty of trustees of subsidiary corporations to their parent was unclear. In addition, it has proved difficult to obtain adequate information regarding the operation of for-profit subsidiaries. The result has been an atmosphere of distrust. For example, the Massachusetts attorney general attempted unsuccessfully to block efforts by a charitable corporation to sell its hospital facility to a for-profit corporation, even though the hospital's trustees planned to treat the proceeds as endowment and to operate a grant-making health care foundation. The attorney general did succeed in preventing the sale of a medical facility and use of the proceeds for the benefit of its parent. In neither case was there precedent for approving or disapproving the proposed action, and the resulting uncertainty had a negative effect on relations between the attorney general and the charitable community.

Recent Developments in Accountability

The State Scene. Developments in the late 1980s give us some insight as to where we are and where we might be in the year 2000 and thereafter. The enforcement tools have not changed. State programs to supervise the general activities of charitable organizations have not expanded. In fact, there has been some contraction in the scope of the programs in Ohio and California. However, state officials have established better communications among themselves and with the Internal Revenue Service and have unified reporting requirements, principally by using IRS forms 990 and 990 PF as the basic vehicles for obtaining information.

The major expansion of regulation at the state level has been in connection with the regulation of solicitation. There are now thirty-six states with reporting statutes, ten of these enacted or substantially revised since 1986. Much of the impetus for this recent expansion came with the adoption in 1987 by the National Association of Attorneys General of a Model Act to Regulate Solicitation. The act is not free of controversy. The higher education community has mounted efforts to be exempted from its provisions, and it contains restrictions on paid solicitors that were declared unconstitutional by the U.S. Supreme Court in its 1988 *Riley* decision.

An important recent development at the state level has been a widespread reappraisal of the basis for the exemption from state and local property and income taxes granted to charities. The initial focus was on alleged business activities of certain athletic clubs, but it was soon expanded to encompass charitable organizations previously considered inviolate, such as hospitals and health-related entities. Some of the impetus for this reappraisal was traceable to the activities of the U.S. Small Business Administration, which in 1980 began an effort to halt what it perceived as harmful advances of the nonprofit sector into commercial pursuits. This effort has included organizing businesspeople to sponsor local and state initiatives to remove tax exemption for charities engaged in "commercial activities."

Another recent development in the states ironically was directed toward alleviating the liability of charitable fiduciaries rather than increasing their duties. In a direct response to widespread and growing fears that charitable fiduciaries would be subject to personal liability for failure to monitor adequately the activities of agents, coupled with a drastic increase in the cost of liability insurance, bills were introduced in the legislatures of almost every state granting immunity in suits seeking monetary damages for negligence and, in some cases, for gross negligence or expanding the scope of existing immunity statutes.

The Federal Scene. In the chronology of the federal government's relations with tax-exempt organizations, 1987 will undoubtedly be associated with the name of Representative J. J. Pickle (D-Texas), just as the names Walsh, Reece, Cox, and Patman are associated with earlier congressional investigations of exempt organizations and, particularly in those earlier investigations, private foundations. Pickle, as chairman of the House Ways and Means Oversight Subcommittee, held three sets of hearings on the activities of exempt organizations during the spring and fall of 1987. The first, held in March, dealt with political and lobbying activities. The committee heard testimony indicating that funds obtained from sales of arms to Iran were funneled through exempt organizations and used to oppose candidates for political office in contravention of Internal Revenue Code provisions. At the conclusion of the hearings, the oversight subcommittee issued thirteen legislative recommendations. These ultimately became part of the Ways and Means Committee's revenue reconciliation bills of 1987, which, with certain amendments adopted during conference, became part of the revenue act that was enacted on December 22, 1987.

The new provisions are noteworthy because of the patterns of regulation they contain. They have expanded accountability by requiring that all exempt organizations, not just private foundations, make forms 990 and 1023 available for public inspection at the organization's offices. They extend excise taxes on organizations and their managers that were previously imposed only on private foundations to apply to publicly supported charities that engage in certain prohibited political or lobbying activities. They impose point-of-solicitation disclosure requirements on certain tax-exempt organizations, again with excise taxes on the organization and its managers as the penalty for noncompliance. Finally, they provide the Internal Revenue Service with broad new powers to obtain information regarding transactions with affiliated entities and to assess taxes and seek injunctions to prevent "flagrant abuses" of the prohibition against making political expenditures.

The second set of hearings, which were held in May, focused on competition with the private sector and the unrelated business activities of exempt organizations. Testimony by government officials and members of the private sector evidenced a dramatic change in public attitude toward exempt organizations and presaged not only changes in the regulatory pattern but also a reappraisal of the rationale for exemption. This was in part a reaction to changes in the scope and nature of exempt organization activities already described, but it was spurred in large part by the Small Business Administration's campaign. A uniform theme in all of the testimony was the lack of information on the exact scope of business activities—whether related or not. In his testimony before the subcommittee, Commissioner of Internal Revenue Lawrence B. Gibbs stated his belief that "unfair competition" would be an unworkable standard for monitoring business activities and that, with the expanded audit activities already in place, the IRS could meet the call for better regulation.

Testimony by representatives of the Treasury Department identified seventeen major issues relating to business activities of exempt organizations that they felt needed review. They made no specific legislative recommendations, but the detailed discussion of problem areas indicated a likely basis for future legislative changes. None individually would depart from the existing regulatory pattern. However, Assistant Treasury Secretary O. Donaldson Chapoton provided a new rationale for tax exemption that was noteworthy. After remarking that the services provided by exempt organizations are similar to those provided by government and that limits on the scope of exemptions are appropriate and necessary, he stated: "This nation has prospered through its reliance on a private, market-based economy to supply necessary goods and services. The role of government generally has been restricted to those socially important activities not adequately supported by the private sector. The role of the quasi-governmental, not-for-profit sector should similarly be restricted to that of supplementing, and not supplanting, the activities of for-profit businesses. Thus, tax exemption for public charities should be restricted to those areas where the quality or quantity of goods and services that would be produced strictly through market forces is inadequate." (United States, 1987).

This view draws from and complements the position of several economists and political scientists, who base their position, however, on the issues of efficiency and the proper role of the tax system rather than the needs of the private sector. Their view was exemplified in testimony presented to the oversight subcommittee on June 30, 1987, by Henry Hansmann of Yale Law School, who argued that exemptions should be granted only to organizations substantially dependent on contributions from the general public or, in the case of those that rely primarily on fees for services (such as hospitals, day-care agencies, health maintenance organizations, and fitness centers), only if there is insufficient competition from the private sector to ensure that the services will not be provided by for-profit organizations at a lower price.

The third set of hearings conducted in 1987 by the subcommittee dealt with the financial dealings of what are described as television ministries. Under existing law, religious organizations need not seek an advance determination of tax-exempt status to qualify for exemption as do other organizations. In addition, they are exempted from annual filing requirements and protected from IRS audit unless the IRS has met certain specific standards. During the hearings, the commissioner and his aides pointed to the severe limits on the ability of the IRS to monitor churches, particularly the lack of any requirement for them to seek an initial determination of tax-exempt status. Testimony was presented suggesting that certain religious organizations should be subjected to expanded reporting requirements. Several church representatives indicated agreement, but others raised objections on constitutional grounds. The general sense of the hearings was that a number of members of Congress would be willing to reconsider the propriety of the current broad exemption of religious organizations from the regulatory process.

In November 1986, the Treasury Department released proposed regulations under Internal Revenue Code Section 501(h), enacted ten years previously, which permits certain tax-exempt charities to elect to be subject to dollar limits on the amounts they may properly spend for lobbying. The proposed regulations were sufficiently restrictive to arouse widespread concern and to cause several members of Congress to call for their withdrawal. In response, the commissioner of internal revenue agreed to postpone final promulgation and arranged for further study. He also appointed an eighteen-member Advisory Group on Exempt Organizations, which met during 1987 and 1988 to discuss the lobbying provisions as well as the other current issues regarding exempt organizations. The willingness of the IRS to work openly with representatives of the independent sector on issues of common concern was a new development, offering hope of improved regulation in the future. In December 1988, the Treasury Department issued reproposed regulations that replaced most of the heavily criticized provisions in the original set of regulations, proposed in 1986, and substantially met most of the criticisms raised of them.

A final development at the federal level to be noted was a proposal to impose a 5 percent excise tax on the investment income of tax-exempt organizations. This was one of several revenue-raising options proposed by the staffs of the House Ways and Means Committee and the Joint Committee on Taxation. Protests from all segments of the independent sector were immediate, and the provision was not among the final options considered by the tax-writing committees. Nonetheless, one of the Treasury Department recommendations to the oversight subcommittee at its hearings on competition was to remove the tax exemption for passive income (dividends, interest, royalties, and rent) of social welfare organizations, trade associations, and labor unions, increasing the likelihood of taxes being imposed on this source of income in the future.

Issues for the Future

Each of these developments presages changes in the regulation of charities at both state and federal levels—some immediate, others long-term. Reliance on the tax laws as the primary source of regulation is not likely to change. Attempts to refine regulatory tools, however, are likely to continue. One can quite easily predict further expansion of some existing rules that govern publicly supported charities, particularly those directed against self-dealing and taxable expenditures, encompassing as they do excessive compensation and other forms of private benefit that have previously been subsumed in the concept of private enurement. It is also likely that many, if not all, of the specific suggestions relating to the unrelated business income tax identified by the Treasury Department as warranting additional study will be enacted. Cooperation between the Internal Revenue Service and the independent sector is greater than it has ever been. This is likely to ensure that new rules will be enforced with greater understanding of their purpose and more appropriate application by the regulators.

However, improved enforcement tools and their more rational application will not stop the ongoing reassessment of the basis for exemption. If the result is to remove exemption from all but those charities that rely primarily on contributions or that do not conduct ''commercial'' activities, two further major changes are likely to occur. First, the federal government will concern itself with the regulation of solicitation, and, for those charities relieved from federal regulation by virtue of being subject to tax, state regulators will likely attempt to fill the gap by enforcing the common-law fiduciary rules. Thus, the basic question of who is to regulate—the federal government or the states—may be answered in new ways. In regard to solicitation, proposals have been made from time to time since the 1970s to require point-of-solicitation disclosure of fund-raising costs as a condition of continued tax exemption or use of the mails. Now that the Supreme Court has held state requirements of this nature unconstitutional, the proponents of stricter regulation may well look to the Congress to accomplish what they cannot do under state law.

The second long-term development will come as a result of broader recognition that the Internal Revenue Service is not the most appropriate agency to regulate the independent sector. It lacks the more refined tools for compelling compliance available to state equity courts. It is not well placed to police disclosure provisions. Even if granted equity-type powers, its staff is neither by training nor by inclination suited to enforcement that is not designed to raise revenue. Just as the rules governing employee benefit plans are enforced in part by the IRS and in part by the Labor Department, so may charities find themselves subject to the jurisdiction of another agency. The Federal Trade Commission and the U.S. Postal Service have already been suggested as appropriate agencies to police solicitations, and the Federal Communications Commission might regulate television ministries. Alternatively, Congress may decide that a separate enforcement agency should be established. The issue of federal preemption of state law would then require reexamination. Some of these regulatory possibilities were raised and discussed in various of the Filer Commission papers (Commission on Private Philanthropy and Public Needs, 1977). They warrant another look.

This, then, is the start of a research agenda for the future. It should also include a fresh look at the effectiveness and propriety of regulatory measures to deal with public solicitations. No studies have been conducted to determine whether point-of-solicitation disclosure of fund-raising costs actually affects giving patterns. Programs to improve public understanding of the "costs" of fund raising are just now under way. We need to know whether these programs will lead to better-informed contributors. We should also consider whether there is sufficient evidence of abuse to warrant expanded regulation designed to protect contributors—weighing the increased costs to government and to the charities against the benefits sought, particularly if the regulatory pattern will involve fifty different laws in fifty different states.

The greatest need for information, however, relates to the "business activities" of exempt organizations. This need was the one common thread in the testimony presented at the 1987 hearings on competition. Lack of knowledge of the scope of nonprofit and for-profit activities of exempt organizations undoubtedly contributed to the misunderstandings expressed by some members of Congress, who seemed to believe that the conduct of unrelated activities that were subject to tax was per se improper. In fact, the enforcement problem appears to be not with the filers but with those who do not understand or who ignore the rules. The larger problem, however, is the extent to which exempt organizations have established for-profit companies and whether, in so doing, they have diverted funds or attention, or both, from their original mission to the detriment of the sector.

In terms of the standards by which we measure accountability, the major unresolved issue at present is the extent to which and the manner in which we permit "business activities." There is a tension here between two opposing views: on one side there are those who believe that the business of charity is charity, not business, and that the adoption of business techniques and standards deter managers from the true goals of the sector and on the other side are those who believe that charities will not survive unless they apply the techniques and standards of the business sector to their activities. This is undoubtedly as much a philosophical as an economic or legal issue. In terms of the study of accountability, it needs to be addressed from each of these perspectives. It is likely that a middle ground will emerge. We will demand use of private-sector techniques to ensure efficiency while retaining the overarching dedication to public benefit that is the essence of philanthropy as the ultimate standard for accountability. New standards will, in turn, require new enforcement tools. In devising them, we must ensure that the need for them has been demonstrated, that the costs they impose in terms of limiting independence are outweighed by that need, and that they represent the least obtrusive measures that can be devised. This ultimately is the challenge that accountability has always posed for the independent sector and that it will continue to pose in the year 2000 and after.

References

Commission on Private Philanthropy and Public Needs. *Research Papers of the Commission on Private Philanthropy and Public Needs.* Vols. 1–5. Washington, D.C.: U.S. Department of the Treasury, 1977.

Fremont-Smith, M. R. *Foundations and Government: State and Federal Law and Supervision.* New York: Russell Sage Foundation, 1965.

Hopkins, B. R. *The Law of Tax-Exempt Organizations.* (5th ed.) New York: Wiley, 1987.

Riley v. *National Federation of the Blind of North Carolina, Inc.,* 56 U.S.L.R. 4869 (U.S. June 29, 1988) (No. 87–328)

United States. Congress. Hearings Before the Subcommittee on Oversight of the Committee on Ways and Means, HOR, 100th Cong., 1st Sess. 11(1987). Statement of the Hon. O. D. Chapoton, Department of the Treasury.

PART TWO

△ △ △ △ △ △ △ △ △ △ △ △ △ △ △

The Commercialization
of the Nonprofit Sector

Among the effects of the decline in federal funding to nonprofits that are identified by several of the contributors in Part One is the trend among nonprofits toward deriving more resources through increasing fees and charges or serving a clientele that can pay for services. The contributors in this part address this trend toward commercialization of the sector, which has become a public-policy issue in Congress and is fueled by charges of unfair competition between nonprofits and small business.

The issue is important, for it has led researchers and policy makers to examine what the fundamental roles of nonprofits are or ought to be. It also demonstrates the basic ignorance that most people have about the law relating to tax-exempt organizations. Although many types of organizations, such as lobbying organizations and mutual benefit membership societies, can be tax-exempt, only organizations serving religious, educational, scientific, or other charitable purposes are defined as charitable, tax-exempt organizations under Internal Revenue Code Section 501(c)(3). These institutions have a public purpose and thus can receive tax-deductible contributions from individuals and corporations. Nothing in the law states that such organizations cannot charge fees or that they are incorporated solely to serve the unfortunate or poor. There is a law, however, that covers unrelated business income derived by nonprofits. This income must be taxed at the prevalent corporate rate.

Some of the contributors to this part review the history and public policy relating to tax exemption and its implications in this era of the trend toward commercialization. While some contributors argue that charitable organizations are acting within the scope of their missions when they charge fees for various activities in the public interest, others argue that the law ought to be changed or that the criteria for determining service in the public interest should be based not on the incorporation status of organizations but rather on their performance.

Underlying many of the arguments in these chapters is the recognition that for-profit organizations have moved into services formerly offered primarily by nonprofits. The debate among the contributors stems from their interpretation of current law or their recommendations to change the law relating to tax exemption. The fundamental issue they are debating is how the public interest ought to be defined. Some argue that tax-exempt status should be narrowly limited to organizations that receive most of their resources through donations; others argue that organizations serving public purposes in arts, health, or education that rely on fee income still are engaged in public service, and that tax-exempt status ensures a focus on such service rather than on profit. The resolution of this debate could have a profound effect on the structure of the nonprofit sector in the future.

△ △ △ △ △ △ △ △ △ △ △ △ △ △ △

The Two Nonprofit Sectors: Fee for Service Versus Donative Organizations

By the year 2000, there will be two relatively distinct nonprofit sectors in the United States. The first, which we might call the philanthropic nonprofit sector, will comprise donatively supported organizations such as charities for the relief of the poor and distressed, cultural organizations such as museums and performing-arts groups, and institutions dedicated to research and higher education. The second nonprofit sector will comprise the so-called "commercial" nonprofits (Hansmann, 1980)— that is, nonprofits that receive virtually all of their income from the sale of services rather than from donations and that frequently compete directly with for-profit firms. This second nonprofit sector, which we might call the commercial nonprofit sector, will include, for example, most nonprofit hospitals, health maintenance organizations, medical testing labs, nursing homes, health and life insurance companies, day-care centers, and fitness centers. This commercial nonprofit sector scarcely existed in 1900; by the year 2000, it is likely to account for more than two-thirds of the nonprofit sector as a whole.

Reasons for the Emergence of the Second Nonprofit Sector

In considerable part, the second nonprofit sector has evolved out of the first one. Hospitals provide the most important, con-

91

spicuous, and well-analyzed example. Until this century, nonprofit hospitals were philanthropic institutions devoted primarily to the care of the poor and were dependent on donations for most of their income. But a series of revolutions in the technology and financing of health care changed that situation radically in recent decades, to the point where now the prosperous as well as the poor use hospitals, and where the overwhelming majority of hospital patients, rich or poor, are able to pay, either directly or through private or public insurance, for the services they receive. Consequently, most nonprofit hospitals today receive virtually no meaningful amount of donative income and have become purely commercial nonprofits (Gray, 1986).

Now that the function of providing subsidized care for the poor has largely been taken away from them, nonprofit hospitals may be considered anachronistic, providing no important services that are not provided as well or better by for-profit hospitals. Nevertheless, even after two decades of strong competition from chains of aggressively expansionist for-profit hospitals, the market share of nonprofit hospitals remains almost exactly what is was twenty-five years ago and shows little sign of declining in the future (American Hospital Association, 1987). This strong resilience of the nonprofit hospitals long after their raison d'être has disappeared is probably due to several factors.

First, despite the claims of their detractors (for example, Herzlinger and Krasker, 1987), nonprofit firms evidently often operate with considerable efficiency when faced with financial stringency and hence cannot easily be driven out of business simply through competition from for-profit firms. Second, the capital that is invested in nonprofit firms cannot be withdrawn and invested in other industries without great difficulty; consequently, whether or not that capital is bringing in a market rate of return, it tends to remain locked into the industry. Third, nonprofit hospitals continue to have the advantage of tax exemption and various other public-policy preferences, though the available empirical evidence is ambiguous as to whether these subsidies have had a strong effect on their market share (Hansmann, 1987b). And fourth, administrators and medical staff affiliated with existing nonprofit hospitals probably have a stake in retaining the nonprofit form, which may offer them greater control, financial remuneration, and protection from competition than would for-profit firms.

Not all commercial nonprofits have evolved from philanthropic ones, however. There are some industries in which commercial nonprofits have played an important role in the industry from its inception. One of the clearest and most interesting instances of this, and one of the oldest as well, is consumer savings banking (Hansmann, forthcoming; Rasmussen, 1988). That industry, which first took shape at the beginning of the nineteenth century, was initially populated almost exclusively by nonprofit firms, in the form of mutual savings banks. (Despite their name, mutual savings banks, unlike mutual savings and loan associations, are not consumer cooperatives but rather are true nonprofits with no elements of depositor ownership.) Here the nonprofit form served a fiduciary role toward the bank's depositors, providing important protection for them at a time when stock banks were too risky for ordinary citizens to trust with their live's savings.

In time, however, state and federal regulation, as well as the increasing maturity of the banking industry itself, endowed stock banks with a degree of trustworthiness comparable to that of nonprofit banks. Indeed, with the adoption of federal deposit insurance in the 1930s, mutual savings banks lost their comparative advantage entirely and became anachronistic. Yet they have continued to occupy a significant place on the economic scene for another half century, probably for reasons similar to those outlined above in the case of hospitals.

There are many other industries heavily populated with commercial nonprofits that seem to have followed one or the other of these patterns of evolution. Indeed, both patterns may be present in many industries. For example, the commercial nonprofits that are found today in the nursing-home industry and the day-care industry seem to have evolved in part from firms that originally were established as philanthropic entities, although it also appears that many of these firms were essentially commercial nonprofits from their founding and presumably adopted the nonprofit form to offer some extra degree of assurance to prospective customers that they would provide quality care.

As I have already suggested, the two industries that I have focused on as examples here, hospital care and savings banking, are industries in which commercial nonprofits appear today to serve no functions that cannot be served as well or better by for-profit firms. And the same conclusion could be drawn about commercial nonprofits in other industries, such as health maintenance organizations, health insurance, and medical testing. Yet we cannot safely conclude that commercial nonprofits are always nonfunctional. There may well be some industries in which commercial nonprofits today serve much the same role that they served in the savings bank industry in its early stages, providing a degree of fiduciary protection for customers against opportunistic behavior in an environment where consumers are for some reason in a poor position to police the quality of service that a firm promises or delivers. For example, although there is much debate on the subject, some commercial nonprofits may be serving such a function today in the nursing care and day-care industries (Hansmann, 1987a).

In any event, the tendency of nonprofit firms to become embedded once they are established indicates that, in the absence of any changes in public policy, we are likely to face a constantly growing population of commercial nonprofits, many of which will be anachronistic. Indeed, given the tendency of government to take over many of the functions traditionally performed by charity, philanthropic nonprofits are likely to find their role continually shrinking as the number of commercial nonprofits expands.

The Response of the Law

Having surveyed some of the reasons for the emergence of the two nonprofit sectors, we can begin to consider how public policy has been responding to this development and how it is likely to respond in the future. Although the pattern is slightly complicated, we can say in general that, if current trends continue, by the year 2000 the two nonprofit sectors are likely to be strongly distinguished in law as well as in fact.

Tax Law. This tendency is most conspicuous in the area of taxation. In principle, the federal corporate income tax presumes that all nonprofit corporations are taxable unless they can establish that they fit into one or another specific exemption set out in the Internal Revenue Code. In practice, however, the definitions have traditionally been interpreted so broadly as to encompass nearly all nonprofits of any financial significance. And the same has largely been true of state property and sales taxes. In effect, nonprofits as a class have been presumed exempt, and only special types of nonprofits have ever been taxed. In general, the words *nonprofit* and *tax-exempt* have been synonymous.

The emergence of the second nonprofit sector has now begun to threaten this regime seriously. Many of the new commercial nonprofits appear so clearly to be providing services that are no different from those offered by for-profit firms that continued tax exemption is conspicuously difficult to rationalize (Hansmann, 1981a). And, in fact, Congress has recently taken strong action in this regard, withdrawing tax exemption in 1986 from nonprofit organizations "providing commercial-type insurance" (Internal Revenue Code Section 501(m)—which has been interpreted to include, for example, Blue Cross/Blue Shield. There is good reason to believe that this is simply the beginning of an assault on the exemption for many types of commercial nonprofits. At least one member of Congress has already proposed withdrawing tax exemption from nonprofit hospitals (Jaschik, 1987), for example, and it is reasonable to suspect that the exemption for hospitals will soon come under much broader attack. And if nonprofit hospitals lose their exemption, federal corporate tax exemption for most or all of the second nonprofit sector may then be in doubt. The same applies, moreover, to state and local taxes, including not just state corporate income taxes but also property and sales taxes. Indeed, some states have already begun to restrict exemption for hospitals (*Utah County* v. *Intermountain Health Care, Inc.,* 709 P.2d 265 [Utah 1985]), fitness centers (Davis, 1986), and other types of commercial nonprofits.

As a result of this development, serious thought will have to be given in the years ahead to defining the appropriate scope of tax exemption. Should all commercial nonprofits be denied exemption, thus in effect extending the exemption only to donative nonprofits? Or should some commercial nonprofits still be exempt? If so, which ones? Should the tax code try to track the distinction, suggested above, between commercial nonprofits that are anachronistic and those that continue to perform a role that distinguishes them from for-profit firms? Would such a distinction be administrable—for example, in the form of a commerciality test of some type? Does it make most sense for the legislature to proceed on an industry-by-industry basis here, as it has in the case of insurance? (see Hansmann, 1981a).

Note, moreover, that many of the new commercial nonprofits continue to obtain their exemption under the general exemption granted "charities." For example, the nonprofit insurance companies from which Congress recently withdrew exemption had previously been exempted as charities. Thus, the refashioning of tax law to deal with the second nonprofit sector is going to force legal scholars and lawmakers to think more seriously about what is meant by the concept of charity—a task that is about four hundred years overdue.

Wherever the line is ultimately drawn between exempt and nonexempt nonprofits, in the end there is likely to be a large portion of the nonprofit sector that is nonexempt. Indeed, perhaps the great bulk of the sector will be nonexempt. And if this happens, the distinction between exempt and nonexempt organizations will come to be a highly visible line of demarcation between the two nonprofit sectors.

What would happen to the size and scope of the second nonprofit sector if tax exemption were withdrawn from it? It is hard to say. On the one hand, the existing empirical work suggests that the market share of nonprofit firms is relatively more sensitive to tax exemption than is that of for-profit firms (Hansmann, 1987b). On the other hand, experience with nonprofit-seeking firms in other sectors, such as mutual insurance companies, suggests that once such firms are well established, the absence of tax exemption or other perquisites does not inhibit their ability to maintain their share of the market (Hansmann, 1985). It is quite possible that the nonprofit hospitals, nursing homes, day-care centers, health maintenance organizations, home health care agencies, and other institutions that populate the second nonprofit sector will come to appear to us much as mutual insurance companies do now—that is, as essentially commercial entities that do not much differ from their for-profit competitors and that are not treated much differently by public policy.

Other Forms of Special Treatment. Even if, as predicted above, tax exemption is ultimately withdrawn from most or all of the second nonprofit sector, the donatively supported nonprofits that make up the first nonprofit sector seem likely to retain their exemption (and probably the charitable deduction as well). But a different pattern is emerging in other areas of the law where nonprofits have heretofore received special treatment. In a number of these areas, the response to the rise of the second nonprofit sector has been to withdraw preferential treatment not just from the commercial nonprofits that constitute that sector but from *all* nonprofits. Labor law is an example. Prior to 1970, virtually all nonprofit organizations were exempted from federal labor law. But in that year, the National Labor Relations Board (NLRB) began to use its discretion to withdraw this exemption from selected nonprofits (Cornell University, 183 National Labor Relations Board 329 [1970]). A critical step in this process was Congress's decision in 1973 to pass legislation specifically withdrawing labor-law exemption from nonprofit hospitals (Public Law 93-360, amending Section 2(2) of the National Labor Relations Act)—a decision presumably based on the increasingly commercial character of nonprofit hospitals. Yet the process did not stop there, and by 1976 the NLRB had proceeded to withdraw exemption from *all* nonprofits, including even small charities supported entirely by donations (*St. Aloysius Home,* 224 National Labor Relations Board 1344 [1976]).

Moreover, a similar process seems under way in other areas, from antitrust law (*NCAA* v. *Board of Regents,* 104 S. Ct. 2942 [1984]) to subsidized postal rates (39 U.S. Code Annotated Section 3626). Thus, the rise of the second nonprofit sector is threatening the privileges of the traditional philanthropies as well.

Corporate Law. Nonprofit corporation law has also been struggling to come to grips with the emergence of two distinct nonprofit sectors. In particular, the American Law Institute has recently released a new Model Nonprofit Corporation Act, which is being proposed for enactment by states throughout the country. In contrast to most existing nonprofit corporation statutes, this act formally splits all nonreligious nonprofits into two different categories. Traditional charities are to be included in the first of these categories, while social clubs and other membership organizations are to be included in the second. Just where most commercial nonprofits are to go in this scheme is presently quite unclear. But there are indications that many of them are intended to be put into the second category, thus creating a further division between the two nonprofit sectors (Hansmann, forthcoming).

Mixed Cases

So far we have been speaking of a growing divergence between two different types of nonprofit organizations. But much the same development is also occurring *within* individual nonprofits. Without giving up their reliance on donative support, many philanthropic organizations in the first nonprofit sector are engaging in increasing amounts of commercial activity to increase their income. It is commonly said that the reason for this is that nonprofits have recently become financially hard pressed as a result of cutbacks in public and private support. There is probably some partial truth to this; nonprofits seem to struggle hard to maintain their established level of activity and seek actively to find new sources of funding to take the place of older sources that are suddenly lost. But it seems mistaken to infer that, in general, nonprofits engage in commercial activity in proportion to the degree to which demand for their charitable and other unremunerative services exceeds the available sources of philanthropic funding. For it would follow from such an explanation that the commercial activity of nonprofits should have been most extensive not now but rather earlier in the century, when the need for the charitable services and public goods provided by nonprofits was far greater and the sources of private and public support for the nonprofit sector were much smaller than they are today. A better explanation for the long-term trend toward expanding commercial activity on the part of otherwise philanthropic nonprofits is that in part it is a response to the tax and other advantages that have come to be afforded such activities and in part it reflects the increasing sophistication and legitimation of commercial activity by nonprofits in general that have resulted from the rapid expansion of the second (principally commercial) nonprofit sector.

In any event, the same problems that are arising between the two nonprofit sectors are also appearing within individual organizations. Thus, to take one conspicuous example, the taxation of unrelated business income has recently become a very lively topic of debate (United States, 1987).

Implications for Policy

Issues Facing Nonprofit Managers. As a consequence of the emergence of the second nonprofit sector, managers of nonprofit organizations are now faced with large and difficult questions about the purposes their organizations are to serve. Managers of the new commercial nonprofits, in particular, must constantly ask themselves whether, and why, the fact that they are non-profit affects what their organization is doing—and, most importantly, how it affects what their organization *should* be doing. Should a nonprofit hospital try hard to provide services that are somehow different from those offered by a for-profit hospital? Should the YMCA's fitness centers offer services that are clearly different from those offered by for-profit fitness centers? If so, just *how* should their services be different? If not, why are they nonprofit, much less tax-exempt, and should they consider altering their form from a nonprofit corporation to a business corporation? In short, organizations within the second nonprofit sector are faced with a massive identity crisis, and the managers of these institutions are somehow going to have to deal with it. Moreover, even a minor identity crisis of this sort affects the managers of traditional philanthropies every time they decide whether to undertake a new commercial venture.

Issues Facing the Organized Nonprofit Sector. The emergence
of two distinct nonprofit sectors creates a dilemma for national
and local organizations that seek to represent the interests of
the nonprofit sector as a whole. For, as we approach the year
2000, the interests of the two nonprofit sectors may increasingly
diverge. For example, rather than fighting to retain special subsidies and preferences, such as tax exemption, for *all* nonprofits,
it may be in the interest of the first nonprofit sector—the philanthropic nonprofits—to protect itself by, as it were, throwing
the second nonprofit sector to the wolves. More particularly,
the traditional philanthropies may wish to lobby for the establishment of a clear line between those nonprofits that will continue
to benefit from special preferences, such as tax exemption, and
those that will not and to place the commercial nonprofit sector
on the far side of the line. The alternative could be that preferences will ultimately be lost for *all* nonprofits, including the
philanthropic ones. In short, when it comes to preferential treatment for nonprofits, it may be rational for the philanthropic
nonprofit sector to conclude that, if united we stand, then united
we will fall.

A divergence of interests between the two nonprofit sectors may also emerge in corporation law, though here it is likely
to take a slightly different form. For example, while it will be
in the interest of many commercial nonprofits to be governed
by the relatively permissive mutual benefit provisions of the new
Model Nonprofit Corporation Act, it may be in the interest of
the philanthropic nonprofits to have the commercial nonprofits,
like the philanthropic nonprofits, governed by the more stringent
public benefit provisions, thus reducing the likelihood of op-
portunism and fraud on the part of commercial nonprofits that
might tarnish the public image and detract from the public support of the nonprofit sector as a whole.

Issues Facing Lawmakers. The evolution of the two nonprofit
sectors also continues to face lawmakers with serious issues of
public policy. I have argued elsewhere (for example, Hansmann,
forthcoming) that there are strong reasons for the organizational
law of nonprofits (in particular, nonprofit corporation law) to
abandon the newly emerging tendency toward establishing dif-

ferent categories of nonprofits with different standards and to impose instead a uniform set of relatively strict fiduciary constraints on all nonprofits, regardless of whether they are in the first or the second nonprofit sector. Similarly, it makes sense for regulatory law (such as securities law and antitrust law) to abandon the remaining distinctions among different types of nonprofits and to treat them all similarly, whether they are in the first or the second nonprofit sector—and moreover to treat them essentially the same as for-profit firms. In contrast, tax law should continue its present trend toward ever greater discrimination between the first and second nonprofit sectors, reserving privileged treatment only for the former, which will be an increasingly smaller subset of all nonprofits. Whether these or other views will prevail, however, remains uncertain.

Conclusion

The very forces that have caused the nonprofit sector to grow so rapidly in recent decades have also led to important shifts in the composition of that sector. Those changes are likely to continue between now and the year 2000, leaving us with an even more diverse—and divided—set of organizations than we have now. As a consequence, there will be difficult questions of policy to be addressed in the years to come, both for lawmakers and for leaders within the nonprofit sector itself.

References

American Hospital Association. *Hospital Statistics.* Chicago: American Hospital Association, 1987.

Cornell University, 183 National Labor Relations Board 329 (1970).

Davis, N. "The Competition Complex." *Association Management,* Aug. 1986, p. 24.

Gray, B. (ed.). *For-Profit Enterprise in Health Care.* Washington, D.C.: National Academy Press, 1986.

Hansmann, H. "The Role of Nonprofit Enterprise." *Yale Law Journal,* 1980, *89,* 835–901.

Hansmann, H. "The Rationale for Exempting Nonprofit Organizations from the Corporate Income Tax." *Yale Law Journal,* 1981a, *91,* 54–100.

Hansmann, H. "Reforming Nonprofit Corporation Law." *University of Pennsylvania Law Review,* 1981b, *129,* 497–623.

Hansmann, H. "The Organization of Insurance Companies: Mutual Versus Stock." *Journal of Law, Economics, and Organization,* 1985, *1,* 125–153.

Hansmann, H. "Economic Theories of Nonprofit Organization." In W. W. Powell (ed.), *The Nonprofit Sector: A Research Handbook.* New Haven, Conn.: Yale University Press, 1987a.

Hansmann, H. "The Effect of Tax Exemption and Other Factors on the Market Share of Nonprofit Versus For-Profit Firms." *National Tax Journal,* 1987b, *40,* 71–82.

Hansmann, H. "The Evolving Law of Nonprofit Organizations: Do Current Trends Make Good Policy?" *Case Western Reserve Law Review,* forthcoming.

Hansmann, H. "The Role of Commercial Nonprofits: The Evolution of Savings Banks." In H. Anheier and W. Seibel (eds.), *The Nonprofit Sector: International and Comparative Perspectives.* Berlin: Walter de Gruyter, forthcoming.

Herzlinger, R., and Krasker, W. "Who Profits from Nonprofits?" *Harvard Business Review,* Jan.-Feb. 1987, pp. 93–106.

Jaschik, S. "Congressman Advocates End to Tax Exemption for Non-Profit Hospitals." *Chronicle of Higher Education,* July 22, 1987, p. 1.

Rasmussen, E. "Stock Banks Versus Mutual Banks." *Journal of Law and Economics,* 1988.

United States. Congress. Hearings Before the Subcommittee on Oversight of the Committee on Ways and Means, HOR 100th Cong. 1st Sess. 11 (1987). Statement of the Hon. O. D. Chapoton, Department of the Treasury.

Utah County v. *Intermountain Health Care, Inc.,* 709 P.2d 265 (Utah 1985).

7

△ △ △ △ △ △ △ △ △ △ △ △ △ △ △

The Complexities of Income Generation for Nonprofits

Nonprofit organizations rarely survive on donations alone. In fact, few nonprofits even receive a substantial portion of their revenues from donations. Among a random sample of 274 tax-deductible organizations that I surveyed for the tax years 1973–1975 (Weisbrod, 1988), some 38 percent of tax-deductible nonprofits received 10 percent or less of their revenues from donations; half received less than 25 percent from donations. Nonprofits are typically involved in a variety of fund-raising markets to make up the balance of revenues. Often they encounter the proprietary sector of the economy as they pursue other sources of revenue. Small businesses particularly resent nonprofits' for-profit endeavors. Responding to numerous complaints from the small-business community, Frank Swain, the Small Business Administration (SBA) chief counsel for advocacy, said, "Small private businesses are laboring under a tax code which taxes them but not some of their competitors—nonprofit organizations doing business for profit" (Swain, 1983). The SBA and various industry groups within the small-business community increasingly refer to nonprofits as "unfair competition."

    This criticism of nonprofits combines both factual and normative issues. In this policy debate, the following questions need

Note: This chapter draws heavily from Chapter 6 of my book *The Nonprofit Economy* (Cambridge, Mass.: Harvard University Press, 1988).

answers: Is there substantial competition between nonprofit organizations and proprietary firms? Is the competition growing? What forms is it taking? Is such competition ''unfair,'' and how should fairness be defined? What should be the limits on what nonprofits may do to raise revenues? And, if the competition is unfair to the proprietary firms, is it also inefficient or otherwise undesirable from the point of view of society as a whole? Only if it is should public actions be taken to restrict the inventiveness of nonprofits in their search for new activities, markets, and resources.

Competition

Supporters of both the nonprofits and the proprietary organizations agree that cutbacks in federal funding, beginning around 1980, have led an increasing number of nonprofits to seek new revenue by engaging in profit-making activities (Schmidt, 1983; U.S. Small Business Administration, 1984). A community group in Milwaukee, for example, has purchased a launderette in hopes of generating profits that can then be used for its community welfare activities (Norman, 1982). Other for-profit endeavors of nonprofit organizations include a commercial weatherization and home-improvement company, a food-management service for hospitals and schools, a restaurant (Cox, 1985), a construction and home-improvement company, a commercial greenhouse business (Grantsmanship Center, 1984), and a national for-profit development company that builds festival marketplaces in smaller cities (Fulton, 1985). Even public television, its government funding having been sharply cut, has resorted to dramatically new measures for raising revenues (Mayer, 1982). A recent book, intriguingly titled *Enterprise in the Nonprofit Sector* (Crimmins and Keil, 1983), includes two words in its title that any people have traditionally regarded as contradictory: *enterprise* and *nonprofit*. But they are no longer contradictory. ''Sixty-nine percent of the organizations we surveyed have given birth to new [profit-making] enterprise within the past twelve years,'' the authors assert (Crimmins and Keil, 1983, p. 14).

Commercial activity by nonprofits is not new; data on revenue sources of nonprofits in the mid 1970s make it clear that even then there was substantial dependence on nondonative revenues—either from membership dues or from some form of sales. As early as 1908, the Metropolitan Museum of Art opened a sales shop; and before that it sold copies of photographs from its collections. One of the best-known examples of sales of goods to generate income for a nonprofit organization is the annual Girl Scouts cookie sale. The Girl Scouts of America sold 125 million boxes of cookies for gross revenue of over $200 million in 1982 (Skloot, 1987).

Some of the new activities of nonprofits are leading to questions about the grounds for tax exemption. Some of these activities are so clearly unrelated to the organization's exempt purpose that they are organized into separate for-profit entities, and the net income is subject to taxation as "unrelated business income" (UBI). (For a number of examples of nonprofits that have formed for-profit subsidiaries and their reasons for doing so, see Mier and Wiewel, 1983.) In other cases, the new activity may be in a "gray" area, neither clearly unrelated nor clearly related to the charitable purposes of the organization. This is likely to constitute a growing administrative problem for the IRS, as financially hard-pressed nonprofits increasingly probe the outer limits of exempt-income activities. A 1985 report by the U.S. General Accounting Office (GAO) points out that this is already a problem. The IRS does not have sufficient information on compliance with the tax on unrelated business income to develop profiles of noncompliant tax-exempt organizations (Finch, 1985). The GAO report notes the limited staff available to the IRS for investigations, the "increasing UBI activity," and the substantial rate of noncompliance that their audit disclosed. Measured in dollars, noncompliance with the tax on unrelated business income was estimated at 25 percent for social welfare organizations, 58 percent for charitable and educational organizations, and 61 percent for business leagues (Finch, 1985).

When nonprofits seek profitable enterprises, they almost inevitably move away from charitable and collective types of services and into the sale of goods. Recent research supports the expectation that when the budgets of nonprofit organizations are squeezed, they respond by shifting attention to sales of goods in private markets. Jerald Schiff and Burton Weisbrod (1986) have hypothesized that nonprofits pursue the goal of maximizing their output of "charitable" services, subject to the necessity of at least breaking even financially. They see nonprofits as potential providers of two kinds of goods or services—charitable and "private." The organization managers and directors prefer to produce the charitable good, which is financed by private donations and by government support, but they may resort to selling private output to "cross-subsidize" their charitable activities. This model of behavior implies that the private business sector does, indeed, have something to fear from nonprofits— but the underlying cause is reduction in government support for nonprofits.

A change in government expenditures can have a number of effects on nonprofits: (1) a direct revenue effect of the change in government spending; (2) a "crowding out" effect on private donations; (3) a revenue-source substitution effect, which gives rise to private firms' fears of nonprofits' competition; (4) a fund-raising effect (changes in government spending affect the amount of money nonprofits spend on soliciting private donations); and (5) exit/entry effects (government budget cuts can affect the number of operating nonprofit organizations).

Utilizing data from tax returns of the more than 11,000 social welfare nonprofits in the United States between 1973 and 1976, Schiff and Weisbrod (1986) estimated the effects of changes in various types of government welfare spending—cash transfers, purchases from nonprofits, and direct governmental provision of services—on these five variables. The study allowed for interactive effects whereby, for example, a cut in government purchases from nonprofits could affect the level of an average nonprofit organization's revenue in a number of ways—directly decreasing it and indirectly either increasing it or diminishing it further as nonprofits changed their fund-raising expenditures and their efforts to sell private goods for the purpose of cross-subsidization. [That is, starting with a system of four structural equations positing the factors affecting an average nonprofit's receipts from (1) donations and from (2) sales, its (3) level of fund-raising expenditures, and (4) the total number of welfare nonprofits in a state, Schiff and Weisbrod, 1986, estimated reduced form equations that reflect the interactive effects.]

Most of the expected effects have occurred. Changes in government welfare expenditures do exert a statistically significant impact on the level and composition of revenues—the proportions of revenues from donations and from sales—for nonprofit welfare organizations. The effects on nonprofits differ, however, depending on whether governments increase or decrease their cash transfers, their direct provision of welfare services, or their purchases of welfare services from nonprofits. When governments reduce their direct provision of social services, the nonprofit sector responds by increasing its commercial sales activities. A 10 percent cut in government social service spending causes nonprofits to increase sales by an estimated 1.3 percent.

This finding, that reduced government spending leads to increased sales efforts, is derived from the study of only welfare organizations. The general question, though, of how nonprofits' sales activities respond to changes in the availability of various forms of public and private revenue remains open. For example, the Schiff-Weisbrod research also found that cuts in other forms of governmental welfare spending—cash transfers—do not bring adjustments that increase nonprofits' sales revenues.

The question of whether nonprofits should be restricted, taxed, or even prohibited from competing with the proprietary sector is coming under the spotlight in the policy arena. A recent survey by the congressional General Accounting Office showed, for example, that 84 percent of private research firms and 90 percent of racket-sport firms claim that nonprofit, tax-exempt universities and fitness facilities compete unfairly with them (Schmedel, 1987b). A critic of university-based commercial research activities, for example, claimed that "Colleges and universities and independent nonprofit organizations offer [research] services in competition with for-profit firms as a by-product of tax-exempt 'basic' research and education functions. . . . Faculty entrepreneurs are able to underprice local firms because they do not have to factor equipment and other capital costs into their prices'' (U.S. Small Business Administration, 1984, pp. 18–19).

Another nonprofit entity, the nonprofit hospital, is expanding "vertically" beyond conventional hospital services into a growing number of for-profit activities. Laundry services and hearing aids are but two examples of activities into which nonprofit hospitals and clinics have expanded (U.S. Small Business Administration, 1984). In the Philadelphia area, three nonprofit hospitals have begun manufacturing prosthetic devices, bringing them into direct competition with private manufacturers of artificial limbs (U.S. Small Business Administration, 1984).

An overall indicator of the competition between proprietary and nonprofit organizations in various industries is the importance of sales revenues to the nonprofits. When nonprofits generate revenues through sales, they are ordinarily providing outputs in competition with proprietary firms, whereas when they receive donations, they are usually providing outputs that differ from what the proprietary market provides. (At times, proprietary firms may receive donations to be used for much the same purposes that nonprofits would use them for. In such cases, however, it is difficult for donors to monitor the nature of the outputs and to whom they are distributed.) Thus, the average nonprofit in the field of legal aid is not very competitive with its proprietary counterparts, for these nonprofits receive only 3 percent of their revenues from "sales." In scientific research, by contrast, the average nonprofit appears to be much more like its proprietary counterparts, for it receives 86 percent of its revenues from sales.

When nonprofits seek to sell outputs profitably in order to fund other activities (that is, to cross-subsidize), they must find outputs that are both salable and profitable. The position that public policy should take concerning these activities depends on the effects on society of permitting or restricting them. Should there be any constraints on the type or level of profit-making activities by nonprofits? One issue is the kinds of money-generating activities nonprofits are likely to engage in if they are not restricted. Another is whether it is both economically efficient and equitable that those activities be pursued. Finally, how does the tax system influence the direction of nonprofits' expansion into new areas? Currently, the system taxes nonprofits' unrelated business income as ordinary corporate profit, and for some classes of nonprofits, it limits the proportion of total revenue that may be derived from such activities that are unrelated to the organization's exempt purpose.

The public-policy choices for the future are between a smaller, more "pure" set of nonprofits that are financed by donations, which will leave the organizations less constrained in their activities, and a larger nonprofit sector that receives more revenue from commercial sales of private-type goods or from those government and private contributions that come with tighter "strings" attached. In my judgment, public policy cannot adopt tax or other measures that drive nonprofits into private-goods markets without compromising nonprofits' principal rationale for existing—their contribution to social welfare. But evidence on this issue is scant.

The cries of unfair competition by the private sector result partly from judgments about how to define a nonprofit's unrelated business income. With this income fully taxable, nonprofits are somewhat discouraged from engaging in the activities that generate it—that is, activities that are not "substantially related" to the "charitable, educational, or other purpose which fixes the basis for its exemption under Internal Revenue Code Section 501" (Internal Revenue Code Section 513). Depending on how broadly or narrowly the IRS interprets the "exempt purpose" of the organization, the nonprofit will have a larger or a smaller domain in which it can compete with proprietary firms at a competitive tax advantage.

The tax law did not always restrict, tax, or otherwise handicap nonprofits' revenues as it now does. In 1948, when a group of alumni donated the Mueller Macaroni Company to the New York University (NYU) Law School, Mueller's profits were given tax-exempt states because NYU was a nonprofit organization (Rose-Ackerman, 1982). But two years later, in an apparent attempt to deal with the "unfair competition" issue, Congress amended the Internal Revenue Code to exempt from taxation only the "related" business ventures of nonprofits. The legislative report stated explicitly that "The problem at which the tax on unrelated business income is directed is primarily that of unfair competition" (S. Rept. 2375, 81st Cong., 2d sess., 28–29, 1950). Concerns about "unfair" competition by nonprofits somehow became translated into concerns about business activity that was not "substantially related" to the exempt purpose.

Administrators and courts have found it very difficult to deal with many specific situations in which they have had to apply the "substantially related" concept. One circuit court judge referred to "hair-splitting" decisions in a case involving the question of whether sales by a nonprofit hospital's pharmacy to private nonhospitalized patients of physicians on the hospital staff were tax-exempt (*Hi-Plains Hospital* v. *United States,* 670 F.2d 528 [5th Cir. 1982]). A former commissioner of the Internal Revenue Service, Sheldon Cohen, expressed the frustrating complexity of distinguishing taxable from nontaxable income of nonprofit organizations: "Nonprofits are a whole can of worms that Congress has yet to look at in a broad way. I have been blowing the trumpet for years to get lawmakers to spell out clearly what should be tax-exempt and what should not be" (Maloney, 1978, p. 7).

The ambiguity of a nonprofit's exempt purpose could be decreased, of course, by a change in the law or its administration. The exempt purpose could be defined more precisely and narrowly. Currently, nonprofits are granted exempt status for such broad purposes as education or community development. How broad should the definition of a nonprofit's exempt purpose be? Proprietary firms would like it to be narrower, so that nonprofit organizations would be more restricted. Nonprofits would like it to be broader, giving greater flexibility. Weighing such conflicting arguments is very difficult. The perspective of a tax-collection agency—such as the IRS—is not the most appropriate one for this balancing.

Another question—seemingly technical, but of considerable import—is how a nonprofit organization's "net income" from an unrelated business activity should be calculated. In particular, how should costs be allocated between its exempt and nonexempt ("unrelated") activities? When a nonprofit is producing both, it can exercise discretion in the way it allocates certain costs—such as for capital equipment, office space, and salaries—that apply to both. It has the incentive, of course, to allocate as much of these costs as possible to the otherwise-profitable unrelated business activities, so as to minimize reported taxable net income and hence tax payments. Thus, nonprofits that may appear to make little profit on their unrelated business activities, where they compete with proprietary firms, may actually make substantially greater profits. This is an additional source of administrative headache for the IRS.

Through a variety of tax laws and subsidy programs, nonprofits are treated as worthy of explicit encouragement. At the same time, there have been actions that effectively reverse such institutional encouragement. A recent decision by the U.S. Office of Management and Budget (OMB), for example, resolves, at least for now, one element of the unfair competition debate. It involves competitive bidding between nonprofit and for-profit firms for federal government contracts. Proprietary firms have argued that their bids are higher simply because they must pay federal, state, and local taxes that their nonprofit competitors do not. In August 1983, the OMB altered its rules on bidding for federal government contracts. Any federal government agency is now required to take into account, in awarding a contract, an estimate of the tax revenue forgone if the contract is awarded to a nonprofit: "If the apparent low bidder or offeror is a tax-exempt organization, the contract price must be adjusted by an amount equal to the Federal, state and local income taxes that would be paid by the lowest non-tax-exempt bidder or offeror. This adjustment is necessary to determine which bidder or offeror has the lower overall cost to the Government" (Executive Office of the President, 1983). The rules also specify how the federal government is to act in the case of a tie between a nonprofit tax-exempt organization and one that is not. If the tax-adjusted price is identical to the non-tax-exempt organization's price, the non-tax-exempt organization is the winner.

There is a paradox here. Society seems to have an unarticulated but de facto policy that sees an important difference between the social desirability of nonprofit activities when they are supported by donations (much of which is contributed indirectly, through the tax system, by taxpayers in general) and when they are supported by sales of goods in private competitive markets. It is important to learn more about whether the source of revenue actually affects the nature of output. This is one more example of the weak analytical and factual base that now underlies policy toward nonprofits.

Do Nonprofits Have a Net Advantage?

However the nonprofits use the funds generated from competitive sales, another important factual question is just how great is the alleged advantage that nonprofits have when they compete with proprietary firms. This, after all, is presumably the basis of the unfair-competition complaint. That complaint rests on more than simply the exemption from profit tax and the deductibility of donations to some nonprofits. Beyond the tax deductibility of donations for some nonprofits and the exemption from corporate profit taxation for all, nonprofits have both advantages and disadvantages in any potential competition with proprietary firms. There are numerous legal rules that define what can be done with the resources commanded by nonprofits. Some of these rules are more restrictive than those confronting for-profit firms; others are less restrictive.

On one hand, nonprofits may not lawfully pay out any surplus or profit to anyone associated with the organization. This "nondistribution" constraint means that the organization is effectively cut off from the market for equity capital. According to the IRS, the "prohibition of inurement, in its simplest terms, means that a private shareholder or individual cannot pocket the organization's funds except as reasonable payment for goods and services" (Hopkins, 1977, p. 128) Excessive wages or salary, rental charges, or purchase price of property would be evidence of private enurement, although the cost of determining what is "excessive" serves as a clear obstacle to IRS enforcement. For example, it took five years, ending in April 1988, for the IRS to develop the case against the PTL Ministry, in which the tax-exempt status was withdrawn, in part because Jim Bakker was allegedly paid a salary that was nearly $1 million more than was "reasonable" for at least three years.

Charitable nonprofits—those that may accept tax-deductible donations—are also severely limited in their freedom to engage in lobbying or other political activities involving attempts to support or oppose a particular candidate or to influence legislation. These constraints are comparatively recent. The prohibition on participation in political campaigns originated in a Senate floor amendment added by Lyndon Johnson in 1954. Johnson apparently believed that a foundation in Texas had provided financial support to his opponent in an election. Limitations on attempts to influence legislation originated earlier, though, in a 1934 Senate floor amendment; the sponsor indicated irritation with the activities of one specific nonprofit organization, the National Economy League (Hopkins, 1977).

The limitation on legislative lobbying—which does not apply to proprietary firms—has posed enforcement problems that attenuate its effectiveness. Internal Revenue Code Section 501(c)(3) states that "no substantial part of the activities" of a charitable organization may be used for "carrying on propaganda, or otherwise attempting, to influence legislation." The term *substantial* is obviously imprecise. It has been interpreted to mean more than 5 percent of an organization's time and effort; under the Tax Reform Act of 1976, however, most charitable organizations (although not churches or some others) have the option of electing to be governed by specific expenditure limitations rather than the vague "substantial" criterion. Under this option, an organization is permitted to spend on lobbying up to 20 percent of the first $500,000 of its expenditures (exclusive of fund-raising expenses), 15 percent of the next $500,000, and 5 percent of expenditures beyond that, with a maximum total of $1 million per year. And expenditures aimed at influencing the public regarding legislative matters are limited to 25 percent of the total amount spent on lobbying (Hopkins, 1977). Even now, charities are under increasing pressure to restrict lobbying; indeed, the definition of *lobbying* continues to be a source of contention. For over two years the IRS has been working on a revision of its administrative rules applicable to the rights of charities to communicate with legislators and public officials. The version proposed in 1986 would, in the view of the sixteen members of the Senate Finance Committee, "severely limit the rights of charities to communicate with legislators and public officials" (Schmedel, 1987a). A revised administrative rule has been circulated and is receiving more favorable comments, particularly from charitable organizations; the period for comments ended in March 1989 (Accetura, 1989).

The nonprofits, charitable or other, however, are not subject to some constraints that are commonly believed to exist. Most notably, they are not restricted in the amount of profit they may make; restrictions apply only to what they may do with the profits—essentially limiting their use to the purchase of more resources for the organization.

Nonprofits also have a number of tax and subsidy advantages over proprietary firms. Government tax subsidies extend beyond the corporate income tax exemption and, for some, deductibility of donations to them. Other areas of special treatment or exemption include Social Security, unemployment insurance, the minimum wage, securities regulations, bankruptcy, antitrust, unfair competition, copyright, and postal rates. But even this impressive list is incomplete. On August 27, 1982, a law was signed requiring large firms that are granted patents to pay a user fee equal to 100 percent of the costs incurred by the federal government in awarding the patent; but nonprofit organizations (as well as small firms and independent inventors) need pay only 50 percent. And certain nonprofits—the charitable organizations that are tax-exempt under Section 501(c)(3) of the Internal Revenue Code—are exempted from the section of the Organized Crime Control Act that prohibits gambling businesses.

Many nonprofit organizations also benefit from favored tax treatment by the states in which they operate. Most states exempt them from paying sales taxes on their purchases and from paying property taxes. The property tax exemption has often been the source of considerable hostility between large nonprofit institutions, such as universities, and local government officials who are obliged to provide police, fire, and other public services to the nonprofits but receive no property tax payments in return. Sometimes the nonprofits make voluntary payments in lieu of property taxes, but even then the amount of the payment is frequently debated. And the exemption from property taxation may induce nonprofits to utilize more capital-intensive and land-intensive production processes than do proprietary firms, which must pay such taxes.

Considering all these differences between nonprofit and proprietary organizations, what is the net effect on competition between them? In one sense, the answer is clear: Nonprofits enter into competition with proprietaries only when they expect to be able to compete profitably. They compete with travel agencies, testing laboratories, and hearing-aid sales, but not with mining companies, steel mills, and home-appliance stores.

Only a little is known about the quantitative importance of the various subsidies that are provided to nonprofits. However, because subsidies differ from state to state—even though the federal portion is the same across all states—it is possible to determine whether there is a systematic relationship between the magnitude of a state's subsidy to a nonprofit organization— for example, through exemption from property and sales taxation—and the size of the nonprofit sector relative to the proprietary sector in that state. This information helps answer the question of what effect various public subsidies have on the ability of nonprofit organizations to survive and to compete with proprietary firms.

The higher the level of a state's taxation of private business, the greater the competitive value to a nonprofit organization of exemption from those taxes. Thus, nonprofits in effect receive greater subsidies in states that have higher rates of property, sales, and corporate income tax than they do in states with lower tax rates. Not surprisingly, research shows that nonprofits have a larger market share in the higher-tax states (Hansmann, 1985). In the competition between nonprofit and proprietary firms, tax exemption of nonprofits makes a difference. Moreover, some exemptions affect nonprofits' incentives. For example, exemption from property taxation makes it particularly attractive for nonprofits to locate in central-city areas, where property tax rates are usually high.

Given that tax and other subsidies to nonprofits enhance the ability of nonprofits to compete, is there something "unfair"? Should laws or their administration be changed so as to reverse the inroads of nonprofits into proprietary markets? Two separable issues in this debate are competition in the specific industry for which the nonprofit has been given exempt status and competition in activities unrelated to those for which exempt status was given. There is also a considerable gray area between the two.

The first arena of competition might seem to be uncontroversial. Congress has determined that the nonprofit form of organization should be encouraged—that is, subsidized—to engage in certain activities. If those subsidies give the nonprofits a competitive advantage, that is the intent. If proprietary firms are handicapped or even driven from the market, so be it.

However, this model of the legislative process is too simple. It assumes that government has determined that the nonprofit form of institution is socially preferred on either efficiency or equity grounds but that nonprofits would not exist to an appropriate degree without subsidization. Government is credited with considerable knowledge and a decision process that leads to maximization of "social welfare." But the facts are far from clear. Evidence that nonprofit hospitals, for example, are more "public-serving" than are proprietary hospitals or that nonprofit schools, nursing homes, day-care centers, or publishers deserve more encouragement than do their proprietary counterparts is by no means overwhelming. It is fair to say that serious attempts to detect the social rationale for encouraging nonprofits in particular areas of economic activity, at least outside the field of health care, have been scant and indecisive (Gray, 1986; Weisbrod and Schlesinger, 1986).

The potential advantage that nonprofits have over proprietary firms in appealing to poorly informed consumers suggests that neither the nonprofit nor the proprietary form is likely to be preferred by all consumers. Poorly informed consumers may prefer dealing with a nonprofit because the constraint on the organization's distribution of profit reduces its incentive to act opportunistically. Better-informed consumers, however, have no such institutional preference and will choose to deal with any organization, regardless of ownership form, that provides the desired outputs at the lowest price. Since public subsidies to the nonprofit sector may reduce the number of proprietary firms, well-informed consumers find the competitive advantage granted to nonprofits counterproductive, inefficient, and unfair.

The second arena for competition is in markets for unrelated outputs—where nonprofit organizations seek to reap profits in order to cross-subsidize their "primary," exempt activities. Here the issue of "fairness," as the affected proprietary firms see it, or of economic efficiency, as an analyst with an economic-welfare perspective might view it, is cloudy at best. The issue of how far nonprofits should be permitted to reach out to compete with proprietary firms can be viewed as a question of which fund-raising methods nonprofits may use. From an economic-efficiency perspective, the desirability of permitting nonprofits to expand into activities that are less central to their exempt purposes involves two sorts of interdependencies: in costs, between a nonprofit's costs of producing its primary outputs and its costs of producing various other outputs, and in revenues, between a nonprofit's ability to generate revenues from its primary activities and its ability to obtain revenues from other outputs.

If there were no such interdependencies—that is, if both production costs and revenues for a narrower "charitable" activity, X_1, and another activity, X_2, were independent of each other—a nonprofit producer of X_1 would have no advantage in the market for X_2; it would have to compete with for-profit firms in the latter market, where consumers would patronize the more efficient suppliers, regardless of ownership type. But the assumption of independence is not likely to hold. Nonprofits that seek new product markets where they can make profit to augment their revenues from donations and other sources will select precisely those products and services where their initial, subsidized production of X_1 provides the greatest competitive advantage.

The advantage could involve costs. Consider a proprietary firm engaged in product testing or archaeological work that complains about competition from a nonprofit university because the university can employ graduate students inexpensively since they are already on campus for their education. The firm is arguing, in effect, that graduate students are joint inputs to the production of both their own education and these other research activities. It should come as no surprise that the university would find it efficient and profitable to make use of just such cost-saving opportunities, rather than to engage in any of a myriad of other production activities in which the resources utilized in its educational activities would give it little or no competitive advantage.

Such joint-cost economies represent real efficiencies, but they are also the basis of a public-policy dilemma. Given that an organization—in this case, a university—is producing tax-exempt outputs, it can be economically efficient for it also to produce certain other outputs. But at the same time, expansion into the other markets brings the subsidized organization into direct competition with unsubsidized forms in the proprietary sector of the economy. For-profit firms may claim unfair competition; yet that competition is efficient, given the initial judgment that there are certain educational activities that merit subsidization through nonprofit organizations.

Joint costs may seem to be a technical matter that can be handled by accountants and that involves no major policy choices, but such a view is incorrect. If a nonprofit organization engages in both tax-exempt and taxable activities, the allocation of its costs between the two can have important implications for the organization's taxes and, hence, its ability to compete profitably with private business. If the nonprofit can charge much of the joint costs to the for-profit activities, it can reduce, if not eliminate, its accounting profit and, hence, its tax liability on unrelated business income, even though the activity is actually quite profitable. By the same token, private or public contributions for the nonprofit's "main" (exempt) activities permit purchase of resources that can be used jointly in both that and other activities; thus, if nonprofits are permitted to extend their activities, donors' contributions constitute a "joint subsidy" for all of the organization's activities—whether intended or not—including those that are not directly related to its principal exempt purposes.

Nonprofits seeking additional revenues can be attracted to particular new activities not only because of cost interdependencies but also because of consumption interdependencies in demand. Thus, consumers who are obtaining X_1 from a nonprofit organization may also prefer to purchase other, X_2 goods and services from it. Indeed, a nonprofit organization in search of profits will seek out just such relationships. For example, patients leaving a hospital may prefer to buy prescription drugs from a pharmacy at the hospital rather than from another down the block; university students may prefer to deal with a travel agency on campus; museum-goers may prefer to patronize the museum shop rather than to shop elsewhere. If consumers do prefer to purchase a variety of goods and services from the same source, then to restrict a nonprofit's outputs would hurt consumers. Yet to permit the nonprofit to expand its activities would hurt proprietary producers. (Whether the nonprofit "provides" the service directly or contracts it out is not important. Even in the latter case, the nonprofit would presumably benefit virtually as much from the rent it could realize as from the profit it could earn.)

A number of proposals are now being considered to reduce competition by nonprofit organizations with proprietary firms. The interdependencies in production costs and in consumer demands make it very complex to evaluate the proposals from an overall societal perspective. One plan to limit nonprofit business activities would increase the tax rate on the first dollar of unrelated business income of the nonprofits, setting it at the highest marginal corporate tax rate rather than at the lowest. Another would totally prohibit unrelated business activities. Still another would alter the criteria for determining what is an "unrelated trade or business," so that the IRS would consider not only whether an activity is "substantially related" to the organization's exempt purpose, as it does now, but also its impact on proprietary firms. There is also a proposal to amend the Federal Trade Commission Act, which exempts nonprofits from the restrictions on unfair competition. (For a discussion of these and other measures, see U.S. Small Business Administration, 1984.)

Complaints of unfair competition do not come only from the private sector. Nonprofits, too, claim that business has entered such customarily nonprofit fields as health and child care. There may well be a tendency for each form of organization to argue that incursion of the other form into an activity dominated by it is "unfair," but surely the appropriate social roles for the private and the nonprofit sectors cannot be determined on the basis of which form of organization was "first"—even if that were clear.

Conclusion

Expansion of nonprofits' commercial activities is both understandable and troubling. Nonprofits do not have access to the market for equity capital, which is a mainstay of for-profit firms. Insofar as nonprofits provide public-type goods they face the problem of free-rider behavior, which restricts their ability to sell outputs to individual consumers, the ultimate source of revenues for proprietary firms. By contrast, for-profit firms find it costly, if not impossible, to obtain donations, which are enormously important for nonprofit organizations.

Subject to these varied constraints on fund raising, any organization can affect the amount of money it receives from each source. A proprietary firm can affect its revenue from sales by changing the level and quality of output, as well as its price, assuming that it does not operate in a perfectly competitive market. A nonprofit organization can affect the amount of donations it receives by engaging in fund-raising activities; it can also augment its resources by producing goods and services that can be sold at a profit. When nonprofits move into these "secondary" markets, they act more and more like proprietary firms, and they become increasingly competitive with the proprietaries. This truly poses a dilemma for public policy. My own judgment is that the important social role of nonprofits would be better served if they became less dependent on commercial revenue and instead were assisted, through tax and other policies, to obtain more revenue through donations. Shifting from tax deductibility of charitable giving to a tax credit is worthy of serious consideration, but that is a subject for another day.

References

Accetura, P. (Internal Revenue Service). Telephone conversation with author, March 30, 1989.

Cox, M. "At Some Eateries, People Just Eat; at This Cafe, They Also Do Good." *Wall Street Journal,* Sept. 18, 1985, p. 25.

Crimmins, J. C., and Keil, M. *Enterprise in the Nonprofit Sector.* Washington, D.C.: Partners for Livable Places and the Rockefeller Brothers Fund, 1983.

Executive Office of the President, U.S. Office of Management and Budget. *Supplement to OMB Circular No. A-76 (Revised), Performance of Commercial Activities.* Washington, D.C.: Executive Office of the President, Office of Management and Budget, 1983.

Finch, J. C. "Where Is IRS Likely to Look in 'Unrelated Business Income' Audits?" *Philanthropy Monthly,* 1985, *85,* 13–16.

Fulton, W. "The Robin Hood of Real Estate." *Planning,* May 1985, pp. 4–10.

Grantmanship Center. *Business Ventures for Nonprofits, 1984 Schedule.* Los Angeles: Grantsmanship Center, 1984.

Gray, B. (ed.). *For Profit Enterprise in Health Care.* Washington, D.C.: National Academy Press, 1986.

Hansmann, H. "The Effect of Tax Exemption and Other Factors on Competition Between Nonprofit and For-Profit Enterprise." Unpublished manuscript, Program on Nonprofit Organizations, Institution for Social and Policy Studies, Yale University, July 1985.

Hopkins, B. R. *The Law of Tax Exempt Organizations.* (2nd ed.) Washington, D.C.: Lerner Law Book Company, 1977.

Maloney, L. "Special Report: For Many There Are Big Profits in 'Nonprofits.' " *U.S. News and World Report,* Nov. 6, 1978, p. 7.

Mayer, J. "Survival Tactics: Cuts in Federal Aid Lead Public TV to Try a Bit of Free Enterprise." *Wall Street Journal,* Mar. 10, 1982, p. 1.

Mier, R., and Wiewel, W. "Business Activities of Not-for-Profit Organizations." *American Planning Association Journal,* Summer 1983, pp. 316–325.

Norman, J. "Lean times for Largess." *Milwaukee Journal,* Oct. 17, 1982, Business section, p. 1.

Rose-Ackerman, S. "Unfair Competition and Corporate Income Taxation." *Stanford Law Review,* 1982, *34,* 1017–1039.

Schiff, J., and Weisbrod, B. A., "Government Social Welfare Spending and the Private Nonprofit Sector: Crowding Out, and More." Unpublished manuscript, Department of Economics, University of Wisconsin, Madison, Nov. 1986.

Schmedel, S. R. "Charities Lobby Hard to Save Their Right to Lobby." *Wall Street Journal,* Mar. 11, 1987a, p. 1.

Schmedel, S. R. "Does Charity Trespass on Business's Territory, or Vice Versa, or Both?" *Wall Street Journal,* Mar. 18, 1987b, p. 1.

Schmidt, S. T. "Survival of Nonprofits May Depend on Their Entrepreneurial Savvy." *Washington Post,* July 27, 1983, p. C15.

Skloot, E. "Enterprise and Commerce in Nonprofit Organizations." In W. W. Powell (ed.), *The Nonprofit Sector: A Research Handbook.* New Haven, Conn.: Yale University Press, 1987.

Swain, F. *SBA News,* No. 83-41. Washington, D.C.: U.S. Small Business Administration, 1983.

U.S. Small Business Administration. *Unfair Competition by Nonprofit Organizations with Small Business: An Issue for the 1980s.* (3rd ed.) Washington, D.C.: U.S. Small Business Administration, 1984.

Weisbrod, B. A. *The Nonprofit Economy.* Cambridge, Mass.: Harvard University Press, 1988.

Weisbrod, B. A., and Schlesinger, M. "Public, Private Nonprofit Ownership and the Response to Asymmetric Information: The Case of Nursing Homes." In S. Rose-Ackerman (ed.) *The Economics of Nonprofit Institutions: Studies in Structure and Policy.* New York: Oxford University Press, 1986.

JAMES M. FERRIS
ELIZABETH GRADDY

△ △ △ △ △ △ △ △ △ △ △ △ △ △ △

Fading Distinctions Among the Nonprofit, Government, and For-Profit Sectors

The voluntary nonprofit sector has traditionally played roles in addition to service provision that are distinct from those of the public and the for-profit sectors, such as pioneering in service delivery, promotion of volunteerism, and advocacy (Kramer, 1981). As a consequence, the government has adopted public policies favorable to the nonprofit sector. The primary benefit of such policies accrues from the favorable tax treatment conferred on the nonprofit sector; that is, the tax-exempt status of the organizations and the tax deductibility to donors of charitable contributions made to them. Fostering the nonprofit sector and its unique contributions is not without cost. This preferential treatment at the federal level alone is estimated to entail a cost to the government in terms of lost tax revenues of $12 billion (U.S. Office of Management and Budget, 1987).

  Considerable attention has been given in recent years to changes in the nonprofit sector, particularly increased government dependency and commercialization. As nonprofits increasingly resort to the traditional revenue sources of the public sector (grants) and the for-profit sector (fees for services), they tend to mirror them. These changes are perceived as having eroded the distinctive roles of the nonprofit sector, at least in some industries. If the difference between the behavior of nonprofit organizations and that of either the public or for-profit sectors has indeed faded, the wisdom of public policies designed to support the nonprofit sector comes into question.

To assess public policy toward nonprofits requires an examination of the extent to which the distinctive roles of the nonprofit sector have eroded, the extent to which current policies are predicated on such roles, and an evaluation of the possibilities for designing public policies to stimulate those roles; that is, policies based on behavior rather than legal definitions of nonprofit status. This chapters begins to address these questions. First, we discuss the nature of the public, nonprofit, and proprietary sectors. Second, we consider the extent to which financing affects sectoral distinctions, using two industries, hospitals and higher education, as illustrations. Finally, we consider the rationale for and implications of current policies and possible policy changes. In order to make this task more manageable, we limit our discussion to public charities—nonprofit organizations that deliver services that are socially desirable; that is, provide collective benefits.

Public, Nonprofit, and For-Profit Organizational Behavior

Although the activities of the three sectors have never been mutually exclusive, historically they have been quite distinct. Their behavior largely reflects the missions assigned to them and the corresponding economic, legal, and political constraints within which they operate.

Proprietary organizations form to produce goods and services and make them available to consumers for a price. For-profit firms respond to the preferences of consumers as reflected by their willingness to pay for services. Owners' property rights to the profits—that is, the difference between the price that consumers pay for the product and the production costs—provide the incentive for undertaking such activity. For goods and services that are excludable and rival in consumption, such arrangements are efficient. However, goods and services that are nonexcludable or nonrival in consumption are not efficiently handled by the for-profit sector. Nonexcludability makes it difficult for suppliers to exact a price from consumers. Nonrivalry permits the revealed preferences of consumers to understate the true benefits to society. If either condition exists, the delivery of such services via the for-profit sector will result in an inefficient resource allocation; that is, an undersupply. Consequently, the responsibility for the delivery of such goods and services should not be left to the market. There is also a need to augment the workings of the market when society decides that access to the market for particular goods and services—for example, education and health care—is limited for those with low incomes.

Whether markets fail to deliver the efficient output level or "unduly" limit access, decisions about the supply of these goods and services require collective action. Most discussions focus on the government sector as the primary vehicle for collective action. Society's preferences for such goods and services can be voiced through political processes. Once the level of output is chosen, government can then use its power to raise revenues to finance the goods and services and arrange for their delivery. Of course, collective action does not necessarily translate into government action. The voluntary nonprofit sector is an alternative. Throughout time, especially in American society, there has been a strong reliance on voluntary action to meet collective interests. Voluntary organizations are an effective vehicle for pooling resources to make available goods and services that would not otherwise be supplied. Individuals, on their own volition, can act collectively to provide such goods and services. In fact, as Weisbrod (1977) notes, provision of goods and services by voluntary organizations often predates governmental provision. As an increasingly large number of individuals value the good or service, government often assumes the responsibility for delivery of the service. In addition, if such government action fails to fully satisfy the demands of some individuals, it is possible for them to augment government provision via voluntary nonprofit organizations.

Explaining the behavior of nonprofit organizations is much more difficult than explaining the behavior of public or proprietary organizations because of the greater heterogeneity of the nonprofit sector. This heterogeneity is reflected in the lack of a strong consensus about the motivations of nonprofit managers, in contrast to the general consensus about the motivation of public managers (budget maximization) and for-profit managers (profit maximization). The common thread among nonprofit organizations is not a specific objective function but their acceptance of the nondistribution constraint. Numerous models have been developed to reflect various characteristics of nonprofit organizations. Models focusing on output maximization, donations, quality, principal-agent problems, and cross-subsidization have been summarized by James and Rose-Ackerman (1986). They conclude from their review that, under certain conditions, nonprofit managers enjoy greater discretion than their counterparts in the for-profit sector. This expanded discretion results from donations not tied to specific outputs and from barriers to entry for new nonprofit organizations. Nonprofit managers can use their discretion to influence the selection of inputs and choices of outputs. This conclusion is consistent with the theories of nonprofit organizations that suggest that managers self-select into the nonprofit sector because of their strong preferences about product quantity and quality as opposed to monetary rewards (Young, 1986).

Governmental acceptance of the responsibility for service delivery does not obviate the role of nonprofit organizations in service provision. A distinctive feature of the nonprofit sector is ideology. Many nonprofits are interested not simply in the delivery of a certain quantity of a service but also in the quality of the service. These preferences are often based on deeply held beliefs. For example, James (1987) argues that a primary motivation for the development of the nonprofit educational sector in different societies is the interest in imparting a religious education. This suggests that nonprofit educational sectors characterize countries with a greater degree of religious entrepreneurship. Her empirical analysis of the sector both within countries and across countries supports this proposition. As long as preferences with respect to product quality are heterogeneous, nonprofit organizations are a mechanism for responding to them. In effect, the nonprofit sector provides diversity that allows individual choice, in contrast to public production, which typically delivers a uniform service.

Government has long recognized the value of such activity by conferring special tax benefits on nonprofit organizations. If an organization wishes, it can apply for such status. In exchange, however, it must accept certain constraints. Although the organization may accrue profits, it is prohibited from distributing the profits. A corollary to the nondistribution constraint is the reasonable-compensation constraint—officers and managers of the voluntary organization cannot be compensated in amounts above reasonable levels. This is intended to prevent the distribution of residuals through compensation premiums.

Funding and the Behavior of Nonprofit Organizations

Given the distinctive missions of the sectors and the legal constraints within which they operate, the economic base for proprietary, nonprofit, and public organizations are quite different. Public bureaus rely almost exclusively on revenues provided by their enabling government or grants from other governmental entities. The main source of revenues for proprietary organizations is consumer purchases. Consumers are typically individuals, but they may also include governments, such as through service contracting. Nonprofit organizations have traditionally relied on donations as a primary source of revenue, although they have also charged fees for services as well as received government grants, especially in more recent times. This diversification of revenues is one of the reasons for the fading of the distinctions between the nonprofit sector and government or business. Despite the nonprofit sector's continued use of donations of money and time, they appear to be increasingly relying on governmental grants and fees for services. The precise cause of this change is uncertain, but it seems reasonable to speculate that it is based on the desire of nonprofit organizations to ensure their survival by diversifying their financial base.

Revenue diversification reduces the threat to organizational survival in the event that charitable contributions decline. Moreover, it enables the organization to expand its constituencies, thereby increasing political support.

Revenue diversification by nonprofit organizations can be expected to produce changes in their behavior. Resource-dependency theory suggests that in order to secure the resources necessary to survive, organizations will alter their structure and change their goals, thereby changing their behavior (Pfeffer and Salancik, 1978). For example, in an analysis of unplanned change in nonprofit organizations, Powell and Friedkin (1987) conclude that external forces are likely to exert influence on organizational behavior when an organization faces a financial shortage, serves a constituency that lacks political clout, or is involved in activities that become increasingly complex. Although the cases examined by Powell and Friedkin involve individual organizations, it is reasonable to assume that their findings reflect trends that affect particular segments of the nonprofit sector.

The implications of resource-dependency theory underscore the ongoing debate about issues of autonomy and commercialization of nonprofits. In essence, there is a potential conflict between the established goals of the organization (that is, of its governing board, donors, and managers) and the goals of the newer revenue sources (government bureaus or fee-paying individuals). Despite the fact that nonprofits have been able to subsidize nonpaying clients or nonprofitable activities with revenues collected from paying consumers (James, 1983) and have been able to expand their activities via government grants and contracts (Salamon, 1987), the potential conflict between goals and revenues causes considerable concern. Some fear that as governments rely on nonprofit organizations to help in the delivery of services through grants and contracts, the independence of the nonprofit sector is threatened. There is concern that, in competing for government grants and contracts, nonprofits will become unduly influenced by the needs and requirements of government bureaus. In addition, it is feared that as nonprofits increasingly generate revenues through charges for services, they may neglect their original mission and ultimately lose their legitimacy. Evidence on the impact of changing funding sources on the behavior of nonprofit institutions and their relationships with public and for-profit organizations is rather limited. To illustrate the potential effects of changing funding patterns, we examine two industries in which different responses to changes in funding sources have resulted in different sectoral relationships and outcomes.

Financing and Sectoral Relationships: Two Cases

To explore how external financing decisions and organizational responses can affect sectoral relationships, we examine the hospital and higher education industries. These two cases are chosen because data are available about their activities over a considerable period of time and there has been an ongoing debate about the role of nonprofit hospitals and universities. We wish to emphasize that these cases are only illustrative and should not be construed as representative or exhaustive.

Hospitals. Sectoral relationships and outcomes within the health care industry, particularly hospitals, have undergone major changes (Marmor, Schlesinger, and Smithey, 1987). In the early part of this century, state, local, and nonprofit hospitals played the predominant role in the delivery of health care. In 1928, hospitals operated by state and local governments accounted for 12.5 percent of all hospitals (general and short-term specialty) and 24.1 percent of hospital beds. By 1980, the percentage of hospitals operated by the state and local sector had increased to 29.5, but their percentage of beds had decreased to 20.5. The nonprofit sector operated 43.9 percent of the hospitals with 58.6 percent of hospital beds in 1929. The share of the nonprofit sector rose to 57.6 percent of hospitals and 70.3 percent of beds in 1980. The share of the proprietary sector diminished over the same period, from 43.6 percent of hospitals and 17.3 percent of beds to 13 percent and 9.2 percent, respectively (Hollingsworth and Hollingsworth, 1986). Although much attention is currently focused on for-profit medicine, nonprofit hospitals still dominate the industry in terms of market share.

Differences in the relative market shares of the three sectors, however, conceal behavioral changes that have been occurring. Despite the increased nonprofit market share, the three sectors have increasingly similar input and output characteristics. In a recent study, Hollingsworth and Hollingsworth (1986) compared the three sectors in terms of operating and performance measure for three years—1935, 1961, and 1979. Although distinctions among the three sectors continue to exist, they note the increasing similarity among different types of hospitals in terms of hospital size, percentage of hospitals professionally accredited, length of stay, occupancy ratios, full-time-equivalent staff per bed, technological complexity, costs per bed, and assets per bed. Moreover, they are also more alike in the types of patients treated and the types of care delivered. Of these measures, distinctions among cost indicators, occupancy, and length of stay have faded the most.

What are the reasons underlying the increasingly similar behavior of the three sectors? Hollingsworth and Hollingsworth acknowledge that the trend toward convergence reflects, in part, the increasing acceptance of medical technology, the standardization effects of accreditation, and the consensus about medical training methods. However, they believe that a greater source of similarities is the change in the funding sources of hospitals. In the early part of the period, public hospitals were funded primarily by state and local tax revenues, voluntary hospitals were funded primarily by charitable contributions, and for-profit hospitals were funded mostly by charges paid by patients. The different funding sources reflect different constituencies. Consequently, it is not surprising that in the early 1900s the behaviors of the three sectors were quite distinct. More recently, however, with the emergence of third-party reimbursement, the funding sources of the three sectors have become more similar. Revenues have been increasingly derived from fees paid by insurance companies, Blue Cross, Medicare, or Medicaid, which have no preference for nonprofit hospitals over for-profit or public hospitals. In addition, the neutrality of insurers toward the sectors reduces the case-mix differences among them. Consequently, the distinctive behaviors of public, nonprofit, and proprietary hospitals have blurred.

Universities. The higher education industry has experienced tremendous growth since the 1950s, resulting in changes in the relative market shares of the public and nonprofit sectors. The growth was a response to increased demand for higher education fueled initially by the GI Bill and later by demographic forces. The demand was also affected by the emerging perception of a college degree as a vehicle for upward mobility. Although both sectors have grown, the expansion to accommodate the increased demand was carried out primarily in the public sector. Consequently, the relative market share has changed. In 1950, the nonprofit sector accounted for 66 percent of universities and colleges and 51 percent of degrees. By 1982, the nonprofit share of the market had slipped to 54 percent of higher education institutions and 36 percent of degrees (American Council on Education, 1987, pp. 110, 152). Nevertheless, the distinctive roles of public and nonprofit institutions have not diminished to any great extent.

The fact that the public sector accommodated the majority of the increased demand reinforced the distinctive roles played by the public and nonprofit sectors. Public universities and colleges, with low tuition, provide education to large numbers of students, particularly students with limited income. Thus, they play a large role in ensuring that students with the appropriate academic credentials have access to higher education. In addition, public higher education provides an array of services to the public at large by generating professionals and knowledge aimed at stimulating state economic development. On the other hand, nonprofit institutions are viewed as providing more diverse educational programs. The segmentation of the sector into research, liberal arts, and urban institutions, each with different missions, is evidence of this diversity (Geiger, 1986).

The differing roles of the two sectors correspond to their funding sources. Nonprofit institutions receive the largest portion of their revenues from private sources. Tuition and fees accounted for 41.6 percent of revenues in 1950; this figure has decreased slightly, to 37.5 percent in 1982. Governments provided only 11.2 percent of revenues in 1950, although this had increased to 19.5 by 1982, primarily as a result of increases at the federal level. In contrast, public institutions are highly dependent on government revenues. In 1950, they received 51.9 percent of their revenues from public funds (9.6 percent from federal sources, 37.4 percent from state sources, and about 4 percent from local sources). By 1982, public support increased to 60.3 percent (11.4 percent from federal sources, 45.3 percent from state sources, and about 4 percent from local sources). Income from tuition and fees was only 18.5 percent in 1950 and decreased to 13.5 percent by 1982 (Nelson, 1978, pp. 70–71; American Council on Education, 1987, pp. 46–49). Thus, despite the expansion in the higher education industry, the revenue patterns of the two sectors have remained essentially the same. Not surprisingly, the two sectors still continue to make distinct contributions to higher education.

Summary. Although causality is difficult to establish, the correlation in these two cases between financial sources and mission is evident. The sectoral differences in the market for higher education might well have diminished if states had decided to accommodate the rising demand for its services by providing financial incentives and support for expansion to both nonprofit and public institutions rather than concentrating on the expansion of existing public institutions or the creation of new ones. In fact, it seems reasonable to suggest that in the absence of federal student aid programs, which are neutral with respect to sector, the sectoral differences would have been accentuated over this period. The evolution of the hospital industry provides a sharp contrast. The increased demand for hospital care has been accommodated in all three sectors by third-party reimbursement rather than simply an expansion of the public hospital sector. Consequently, all three sectors are able to compete for fee-paying patients. This has resulted in the diminution of differences among the nonprofit, public, and proprietary hospitals.

This discussion of the relationship between financing and mission brings into question public policies that assume the distinctiveness of the nonprofit sector. It may be that in some industries the unique roles of the nonprofit sector may no longer exist. In that case, blanket support of the nonprofit sector may be unjustified. In order to assess whether such policies are warranted, we next consider the rationale for current policies and future prospects for these policies.

Implications for Public Policy

The most important public policies with respect to the nonprofit sector are their treatment under the tax codes: federal, state, and local. Simon (1987) has estimated that in 1985, nonprofits generated $100 billion in revenues exempt from federal income tax, held $300 billion in property exempt from state and local property taxes, and received $50 billion in contributions that were deductible by the donors from their federal and state income tax liabilities. Thus, tax advantages conferred on the nonprofit sector represent a substantial monetary value to nonprofits. At the same time, they entail a considerable tax expenditure—that is, a loss in tax revenues—by the public sector. The magnitude of these tax expenditures, in conjunction with an emerging perception of the nonprofit sector's loss of distinctiveness, raises two questions: (1) Should the nonprofit sector continue to receive tax preferences? (2) If so, what is the proper basis of such preferences? We address these questions by considering the rationale for current policies and speculating about future policies.

Rationales for Current Tax Policies. Justification of the favorable treatment of nonprofit organizations has taken two different approaches: proper definition of the tax base and the desirability of stimulating nonprofit-sector activity via subsidies.

The tax-base rationales vary by the type of tax (individual income tax, corporate income tax, or property tax) and the recipient of the tax advantage. Simon (1987) reviews the numerous arguments. For example, the deductibility of individuals' charitable contributions is defensible on the groups that such contributions are not included in the Haig-Simons definition of taxable income. According to this definition, taxable income is the sum of the individual's consumption and the accumulation of wealth. The individual's net worth is not increased as a result of the contribution. Thus, the question is whether the contribution represents a form of consumption. If one views nonprofit organizations as a response to unsatisfied collective demands, one might argue that it does. However, since the individual does not benefit directly from the contribution, most analysts do not consider it consumption. Likewise, since contributions by corporations are not a form of profit, there is reason to provide deductions from the corporate income tax.

The reasoning underlying the defense of the tax-exempt status of nonprofit organizations is somewhat different. Bittker and Radhart (1976) argue that nonprofits should not be taxed under corporate income tax statutes because the corporate tax is based on income-generating activities pursued for personal gain and, thus, is not relevant to nonprofit entities. Although there is merit to the tax-base arguments, they do not appear to have been definitive in shaping public policy, particularly in the formative years. The specific design of the tax system— for example, the limits on deductibility—does not appear consistent with this line of reasoning.

The more noteworthy defense of the nonprofit sector's tax advantages is related to the notion of government support. The rationale for supporting the nonprofit sector is based on the concept that the services delivered by such organizations are collective in nature. In effect, the services yield benefits that are not restricted to the donors or the clients. Thus, in order to achieve a more efficient outcome, public action is required. There are two principal forms such action may take: direct public delivery and public support of private delivery. The former is preferable if the services are nonexcludable or the majority of the benefits derived from the service are nonrival. On the other hand, if the service has a mix of collective and private benefits and is excludable, the private sector, either for-profit or nonprofit, can organize the production and exchange of the service. The public sector, in turn, can bolster the activity via grants or tax subsidies. The historical record is replete with evidence for the support rationale. In fact, Simon (1987) quotes a recent Supreme Court opinion that asserts that tax exemption and deductibility are a form of subsidy having effects similar to government spending programs (461 U.S. at 544–545).

The tax-subsidy approach allows public policy to build on private behavior. Donors influence the value of the preferential tax treatment to nonprofits by the amount of contributions they make. In addition, clients who purchase services influence the value of the exemption afforded directly to the organization. Consequently, organizations that satisfy their constituents' preferences are rewarded. This results in diversity, one of the acclaimed attributes of the nonprofit sector. On the other hand, it relegates the public sector to a rather passive role. Moreover, rather than allocating resources for collective purposes via the government arena, it allows for a determination of allocation by individual behavior. This behavior is limited, in practice, to relatively high-income individuals, since lower-income individuals are less likely to contribute because of their limited household budgets in general and the relatively higher price of giving for them that results from the use of tax deductions rather than credits. Thus, to the extent that there is a collective interest in the activity, a sizable portion of the population is effectively precluded from participation. The basic issue then is whether support for activities of the nonprofit sector should be assigned to the "domain of rights" or the "domain of dollars" (Okun, 1975).

Future Public Policies. Two propositions underpin current public policy toward the nonprofit sector: (1) the nonprofit sector performs functions that are socially desirable and, hence, deserving of public support; and (2) such support will primarily be in the form of tax subsidies. Unless such propositions are rebuffed, future policies are unlikely to depart radically from current policies, but neither are they likely to remain unchanged.

Our discussion of the fading distinctions among the three sectors hints at the possibility that support for public subsidy of nonprofit organizations is being undermined. Although the nonprofit sector has played a critical role in the development of American society, there is concern that the distinctiveness of the nonprofit sector, at least in some industries, is eroding. If the nonprofit sector begins to resemble public organizations, one may question whether it is desirable for public policy to create competition or underwrite duplication of public agencies without providing the means for public accountability. Likewise, if the nonprofit sector begins to resemble the proprietary sector, one may question whether it is useful for the public sector to underwrite activities that the for-profit sector is able and willing to organize, thus providing unfair competition. It is unlikely, however these questions are answered, that the public policy of subsidizing the nonprofit sector via the tax system will be revoked. The differences among the sectors are not likely to be completely eradicated, but they will probably be minimized. The public-policy question then is at what cost such distinctions should be supported. Consequently, it is likely that the various tax provisions will be subject to increased scrutiny. Such scrutiny may lead to a more discriminating application of tax subsidies.

If one accepts the assumption that the distinctiveness of the nonprofit sector is desirable, public officials are likely to look for policies designed to maintain that distinctiveness. The nonprofit status of an organization is not immutable. For example, in the hospital industry, an increasing number of nonprofit hospitals are converting to for-profit status. In addition, some local governments have chosen to spin off their hospitals to specifically created nonprofit foundations. Likewise, at various times nonprofit universities have been converted to public universities. Although there are a variety of reasons for such changes, financial considerations appear to be overriding. By altering their legal form, organizations enhance their access to financing sources. For-profit status opens up equity markets as a funding source. Government status enables an organization to compete for part of the public budget. This suggests that the conferral of tax benefits needs to be based on performance rather than merely a legal definition. In effect, industry classification and the willingness of directors to accept the nondistribution and reasonable-compensation constraints should be considered necessary but not sufficient conditions for tax subsidies. Failure to target tax preferences to organizations that make a distinctive contribution is likely to erode public support for these policies. Dimensions of performance that could provide a basis for a more selective treatment of nonprofits are the extent to which they deliver services to the poor; contribute diversity as reflected by direct public support—that is, donations; serve as a direct substitute for public production—that is, government contracts or grants; or some combination thereof.

The adoption of a performance-based determination of tax-exempt status would entail costs. It would impose reporting requirements that organizations may feel are intrusive and burdensome. In addition, it would require an administrative structure to monitor the organizations as well as to systematically review the validity of the preferential treatment. To the extent that this is done by the Internal Revenue Service, the additional costs would be minimal; alternative administrative arrangements are likely to be more expensive. At the same time, additional benefits, in terms of added revenues as well as more socially desirable outcomes, would accrue. The wisdom of adopting performance-based tax preferences depends on whether the gains from the better targeting of the tax subsidy and the sector's increased legitimacy are sufficient to justify the increased administrative and compliance costs and the potential loss of the nonprofit sector's autonomy.

Conclusion

Although this analysis has been speculative, it does outline the issues that need to be addressed as public policies toward the voluntary nonprofit sector are reconsidered. They include both positive and normative questions. First, is the performance of nonprofit organizations distinguishable from that of public bureaus or firms? Second, if it is, to what extent is society willing to support the unique contributions of the nonprofit sector through public policies? Third, is it feasible to formulate and implement public policies that encourage only the desirable contributions of the nonprofit sector, rather than the nonprofit sector as a whole? The answers to these questions are likely to shape the debate about the future of public policies toward the nonprofit sector.

References

American Council on Education. *1986–1987 Factbook on Higher Education.* Washington, D.C.: Macmillan, 1987.

Bittker, B. I., and Radhart, G. K. "The Exemption of Nonprofit Organizations from Federal Income Taxation." *Yale Law Journal,* 1976, *85* (3), 299–358.

Geiger, R. "Finance and Function: Voluntary Support and Diversity in American Private Higher Education." In Levy, D. C. (ed.), *Private Education: Studies in Choice and Public Policy.* Oxford, England: Oxford University Press, 1986.

Hollingsworth, J. R., and Hollingsworth, E. J. "A Comparison of Non-Profit, For-Profit and Public Hospitals in the United States: 1935 to the Present." Working paper no. 113, Program on Nonprofit Organizations, Institution for Social and Policy Studies, Yale University, June 1986.

James, E. "How Nonprofits Grow: A Model." *Journal of Policy Analysis and Management,* 1983, *2* (3), 350–365.

James, E. "The Public/Private Division of Responsibility for Education: An International Comparison." *Economics of Education Review,* 1987, *6* (1), 1–14.

James, E. and Rose-Ackerman, S. *The Nonprofit Enterprise in Market Economics.* New York: Harwood Academic Publishers, 1986.

Kramer, R. *Voluntary Agencies in the Welfare State.* Berkeley: University of California Press, 1981.

Marmor, T., Schlesinger, M., and Smithey, R. "Nonprofit Organizations and Health Care." In W. W. Powell (ed.), *The Nonprofit Sector: A Research Handbook.* New Haven, Conn.: Yale University Press, 1987.

Nelson, S. "Financial Trends and Issues." In D. W. Breneman and C. E. Finn, Jr. (eds.), *Public Policy and Higher Education.* Washington, D.C.: Brookings Institution, 1978.

Okun, A. *Equality and Efficiency: The Big Tradeoff.* Washington, D.C.: Brookings Institution, 1975.

Pfeffer, J. and Salancik, G. R. *The External Control of Organization.* New York: Harper & Row, 1978.

Powell, W. W., and Friedkin, R. "Organizational Change in Nonprofit Organizations." In W. W. Powell (ed.), *The Nonprofit Sector: A Research Handbook.* New Haven, Conn.: Yale University Press, 1987.

Salamon, L. M. "Partners in Public Service: The Scope and Theory of Government-Nonprofit Relations." In W. W. Powell (ed.), *The Nonprofit Sector: A Research Handbook.* New Haven, Conn.: Yale University Press, 1987.

Simon, J. G. "The Tax Treatment of Nonprofit Organizations: A Review of Federal and State Policies." In W. W. Powell (ed.), *The Nonprofit Sector: A Research Handbook.* New Haven, Conn.: Yale University Press, 1987.

U.S. Office of Management and Budget. "Special Analysis G— Tax Expenditures." In U.S. Office of Management and Budget, *Budget of the United States Government, 1988.* Washington, D.C.: U.S. Government Printing Office, 1987.

Weisbrod, B. A. *The Voluntary Nonprofit Sector.* Lexington, Mass.: Heath, 1977.

Young, D. "Entrepreneurship and the Behavior of Nonprofit Organizations." In S. Rose-Ackerman (ed.), *The Economics of Nonprofit Institutions: Studies in Structure and Policy.* New York: Oxford University Press, 1986.

9

△ △ △ △ △ △ △ △ △ △ △ △ △ △ △

Cash Cows or Sacred Cows: The Politics of the Commercialization Movement

> We are ready to enter any profession except perhaps the oldest one in order to make enough money to keep public radio on the air. (National Public Radio president Frank Mankiewicz, faced with cuts in federal support.) [Tucker, 1982.]

The pursuit of commercial revenue by nonprofit organizations is a much discussed if not uniformly lauded activity within the philanthropic and public-policy worlds. Managers of nonprofit organizations seek sources of reliable and abundant funds—cash cows—that will replace dwindling government funding so that they can devote their full attention and resources to the organization's central goals. At the same time, they want to maintain the philanthropic character of their organizations and the economic perquisites that accompany that character: they want to remain sacred cows and preserve the donative support that they receive from the public and the tax exemptions that they obtain from government.

    Commercial activity appears to blur the distinction between the business and nonprofit realms. To the general public,

Note: The author wishes to thank the John D. Rockefeller III Fellowship at the Yale University Program on Non-Profit Organizations for supporting the research that led to this chapter.

140

which equates nonprofit organizations with charity, consumer activity is at least incongruous, if not inappropriate. To the scholar attempting to discover the basis of the division of labor among the nonprofit, government, and business sectors, the pursuit of earned income adds a layer of complexity to the requisite analysis. Most of the published examinations of this topic are confined to prescriptions of managerial how-to's, policy analyses of the equity of competition between nonprofit organizations and for-profit firms, and considerations of whether commercial activities represent a viable source of funding for nonprofit organizations. Little of a theoretical nature has been written that examines the role of this activity from an economic or political perspective. The scholarly literature that attempts to explain why some services are supplied by conventional business organizations, some by government bureaucracies, and others by nonprofit organizations has not focused on commercial activities.

This chapter examines the existing models of the nonprofit sector to see how well they account for the apparent anomaly of commercial activity. The models best equipped to explain commercial activity are those that emphasize the cross-subsidizing character of nonprofit activity (that is, the use of revenues from one activity to support another). However, the role of politics needs greater emphasis at both the organizational and sectoral levels if the current models are to be successful. This chapter will only amend and reorder portions of the existing theories of nonprofit organizations. It is an argument that political factors—never entirely absent from discussions of nonprofits—are at the core rather than the periphery of what nonprofits are about. In other words, nonprofits are not well characterized as service organizations unimportantly different from their for-profit analogues.

With respect to commercial activities, the political character of nonprofits has three dimensions: the ideologically driven behavior at the organizational level that generates the "mission-oriented" character of many nonprofits, the impact of macro-political phenomena such as changes in national policy and institutions on the incentives and constraints facing individual organizations, and the efforts of nonprofits to influence policy bearing on them. Political factors are highlighted because the dominant approach to the analysis of nonprofit organizations—economic modeling—underemphasizes this dimension of the sector. This chapter uses the puzzle posed by commercial activities to argue that economic models fail to capture critical dimensions of the nonprofit sector.

The analysis begins with a simple taxonomy of nonprofit commercial activities. Some of the more prominent economic models of nonprofit organizations are outlined, and the extent to which they capture the role of commercial activities is examined. The role of politics in theories of political economy and of the nonprofit sector is then discussed. Commercial activities are shown to be best understood against the background of changing national policy. Four political phenomena that shape commercial activity of nonprofits are examined in detail: government funding of nonprofit organizations and the resulting expansion of the nonprofit sector and the incursion of for-profit firms into traditionally nonprofit industries; privatization and the contraction of the nonprofit sector; tax policy; and controversies about competition between business and nonprofits. The chapter concludes with some comments about the implications of this recasting of nonprofit theories for public policy.

Commercial Activities

Broadly speaking, there are three categories of commercial activities: unrelated business activities, fee-for-service activities, and related commercial activities. These labels are an elaboration of a widely used nomenclature for nonprofits developed by Hansmann (1980). He labels nonprofit organizations that receive most of their funding through contributions as donative nonprofits and those that receive most of their funding through fees for services as commercial nonprofits. The term *commercial activities* is used here to designate a broader group of nondonative financing sources; Hansmann's terminology is followed when referring to nonprofit *organizations*.

Unrelated Business Activities. The goal of these activities is unrelated to the basic mission of the nonprofit. The key purpose is the subsidization of the basic mission through the pursuit of profits in the market. While unrelated business activities are not associated with the direct accomplishment of the mission of the nonprofit, they may be intimately related to its particular competencies. That is, nonprofits will often choose business ventures that exploit their organizational expertise or piggyback on their existing physical capital (Nielsen, 1986). For example, if a nonprofit organization has facilities that go unused during certain time periods, those facilities may be used to generate revenue.

Fee-for-Service Activities. The services in these instances are mission services, but unlike the case of services provided by more traditional charities, the recipients are also the source of financial support. Many traditional nonprofit organizations charge for their basic services, and more and more nonprofits are beginning to move in this direction. Income from fees for services is labeled "program service fees" by the IRS. University tuition and fees for psychological counseling or job training fit into this category.

Related Commercial Activities. These activities are the source of much of the current political conflict between nonprofit organizations and small business, especially regarding the tax code. They are services that accomplish auxiliary purposes of a nonprofit organization; typically, related commercial activities are carried out to serve the various constituencies of a nonprofit organization. These sorts of activities range from university-operated laundries to museum gift shops to the YMCA's health clubs.

    Nonprofit organizations can carry out these different types of commercial activities either through an arm's-length subsidiary or directly under the auspices of the nonprofit itself. Entirely unrelated business activities are frequently carried out by subsidiaries, while fee-for-service activities are engaged in directly by the nonprofit, because the services constitute its very mission.

Economic Theories of Nonprofit Organizations

For those that ponder the proper boundary between the public and the private domains, nonprofit organizations stand as an anomaly: they are private organizations explicitly performing public tasks. This anomaly attracts the interest of economists, who have developed most of the synoptic analyses of the nonprofit sector. They are intrigued and puzzled by the existence of nonbusiness, nongovernmental organizations operating in the economy. Their efforts to analyze nonprofit organizations using neoclassical microeconomics place them squarely in the midst of debates about political economy. In bringing their disciplinary tools to bear on nonprofit organizations, they are explicitly characterizing as economic entities what many people would consider to be nonmarket institutions.

Economic Models Applicable to Commercial Activities. The theories developed by economists to explain nonprofit organizations are roughly of two types: those that seek to explain the role that such organizations play in the economy and society and those that seek to identify and account for the distinctive types of behavior in which such organizations engage (Hansmann, 1987). Some economists describe these two types of theories as addressing the demand for and supply of nonprofit organizations, respectively.

Among the theories that try to explain the social role of nonprofits, a dominant approach is that of contract failure. The major proponent of contract failure theory is Henry Hansmann. He argues that "nonprofits arise in situations in which, owing either to the circumstances under which a service is purchased or consumed, or to the nature of the service itself, consumers feel themselves incapable of accurately evaluating the quantity or quality of the service that a firm produces for them" (Hansmann, 1987, p. 29). Because nonprofit organizations face a nondistribution constraint—that is, the prohibition on the distribution of net earnings to individuals that exercise formal control over the organization—they are appropriately structured to provide such services. A for-profit firm has both the opportunity and the incentive to exploit the customer in these circumstances. Because of the nondistribution constraint, a nonprofit organization lacks this opportunity.

According to the contract-failure theory, the nondistribution constraint resolves problems of market failure resulting from differences in the information available to the parties involved in the transaction. The implication is that commercial nonprofits providing services on a fee basis are not any less legitimately nonprofit than traditional donative nonprofit organizations. Thus, Hansmann's theory readily accommodates one of the three sorts of commercial activity under consideration in this chapter. It does not provide as ready an explanation for cash cows.

James (1983) offers a sophisticated analysis of the behavior of nonprofits that is compatible with Hansmann's theory. She characterizes nonprofit organizations as consumer-producer hybrids. In this model, nonprofits engage in a variety of activities, each of which has a different utility and profitability to the organization. The activities fall into three combinations of utility and profitability. Some activities yield positive marginal utility but negative profit to the organization. They are deficit-producing. Those in the second class have negative utility but produce a profit. Finally, some activities yield profit but are of neutral utility. The first category is the set of activities that form the crux of nonprofit charitable endeavor—those services that cannot support themselves in the marketplace. James describes them as implicit consumption—that is, the nonprofit organization's raison d'être is to perform these activities because the members of the organization enjoy the work, obtain social legitimacy or kudos for their efforts, or simply satisfy an altruistic impulse. The two other types of activity—which are profitable—cross-subsidize the implicit consumption.

Rose-Ackerman (1987) elaborates a model that, by focusing on the relationship between donors and managers of nonprofits, provides the framework for showing how nonprofit managers may choose to pursue commercial activities rather than seek other funding sources. She suggests that these managers are more interested in the choice of product mix that their organizations produce than are their for-profit counterparts. Rose-Ackerman argues that the character of the nonprofit's output will respond to the character of the revenue: if revenue from an unconstrained source becomes less available, the nonprofit will be forced to shift to a source with more strings attached. This model suggests that commercial revenue will be pursued (1) when its pursuit is relatively lucrative (that is, it provides high marginal return) and (2) when it is relatively less constraining on the output that the manager seeks to produce than are other sources. In the face of low but positive marginal return, managers may choose to devote their resources to service quality instead of pursuit of revenue. This model can be viewed as an elaboration of the utility-profitability model of James.

It is interesting to note that in the models of nonprofit managerial behavior suggested by James and by Rose-Ackerman, the activities that the nonprofit organization uses to subsidize its deficit-producing activities need not be for-profit ventures. For instance, the set of examples that James uses to illustrate her model includes both situations where the subsidizing activity is unrelated to the organization's mission and instances where the subsidizing activity is centrally and uncontroversially related to the organization's mission. An example of the latter is provided by James's analysis of the relationship of undergraduate to graduate education in universities, where, she argues, undergraduate education produces a surplus that supports the cost of graduate education (James, 1983). Note that the subsidizing activity is a conventional, nonbusiness source of income in this case. The commercial character of the subsidizing activity is irrelevant to these models.

The cross-subsidization model (potentially) put redistribution at the center of consideration, whereas the contract-failure models view redistribution simply as one preference exercised in the market. The cross-subsidizing behavior could be taken as a normative criterion for nonprofit status or at least for tax subsidy. It would then entail a critical stance toward nonprofits that rely wholly on fees for services because they provide no services needing subsidy. The normative question of commercial nonprofits in the context of the controversy about competition between small business and nonprofit organizations is discussed in the final section of this chapter.

Allocative and Nonallocative Exchange. In addition to the specific limitations that the various economic models face in accounting for commercial activities, there are broader difficulties that these models pose for the analysis of nonprofits and their cash cows. The functional characterizations that Hansmann and James provide for nonprofit organizations transform those organizations into a species of market organization. It is that accomplishment that provides the impression that the blush has been removed from these organizations. To put it crudely, donations to CARE are just purchases of hunger relief. They are one among innumerable kinds of market transaction. The way to evaluate them, therefore, is in terms of their allocative efficiency.

The economic models discussed in this chapter characterize nonprofits as allocative mechanisms. Some nonprofits are clearly redistributive mechanisms. The confusion here is analogous to conflating the allocative activities of the government (that is, economic transactions viewed from the perspective of optimal use of resources, or Pareto-efficiency), such as garbage collection, with the redistributive ones (that is, transactions viewed from the perspective of equity), such as progressive taxation or welfare services.

It may be legitimate to evaluate the allocative *dimension* of donative nonprofits, but that is not the same as claiming that such organizations exist to perform allocative functions. Consider Hansmann's (1980) characterization of donations as third-party payments for goods provided to more or less irrelevant beneficiaries. For Hansmann, the important characteristic of the nonprofit is that it allows exchange to be made—the donor exchanges money for the execution of charitable services—with the reasonable assurance provided by the nondistribution constraint that the donation will not be pocketed. The beneficiary is virtually absent here. But suppose that we focus instead on the beneficiary by concentrating on the subsidized output of the organization. A donative nonprofit typically provides either less-than-market-price goods and services or zero-price goods and services. As James's (1983) model indicates, the conduct of a nonprofit can be understood only by placing its cross-subsidizing behavior, the behavior that is most likely to be redistributive, at the center of the model. While Hansmann's model is not set up to account for behavioral variation among nonprofit organizations, that difference in orientation does not vitiate the problem that it faces in even beginning to account for important changes in nonprofit behavior, such as when a nonprofit begins to charge clients for services that it previously provided for free.

Making redistributive activities merely a subset of allocative transactions—that is, a preference exercised through purchase from nonprofits—obscures important political issues. The growth of for-profit activities among nonprofit organizations can be seen as a rise in the preponderance of cross-subsidization as a funding mechanism for the delivery of public services. Analysis of the sort that is suggested by James's model illuminates questions of market distortion through non-cost-based pricing or of the fairness of cross-subsidization for the customer purchasing the subsidizing service. It is not conducive, however, to the examination of shifts in the structure of the welfare state, of which this is clearly an important part.

This is not to argue that nonprofits are primarily redistributive social mechanisms. Many types of nonprofits are not: their services do not shift resources from the more well off to the less well off. Arts organizations, such as operas and symphonies, have upper-middle-class and upper-class constituencies and trustees. Universities are viewed by many as functioning to socialize elites. Salamon, Musselwhite, and De Vita (1986, p. 5) note that fewer than one-third of the nonprofit agencies surveyed in the Urban Institute's study of the nonprofit sector indicated that they focused on serving a low-income or poor clientele.

Keeping redistributive issues in the center of analysis of nonprofits has policy implications as well as theoretical importance. In the current controversy about competition between nonprofit organizations and small business, the justification of nonprofit commercial activity hinges on the legitimacy of non-profit cross-subsidization. Characterizing cross-subsidization only as allocative hinders rather than helps the process of establishing normative standards for nonprofit behavior.

This problem is manifest in more concrete form by the fact that neither James's nor Rose-Ackerman's model tells us why large-scale commercial activity did not occur prior to the 1980s. If, as James's model indicates, it is in the very nature of nonprofits to cross-subsidize internally, then why have they not always done so? Rose-Ackerman's model suggests that any revenue source may be left unexploited if the trade-off between constraint and funds is too unappealing. Absent some specification of nonprofit managers' preferences, however, this formulation becomes tautological: commercial revenues are not pursued because other funds were available or the commercial revenues were not worth the constraints they imposed on managerial prerogatives.

Politics, Policy, and Nonprofit Commercial Activity

Politics and policy have importantly shaped the macroenvironment in which nonprofits evaluated their funding options. Neither cross-subsidization, cash cows, nor nonprofits in general can be understood without bringing politics and policy into the story.

There are two different ways in which politics and policy shape nonprofit commercial activity. First, government policy can directly and/or deliberately shape the sectoral division of labor. Salamon (1987) and James (1987) have recently propounded theories in which government-nonprofit relations are made a more central determinant of nonprofit roles. Second, government action taken for essentially unrelated reasons can affect intersectoral relationships.

The emphasis on politics and policy and the associated focus on the way in which government can structure behavior in society in often unintended ways are related to some arguments now being made by neostatist political theorists. Neostatists are interested, as reflected in the title of a recent book (Evans, Rueschemeyer, and Skocpol, 1985), in "bringing the state back in." They propose that states (that is, governments) be studied from a macroscopic perspective: "in this perspective, states matter not simply because of the goal-oriented activities of state officials. They matter because their organizational configurations, along with their overall patterns of activity, affect political culture, encourage some kinds of group formation and collective political actions (but not others), and make possible the raising of certain issues (but not others). . . .When the effects of state are explored from . . . [this] point of view . . . the investigator looks more macroscopically at the ways in which the structures and activities of states unintentionally influence formation of groups and the political capacities, ideas, and demands of various sectors of society" (Evans, Rueschemeyer, and Skocpol, 1985, p. 21).

This aspect of the neostatist approach holds out the potential for explaining what nonprofits and their cash cows have in common in spite of the diversity of industries in which they operate. From this perspective, nonprofits and cash cows need not share functional characteristics in all times and all sectors. Instead, their commonality can grow in response to benefits bestowed or penalties threatened by the state (for example, granting or withdrawing tax exemptions). Organizations can consciously assume the nonprofit form in response to the incentives provided by the state. And those incentives can change over time as the larger political economy and specific government policies evolve. The government policies that so shape the development of nonprofits and cash cows need not be responses to market failure and therefore need not be driven by autonomous economic factors.

There is another way in which the state may be crucial to the analysis of nonprofit organizations. Most theories of the institutional division of labor start with the question "why not the market?" The answer is typically one variant or another of market failure. While the characterization of certain goods and services as not being amenable to market provision because, say, they are public goods (in the microeconomic sense of that term) may be transhistorical or transcultural, government and other institutions can play a crucial role in altering the environment in which the good is produced or consumed so that it may be capable of being provided through marketplace means.

Karl Polanyi (1944) propounded a thesis related to this in *The Great Transformation,* in which he argued that the establishment of free wage labor markets in the eighteenth and nineteenth centuries was not a natural development but rather the result of protracted political struggle and deliberate institutional change. By the same token, the character of goods and services may be altered by public policy so as to change the characteristics that make them less amenable to market provision.

Similarly, markets do not function where the consumers lack the income with which to make purchases. In order for their needs or demands to be met, they must be subsidized in some manner. The cross-subsidization that occurs within nonprofits is one way to meet those needs. Government subsidy of providers is another. And direct government subsidy of the consumers is a third. The point here is that government has the potential for shifting sectoral assignments through changes in the methods of subsidization. While answering the question ''why not the market?'' is illuminating insofar as it tells us that some goods are not amenable to marketplace provision, it avoids the larger question of why the character of those goods evolves.

Theories of Nonprofit-Government Relations. Before turning to the discussion of the specific political phenomena that influenced nonprofit commercial activity, it is useful to look at the theories that model nonprofit-government relations. Salamon (1987) and James (1987) both argue for a revision of economic theories of the nonprofit sector that characterize the sector as a residual set of institutions arising as a result of the failure of either the market or the government to meet social needs.

Salamon maintains that nonprofits historically existed in partnership with government rather than in competition. He describes the respective roles of government and nonprofits as policy formulation and policy delivery, and he adduces a variety of historical evidence to indicate that such a complementary relationship can be dated back to prerevolutionary times in the United States (Salamon, 1987, p. 101). The evolution of the respective roles in public service has been from *provision by nonprofits* to *provision by government.*

The shift in responsibilities has arisen not in response to

government or market failure, as other theorists have claimed, but in response to the inadequacies of nonprofit provision. Salamon labels such inadequacies *voluntary failure* and specifies four sources of failure: insufficiency, particularism, paternalism, and amateurism. He also discusses the strengths of nonprofits vis-à-vis governments, thereby explaining the benefits gained by collaboration. But it is the account of the shift of provision from nonprofits to government that is interesting here because of its relative novelty among theorists of the nonprofit sector and because of its historical verisimilitude. Salamon combines the explanation for the growing role of the state with the differentiated characterization of government and nonprofit roles to arrive at a theory that avoids ascribing a residual role to nonprofits. It is a theory that makes sense of the current character of nonprofit funding, with its dependence on government funding and its surprising lack of donative support.

Estelle James, in a recent comparative international study of nonprofit sectors, has been led to amend the economic emphasis on nonprofit organizations as a response to market failure as well. Like Salamon, she finds differentiated roles for nonprofits and government: "whereas government is a substitute for NPOs [nonprofit organizations] in production, it is a complement in financing" (James, 1987, p. 397). James posits two variables that explain why certain services are provided by the private sector rather than government: excess demand and differentiated demand for public or quasi-public goods. The former occurs where citizens find certain services underprovided by government and turn to private production to obtain those services. The second demand-side variable, differentiated tastes, occurs where government production is constrained by a broad range of tastes with regard to the kind rather than the quantity of public services. James specifies four conditions under which private-sector production occurs and then goes on to argue that private production typically takes place under nonprofit rather than for-profit auspices primarily because ideologically motivated groups and individuals, especially those affiliated with organized religion, seek to maximize the number of their adherents. The nonprofit form allows for behavior not compatible with profit maximization. For example, below-cost provision of educational services attracts pupils and is possible only with an organizational form that is conducive to cross-subsidization. Other factors, such as access to low-cost labor, client trust and loyalty due to ideological affiliation, and government subsidy secured through exercise of political power, cement the advantage that the nonprofits have over for-profits in provision of the relevant services.

James's model builds on her earlier analysis of cross-subsidization in that it relies on ideological components in the development of the supply of nonprofit services. In her earlier model, this would be called organizational consumption. The later model is much more sophisticated in that it posits ideological interests on the part of consumers and characterizes government as more than a competing multiproduct nonprofit organization.

Against the background of the economic and political theories of the nonprofit sector sketched above, a review of some of the concrete developments in national policy and in the nonprofit sector that have contributed to the emergence of increased commercial activity will evince a clear role for the impact of politics and policy on nonprofits and their cash cows. The developments include changes in government funding, privatization of social services, changes in tax policy, and controversies about competition between business and nonprofits. The first three phenomena are treated in the remainder of this section; the fourth is discussed briefly in the concluding section of this chapter.

Government Funding and Expansion of the Nonprofit Sector. Increases in government spending on social services (in the broadest sense of that term) had two very important impacts on the nonprofit sector and on the sector's commercial activities. First, increases in government funding of nonprofits in the post–World War II period stimulated the growth of the nonprofit sector. New organizations were created in response to this stimulus, and existing organizations expanded. When, several decades later, the Reagan administration reduced that funding, the organizations threatened by those cutbacks sought new revenue

sources to replace government funding. Commercial revenue
was one source of alternative funding.

Second, in a variety of social and health care fields, the
government initiated extensive third-party, voucher-type financial support of services in industries where nonprofits were active. In other words, the government gave individuals money
with which to buy services from providers that were either nonprofit, for-profit, or governmental institutions. The most notable
of these programs is Medicare, the federal health insurance program for the aged. Client populations that previously had been
served only through subsidized provision by nonprofits or the
government could now be served by for-profit firms. The provider organization no longer needed to obtain and furnish the
subsidies on behalf of the clientele; the clientele brought the subsidies with them. The result was that in a number of industries
it was now profitable for conventional businesses to compete
with traditional nonprofit social service and health care providers. Competition between nonprofits and business resulted.
Political controversy followed. The effects of increases in government funding thus produced political and economic repercus-
sions that are central to the circumstances that shaped the pursuit of commercial revenue by nonprofits in the 1980s.

Nonprofit organizations providing personal social services
began to obtain a significant portion of their funding from the
government in the 1960s. In particular, the 1967 amendments
to the Social Security Act, which provided grants that matched
triple the value of funds donated to nonprofit social service agencies, increased both nonprofit reliance on government funding
and the size of this portion of the nonprofit sector. Nonprofit
social service agency reliance on government funding was further increased in 1974, when Title XX of the Social Security
Act broadened the criteria for eligibility for receipt of personal
social services (Kramer, 1982). Similarly, the Educational Television Facilities Program and the establishment of the Corporation for Public Broadcasting in the 1960s stimulated the growth
of nonprofit broadcasting.

Public subsidy stimulated the growth of nonprofit health
care providers in several ways. Direct funding of providers that
served the poor just after World War II spurred nonprofit

growth, as did the system that replaced it: Medicare and Medicaid. These programs subsidized the patient directly and the provider indirectly by stimulating demand. This form of support also encouraged for-profit provision. Some federal health care funding was designed specifically to stimulate the growth of nonprofit institutions. The Hospital Survey and Construction Act of 1946, known as the Hill-Burton Act, subsidized a variety of nonprofit and public health care facilities, especially short-term-stay general hospitals (Marmor, Schlesinger, and Smithey, 1987, p. 226; Starr, 1982, pp. 348–351).

Privatization. Privatization has a double importance to the analysis of cash cows. As an empirical matter, withdrawal of government funding has stimulated nonprofit commercial activity. As a theoretical and ideological matter, it signals an attempt to alter the institutional division of labor in American society. But it also exposed significant ignorance, even misunderstanding of the character of the nonprofit sector.

The proponents of privatization view nonprofits as an alternative to the state. Salamon's theory of government-nonprofit partnership, discussed earlier, takes the opposite view. His theory grows out of the findings of the Urban Institute's Nonprofit Sector Project, which he directed (Salamon, Musselwhite, and De Vita, 1986). The Urban Institute has been studying the changing role of nonprofit organizations in the United States and especially the relationships between these organizations and government in a large-scale research project for the past six years. The Urban Institute research (Salamon and Abramson, 1982) captured a crucial characteristic of the situation posed by federal budget cuts for nonprofit organizations: they were (and continue to be) caught in a squeeze. On the one hand, the government was explicitly looking to them to step in and provide those services that were being eliminated from the federal budget. This stimulated demand for nonprofit services. On the other hand, federal financial support for nonprofits was reduced; the supply of nonprofit services was thus being curtailed. Finally, the amount of the shortfall was much larger than could be expected to be met by increased donative support of nonprofits.

This research had two great strengths. First, it recognized, as few other analyses of the sector had, that nonprofits received a significant portion of their funds from government and that federal budgets would have direct impact on them. Second, it quantified the magnitudes of the various impacts. As of 1981, government was the largest source of funding for the sector, contributing 41 percent of its revenues. Of the ten subsectors that the project analyzed, six relied more on government revenue than on all other sources combined, and for eight subsectors, government was the largest single source of revenue. In none was donative support the largest source of revenue. Thus, it is not surprising that the budget cuts in the period 1982–1986 produced revenue losses to nonprofit organizations (exclusive of Medicare and Medicaid) of approximately $23 billion in comparison with what they would have received had 1980 spending levels been maintained. That translates into an approximate annual loss of $4.6 billion in ''supply.'' In the same period, cuts in areas in which nonprofits are active have amounted to about $70 billion. This has generated the increased demand for service provision by nonprofits.

Private philanthropy was expected to make up the gap between supply and demand in the support of health, welfare, culture, and the arts. The Urban Institute's research indicates that private giving was able to make up for some of the budget cuts but could not do the whole job. Charitable contributions made up for only 57 percent of the direct revenue losses sustained by nonprofits and only 7 percent of the decrease in government spending in the areas of interest to nonprofits. Looking to the future, the Urban Institute calculated that in order to offset the budget cuts that the administration proposed for fiscal years 1987–1989, private giving would have to *grow* at a rate of 700 to 800 percent higher than its peak rate in recent years to meet the service gap. To offset the direct revenue losses, giving would have to grow at a rate of 200 to 300 percent higher than its recent peak rate.

The recent revision of the tax laws compounded the squeeze facing nonprofits. The new flatter tax rates decrease the economic incentives for charitable giving. At the same time, the abolition of the charitable deduction for nonitemizers and the increase in the floor for itemizers further reduce tax incentives for giving.

The Urban Institute's findings demonstrate that nonprofits had relied on government support and that cutbacks in that support put them in a position where they had great incentive to seek alternative sources of revenue. It is not surprising that this pressure led many of them to pursue commercial revenue. Here it is important to note that it is not the "comparative advantages" of the respective sectors that generate the intersectoral division of labor. Instead, it is the organizational response to macropolitical changes—large-scale federal budget cuts—that produced the result in question.

Tax Policy. Tax policy is important to the discussion of cash cows for three reasons. First, the major portion of government policy on nonprofit organizations is accomplished through tax policy. Some policy is realized through administrative regulation of nonprofits receiving government grants and contracts, and some is achieved through state laws establishing the requirements for incorporation of nonprofit organizations. Nonetheless, most policy, especially policy on commercial activity, is a matter of taxation. Second, as the chief means of government oversight, tax policy regarding cash cows is the locus of political dialogue about the legitimacy of commercial activity. That dialogue, as recorded in congressional testimony, court cases, and ancillary documents, is, unfortunately, the only significant source of historical information on the pursuit of commercial revenue by nonprofits. In this respect, tax policy is important not in itself but as a vehicle for historical inquiry. Third, tax policy limits and shapes the types of commerce that nonprofits can pursue and affects the potential profitability of that commerce.

Broadly speaking, tax treatment of commercial activities has taken two forms: the destination test prior to 1950 and the relatedness test from 1950 onward. Not surprisingly, not until the income tax became an important part of the fiscal landscape with the establishment of the national permanent income tax in 1913 (Witte, 1985) did tax treatment of nonprofits and of cash cows become a political issue. Major policy on the tax treatment of cash cows was first established in 1924 in a U.S. Supreme Court case, *Trinidad* v. *Sagrada Orden de Predicadores* (263 U.S. 578). In a case concerning a religious order that used rental income from substantial landholdings and sales revenue from articles sold to churches and related institutions, the Court found such income to be tax-exempt because of the use to which it was put. According to the destination test, as this criterion was called, the income from commercial activities carried on by nonprofits was tax-exempt as long as that income was used for charitable purposes. The *destination* rather than the *source* of the income was determinative.

It is important to understand that corporate income is now and was at the time of the *Sagrada* decision taxed twice. First, the corporation pays taxes on its net income. Then, shareholders pay taxes on the dividends. Under the destination test, nonprofit organizations owning and operating businesses paid taxes at *neither* point. Regardless of the exemption test used, however, the second level of taxation is generally avoided if the shareholder is a nonprofit organization.

By the early 1940s, both the Department of the Treasury and the Bureau of Internal Revenue (the predecessor to the IRS) were starting to object to the destination test and to consider the tax-revenue and social-policy implications of allowing charities to be extensively involved in business activities. What brought cash cows to the attention of the public, however, was the Mueller Macaroni case. A group of wealthy New York University Law School alumni purchased the C. F. Mueller Company, the country's largest manufacturer of noodles, macaroni, and pasta. The alumni, hoping to provide a source of income that would allow their alma mater to achieve greater prestige in the academic community, acquired the company using techniques that we would now call a leveraged buy-out. While the action differed little from the prewar cases of nonprofit commercial activity, the reaction here was instantaneous and vociferous. *Fortune* Magazine ("The Abuse of Tax Exemption," 1950) and the *New Republic* (Mezerik, 1950) editorialized about the scandalous behavior of charities, and one member of Congress thundered that "if something is not done . . . the macaroni monopoly will be in the hands of the universities" (U.S. Congress, House, 1950, p. 580).

But contrary to some accounts, it was not the Mueller case in and of itself that galvanized Congress and the public. The House Ways and Means Committee initiated hearings in 1947 on the conducting of businesses by tax-exempt organizations. Congress was concerned about cash cows several years prior to the hubbub over Mueller. Even representatives of the nonprofit sector were curious about the extent of commercial activity within their domain.

A form of nonprofit commercial activity that most observers found especially vexing was sale-leaseback of real estate. According to congressional testimony (U.S. Congress, House, 1950, p. 176; U.S. Congress, Senate, 1950, pp. 560–566), colleges and universities were involved in extensive sale-leaseback operations with department stores. For example, in the first widely publicized case, Allied Stores sold the real estate associated with some of its operations to Union College. The college then leased the property back to the department store. In such transactions, the property was typically sold at above market costs, but the nonprofit organization recouped the difference because it paid no real estate taxes or income taxes on the transaction. The department store benefitted from an above-market sale price, a below-market rental rate, and the deductibility of the rental payments.

This arrangement spread rapidly; by 1950, Yale had sale-leaseback arrangements with Macy's in San Francisco and Frank & Seder in Philadelphia; Harvard with Gimbel's; Oberlin College with Montgomery Ward, Sears, and Woolworth; and the University of Pennsylvania with Lit Brothers in Philadelphia. Public ire was generalized and unspecific. Many of the abuses cited were instances of businesses establishing charities or foundations in order to maintain control of corporations in the face of estate taxation or simply to avoid taxation. These cases were conflated with instances where operating nonprofits such as universities pursued commercial revenue.

The policy concerns of Congress centered on two issues: the potential that tax exemption gave nonprofits unfair competitive advantage over taxable businesses and the loss of tax revenues engendered by the removal of industrial and commercial activities from the tax base. Regardless of the technical merits of the complaint about unfair competition, which was contested then as it is now, Congress treated the issue as self-evident and serious. With regard to the impact of nonprofit cash cows on the tax base, the Treasury estimated that tax revenues of about $100 million were forgone through their tax exemption. Other analysts argued that the forgone revenues were closer to $3 or $4 million ("Colleges, Charities and the Revenue Act of 1950," 1951, p. 852; U.S. Congress, Senate, 1950, p. 514).

The result of these revelations and of the concern shown by Congress was a fundamental change in tax treatment of nonprofit commercial activity. Congress established a relatedness test to replace the destination test. Now the standard for taxability was the relatedness of the revenue-raising activity to the nonprofits' basic tax-exempt mission. Commercial activities pursued by nonprofits deemed to be unrelated were subject to the unrelated business income tax (UBIT). If such activities were carried out under the auspices of a separate for-profit corporation—a feeder corporation—revenues from those activities were fully taxable at the corporate rate.

Few changes of significance to the issues treated in this chapter have been made in the taxation of nonprofit commercial activities since 1950. While the tax treatment of foundations was drastically revised in 1969, only technical changes in the relatedness test were made. Some classes of nonprofit organizations, primarily churches, social welfare organizations, and a variety of mutual benefit organizations, that had been previously excluded from the coverage of the unrelated business income tax were now covered by that tax. Also, the tax exemption of rental properties owned by nonprofits was further restricted in order to thwart new, more sophisticated versions of the sale-leaseback tax avoidance (Treusch and Sugarman, 1983, pp. 244–251). These amendments raised no political interest of the magnitude surrounding the 1950 policy changes. Not until the 1980s, with the mobilization of the small-business community over the unfair-competition issue, did this tax-policy issue regain political salience.

The battles over taxation of commercial activities are of importance to theories of the nonprofit sector in three respects. First, the vagaries of the tax code provide opportunities for nonprofits to earn revenue, and, concomitantly, the increasingly stringent treatment of commercial activities limits those activities. Second, attempts by nonprofits to affect tax policy—either to obtain favorable treatment or to mitigate punitive sanctions—provide a link of a political sort between individual nonprofit organizations and the macropolitical environment in which they operate. Third, political conflict between nonprofits and other sorts of institutions and groups, such as small business or ideologically motivated factions, imposes a constraint on individual nonprofit organizations' activities. In the models that characterized nonprofit organizations as institutions that engage in cross-subsidization, we saw that there were generally two classes of activities in which the organizations engaged: mission activities and subsidizing activities. From the perspective of those that operate the nonprofit organization, the identity of the latter activities is unimportant as long as they meet certain minimum criteria of profitability and lack of constraints or disutility. In contrast, the identity of the mission activity is important—it is what motivates the very operation of the organization.

Politics may be integrated into these models by portraying the controversies as the means by which various groups in society either intentionally or unintentionally raise the costs of one of a set of potential subsidizing activities relative to other possible sources of subsidy (for example, the cost of commercial activities versus the cost of donations). The costs can be raised directly as nonprofit managers find that the controversy requires managerial attention or as public disaffection is manifested in decreased financial support. Or the costs may be imposed by the policy that is eventually implemented.

This is not just idle theoretical rumination. The political strategy of the small-business critics of nonprofit organizations explicitly includes a component geared toward changing the public perception of nonprofit organizations in order to influence the profitability of certain sources of revenue (Pillsbury, 1987, p. 39). The "halo effect" is just as much a target as the tax exemptions.

Policy Implications

Recent controversy about competition between nonprofits and small business has engendered intense scrutiny of nonprofit commercial activities and rekindled public debate about the proper role of nonprofits in society. The small-business community complains that the tax exemption and related benefits enjoyed by nonprofits put competing businesses at a disadvantage and that nonprofits should not be "in business" in any event—they should be helping the poor and disadvantaged while relying on charitable support (Business Coalition for Fair Competition, 1985). Nonprofits respond that small businesses also enjoy tax advantages, that nonprofits have never been confined to donative financing, and that service exclusively to the poor would stigmatize recipients (Pires, 1985).

The arguments are analytically complex, and the data needed to arbitrate the issues are currently unavailable (U.S. General Accounting Office, 1987), but the analysis in this chapter provides some positive and normative insights into the debate. To the extent that cross-subsidization is a key feature of nonprofit organizations and that in some way or another nonprofits pursue activities unsupportable in the market, several important inferences can be drawn. First, those nonprofits that support themselves solely through fees for service may not be entitled to tax exemption and related public subsidies and dispensations. Their ability to operate solely on the basis of fees for services implies that their services lack a redistributive or collective component. This criterion would not disallow exemption for nonprofit organizations that operate partially on the basis of this sort of financing or that employ sliding-scale fee systems. Second, the small-business community's attempt to limit nonprofits to donative financing and narrowly defined charitable activity misconstrues what nonprofits are about, currently and historically. If the historical research that is beginning to emerge is correct, pure charities are more a part of American folklore than of the actual American political economy (Hall, 1987).

The discussions of the role of politics and policy in shaping nonprofit commercial activity raises concerns in a different dimension. Advocates of various ideological stripes look to nonprofits to play a vital role in the welfare state. Some conservative privatizers want them to relieve the load on government. Even those not advocating privatization see a crucial role for nonprofits in service delivery, advocacy, or constituent participation. As various forms of financial support available to nonprofits—government funding, charitable deductions, and now commercial cross-subsidization—are successively curtailed, policy makers need to face up to the possibility of the gradual enfeeblement of the nonprofit sector.

This raises an important point about the dispute regarding fairness of competition between small business and nonprofit organizations. While the dearth of data and the complexity of the requisite analysis make conclusions hard to come by, it is probably the case that fairness is not a matter of leveling a tilted playing field, because the field is not tilted but bumpy. That is, the unfairness may not lie so much in the relative advantages that nonprofits have over their small-business competitors—the magnitude of the advantage of tax exemption to nonprofits has yet to clearly established, especially in an analysis that incorporates commensurate small-business tax benefits—as in the fact that small businesses are bearing the burden, through depressed market returns, for a portion of the cost of public services that might be more equitably distributed through the general tax system (Rose-Ackerman, 1986). If nonprofits received more funding from government sources, or if services provided by nonprofits were provided directly by government agencies, then the cost of those services would be spread throughout the tax base rather than being imposed on small business through nonprofit competition. In this sense, small business is bearing an undue portion of the cost of the welfare state.

The policy implications of this perspective on unfairness are complex. First, this perspective relies on the sort of market analysis described by Rose-Ackerman (1986) where subcompetitive returns on investment for an industry have to be established. Second, remedies for the inequities that are found could include (1) more direct government funding for nonprofit organizations in order to decrease their incentives to pursue commercial revenue, (2) a shift to direct government provision of public services, (3) increases in tax deductions for charitable contributions in order to increase donative funding, (4) compensation for small businesses hurt by nonprofit competition, and (5) an explicit choice to reduce the relevant public services by prohibiting certain sorts of nonprofit commercial activity without providing compensating increases in funding for nonprofits or without increasing government provision.

Some of these remedies have obvious drawbacks. The shift to direct government provision undermines whatever virtues nonprofit provision offers by reducing this sector's role. Compensation for small business is administratively complex and suffers from difficulties of establishing clear and legitimate standards of injury. The proposals for greater government funding or increased tax incentives for giving produce fewer negative consequences, but it has been precisely the movement of public policy away from such subsidies that has contributed to the pursuit of commercial revenue by nonprofits. Concern about the federal budget deficit militates against the readoption of these approaches. In the short term it appears that, if small business succeeds in its political quest, the ''remedy'' employed will be limitations on commercial activity and reduced nonprofit services. We will have both fewer sacred cows and fewer cash cows.

This chapter began by pointing out that commercial activities of nonprofit organizations violate our commonplace conceptions of what nonprofits are about. The apparent anomaly of organizations whose distinctiveness rests in their being unlike businesses acting like businesses motivates the two-stage process of this inquiry: first, what exactly do we mean by nonprofit organizations, and second, how well do those answers accommodate commercial activity?

In order for commercial activity to be an anomaly, there must be a coherent notion of ''nonprofitness'' against which to measure the aptness of this particular activity. Throughout this chapter, it has been argued that cross-subsidization is an important, perhaps essential feature of both nonprofits in general and their commercial activities in particular. It provides a plausible behavioral account of much nonprofit activity. It is a ''supply-side'' theory in the terminology introduced earlier. It is less powerful in accounting for demand factors or in explaining the role of nonprofit organizations in society. The analysis of non-profits as cross-subsidizers does not stand as a comprehensive theory of the role of nonprofit organizations. But the behavior in question is more easily understood when the nonprofit sector is viewed against the backdrop of its environment. Some of the models reviewed, such as those of James (1983, 1987) and Rose-Ackerman (1986, 1987) have incorporated the impact of the government and business sectors on nonprofit organizations, but they generally leave out or underemphasize the importance of the macropolitical environment.

One of the theoretical aims of this chapter has been to cast doubt on the notion that nonprofit organizations (or, by implication, government) are a residual category of social organization. Instead, it has been argued that ''nonprofitness'' or ''publicness'' is not simply what ''privateness'' cannot accomplish. By making the argument that macropolitical factors influence intersectoral and intrasectoral behavior, this chapter is making claims about what kinds of factors are important in the analysis of the political economy—it is arguing for the necessity of bringing the state back in.

References

''The Abuse of Tax Exemption.'' *Fortune,* May 1950, pp. 74–77.

Business Coalition for Fair Competition. *Unfair Competition in the States.* Washington, D.C.: Business Coalition for Fair Competition, 1985.

''Colleges, Charities and the Revenue Act of 1950.'' *Yale Law Journal,* 1951, *60,* 851–893.

Evans, P. B., Rueschemeyer, D., and Skocpol, T. *Bringing the State Back In.* New York: Cambridge University Press, 1985.

Hall, P. D. ''A Historical Overview of the Private Nonprofit Sector.'' In W. W. Powell (ed.), *The Nonprofit Sector: A Research Handbook.* New Haven, Conn.: Yale University Press, 1987.

Hansmann, H. ''The Role of Nonprofit Enterprise.'' *Yale Law Journal,* 1980, *89,* 835–901.

Hansmann, H. "Economic Theories of Nonprofit Enterprise." In W. W. Powell (ed.), *The Nonprofit Sector: A Research Handbook*. New Haven, Conn.: Yale University Press, 1987.

James, E. "How Nonprofits Grow: A Model." *Journal of Policy Analysis and Management*, 1983, *2* (3), 350–353.

James, E. "The Nonprofit Sector in Comparative Perspective." In W. W. Powell (ed.), *The Nonprofit Sector: A Research Handbook*. New Haven, Conn.: Yale University Press, 1987.

Kramer, R. "From Voluntarism to Vendorism: An Organizational Perspective on Contracting." Working Paper no. 54, Program on Nonprofit Organizations, Institution for Social and Policy Studies, Yale University, 1982.

Marmor, T. R., Schlesinger, M., and Smithey, R. W. "Nonprofit Organizations and Health Care." In W. W. Powell (ed.), *The Nonprofit Sector: A Research Handbook*. New Haven, Conn.: Yale University Press, 1987.

Mezerik, A. G. "The Foundation Racket." *New Republic,* Jan. 30, 1950, pp. 11–13.

Nielsen, R. P. "Piggybacking Strategies for Nonprofits: A Shared Costs Approach." *Strategic Management Journal*, 1986, *7*, 201–215.

Pillsbury, M. "Competition Between the Nonprofit and For-Profit Sectors." Unpublished master's thesis, School of Business, New York University, 1987.

Pires, S. *Competition Between the Nonprofit and For-Profit Sectors.* Washington, D.C.: National Assembly of National Voluntary Health and Social Welfare Organizations, 1985.

Polanyi, K. *The Great Transformation.* Boston: Beacon Press, 1944.

Rose-Ackerman, S. "Unfair Competition and Corporate Income Taxation." In S. Rose-Ackerman (ed.), *The Economics of Nonprofit Institutions: Studies in Structure and Policy.* New York: Oxford University Press, 1986.

Rose-Ackerman, S. "Ideals Versus Dollars: Donors, Charity Managers, and Government Grants." *Journal of Political Economy,* 1987, *95* (4), 810–823.

Salamon, L. M. "Partners in Public Service: The Scope and Theory of Government-Nonprofit Relations." In W. W. Powell (ed.), *The Nonprofit Sector: A Research Handbook.* New Haven, Conn.: Yale University Press, 1987.

Salamon, L. M., and Abramson, A. J. *The Federal Budget and the Nonprofit Sector.* Washington, D.C.: Urban Institute Press, 1982.

Salamon, L. M., Musselwhite, J. G., and De Vita, C. J. "Partners in Public Service: Government and the Nonprofit Sector in the American Welfare State." Paper presented at the INDEPENDENT SECTOR Spring Research Forum, New York, Mar. 1986.

Starr, P. *The Social Transformation of American Medicine: The Rise of a Sovereign Profession and the Making of a Vast Industry.* New York: Basic Books, 1982.

Treusch, P. E., and Sugarman, N. *Tax Exempt Charitable Organizations.* (2nd ed.) Philadelphia: American Law Institute–American Bar Association, 1983.

Tucker, W. "Public Radio Comes to Market." *Fortune,* October 18, 1982, p. 207.

U.S. Congress. House. Committee on Ways and Means. *Hearings on the Revenue Revisions of 1950.* 81st Cong., 2d sess., Feb. 10, 1950.

U.S. Congress. Senate. Committee on Finance. *Hearings on the Revenue Revisions of 1950.* 81st Cong., 2d sess., 1950.

U.S. General Accounting Office. *Tax Policy: Competition Between Taxable Businesses and Tax-Exempt Organizations.* GAO/GGD-8-40BR. Washington, D.C.: U.S. General Accounting Office, 1987.

Witte, J. *The Politics and Development of the Federal Income Tax.* Madison: University of Wisconsin Press, 1985.

10

△ △ △ △ △ △ △ △ △ △ △ △ △ △ △

The Use of
For-Profit Subsidiary Corporations
by Nonprofits

Disputes concerning the commercial activities of exempt organizations date to the introduction of the income tax and have continued throughout the evolution of the tax laws. As a result of these disputes, Congress has twice focused on exempt organizations' commercial activities and charges of "unfair competition," once in 1950 and again in 1969. Despite the years of controversy, Congress's efforts, and numerous court decisions, it now seems likely that this issue will once again be scrutinized ("Rep. Rostenkowski Announces . . . ," 1987). One recurrent aspect of the debate has been the utilization of taxable subsidiary corporations by exempt organizations. This subject is ripe for policy review as the use of taxable subsidiaries has increased dramatically during the 1980s. This chapter will trace the evolution of the use of taxable subsidiaries, identify the reasons for their proliferation, and examine the policy ramifications of this development.

The Early Years: The Debate Begins

In 1913, the year in which the Sixteenth Amendment to the Constitution was ratified, giving Congress the "power to lay and collect taxes on income," a dispute arose between the insular collector of internal revenue of the Philippine Islands (which were then a U.S. territory) and a Philippine religious corporation over the commercial activities of that corporation. The corporation derived its income from interest, rents, and dividends as well as from the sale of wines, chocolates, and other articles purchased and supplied for use in its churches and schools. The tax collector took the position that the corporation was not ''operated exclusively'' for religious purposes but rather was operated in part for commercial purposes in that it used its properties to produce income and traded in various goods. This dispute was resolved in the organization's favor eleven years later. In *Trinidad* v. *Sagrada Orden de Predicadores* (263 U.S. 578 [1924]), the U.S. Supreme Court enunciated the ''destination of income test'' and held that the destination of the income—not the source—was the ultimate test of the right of exemption.

During the next two decades, the Internal Revenue Service was involved in similar disputes with charitable organizations that engaged in transparently profit-making activities. In one of the most celebrated cases (*C. F. Mueller Co.* v. *Commissioner,* 190 F.2d 120 [1951]), a corporation engaged in the manufacture and sale of macaroni was acquired and merged into a corporation organized to benefit the School of Law of New York University. The IRS's assertion that this entity was neither organized nor operated exclusively for a charitable purpose was again thwarted by the destination-of-income test. By the time the Third Circuit Court of Appeal rendered its opinion in that case, however, the law had been changed. Congress had already reacted to complaints that exempt organizations were engaged in profitable business activities in competition with taxable entities: ''the involvement of educational institutions in the field of banking, real-estate, commerce, and industry goes merrily on. Universities own haberdasheries, citrus groves, movies, cattle ranches, the Encyclopaedia Brittanica (owned by the University of Chicago), and a large variety of other enterprises. The University of Wisconsin controls patent pools and collects royalties. Universities and colleges, together with foundations, have an annual income from their business activities of well over a half billion dollars annually. Were this income not tax-exempt, they would pay $173,000,000 in Federal Taxes annually" (*Congressional Record*, 1950, pp. 9273–9274).

The Revenue Act of 1950: The Debate Continues

The Revenue Act of 1950 devised a scheme to deal with the issue of unfair competition between taxable and exempt entities. The first part of the scheme was the enactment of the "feeder" provisions of Section 502 of the Internal Revenue Code (IRC) to overturn the destination-of-income test (feeders are business organizations that "feed" income to a tax-exempt organization). Section 502(a) provides that an organization "operated for the primary purpose of carrying on a trade or business for profit shall not be exempt from taxation under section 501 on the ground that all of its profits are payable to one or more organizations exempt from taxation under section 501." Congress noted that "such an organization is not itself carrying out an exempt purpose. Moreover, it is obviously in direct competition with other taxable businesses" (U.S. Congress, House, 1950, p. 41; U.S. Congress, Senate, 1950, p. 35).

The second part of the scheme to deal with the issue of unfair competition was the imposition of the regular corporate income tax on active business income that arises from activities that are "unrelated" to an organization's tax-exempt purposes. This new "unrelated business income tax" was directed at unfair competition conducted by charitable organizations, labor organizations, and business leagues:

> The problem at which the tax on unrelated business income is directed is primarily that of unfair competition. The tax-free status of section [501] organizations enables them to use their profits tax-free to expand operations, while their competitors can expand only with the profits remaining after taxes. Also, a number of examples have arisen where these organizations have, in effect, used their tax exemptions to buy an ordinary business. That is, they have acquired the business with little or no

investment on their own part and paid for it in installments out of subsequent earnings—a procedure which usually could not be followed if the business were taxable.

In neither the House bill nor your committee's bill does this provision deny the exemption where the organizations are carrying on unrelated active business enterprises, nor require that they dispose of such businesses. Both provisions merely impose the same tax on income derived from an unrelated trade or business as is borne by their competitors [U.S. Congress, Senate, 1950, p. 27].

In devising this scheme to deal with unfair competition, Congress was specifically concerned with "active" business income. It excluded from taxation the types of income that had traditionally been considered "passive" in nature; that is, dividends, interest, royalties, and rents (Internal Revenue Code Sections 512(b)(1)–512(b)(3)). It soon became clear, however, that transactions could be structured to use subsidiary corporations so as to avoid the unrelated business income tax.

Within months of passage of the Revenue Act of 1950, for example, the Amon Carter Foundation formed a wholly owned subsidiary corporation and transferred to it certain oil and gas leases and related machinery. It was apparent that the new unrelated business income tax rules would subject the foundation to taxation if it operated the business. Moreover, the destination-of-income test was no longer available to shield the subsidiary from taxation. Accordingly, the business operation was structured so that the new taxable subsidiary corporation operated the business and paid "income" on the oil and gas properties to the foundation in the form of overriding royalties. The foundation claimed an exclusion from the unrelated business income tax rules on the basis of the "passive" nature of the royalty income. The IRS objected, but was unsuccessful in its assertion that, in substance, the subsidiary corporation had no separate existence (*Amon G. Carter Foundation* v. *United States,* 58–1 U.S.T.C. (C.C.H.) 9342 [N.D. Tex. 1958]).

In a similar case, the Robert A. Welch Foundation transferred a taxable "working interest" in oil and gas properties
to its controlled taxable subsidiary corporations and subsequently
reported income from these properties as nontaxable royalties.
The IRS asserted unsuccessfully in the Fifth Circuit Court of
Appeal that the foundation's income should be characterized,
in substance, as a taxable "working interest" (*United States* v.
Robert A. Welch Foundation, 334 F.2d 774 [5th Cir. 1964]). The
IRS subsequently announced in a 1969 revenue ruling that it
would not follow the Fifth Circuit's opinion.

The Tax Reform Act of 1969: The Debate Continues

By the time the IRS's 1969 revenue ruling was published, Congress was again responding to complaints of unfair competition
between exempt and taxable entities. In this context, there were
two basic concerns. The first was the extensive involvement of
private foundations—privately supported charitable organizations—in the business sector. Congress feared that charitable
concerns had become secondary to business concerns. The Senate
Finance Committee cited the example of a foundation that was
found to control eighteen operating businesses, including a $10
million newspaper, the largest radio station in the state, a $20
million insurance company, a lumber company, several banks,
three large hotels, a garage, and a number of office buildings
(U.S. Congress, Senate, 1969, p. 39) Congress reacted in the
Tax Reform Act of 1969 by imposing severe limitations on the
ability of private foundations to maintain holdings in business
enterprises:

> Those who wished to use a foundation's stock hold-
> ings to acquire or retain business control in some
> cases were relatively unconcerned about produc-
> ing income to be used by the foundation for char-
> itable purposes. In fact, they might have become
> so interested in making a success of the business,
> or in meeting competition, that most of their at-
> tention and interest was devoted to this with the

result that what was supposed to be their function, that of carrying on charitable, educational, etc. activities was neglected. Even when such a foundation attains a degree of independence from its major donor, there is a temptation for its managers to divert their interest to the maintenance and improvement of the business and away from their charitable duties. Where the charitable ownership predominates, the business may be run in a way which unfairly competes with other businesses whose owners must pay taxes on the income that they derive from the businesses. To deal with these problems, Congress concludes it is desirable to limit the extent to which a business may be controlled by a private foundation [Joint Committee on Internal Revenue Taxation, 1970, p. 41].

Congress's second basic concern was that many of the other exempt organizations that were excepted from the unrelated business income rules (including churches) were engaging in or were apt to engage in unrelated business. Congress responded by expanding the coverage of the unrelated business income tax to virtually all exempt organizations. In addition, there were changes limiting the types of income excepted from the unrelated provisions. One such provision was designed to prevent parent-subsidiary corporate transactions from escaping taxation through the use of sophisticated interest, rents, annuity, and royalty schemes. Specifically, IRC Section 512(b)(13) was amended to provide a "controlled organization test"; that is, a test providing that when a tax-exempt organization owns more than 80 percent of a taxable subsidiary, the interests, annuities, royalties, and rents received by it from the subsidiary are to be treated as unrelated business income and are subject to tax. This, of course, was a legislative response to those earlier cases where exempt organizations caused the profits of their controlled corporations to be passed on to them in the passive form, thereby avoiding the tax on the subsidiaries' income: "In certain cases exempt organizations do not engage in business directly but do so through nominally taxable subsidiary corporations. In many such instances the subsidiary corporations pay interest, rents or royalties to the exempt parent in sufficient amount to eliminate their entire income, which interest, rents, and royalties are not taxed to the parent even though they may be derived from an active business. This problem is remedied under the bill by removing the exemption from the unrelated business tax for passive income if it is in the form of interest, rents, and royalties received from controlled corporations" (U.S. Congress, House, 1969, p. 49; U.S. Congress, Senate, 1969, p. 73).

This statutory change did not put the practice to rest. Indeed, two years after the 1969 amendment, the IRS assessed taxes against the Mabee Foundation. In that instance, the Mabee Petroleum Corporation—a wholly owned taxable subsidiary corporation of the Mabee Foundation—engaged in the production and sale of oil and gas through ownership of oil and gas leases. The foundation, as holder of the overriding royalty interests, received payments directly from the oil purchasers rather than indirectly through its subsidiary, which would have been the customary method of receiving such payments. While admitting that the subsidiary was a "controlled organization," the foundation argued that the overriding royalties should be excluded from unrelated business taxable income because the income was not "derived from" the subsidiary within the purview of IRC Section 512(b)(13) but rather was derived from the oil purchasers directly. Neither the trial court nor the appellate courts found this argument convincing. Indeed, the Tenth Circuit Court of Appeal described the method of payment as a "scheme . . . within the manipulations which Congress sought to tax": "It is of no consequence that Foundation and Petroleum had arranged for Foundation to receive the money directly rather than through Petroleum. Petroleum produces and markets the gas and oil to generate the production income upon which Foundation's overriding royalty income is based. Taxation does not depend on the mechanical formality of whether the overriding royalty income was paid through the controlled organization generating the income or directly to the charitable recipient. It appears clear beyond peradventure that Congress intended to tax a charitable organization's receipt of customary 'royalties' from a 'controlled organization''' (*The J. E. and L. E. Mabee Foundation* v. *United States,* 533 F.2d 521 at 524 [10th Cir. 1976]).

The 1980s—Exempt Organizations Change: The Debate Intensifies

The interest of exempt organizations in utilizing taxable subsidiary corporations increased significantly in the past decade. A decline in traditional funding sources and an increase in demand for services forced many exempt organizations into the commercial arena (McGovern, 1986). The Urban Institute's Nonprofit Sector Project, for example, found that federal support for the nonprofit sector declined an estimated $4.5 billion between 1980 and 1984 and that this decline was offset in large part by commercial sources of income (Salamon, 1984).

To survive in a dramatically changing economy, many Section 501(c)(3) organizations began to revise their corporate structures. The increased use of taxable subsidiary corporations was a part of this strategy. For example, the IRS issued 593 private letter rulings to Section 501(c)(3) organizations that operated in tandem with taxable subsidiary corporations between 1977 and 1986. In comparison, there had been only 8 equivalent rulings issued in the previous ten-year period. (These statistics were obtained through an automated search of a private letter ruling data base.)

This change was most notable in the health care sector; 435 of the 593 rulings involved health care organizations. Nonprofit community hospitals particularly felt the brunt of a changing economy. Goverment, business, and third-party payers sought to control health care costs that had escalated wildly in past years of high inflation and double-digit interest rates. In addition, the federal government moved away from a cost-reimbursement system under the Medicare program to a prospective-payment system based on preset prices. As this financial reimbursement system was changing, nonprofit hospitals were faced with competition for patients and doctors from chains of aggressive for-profit corporations. In order to survive in a changing, heavily regulated, and intensely competitive environment, nonprofit hospitals began to diversify by reorganizing into multientity structures (McGovern, 1987). In most instances, a taxable subsidiary corporation was included in the new system.

Subsidiary corporations continue to be utilized in these systems to structure transactions so that income flowing between the corporations can be characterized as nontaxable passive income. In the early 1980s, for example, the IRS district director in Detroit sought advice from the IRS's national office about a parent-subsidiary corporate transaction in a hospital system that sought to escape the unrelated business income tax through the use of a sophisticated rent arrangement similar to the one used in the Mabee Foundation case. The transaction involved a tax-exempt parent holding company that controlled two wholly owned subsidiaries: a tax-exempt hospital and a for-profit pharmacy and optical shop. The hospital leased space in its facility to the for-profit pharmacy and optical shop. Rental payments from the for-profit entity were made to the tax-exempt hospital and not to the parent corporation. As the hospital did not control the for-profit subsidiary, the parent corporation claimed that the rent payments to the hospital were not subject to Section 512(b)(13) or the unrelated business income tax. As in the Mabee Foundation case, this scheme was an attempt to structure the transaction so that typically "passive" income payments are received from third parties rather than from the exempt organization's controlled corporation. It was the opinion of the IRS's Office of Chief Counsel, however, that the interposition of a wholly owned entity between the exempt controlling organization and the wholly owned source of the payments may be disregarded for purposes of applying the unrelated business income tax. Accordingly, rent payments to the hospital were deemed subject to Section 512(b)(13) and the unrelated business income tax. (General Counsel Memorandum 38878, July 16, 1982. A general counsel memorandum (GCM) is a legal opinion of the Office of Chief Counsel that is based on the particular issues and facts of a specific case. GCMs are not intended for precedential use and do not represent the official agency position.)

1987: Congressional Hearings

On September 12, 1986, the House Ways and Means Committee announced a hearing to review the federal tax treatment of commercial and other income-producing activities of tax-exempt organizations and related entities (U.S. Congress, House, 1986). Five days of hearings were held in June 1987. The deputy assistant secretary for tax policy of the Treasury Department presented the government's policy views on the appropriate tax treatment of income-producing activities of exempt organizations and related entities (Chapoton, 1987). This testimony, which was comprehensive in scope, made two recommendations for revision of the tax laws that pertain to the use of taxable subsidiary corporations.

The first recommendation was to revise the controlled organization test of Section 512(b)(13). Treasury noted that an exempt organization could own 100 percent of the voting stock of a subsidiary, 99 percent of the total value of a subsidiary, but only 79 percent of a single class of nonvoting stock and not technically fall within the definition of a controlled organization. Treasury's recommendation was that the definition of a controlled organization should be changed to include an organization in which the parent exempt organization has more than a 50 percent interest, measured by either voting power or value. In addition, Treasury suggested that application of the ownership attribution rules be enacted so that a subsidiary controlled by an affiliate of an exempt organization would be covered.

Treasury also suggested that consideration be given to aggregating the activities of an exempt organization and its susidiaries. Under present law, a Section 501 (c)(3) organization can engage in a business as a substantial part of its activities so long as the operation of the business is in furtherance of its exempt purpose and it is not organized or operated for the "primary purpose" of carrying on an unrelated business. Treasury recommended that, in appropriate cases, the activities of an exempt parent and its subsidiaries should be aggregated to test for the exempt organization's primary purpose (especially where management of the subsidiary is fully integrated with that of its parent). These recommendations were subsequently endorsed in an October 15, 1987, letter to the chair of the House Ways and Means Subcommittee on Oversight from four Republican members of that subcommittee ("Initial Recommendations . . . ," 1987). Given this endorsement, they are likely to receive serious consideration by the full Ways and Means Committee.

1989 and Beyond: Will History be Repeated?

In 1950, Congress attempted to create rules that would prevent exempt organizations and their subsidiaries from competing unfairly with taxable businesses. Nineteen years later, in 1969, Congress recognized that the problem had not been solved by its 1950 legislation and created additional rules to restrict exempt organizations' use of taxable subsidiaries. Now Congress may find it necessary to enact yet more legislation attempting to prevent exempt organizations from using taxable subsidiaries to unfairly compete with other taxable businesses. Certainly, Congress's current concerns in this area are nearly identical to the concerns that it expressed prior to enacting legislation in both 1950 and 1969.

Perhaps, then, the basic issue to be considered as Congress ventures into its third major review of the tax laws dealing with the issue of unfair competition is whether perceived abuses can be dealt with through continued microscopic revisions to a very comprehensive tax law. This chapter has demonstrated that exempt organizations have, over the years, utilized creative tax planning to cause the profits of their controlled corporations to be passed on to them in passive form, thereby avoiding the tax on the subsidiaries' income. Previous congressional responses have not been successful in dealing with this situation. If history is a guide, the suggested revision to the controlled-organization test of Section 512(b)(13) may prove once again to be only a temporary obstacle to those seeking to characterize income as passive (that is, nontaxable) in nature. Indeed, it must be questioned whether any controlled-organization test will be effective with respect to the new "systems" of exempt entities. As indicated earlier, the recent explosive use of taxable subsidiary corporations has been primarily in the hospital area, where the single exempt entity has spawned a system of related exempt and taxable entities. While Section 512(b)(13) applies only to transactions between a parent corporation and a controlled corporation, it is questionable whether that statute, or any revision to that statute, will be effective in dealing with a potentially unlimited number of transactions that can be structured between brother-sister corporations in a system of exempt entities.

Similarly, the proposed commercial activity aggregation rules may not be effective in the hospital area. The difficulty of applying a primary-activity test in the hospital area is that the gross income from hospitals is larger than that of any other type of public charity (U.S. Internal Revenue Service, 1985–86). Thus, hospitals will be able to aggregate a significant amount of business activity without failing a "primary purpose" test.

If perceived abuses cannot be effectively addressed through continued microscopic revisions of a very comprehensive tax law, the alternative is macro change. In looking for an effective macro change, the obvious model is the excise taxes imposed on private foundations in the Tax Reform Act of 1969. The excess business holding rules were specifically designed to deal with business involvement of privately funded Section 501(c)(3) organizations (IRC Section 4943).

There are current indications that an extension of these rules to public charities may be appropriate. For example, one concern expressed in 1969, that charitable interests of private foundations had become secondary to business interests, is closely parallel to similar concerns expressed about public charities today. A former director of the Urban Institute, for example, offered the following opinion on the findings of the institute's

Nonprofit Sector Project: "As government support declines, private charity fails to fill the gap, and organizations turn increasingly towards commercial sources of income instead, the sector's willingness and ability to serve those in greatest need may decline, undermining the sector's raison d'être in the process" (Salamon, 1984, p. 23). In addition, the opinion of one noted commentator on exempt organizations suggests that the point for macro change has already been reached:

> [3] Subsidiaries and Subordinates. . . . So for now, the quietly efficient, multi-tiered charitable enterprise, selling its related and unrelated goods, service or facilities, to charitable classes of the public, to customers generally and to governmental units, does not see the Service as a threat to its integrity, but merely as an unruly, but manageable, partner. Congress seems unlikely to act on its own initiative, the Treasury Department seems unwilling to spend its meager resources in yet another study, and the public does not seem to sense that the magnitude threatens its peace and good order. The business community seems to be the only remaining interested party; and since it appears that the economy is sufficiently expansive to be hospitable to all newcomers, regardless of cloak or mantle, that community seems content to absorb or accommodate its charitable competitors [Lehrfeld, 1984, p. 26-1].

It is critical, however, that this suggestion be scrutinized with extreme caution. To begin with, there is a lack of data about the extent of commercial activity of exempt organizations. (Despite a comprehensive search, the General Accounting Office (GAO) could not find such data. GAO examined the IRS's Statistics of Income and Exempt Organizations Business Master File data bases. In addition, GAO examined studies by the Bureau of the Census in 1977 and 1982, the Urban Institute in 1982, the Partners for Livable Places and the Rockefeller Brothers Fund in 1982, the INDEPENDENT SECTOR in 1984, the

Small Business Administration in 1984, and the National Assembly of Voluntary Health and Welfare Organizations in 1985. GAO/GGD-87-40BR.) Moreover, while it is clear that federal support for the exempt sector has declined dramatically in recent years, and while it is also clear that sophisticated exempt organizations have entered the commercial arena in response to this decline, it is not known whether the priority of these organizations is the bottom line or the provision of services. Historically, the major initiatives in addressing significant issues of medical care, housing, education, and employment have emanated from the exempt sector. If the economic base of today's exempt organization is dramatically slashed without a consideration of ways to continue these contributions, major difficulties may arise in the provision of social services in the future, particularly during a recession or when the business economics of the marketplace are otherwise unfavorable.

References

Congressional Record. Statement of the Honorable Robert L. Doughton, Chair, Committee on Ways and Means, HOR. 1950, *96,* pt. 7, pp. 9273-9274.

"Initial Recommendations by House Ways and Means Oversight Subcommittee Republicans on Unrelated Business Income of Tax-Exempt Organizations." *Daily Tax Reporter,* Oct. 27, 1987, p. 7-1.

Joint Committee on Internal Revenue Taxation. *General Explanation of the Tax Reform Act of 1969.* Washington, D.C.: U.S. Government Printing Office, 1970.

Lehrfeld, W. J. "Dealing with Investors and Other Methods of Generating Income: Tax Aspects of Revenue Producing Activities." *Institute of Federal Taxation,* 1984, *42,* 26-1.

McGovern, J. J. "The Changing Character of Exempt Organizations." *Philadelphia Monthly,* 1986, *19,* 19.

McGovern, J. J. "Restructured Nonprofit Hospitals." *Tax Notes,* 1987, *35* (4), 405.

"Rep. Rostenkowski Announces 1988 Agenda for Ways-Means Oversight Committee." *Daily Tax Reporter,* Dec. 21, 1987, p. G-1.

Salamon, L. M. "The Results Are Coming In." *Foundation News,* 1984, *25,* 16–17.

U.S. Congress. House. H. Rept. 2319, 81st. Cong., 2d sess., 1950.

U.S. Congress. House. H. Rept. 91-413, pt. 11, 81st Cong., 2d sess., 1969.

U.S. Congress. House. Committee on Ways and Means. Press Release #25, Sept. 12, 1986.

U.S. Congress. House. Hearings before the Subcommittee on Oversight of the Committee on Ways and Means. 100th Cong., 1st sess., 1987. Statement of the Honorable O. D. Chapoton, Department of the Treasury.

U.S. Congress. Senate. S. Rept. 2375, 81st Cong., 2d sess., 1950.

U.S. Congress. Senate. S. Rept. 91-552, 81st Cong., 2d sess., 1969.

U.S. Internal Revenue Service. *IRS Statistics of Income Bulletin,* Winter 1985–86, p. 26.

11

DENNIS R. YOUNG

△ △ △ △ △ △ △ △ △ △ △ △ △ △ △

Beyond Tax Exemption:
A Focus on Organizational
Performance Versus Legal Status

It is now well appreciated by scholars and others concerned with contemporary nonprofit organizations that the nonprofit sector struggles with an identity crisis. Indeed, Jon Van Til (1988) has written a book devoted solely to coping with this question from a theoretical standpoint. The sector is easily designated by what it is not, but it has been difficult to find a term that describes it positively. *Voluntary sector, independent sector,* and *mediating institutions,* for example, are the most popular terms, yet they belie the realities and complexities of modern-day non-profit organizations, as significant numbers of these organizations rely on paid staff, are highly dependent on the public and business sectors, and serve not merely as intermediaries but as primary service providers.

The *third sector* is another term that has been employed, if not with great enthusiasm, by those who seek an accurate if bland and neutral description. Yet even this term has its problems, for there are several dimensions along which the sectors may be ordered, and it is not clear that the nonprofit sector comes out third on each one. Certainly if measured in terms of the volume of economic activity—for example, by income, expen-

Note: The author wishes to thank Avner Ben-Ner, Peter Dobkin Hall, and Virginia Hodgkinson for their helpful comments on earlier drafts of this chapter.

ditures, assets, or employment (but not volunteering)—the non-profit sector is third to business and government. But other ways of keeping score are equally valid. For example, a number of scholars suggest that the historical tendency has been for non-profit organizations to precede the development of profit-seeking or governmental institutions in particular fields. Bremner (1960), Weisbrod (1977), and Mason (1984), for example, suggest that nonprofit activity foreshadows governmental initiative, while Mason (1984), Greene (1977), and others observe that nonprofits often break the economic ground for business. While there is no scholarly consensus that this is the dominant mode of his-torical development of the sectors, this view would argue for calling the nonprofit sector the *first sector.*

Alternatively, one can view the sectors from a normative point of view, as suggested by Gamwell (1984). As Van Til (1988) points out, Gamwell finds nonprofit institutions to have high societal purpose and to be morally superior or "teleologi-cally prior"; hence, from this viewpoint also, the nonprofit deserves to be called the *first sector.*

Perhaps the most troublesome dimension on which the nonprofit sector tends to rank third is its treatment in positive social science theory, especially economic theory. The best-known economic theories of the sector, those developed by Weisbrod (1977) and Hansmann (1980), essentially view the nonprofit sector as a residual one, resulting from failures of government, on the one hand, and the private marketplace, on the other hand. According to these frameworks, nonprofit or-ganizations arise to provide services that the first and second sectors have difficulty in providing. Recently, however, Salamon (1987) has put the shoe on the other foot, specifying a theoretical framework that he calls "voluntary failure." In this view, governmental activity is seen to arise out of the inadequacies of voluntary provision. Presumably, a similar construction could be developed to explain the rise of business enterprise.

This chapter discusses the implications of viewing the non-profit as the first sector in a sense that mirrors Salamon's ideas and that parallels one conception of the historical view. Speci-fically, it argues that the nonprofit sector is the more basic, primary sector, constituting the original medium in which organizations in any given field first develop. In this sense, it is a sort of undifferentiated "primordial organizational soup" that, over time, gives rise to certain specialized forms, such as businesses or governmental entities, that eventually occupy their own sectors. It is further argued that this "evolutionary" perspective calls into question the present public-policy treatment of nonprofit organizations. In short, this view suggests that the nonprofit sector, and its "derivative" sectors of business and government as well, contain within themselves a variety of potential motivations and behaviors. This raises the question of whether the label *nonprofit* is the best way of singling out organizations for preferential policy treatment tied to the provision of public benefits. The particular focus of the discussion will be on "mixed industries" in which similar services can be provided by businesses or government agencies as well as by nonprofits.

Terminology

Before elaborating on the foregoing view, it is useful to distinguish among several concepts to be used below: industries, activities, purposes, motivations, constraints, incentives, and behavior.

An *industry* is a collection of organizations that provide the same general mix of services. Some industries cross sectoral boundaries, and many of these, such as the hospital and day-care industries, involve the nonprofit sector. While some industries—for example, professional associations and religious institutions—may involve nonprofit organizations exclusively, in this chapter we will be concerned mainly with industries, such as hospitals, day-care centers, and theaters, in which nonprofits, businesses, and possibly government agencies coexist in the production of services.

Activities are services provided by industries. Organizations in many industries engage in several (usually interrelated) activities. For example, hospitals sponsor research, teach medical students, and provide treatment for the sick; universities educate and do research; and so on.

Purposes are the normative objectives associated with particular varieties of activity and with sectors within industries. For example, certain hospital activities, such as research and charitable care for the poor, are oriented toward the general public good, while other activities, such as elective surgery, emphasize the generation of private benefits. In present public-policy treatment, nonprofits are expected to emphasize activities with more public-regarding purposes.

Motivations are the personal reasons that energize and drive individuals to participate in organizations and their activities. Motivations can range from greed to artistic achievement to altruism or belief in a good cause (Young, 1983).

Constraints are the structural factors associated with given industries and sectors within industries that restrain the pursuit of particular motivations. For example, in the nonprofit sector, the nondistribution constraint is intended to restrain self-enrichment by those in control of the organization. *Incentives* are the reverse of constraints; they are structural parameters designed to encourage rather than discourage pursuit of certain motivations.

Behavior is the actual pattern of service provision in terms of quality, cost, reliability, and distribution of benefits among alternative recipient groups. Behavior results from the interaction of motivations and constraints or incentives and is reflected in the nature of activities and purposes pursued by organizations in an industry.

Given these distinctions, we can now observe that one characteristic of many of the social science theories that seek to explain the existence of nonprofit organizations is that they tend to slide over the differences between the (normative) purposes of an organization, the motivations of its participants, and the resultant organizational behavior. This gives rise to a largely schizophrenic literature on nonprofits: those who analyze the behavior of nonprofits usually base their models on selfish, utilitarian motivations of participants, while those who try to explain the existence of the sector cite normative purposes and assume a sectoral advantage in promoting virtue. Thus, while James (1983), Niskanen (1971), Pauly and Redisch (1973),

Rose-Ackerman (1987), and others explain nonprofit behavior in terms of maximizing income, power, and status or other utilitarian benefits to managers, Hansmann (1980) reasons that nonprofits exist because they are more trustworthy than profit-making businesses, and Weisbrod (1977) argues that nonprofits accomodate the collective good of groups within communities that do not command a political majority. Salamon too sees nonprofits as public-regarding, but in partnership with government, while Berger and Neuhaus (1977) view nonprofits as public-spirited units that connect the powerless individual to the mega-institutions of the public and business sectors. Clearly, it is on the basis of these latter presumed virtues, related to purpose, that nonprofit organizations are granted special public-policy treatment.

How can the two streams of economic literature—behavioral versus theory of existence—be reconciled? The important concept for doing so is the distinction between the purpose of an organization and the motivations that energize it. The rationales for nonprofits developed by Hansmann (1980), Weisbrod (1977), and Salamon (1987) mainly concern purpose and the advantage of the nonprofit form for pursuing certain purposes. But these theories do not speak directly to motivation or behavior, except for Hansmann's argument that the non-distribution constraint enhances nonprofits' trustworthiness by discouraging self-enrichment. Contributions to the literature on nonprofit organizational behavior, on the other hand, generally assume some singular variety of motivation, usually selfish, and put the burden of behavior control on the constraints built into the nonprofit form.

In the view produced here, it is assumed that the incentives and constraints applying to nonprofit (and other types of) organizations are not fully determining of behavior and that motivations do influence behavior. Moreover, it is insufficient to assume that only a single variety of motivation, either selfish or altruistic, exists within a given sector; rather, each sector will accommodate a *distribution* of participant motivations and behaviors, rather than a singular variety. This argument follows from previous work (Young, 1983) in which it was observed that entrepreneurs within a given industry are driven by a variety of motives that ultimately may manifest themselves in organizational behaviors. Those motivations tend to sort themselves out by sector through a process of matching motives to the norms and opportunities of each sector. However, because this sorting process is imperfect and is based on multidimensional sector characteristics, it yields not only modal differences in motivation between sectors but also substantial intrasector variation. Thus, while the motivational content of sectors may differ "on average," sectoral motivation distributions may also overlap substantially. Hence, it becomes important to examine the range of motivations, as well as the modal type of motivation that may be attracted to organizations in each sector, if we are to obtain a full picture of sector behavior as well as intersector differences.

An Evolutionary Model

In developing the notion of the nonprofit sector as the primary sector (primordial soup) from which alternative types of organizations develop, it is argued here that the nonprofit is the most robust sector in terms of the motivations and behaviors that it may encompass and that the business and government sectors, while more specialized, are also motivationally and behaviorally heterogeneous. It is this intrasectoral heterogeneity that ultimately gives rise to the proposition that renewed scrutiny of differential public-policy treatment of the sectors may be desirable. In order to develop this argument, a nominal scenario is suggested through which an industry evolves and differentiates itself into public, business, and nonprofit sectors.

Basically, there are two stages in the chronological development of an industry. In the first stage, an activity is pursued and organized in nonprofit form. At this stage, the activity is experimental, and it is unclear whether it can be made profitable or whether a large enough coalition would support its provision by government. It remains in the nonprofit sector until these questions become clarified (Mason, 1984). One reason for this is the nonprofit sector's intrinsic flexibility. Nonprofits can avail themselves of a wide spectrum of means of support and a wide variety of constituencies (Mason, 1984); hence, they constitute a flexible vehicle for accomodating diverse purposes. This is part of the reason why the nonprofit is "first" in the evolutionary sense described here. Once activities move to the business or government sectors, they experience environments that are somewhat less flexible and tolerant of alternative purposes and concomitant behaviors.

While it is in this first stage, participants with a wide variety of motivations are drawn to the activity, some for its innovative character per se, some for its potential to promote social good, and some for the potential self-enrichment it may ultimately promise. As the activity progresses in this stage, the motivational mix is liable to become more heterogeneous. In particular, as the public good and profit potentials become clearer, more individuals with motives consistent with these interests will be drawn in, even before those potentialities can be realized. The nonprofit form only loosely constrains those who would enter. All that is required is that participant organizations find some viable group of constituents to support them, whether by grants, donations, volunteer labor, member fees, or the like. Thus, a wide variety of motivations may be accommodated within the nonprofit sector at this stage. And to the extent that it is viable, a range of private purposes and self-enriching behaviors as well as public-serving behaviors may be manifested within the sector, because there is no stringent market or political test for survival.

In stage two, the profit potential or political viability of the activity becomes clarified, making it possible for some organizations engaging in the activity to operate within a business framework or within government. Some proportion of existing providers or some new providers then move to these sectors. In the process of this shifting, some of the motivations contained within the nonprofit sector are siphoned into business or government, for several reasons. Although self-enrichment is feasible within the nonprofit framework, it may be more efficiently pursued in the business sector, where explicit mechanisms of ownership and development of capital are in place. Moreover, there is a signaling phenomenon that occurs. In business, self-enrichment is condoned and encouraged. Individuals move so that their motivations match the prescribed norms. A similar argument applies for shifts of activity into government. While the public purpose is served by nonprofit organizations, it may be more efficiently pursued on a larger scale by government because of the nonprofit sector's free-rider problem (Olson, 1965). In addition, while personal power objectives may also be pursued in nonprofit organizations, the potential for reaching these objectives may be richer in the public sector (Young, 1983). As a result, in stage two, the mix of motivations in the nonprofit sector becomes differentiated from that in business or government, within a given industry.

However, there are a number of reasons why this sorting process does not result in a clean separation of motivations by sector and why the nonprofit sector does not always wither away in the evolutionary process herein described. In particular, the business sector may absorb some altruistic or public-spirited motivations as well as self-enriching ones, while the nonprofit sector may retain some selfish motivations.

Consider the mixture of motivations siphoning off to the business sector. In the first place, individuals themselves may internalize a mixture of motives. Since individuals move as whole beings, they will inevitably bring a mix of motives to whatever sector they work in. Second, activities with alternative purposes often cluster together so that when transitions of activity occur, they are accompanied by mixed motives associated with mixed purposes. For example, even in the business sector, hospitals will support research and teaching, and these activities in turn will maintain participation of some with unselfish motives.

Similar arguments apply to the segment of activities "left behind" in the nonprofit sector. While certain levels of self-seeking motivation will be siphoned away from the nonprofit sector, that sector will not be fully "purified." Again, individual people internalize mixed motives. In addition, there is a certain stickiness or inertia to the process of transition. Unless the benefits are very clear-cut and the entry barriers to business quite low, some self-seeking motivations can be expected to remain within the nonprofit context. Third, there is the possibility of willful exploitation of the nonprofit form; that is, although normative signals and explicit structural mechanisms encourage self-seeking behavior to operate in the business sector, some participants may see opportunities to exploit the weaker accountability structure of the nonprofit sector in order to seek their fortunes. Hence, they choose not to select themselves out of that sector.

In summary, it is argued that as industries evolve from their primordial stage-one form in the nonprofit sector to become differentiated into other sectors at stage two, the motivations within the nonprofit sector remain mixed. Moreover, motivations in the derivative (business or government) sectors are also not singular. While there will be average or modal differences among sectors in their motivational mixes, substantial overlaps in these motivational distributions are also likely.

Finally, note that the foregoing argument does not assume a fixed distribution of motivations in an industry over time or that it is possible to identify, in advance, which emerging activities will be profitable. In stage one, there will be considerable uncertainty about the future of an activity. Thus, the activity will attract pioneers and risk takers of various motivational stripes. Only in stage two will profit potential and public benefits become clear. At this stage, new entrants may bring with them different motivations from those of the pioneers and, as a result, may change the motivational mix of the industry over time. Nonetheless, the motivational mixes by sector will remain heterogeneous for the reasons articulated above.

Thus far, however, we have argued only in terms of motives, not in terms of behavior. If constraints within the sectors are so tight as to preclude the manifestation of alternative behaviors, the above argument would be moot. Because businesses must make a profit from sales to survive, and because government activity must conform roughly to the preferences of a political majority or a controlling coalition, one may question whether the foregoing heterogeneous mixes of motivations within sectors are viable in the long run or make any difference in terms of observed behavior. If one views the business or government sector as highly competitive and admitting only of singular varieties of behavior for survival, then the argument for behavioral heterogeneity in the business or government sector is nullified. However, it seems more realistic to argue that competition in these sectors is *not* generally binding. Rather, the model of managerial discretion within which managers of businesses (Williamson, 1963) or government agencies (Niskanen, 1971) have flexibility in their behavior seems more appropriate in many cases.

For nonprofit organizations, the case for managerial discretion seems even stronger. For example, Rose-Ackerman (1987) argues that substantial differences may exist between the preferences of charity managers and those of donors and that the limited choice among charities provides managers with discretion to follow their own preferences. This argument is reinforced by the fact that there are no clear performance criteria analogous to profit or political support by which donors or trustees can hold nonprofit managers accountable. Moreover, the nonprofit sector has no strong motivational filter of its own. All that is intrinsically required for a nonprofit to survive is that it be able fo find some group of people willing to support its aims, good or bad, selfish or altruistic, and that it satisfy (if it so chooses) some very broad and unevenly policed rules to acquire a charter and official tax-exempt status (Simon, 1987). While there are strong religious, service, community-based, artistic, professional, and other traditions within subsectors of the nonprofit community, no strong overall mechanism limits the nonprofit sector to a particular (virtuous) variety of behavior.

Add to this the now well-appreciated facts that (1) the three sectors are highly intertwined in their relationships and dependent on one another for resources and services (Salamon, 1987) and (2) that as circumstances change, or as "errors" in sector choice are corrected, there are movements of activities from the government and business sectors back into the nonprofit sector that entail the same kinds of inertial tendencies and intermixtures of purposes and motives as movements in the other direction (Legoretta and Young, 1986), and you are certain to reach Jon Van Til's (1988, p. 168) conclusion that the acts of nonprofit organizations are not "necessarily clothed in a special robe of virtue. They are human endeavors, and like the rest of them, require questioning, evaluation, and, at times, even regulation."

In summary, an evolutionary theoretical perspective would characterize the nonprofit as the first sector in the sense of its being more basic and general than business or government. The latter institutions arise as specializations to accommodate certain wealth-seeking and political purposes and tolerate a narrower, but still diverse, set of behaviors than the nonprofit arena from which they derive. The nonprofit sector, on the other hand, is purified of selfish motives in some degree by the divestment of activity into other sectors but nonetheless retains a heterogeneous motivational mix and tolerates a variety of behaviors. Since the special policy treatment of nonprofits is based on an assumption of public-spirited, benevolently motivated behavior by these organizations, the evolutionary view suggests that a fresh look be taken at this policy structure.

Policy

If the nonprofit is really the first sector in the evolutionary sense described, and given the implications of this model that both the nonprofit and other sectors will necessarily embody both selfish and public-regarding motivations and behaviors, then one is led to the conclusion that the present system for policy treatment of nonprofit organizations may be misguided. That is, public policy should encourage and reward publicly beneficial behavior wherever it occurs and should not reward selfish behavior in the guise of virtue.

The present policy system, which may be termed "regulation by structure," grants corporate tax exemptions, tax deductibility of charitable contributions, postal benefits, property tax relief, exclusive rights to provide services or receive contracts under certain governmental programs, and other benefits and subsidies to organizations that assume the nonprofit form. (It also offers certain tax and other benefits that only profit-making businesses can use; however, the focus here will remain the treatment of nonprofits.) The conceptual basis for the present policy structure has two complementary parts. First, it is assumed that the nonprofit form itself limits selfish behavior. In particular, as Hansmann (1980) argues, the nondistribution constraint prohibits those in control of a nonprofit organization from appropriating for themselves the financial surpluses of the organization. However, the nondistribution constraint actually inhibits rather than prohibits. In particular, unless that constraint is intensively policed, which it is not in most cases (Simon, 1987), then it will be possible to circumvent the constraint through various channels, including outright cheating (direct profit taking), inflated salaries, self-dealing in the supply of input materials, supplies, and contracted services, or the provision of services that directly benefit those in control. These possibilities are not worrisome if it can be comfortably assumed that the intents and motives of those who engage in nonprofit activity are pure. However, our evolutionary, first-sector theory suggests otherwise.

Compensation for the "leakiness" of a poorly policed nondistribution constraint and justification for the present policy structure are partially provided by another conceptual pillar of the present system—that of screening and signaling. According to this argument, each of the sectors signals certain values represented by its stated norms and supporting opportunity structures. For business, those norms involve wealth creation and self-enriching behavior; for the nonprofit sector, the norms promote the public good and collective action. Signaling theory suggests that organizational participants will seek the context that most comfortably fits and accommodates their orientations and objectives. Hence, there will be a natural sorting of motivations and behaviors into the different sectors, with the business sector, for example, attracting the income maximizers (Young, 1983). An important adjunct consideration to the signaling model, developed by Hansmann (1980), is that the nonprofit form, because of its normative structure, the consequent screening of motivations that this structure sets in motion, and the presence of the nondistribution constraint, serves as a signal to consumers and contributors. These groups, therefore, put their trust in nonprofits and direct their contributions and patronage to these organizations in circumstances where they cannot directly verify the quality and integrity of services for themselves.

While the signaling argument may be generally valid, it also has its "leaks." In particular, the theory describes where the "modal participant" with a given variety of motivation will choos : to operate; it does not argue that a given sector will capture all motivational elements of a given type. Indeed, the first-sector evolutionary theory considered here suggests that motivational orientation and consequent behaviors will not be cleanly separated by sector. On average, behavioral orientations will differ among the sectors, but there will be substantial variation within sectors. As a consequence, the present policy structure will reward some nonprofits that behave inappropriately while it penalizes some business behavior that may be in the public interest. The extent of this dysfunctional pattern is an empirical question; it depends on the extent of the leaks in the nondistribution constraint and the screening process in practice.

What are the alternatives for future policy? One approach is to keep the status quo. If the leaks are relatively small, then it may be better simply to live with the imperfections of the present system. Examples can be cited of serious abuses by nonprofit organizations (Etzioni and Doty, 1976) and of public-spirited behavior by businesses (McKie, 1974), but how important these phenomena are in quantitative terms cannot be determined.

Another nonradical approach, of course, would be to increase the resources devoted to policing the nonprofit sector so as to reduce the serious leaks. This may be desirable if it turns out that a relatively modest investment in investigative machinery ameliorates a significant proportion of present misbehavior. However, this alternative would fail to address the possibility that businesses are inhibited under the present system from pursuing certain publicly beneficial behaviors.

The evolutionary, first-sector theory essentially argues for a different approach, one that would directly reward public-regarding behavior with tax and other benefits and deny such benefits when such behavior was not forthcoming, regardless of sector—in other words, a "sector-neutral" regulatory policy. But what would such a system look like, is it feasible, and how might it be implemented? Two different conceptual bases might be considered: output regulation and process regulation.

A system of output regulation would essentially grant special benefits to those organizations, regardless of sector, that provide designated public services of appropriate quality, cost, and distribution among those in need. Under such a system, hospitals, day-care centers, schools, arts and cultural organizations, and organizations in other industries deemed to encompass a special public purpose or to be subject to "contract failure" deriving from consumer disadvantage would be eligible for policy benefits, regardless of their sector, if they can convince regulators of their special merit. The problem with this alternative, of course, is that it puts a heavy burden on the regulators, one that, in general, they cannot adequately assume. There are several well-known problems with such regulation. The regulatory system may require an enormous allocation of resources to gather necessary information; in collecting such information, it may become intrusive; and it will be subject to corruption by the regulatees. More fundamentally, however, for the kinds of services in which nonprofits have typically been engaged, adequate regulation of output is made highly problematic by the difficulties of measurement. In particular, the subtle aspects of service quality in such areas as day care, health care, and education are not subject to quantitative specification. As the work of Weisbrod and Schlesinger (1986) on nursing homes demonstrates, organizations bent on self-enrichment will toe the line where performance can be measured but will elude accountability where it cannot.

If "regulation by structure" (the present approach) is unsatisfactory, and if regulation of output does not work, is there another alternative? "Regulation by process" is such a possibility. One reason that people (consumers, donors, grantors, government contractors, and so on) rely on nonprofit organizations and entrust them with the provision of sensitive services is that their decision-making processes and records tend to be more open and accessible than those of the other sectors. Nonprofit day-care centers or nursing homes, for example, are more likely to involve parents or children of the elderly in advisory groups or on their boards and to maintain an open-house policy with respect to visitation. Nonprofit universities and health care organizations more commonly participate in professional peer-review processes, and so on. As Nelson and Krashinsky (1973) have argued, this is an essential reason why the nonprofit alternative may be preferable in many cases. And processes tend to be much easier to specify and to verify than outputs. But note that there is no exclusive link between open processes of decision making and a particular corporate form. Many nonprofit organizations are closed and secretive in their deliberations, while many businesses operate quite openly and encourage the participation of consumer-oriented parties. Is there any reason, therefore, that a for-profit day-care center that opens its books to public scrutiny and opens its program for public inspection should be denied the same policy benefits as are granted to the nonprofit center that does the same? And is there any good reason to grant those policy benefits to the nonprofit nursing home that denies such public access? In principle, there is not, assuming that viable processes can be specified that will provide effective oversight.

Pursuit of a policy of regulation by process rather than regulation by structure would require considerable study, industry by industry. The structure and functioning of governing boards, the specification and roles of advisory committees, the use of peer-review and accreditation systems, codes of ethical practice, the processing of complaints and grievances, and the standards for accounting and publication of financial records and program reports would all have to be examined. Moreover, exclusive structures such as accreditation processes that demand nonprofit status as a prerequisite to participation or approval would require revision. Finally, one would have to ask how resource-intensive the regulatory regime would have to be to ensure that applicant organizations could not fool the regulators by displaying a decision-making process on paper that failed to reflect the underlying reality. (This consideration might be of particular concern to those worried about profit-making businesses engaging in duplicity in order to qualify for public benefits.)

In essence, one would have to ask what processes help ensure a good school, a good day-care center, or a good nursing home. And one would have to recognize that even an acceptably open process of decision making would not guarantee good outcomes in all cases. Thus, some basic constraints on measurable aspects of output are likely to be needed to ensure that the state supports only those organizations that produce outputs that are lawful and consistent with public policy. (For example, organizations that practice racial discrimination should no doubt be precluded from public benefits, no matter how openly the decision to pursue such practice might have been reached.)

In the end, one would likely find that, on the whole, the organizations that are now nonprofit would be best accommodated by a process model of regulation for determining policy benefits. However, one must also be open to the likelihood that some businesses would also qualify, that some organizations presently nonprofit would not, and that an overall net improvement in the systems for delivering essential public services could result.

References

Berger, P., and Neuhaus, J. *To Empower People: The Role of Mediating Structures in Public Policy*. Washington, D.C.: American Enterprise Institute, 1977.

Bremner, R. *American Philanthropy*. Chicago: University of Chicago Press, 1960.

Etzioni, A., and Doty, P. *Profit in Not-for-Profit Institutions*. New York: Center for Policy Research, 1976.

Gamwell, F. I. *Beyond Preference*. Chicago: University of Chicago Press, 1984.

Greene, S. *To Promote Voluntarism*. New York: Association of Junior Leagues, 1977.

Hansmann, H. "The Role of Nonprofit Enterprise." *Yale Law Journal*, 1980, *89*, 835–901.

James, E. "How Nonprofits Grow: A Model." *Journal of Policy Analysis and Management*, 1983, *2* (3), 350–365.

Legoretta, J., and Young, D. R. "Why Organizations Turn Nonprofit: Case Studies." In S. Rose-Ackerman (ed.), *The Economics of Nonprofit Institutions: Studies in Structure and Policy*. New York: Oxford University Press, 1986.

McKie, J. W. (ed.). *Social Responsibility and the Business Predicament*. Washington, D.C.: Brookings Institution, 1974.

Mason, D. E. *Voluntary Nonprofit Enterprise Management*. New York: Plenum Press. 1984.

Nelson, R. R., and Krashinsky, M. "Two Major Issues of Public Policy: Public Subsidy and Organization of Supply." In D. R. Young and R. R. Nelson (eds.), *Public Policy for Day Care of Young Children*. Lexington, Mass.: Heath, 1973.

Niskanen, W. *Bureaucracy and Representative Government*. Chicago: Aldine-Atherton, 1971.

Olson, M. *The Logic of Collective Action*. Cambridge, Mass.: Harvard University Press, 1965.

Pauly, M., and Redisch, M. "The Not-for-Profit Hospital as a Physicians' Cooperative." *American Economic Review, 63* (1), Mar. 1973, pp. 87–100.

Rose-Ackerman, S. "Ideals Versus Dollars: Donors, Charity Managers, and Government Grants." *Journal of Political Economy,* 1987, *95* (4), 810–823.

Salamon, L. M. "Partners in Public Service: The Scope and Theory of Government-Nonprofit Relations." In W. W. Powell (ed.), *The Nonprofit Sector: A Research Handbook*. New Haven, Conn.: Yale University Press, 1987.

Simon, J. G. "The Tax Treatment of Nonprofit Organizations." In W. W. Powell (ed.), *The Nonprofit Sector: A Research Handbook*. New Haven, Conn.: Yale University Press, 1987.

Van Til, J. *Mapping the Third Sector*. New York: Foundation Center, 1988.

Weisbrod, B. (ed.) *The Voluntary Nonprofit Sector: An Economic Analysis*. Lexington, Mass.: Heath, 1977.

Weisbrod, B., and Schlesinger, M. "Public, Private, Nonprofit Ownership and the Response to Asymmetric Information: The Case of Nursing Homes." S. Rose-Ackerman (ed.), *The Economics of Nonprofit Institutions: Studies in Structure and Policy*. New York: Oxford University Press, 1986.

Williamson, O. *The Economics of Discretionary Behavior: Managerial Objectives in the Theory of the Firm*. Englewood Cliffs, N.J.: Prentice Hall, 1963.

Young, D. R. *If Not for Profit, for What?* Lexington, Mass.: Lexington Books, 1983.

PART THREE

△ △ △ △ △ △ △ △ △ △ △ △ △ △ △

Underserved Constituencies That the Sector Needs to Serve

Part Three addresses the traditional functions of nonprofit organizations to serve the poor, underserved, or neglected populations in society. Emanating from the Western religious tradition and cultivated by religious social movements in the nineteenth century, the historical mission of many nonprofits was to care for orphans, widows, the poor or destitute, or those who had inadequate representation under law. The most popular conception of the mission and roles of nonprofit organizations stems from this long tradition. Because it has been long secularized through local and national social welfare programs, social scientists tend to forget that the movement to secure public welfare for people in need can be traced to this long religious tradition of social service and advocacy. The tradition includes a social responsibility to care for those who cannot care for themselves, such as children, as well as to advocate for the rights of those who are not given representation, such as the abolition of slavery. It also includes, particularly in more modern times, the ability of groups to help themselves.

The contributors in this part discuss the role of nonprofit organizations in advocacy, in eradicating poverty and famine, and in engaging in self-help to promote better opportunities. In each of these chapters, the fundamental purposes of philan-

201

thropy and voluntary action are discussed through particular examples. They include questions about advocacy as a fundamental role of nonprofits, the neglected role of the recipient in philanthropy, the ability of individuals to sustain help to people suffering from long-term social problems such as famine or intractable poverty, and the necessity of philanthropy and voluntary action to emerge from mutual self-help. Underlying all these chapters is the question of what philanthropy and voluntary action can do best and what needs to be done by government.

12

ROBERT H. BREMNER

△ △ △ △ △ △ △ △ △ △ △ △ △ △ △

Encouraging Advocacy for the Underserved: The Case of Children

Advocacy is at once a traditional and a controversial function of philanthropy. Advocacy for children, in particular, strikes many people as suspect, since it poses challenges to the authority of both the state and parents and usually calls for heavy expenditures from the public purse. Advocacy, like its counterpart in philanthropy, service, changes over time not only in constituencies but also in objectives and methods. This chapter first comments on the relationship between service and advocacy in modern philanthropy and then focuses on some of the agents and problems of recent advocacy movements for children in the United States and their prospects for the future.

Service and/or Advocacy

The strong opposition expressed by the philanthropic community to the regulations proposed by the Internal Revenue Service in November 1986 to implement the Public Charities Lobbying Act of 1976 demonstrated the importance that charitable organizations of all kinds and diverse points of view attach to advocacy and their resistance to governmental attempts to curtail lobbying and other efforts to influence public policy by nonprofit groups. INDEPENDENT SECTOR, whose roots go back to the Coalition of Concerned Charities, which worked for passage of the 1976 law, has taken a leading part in securing revision of the regulations and also in opposing efforts by the Reagan administration to exclude advocacy organizations from the United Way Combined Federal Campaign.

"By devoting its resources to a particular activity, a charity expresses a view about the manner in which charitable goals can best be achieved." This quotation is from a dissenting opinion by Justice Blackmun in a Supreme Court case involving the constitutionality of Executive Order No. 12404 (February 10, 1984) excluding charities seeking to influence the determination of public policy from the Combined Federal Campaign [*Cornelius* v. *National Association for Advancement of Colored People,* S. Ct. no. 84-312, July 2, 1985 (slip opinion)]. Blackmun argued that "Charities working toward the same broad goal, such as 'improved health,' may have a variety of views about the path to the goal." Service charities, for example, believe that the best approach to "improved health care" is through medical research, public education, detection programs, or direct care of the sick. Advocacy organizations, on the other hand, believe the best way to achieve the goal is "by changing social policy, creating new rights for various groups in society, or enforcing existing rights through litigation, lobbying, and political action" (*Cornelius,* 1985, at p. 20).

The difference between service and advocacy charities is seldom absolute. Health and welfare organizations may elect, as a general rule, to follow either the service or the advocacy path, but circumstances may sometimes make it necessary or advisable for them to take the other path. Two of America's most famous voluntary agencies, the New York Association for the Improvement of the Condition of the Poor and the Charity Organization Society of New York, pioneered not only in the development of casework services but also in compaigns for public health, better housing, and welfare reform; their successor, the Community Service Society of New York, decided in 1971 to end individual and family caseworker services in order to concentrate its resources on community services and social reform. The doctrine that prevention is cheaper and better than cure is so widely accepted in principle, if not always observed in practice, that nearly all health and welfare organizations feel an obligation to advocate preventive action ("building a fence at the top of the cliff") instead of resting content with the thankless tasks of picking up the pieces and clearing the wreckage. Service and advocacy are difficult to separate when a charity offers help to the needy in such a way as to demonstrate its need and feasibility and to rebuke public indifference to the people served. Voluntary effort on behalf of a group such as homeless families seems to lead inevitably from provision of temporary shelters to attempts to compel city, state, and national governments to take more vigorous action.

Are voluntary agencies needed, in view of the great expansion of governmental health and welfare activities? This question, raised in 1961, was to come up repeatedly in the Kennedy-Johnson years as federal programs encroached further on the traditional realms of philanthropy and the "lopsided availability of tax dollars over voluntary dollars" for welfare, education, and health became ever more apparent (Hamlin, 1961, p. 4). Before the decade of the 1960s closed, however, both service and advocacy organizations had proved their usefulness, in different ways, in the American version of a welfare state. In each case, the roles assigned to or assumed by voluntary agencies stemmed from fear and distrust of bureaucracy and big government. Not civil servants but employees of voluntary agencies working under grants from or contracts with government delivered the services made available in new fields and to a broader clientele by new federally funded social programs.

Even before enactment of the new social programs, tax-exempt organizations, whose right to engage in legislative lobbying was until 1976 severely limited by the tax code, began to monitor the enforcement of executive orders, existing laws, and court decisions by public officials. The Southern Regional Council, a foundation-supported equal opportunity organization, led the movement to secure more stringent enforcement of civil rights, desegregation, and antidiscrimination laws. In cooperation with other advocacy groups, the council investigated and reported on the misuse by school districts of funds made available by the federal government for compensatory education of poor children. This study, which led the Department of Health, Education, and Welfare to seek to recapture misused funds and to institute and enforce stricter guidelines and standards, inspired coalitions of advocacy groups to monitor federal performance in housing, employment, civil rights enforcement, and many other areas (Fleming, 1972; Caplin and Timbie, 1975).

"Riding herd on government programs," as Harold C. Fleming (1972, p. 5), former director of the Southern Regional Council, called the monitoring process, was a familiar tactic of some advocacy organizations and, of course, was regularly practiced by business, labor, farm, and professional associations. During and after the 1960s, monitoring became much more common as welfare recipients, consumers, the physically handicapped, the developmentally disabled, and the elderly became conscious of their rights and militant in their demands for observance of them. What they wanted, in most cases, was to have the services authorized by statute provided adequately and appropriately. In 1967, a coalition of women's organizations sponsored a study of the extent to which the school lunch program established in 1946 was meeting, or failing to meet, the needs of poor children. The study, *Their Daily Bread* (Committee on School Lunch Participation, 1968), revealed shocking inadequacies in the coverage, financing, and administration of the program: of fifty million school children, only eighteen million participated in the school lunch program, and fewer than two million were able to get free or reduced-price lunches; the poorer the school district, the less likely its children were to be served. The findings of *Their Daily Bread* were given further publicity in *Hunger, U.S.A.* (Citizen's Board of Inquiry, 1968), the report of a citizens' inquiry group that led to the formation of the Senate Select Committee on Nutrition and Human Needs (Kotz, 1969; Mayer, 1972). For almost a decade after 1968, the select committee held hearings, assembled expert testimony, and worked to improve the coverage of the nation's child nutrition programs.

Since the 1960s, public-interest advocates, drawing on the example and experience of organizations such as the National Association for the Advancement of Colored People Legal Defense and Education Fund and the American Civil Liberties Union, have made wise use of litigation as a means of changing public policy. Like monitoring, this is an instance of the use in the public interest of methods long employed by private interests to modify or overturn social legislation or other measures they oppose. The use of litigation in advocacy has been fostered by the establishment of the federal legal services program to meet the needs of the poor and the development of public-interest law firms supported by philanthropic foundations and the federal government rather than by fees from clients. In a recent examination of test-case litigation for children, Robert M. Mnookin (Mnookin and others, 1985, pp. 7-8) asserts that these new institutions, bringing together reform-minded lawyers, have played an important role in expanding the policy-making activity of courts.

Both the expansion of judicial power and the often controversial activities of public-interest lawyers have come under attack by political and academic critics. From the standpoint of philanthropy, public-interest law is interesting and important because it combines service (legal representation) to clients with advocacy of causes and demonstrates their compatibility.

Advocacy for Children

Americans who read the future in the circumstances of today's children worry about the vast numbers of children under six years of age who belong to families living in poverty (20 to 25 percent of all children, 40 percent of Hispanics, more than 50 percent of blacks), about the more than half a million children in homeless families, and about an undetermined number, estimated at several hundred thousand, of "orphans of the living" in foster homes and are concerned that a very large percentage of babies expected to be born in the next decade will have mothers who are unwed teenagers. These and other circumstances will make it more difficult for families to meet their children's needs without assistance from others; they increase the need for advocacy to protect and promote the children's interests but do not necessarily make the advocates' tasks easier or intrusion or intervention in families more welcome.

Friendly critics fault child advocates for substituting talk for action, being unable to agree on goals, attending to the needs of some groups of children while ignoring those of others, and favoring indirect solutions, such as aid to families, rather than programs with a direct impact on children (Sponseller and Fink, 1982). A less friendly critic, Robert H. Mnookin, points out a "troubling paradox": "children need advocates because in most circumstances, young persons cannot speak for and defend their own interests. And yet, because children often cannot define their own interests, how can the advocate know for certain what those interests are? More fundamentally, how can there be any assurance that the advocate is responsive to the children's interests, and is not simply pressing for the advocate's own vision of those interests, unconstrained by clients?" (Mnookin and others, 1985, p. 24). Moreover, Mnookin argues, except in unusual cases, "value and prediction problems make the best interest of children indeterminate for legislators, administrators, and judges alike" (p. 43).

Mnookin's objections can be raised against advocacy for animals, the environment, historic preservation, endangered species, and the mentally ill and incompetent; advocacy advertising by business; and the comments of spokespeople for or against public policy in many areas of social and economic concern. Legislators, administrators, and judges find it hard to agree on what is in the best interest of the human race, the nation, and, in most cases, adults. Advocates for children have not spoken with one voice or monopolized the floor in debates on children's issues. The victories they have won have been achieved after consideration of alternate proposals and are products of what Justice Holmes called "free trade in ideas" (*Abrams* v. *United States,* 250 U.S. 616 (1919), at p. 630).

In the first six decades of this century, child advocacy organizations worked through state legislatures and Congress for child labor, juvenile court, and compulsory education laws, for the establishment of the United States Children's Bureau, for promotion and protection of child and maternal health, for programs to aid dependent children in their own homes, for expansion and improvement of child welfare services by public and voluntary agencies, for equal educational opportunities for minority children, and for extending health care and education to handicapped children. Since 1960, other advocates, often suspicious of the paternalistic, protective approach of traditional "welfare" advocates, have gone to the federal courts to seek recognition for some of the rights adult citizens enjoy under the Bill of Rights and the due process and other clauses of the Constitution (Kahn, Kamerman, and McGowan, 1972, pp. 30–34; Steinfels, 1982, p. 237; Mnookin and others, 1985, pp. 55–57).

The United States Children's Bureau differed from voluntary child advocacy organizations not only in that it was a government agency but also in its broad mission "to investigate and report . . . upon all matters pertaining to the welfare of children and child life among all classes of our people" (Bremner, Barnard, Hareven, and Mennel, 1971, p. 774). In the 1960s, a half century after its founding in 1912, the Children's Bureau's interest in all children, rather than just in those currently deemed at risk, and its concern for the "whole child"—physical, mental, and social—seemed old-fashioned to administrators accustomed to dealing with specific issues in "problem-solving" ways. An executive order issued in 1969, early in the Nixon administration, dismantled the bureau and consigned it to an inconspicuous place in the federal hierarchy. Except on ceremonial occasions, little has been heard from the bureau since then (Bremner, 1983a).

In 1987, Otis R. Bowen, secretary of health and human services, used the occasion of the seventy-fifth anniversary of the founding of the Children's Bureau to disclaim "a federal monopoly on child-caring and protection." Instead, he saluted the achievements of "grassroots individuals and organizations, professional groups, foundations, and voluntary, private and public child welfare agencies" (Reece, 1987, p. 4). Thirteen people received awards in recognition of their contributions to the well-being of American children. Most of the honorees had been active in the movements for the prevention and treatment of child abuse and improvements in child welfare services, especially adoption and foster care (Reece, 1987).

Child Abuse and Adoption Assistance

Child abuse was rediscovered as a social problem in the early 1960s following a decade of research in pediatric radiology that led physicians, more or less against their wills, to conclude that some children had been assaulted by parents or guardians. The extent of the problem and the shortcomings of existing service for the victims were brought to the attention of the Children's Bureau by Vincent De Francis, formerly with the New York Society for the Prevention of Cruelty to Children, who in 1955 became director of the Children's Division of the American Humane Association. During the 1950s, interest in child abuse increased among social workers and pediatricians, and following publication of "The Battered Child Syndrome" in the *Journal of the American Medical Association* (Kempe and others, 1962), popular magazines ran numerous articles on child abuse. In 1963, the Children's Bureau circulated a model state law encouraging the reporting of physical abuse to physicians; the American Academy of Pediatricians and the Council of State Legislatures proposed other versions. Before the end of the 1960s, all states had adopted legislation encouraging or requiring physicians, teachers, and others involved in child care to report suspected cases of child abuse to public authorities (Nelson, 1984, pp. 2–3, 11–13, 39–44; Steinfels, 1982, p. 229).

In 1974, one hundred years after the founding of the New York Society for the Prevention of Cruelty to Children, President Nixon signed the Child Abuse Prevention and Treatment Act into law. The measure, whose principal sponsor was Senator Walter F. Mondale, authorized funds for research and demonstration projects and for discretionary social service grants to the states. It was intended not to eliminate child abuse but to ameliorate the problem by identifying and assisting programs that seemed worthy of further study and replication (Bremner, 1983a, p. 95).

The limited scope of the law, probably all that was attainable at the time of its enactment, has been criticized for treating child abuse as a form of deviance, correctable by therapeutic measures, and for emphasizing its psychological origins, rather than attacking its roots in social and economic injustice (Nelson, 1984, p. 3). On the other hand, state reporting laws and court decisions dealing with child abuse and neglect have come under attack by advocates of family privacy and autonomy (Steinfels, 1982, p. 229; Johnson, 1986, pp. 272–274). The pendulum of public opinion swings back and forth between concern for battered children and resentment of government intrusion in family matters as newspapers report and communities react to, on the one hand, instances of children being murdered or severely injured by parents and, on the other hand, cases of seemingly unwarranted public intervention in private relations between parents and children (Egan, 1988).

Goodwill and moral outrage are not sufficient to solve the complex problems presented by the 200,000 or more cases of child abuse (now often called maltreatment) and neglect coming before American courts—family, juvenile, probate, and general jurisdiction—each year. Since the National Legal Resource Center for Child Advocacy and Protection of the American Bar Association began work with two attorneys in 1979, it has attempted to help the courts improve their procedures in these cases so as to arrive at more equitable and responsible decisions. The center, whose director, Howard A. Davidson, was among those honored at the Children's Bureau's seventy-fifth anniversary, has published a manual for judges in maltreatment and neglect litigation (Davidson and Horowitz, 1986), as well as publications for bar associations, individual attorneys, and social workers. Much of its work in the field has been supported by the National Center on Child Abuse and Neglect, an agency created by the 1974 Child Abuse Prevention and Treatment Act (National Legal Resource Center for Child Advocacy and Protection, 1981; Davidson and Horowitz, 1986).

In 1978, when Congress renewed and widened the scope of the 1974 law, it added a second title, "Adoption Assistance," which laid the groundwork for anticipated reforms in foster care. Representative George Miller of California, who in 1977 brought the "crisis in foster care" to the attention of Congress, declared that a system intended to provide short-term shelter for children during periods of emergency had become a system of indeterminate long-term placements in which little effort was made either to reunite the child's own family or to find a suitable adoptive home. No one defended the defects that Miller cited or questioned their seriousness, but advocates of foster-care reform, including the Child Welfare League of America and the Children's Defense Fund, differed on the changes to be made, and officials of the Carter administration and members of Congress found it difficult to reach agreement on corrective action. In 1980, however, Congress passed and President Carter signed a comprehensive measure providing for encouragement of adoption of hard-to-place children and mandating reforms in foster-care practices and funding (Steiner, 1981, pp. 145–152; Hardin, 1983; Bremner, 1983b, pp. 95–97).

The Adoption Assistance and Child Welfare Act of 1980 has been hailed as "the most important piece of child welfare legislation enacted in the past twenty years, a blueprint for a new combined effort on the part of the judicial, executive, and legislative branches to preserve families, and if necessary, to build new ones" (National Council of Juvenile and Family Court Judges and others, 1987, p. 7). To date, however, the statute remains for the most part only a blueprint, because during the Reagan administration, neither federal nor state governments made a vigorous effort to enforce its mandates or fund the family counseling and mental health services intended to reduce the need for foster care (Miller, 1987).

National and State Advocacy Organizations

Two organizations whose contributions to children were not recognized at the Children's Bureau anniversary celebration were the National Child Labor Committee and the Children's Defense Fund. The former, one of the nation's oldest extant child advocacy groups (founded in 1904), continues to act as a watchdog over child labor legislation but, since 1946, has given increasing attention to helping young people gain employment and work experience. In 1980, for example, the committee completed a compendium of child labor laws in all fifty states, produced a series of guidebooks for supervisors of youth work programs, and helped found the National Youth Employment

Coalition. It currently promotes improvement in cooperative education programs in high schools and employment and training programs for teenage parents. The National Child Labor Committee, which has long taken an interest in the children of migrant farm workers, helped draft the Migrant Education Act of 1967 and has monitored its administration (Romanofsky, 1978, pp. 456–460; National Child Labor Committee, 1984).

The Children's Defense Fund, organized in 1973 with Marian Wright Edelman as president, grew out of the Washington Research Project, an organization of public-interest lawyers, researchers, and public-policy monitors. In the fund's early years, it took an adversarial stance against government, using research and litigation to show families their rights in dealing with bureaucracy and to point out flaws and inequities in federal-state welfare and education programs. In publications such as *Children Out of School in America, Children in Adult Jails, Children Without Homes,* and *Children Without Health Care,* the Children's Defense Fund (1974, 1976, 1978, 1981) showed the gulf between promise and reality in public provision for poor, minority, and handicapped children. Despite its name, the Children's Defense Fund, like its founder, has been more of a family advocate than a doctrinaire supporter of children's rights. *Children Without Homes,* for example, emphasized the need for services to help troubled families in order to keep as many children as possible out of foster care and restore them to their own homes as quickly as possible.

After the Reagan administration's first round of reductions in appropriations for children's programs, the Children's Defense Fund emerged as a vigorous and effective lobbyist against further cuts. Through a monthly newsletter and an annual *Children's Defense Budget,* it has rallied support for the programs and has kept readers advised of the effect of public policy on families and children. The Children's Defense Fund's analysis of the impact on children of the fiscal year 1988 budget characteristically deals with the extent of poverty among children and the increasing inadequacy of basic wages to meet many families' needs (Children's Defense Fund, 1987; Ross, 1983; Poole, 1987).

In addition to the national organizations, there are state-based advocacy organizations for children in thirty-five states. As a general rule, these organizations do not provide services but undertake social action and policy initiatives for poor, minority, and disabled children. Although the roots of the organizations are in the civil rights movements of the 1950s and 1960s, most of them were founded in the 1970s as a result of concern about children out of school and the movement for deinstitutionalization of status offenders. During the 1970s, with grants from the federal Department of Justice, the organizations investigated the number and treatment of children incarcerated in adult jails. In the early 1980s, child advocates at the state, local, and national levels organized a National Coalition of Advocates for Students, which, with support from eight foundations, studied and reported on changes needed in public schools to meet the needs of poor, handicapped, and minority children (Kahn, Kamerman, and McGowan, 1972; Handler and Zatz, 1982; National Coalition of Advocates for Students, 1985).

The state-based organizations focus attention on "vulnerable children and their families who present themselves to public institutions for assistance"; their primary purpose is "to protect rights and gain entitlements for children." They operate on the "trickle-up" theory of social reform, which holds that changes benefiting poor, minority, and disabled children ultimately help *all* children (Kentucky Youth Advocates and the Massachusetts Advocacy Center, 1987, pp. 15, 93, 96).

Conclusion

Every day, the need for advocacy directed toward improving benefits and services for children at both the federal and the state levels is brought home by accounts of children growing up with little reason to face the future with hope. Continuing advocacy for children on a broad front ranging from day care, foster care, education, health, housing, and welfare is essential to counteract "advocacy advertising" presenting the arguments of business corporations against government regulation and intervention and the ostensibly scholarly and authoritative publications of research centers promoting laissez-faire social policy.

The Committee for Economic Development (1987), in a hard-hitting report, *Children in Need,* has pointed out urgent economic reasons for directing more of the nation's resources to meeting the needs of disadvantaged children: "The nation cannot continue to compete and prosper in the global arena when more than one-fifth of our children live in poverty and a third grow up in ignorance. . . . The nation can ill afford such an egregious waste of human resources. . . . Allowing this to continue will not only impoverish these children, it will impoverish our nation—culturally, politically and economically" (pp. 1, 3).

The recommendations of the Committee for Economic Development in *Children in Need* (investment of more public funds in quality child care and preschool education for disadvantaged children and prenatal care and parental instruction for teenagers), as well as evidence from other sources, suggest that day care and education at all levels will be major areas of activity for child advocates in the near future. Improvements in foster care, including monitoring the administration and enforcement of the Adoption Assistance and Child Welfare Act of 1980, will continue to hold high priority. Child advocates will find wide opportunities for action at the state and local levels. "Although all levels of government must strengthen their commitment to assisting children in need," declares the Committee for Economic Development (1987, pp. ix–x), "federal leadership on this issue is crucial at this time to guide reform efforts and to inspire participation from the varied segments of our national community." One way advocates can help correct the "vacuum of leadership" at the federal level is to work for the restoration of the United States Children's Bureau to its former place of importance and influence in the national government and the counsels of the nation.

Advocacy, whether for children, minorities, the handicapped, the homeless, endangered species, or environmental causes, seeks not only to win new programs and services for its clients but also to ensure that existing ones are fully and properly implemented. Its goals are recognition of clients' rights and fair treatment for all of them by both public and private sectors. For these reasons, advocacy is as vital a part of philanthropic

endeavor as service and deserves no less serious attention by
students of the subject.

References

Abrams v. *United States,* 250 U.S. 616 (1919).

Bremner, R. H. "Children's Bureau." In D. R. Whitnah (ed.),
Government Agencies. Westport, Conn.: Greenwood Press,
1983a.

Bremner, R. H. "Other People's Children." *Journal of Social
History,* 1983b, *16,* 83–103.

Bremner, R. H., Barnard, J., Hareven, T. K., and Mennel,
R. M. (eds.). *Children and Youth in America: A Documentary History.*
Vol. 2. Cambridge, Mass.: Harvard University Press, 1971.

Caplin, M. M., and Timbie, R. E. "Legislative Activities of
Public Charities." *Law and Contemporary Society,* 1975, *39* (4),
183–210.

Children's Defense Fund. *Children Out of School in America.* Washington, D.C.: Children's Defense Fund, 1974.

Children's Defense Fund. *Children in Adult Jails.* Washington,
D.C.: Children's Defense Fund, 1976.

Children's Defense Fund. *Children Without Homes.* Washington,
D.C.: Children's Defense Fund, 1978.

Children's Defense Fund. *Children Without Health Care.* Washington, D.C.: Children's Defense Fund, 1981.

Children's Defense Fund. *A Children's Defense Budget: An Analysis
of the FY 1988 Federal Budget and Children.* Washington, D.C.:
Children's Defense Fund, 1987.

Citizen's Board of Inquiry into Hunger and Malnutrition in
the United States. *Hunger U.S.A.* Boston: Beacon Press, 1968.

Committee for Economic Development, Research and Policy
Committee. *Children In Need.* New York: Committee for
Economic Development, 1987.

Committee on School Lunch Participation. *Their Daily Bread.*
Atlanta: McNelley Rudd, 1968.

Cornelius v. *National Association for the Advancement of Colored People
Legal Defense and Education Fund.* S. Court. No. 84–312, July
2, 1985.

Davidson, H. A., and Horowitz, R. M. (comps.). *Legal Advocacy for Children and Youth: Reforms, Trends, and Contemporary Issues.* Washington, D.C.: American Bar Association, 1986.

Egan, T. "Child Abuse Prompts New Look at Laws." *New York Times,* Jan. 1, 1988, p. 5.

Fleming, H. C. "Riding Herd on Government Programs." *Foundation News,* 1972, *29,* 5–9.

Hamlin, R. H. (ed.). *Voluntary Health and Welfare Agencies in the United States: An Exploratory Study by an ad Hoc Citizens Committee.* New York: Schoolmasters' Press, 1961.

Handler, J., and Zatz, J. (eds.) *Neither Angels nor Thieves: Studies in Deinstitutionalization of Status Offenders.* Washington, D.C.: National Academy Press, 1982.

Hardin, M. (ed.). *Children in the Courts.* Boston: Butterworth, 1983.

Johnson, J. M. "The Changing Concept of Child Abuse." In J. R. Peden and F. R. Glahe (eds.), *The American Family and the State.* San Francisco: Pacific Research Institute for Public Policy, 1986.

Kahn, A. J., Kamerman, S., and McGowan, B. *Child Advocacy: Report of a Baseline Study.* Washington, D.C.: U.S. Children's Bureau, 1972.

Kempe, C. H., and others. "The Battered Child Syndrome." *Journal of the American Medical Association,* July 7, 1962, pp. 17–24.

Kentucky Youth Advocates and the Massachusetts Advocacy Center. *Fairness Is a Kid's Game: A Background Study.* Louisville: Kentucky Youth Advocates, 1987.

Kotz, N. *Let Them Eat Promises: The Politics of Hunger in America.* Englewood Cliffs, N.J.: Prentice-Hall, 1969.

Mayer, J. "Toward a National Nutrition Policy." *Science,* 1972, *176,* 237–241.

Miller, G. "State-Sponsored Child Abuse." *New York Times,* Mar. 24, 1987, p. 27.

Mnookin, R. H., and others. *In the Interest of Children: Advocacy Law Reform and Public Policy.* New York: Freeman, 1985.

National Child Labor Committee. "Working for Youth for Eighty Years." *New Generation,* 1984, *64,* entire Winter issue.

National Coalition of Advocates for Students. *Barriers to Excellence: Our Children at Risk*. Boston: National Coalition of Advocates for Students, 1985.

National Council of Juvenile and Family Court Judges and others. *Making Reasonable Efforts: Steps for Keeping Families Together*. San Francisco: National Center for Youth Law, 1987.

National Legal Resource Center for Child Advocacy and Protection. *Child Abuse and Neglect Litigation: A Manual for Judges*. Washington, D.C.: National Center for Child Abuse and Neglect, U.S. Children's Bureau, 1981.

Nelson, B. J. *Making an Issue of Child Abuse: Political Agenda Setting for Social Problems*. Chicago: University of Chicago Press, 1984.

Poole, W. T. "Children's Defense Fund." *Capital Research Center Profiles*, July 1987, entire issue.

Reece, C. "Children's Bureau 75th Anniversary, 1912–1987." *Children Today*, 1987, *16*, 4–7.

Romanofsky, P. (ed.). *Social Service Organizations*. Vol. 2. Westport, Conn.: Greenwood Press, 1978.

Ross, C. J. "Advocacy Movements in the Century of the Child." In E. F. Zigler and others (eds.), *Children, Families and Government: Perspectives on American Social Policy*. Cambridge, England: Cambridge University Press, 1983.

Sponseller, D. B., and Fink, J. S. "Public Policy Toward Children: Identifying the Problems." *Annals of the American Academy of Political and Social Science*, 1982, *461*, 14–20.

Steiner, G. Y. *The Futility of Family Policy*. Washington, D.C.: Brookings Institution, 1981.

Steinfels, M. O. "Children's Rights, Parental Rights, Family Privacy, and Family Autonomy." In W. Gaylin and R. Macklin (eds.), *Who Speaks for the Child: The Problem of Proxy Consent*. New York: Plenum Press, 1982.

13   SUSAN A. OSTRANDER

△ △ △ △ △ △ △ △ △ △ △ △ △ △ △

The Problem of Poverty and Why Philanthropy Neglects It

Philanthropic giving is often labeled as "charity." For most people "charity" conjures up images of the affluent helping the poor (Jencks, 1987, p. 322). Data on the distribution of philanthropic resources suggests, however, that by far the largest segment of philanthropy does not directly serve, advocate for, or organize the poor. This chapter explores this phenomenon. First, the chapter reviews some of the available information on the topic: what do we know about how much of the philanthropic effort is directed toward poverty? What pressures presently exist for increasing attention to poverty? Next, existing history and theory of the philanthropic sector are applied to help us understand more about why attention to poverty has taken the form it has. Finally, how the alleviation and eventual end of poverty might become a higher priority on the philanthropic agenda is considered.

The major argument here is that the relative neglect of poverty by mainstream philanthropy can be explained in part by how scholars and practitioners have conceptualized philanthropy. The focus is on two issues: first, the conceptualization of relations between philanthropy and the state and politics and, second, the conceptualization of relations between donors and recipients. It is suggested that a shift in philanthropic priorities toward more attention to alleviating and ending poverty in the

United States would be facilitated by a reconceptualization of these relations. This chapter is not a reassertion of a traditional notion of charity that the affluent should simply give *more* to the poor than they presently do. Nor is it a hearkening to Reagan's call for a philanthropy that takes over for the welfare state. It is rather suggesting that a philanthropy that places issues of poverty high on the agenda will necessarily be a very different philanthropy from the one we know.

Current Involvement and Pressures for Increased Effort

Two striking figures stand out from a review of available data on this topic: 30 percent of philanthropic organizations serve a clientele of which the majority are poor, and less than 10 percent of philanthropic giving is directed toward those with less access to resources than the donor. The 10 percent figure is an estimate from IRS data by political economist Russell Roberts, quoted by Christopher Jencks in the recent Yale University Press handbook (Jencks, 1987, p. 322). The 30 percent figure has been widely quoted and comes from the by now well-known research of Lester Salamon and his colleagues at the Urban Institute. It is based on a survey of 3,400 nonprofit organizations, including educational and cultural groups (Salamon, 1987, p. 111). The same study found that half of so-called "charitable" organizations serve a clientele of whom only 10 percent are poor.

Other data seem to confirm these figures as being on track. National Committee for Responsive Philanthropy researcher Scott Piepho reported in a recent paper that "a growing body of research suggests that United Ways are oriented toward serving the mainstream of society at the expense of the disadvantaged and disenfranchised" (Piepho, 1987, p. 1). In his review of who gives what to whom, Jencks (1987, p. 322) concludes that "very few of the contributions are charitable in [the] sense [of giving to the poor]." Pablo Eisenberg (1987) wrote in a recent issue of *Foundation News* that, "while there have been some slight increases in money given to the poor, minorities and other disadvantaged, these constituencies and their grassroots organizations are still getting the crumbs of the philanthropic pie" (p. 52). My own research on voluntary social service agencies suggests that the great majority of clients of Family Service Associations—the largest charitable voluntary organization serving families—are middle-class (Ostrander, 1985). A paper presented at the INDEPENDENT SECTOR Spring Research Forum in 1987, also based on the Urban Institute study, showed—as did my research—that during the early to mid-1980s, services to poor from the nonprofit sector actually declined, in part because of decreased government support (Musselwhite and Salamon, 1987, pp. 369–370; Ostrander, 1989).

The relatively small proportion of the total philanthropic effort directed toward alleviating and ending poverty has led several scholars to suggest that the terms *philanthropy* and *charity* ought to be more carefully delineated, with the term *charity* reserved for only that portion of philanthropy that is specifically aimed at the poor (Jencks, 1987, p. 322). Robert Bremner, author of the definitive history of American philanthropy, made a similar suggestion in his 1977 paper for the Filer Commission (Bremner, 1977, p. 98).

James Joseph, president of the Council on Foundations, recently cited as one of the key trends in philanthropy the "increased pressure . . . to meet needs of the most vulnerable groups" (Joseph, 1986, p. 14). One source of pressure in this direction is a real decline in public assistance at a time when poverty increased, during the late 1970s and early 1980s. Poverty researcher Michael Sosin (1986, p. 19) cites a 22 percent decline in Aid to Families with Dependent Children expenditures during the 1970s (in dollars controlled for the rapid inflation of that decade). We saw, of course, increased pressure from the Reagan government for philanthropy to assume more of the responsibility for serving the poor, taking over for a welfare state that Reagan hoped to severely cripple, if not dismantle entirely. Several authors, including myself, have also cited the growing need for nonprofits to legitimate their activities, to show a public on whom they are dependent for resources—whether governmental or nongovernmental—that what they are doing is worthwhile (Douglas, 1987, p. 49; Ostrander, 1989; Sosin, 1986, p. 22).

Another major factor pressing traditional philanthropy to serve the poor, advocate for them, and organize them for social change is the "donee movement" and the kinds of alternative philanthropic groups coming out of that movement. The leading organization in this movement, the National Committee for Responsive Philanthropy (NCRP), was organized in 1977. The committee concerns itself with what it characterized in the first edition of its newsletter as a "considerable imbalance in philanthropic giving with the overwhelming majority of funds going to traditional organizations . . . and a very small proportion to advocacy organizations" serving the interests of "minorities, women and other economically and politically powerless groups" (National Committee for Responsive Philanthropy, 1978, p. 1). As one of its activities, the committee has been among the leaders of a movement to allow non–United Way alternative funds to deduct voluntary philanthropic contributions from paychecks at the workplace. The alternative funds typically focus their donations on the poor and other marginal groups. A recent booklet published by the National Committee for Responsive Philanthropy (1986a), *Charity Begins at Work,* describes the growing effort to institute alternative funds as payroll deductions.

One group of successful United Way alternative funds is the Black United Funds. The National Black United Fund estimates that only 3 percent of United Way funds go to black-controlled groups (National Committee for Responsive Philanthropy, 1986a, p. 37). There are presently eight cities with a Black United Fund, and $4 million was raised in 1984, mostly from payroll deductions. The Black United Fund initiated the fight to open the Combined Federal Campaign for government workers to non–United Way charities, and former National Black United Fund president James Joseph now heads the Council on Foundations.

In addition to the National Committee for Responsive Philanthropy and the Black United Funds, some thirty-three alternative federated funds and a number of foundations are now organized around principles such as "change, not charity" (National Committee for Responsive Philanthropy, 1986a, p. 42). While some of the monies from these funds go to issues not directly related to poverty, such as the environment and nuclear disarmament, it is likely that a significantly higher proportion of resources go to groups advocating for and with poor and low-income people than is the case with more established philanthropies. A Minnesota Twin Cities study found, for example, that while 25–40 percent of United Way funds there benefited the disadvantaged, the figure for the cities' alternative fund (Cooperating Fund Drive) was 77 percent (National Committee for Responsive Philanthropy, 1986b, p. 4).

At appears, therefore, that there is increasing pressure from a declining welfare state, from a growing problem of poverty, from some voluntary social welfare agencies' need to legitimate their activities, and from increasingly influential donee groups for established philanthropy to turn more of its attention to poverty.

What does the general public think about this issue? Emmett Carson (1987), a researcher with the Joint Center for Political Studies, found that from two-thirds to three-fourths of his sample of both blacks and whites said that the middle class is not doing enough to help the poor (p. 3). When asked what they thought was the single most important problem for private charities to try to solve, about one in ten (9 percent of blacks, 11 percent of whites) said that poverty was the most important (p. 17). A recent Rockefeller Brothers Fund study reports a comparable response to a somewhat different question. When asked what was the main reason they gave to a particular charity, 12 percent (the second-highest number) of respondents said "Helps poor, needy, less fortunate" (Hodgkinson and Weitzman, 1986, p. 23). INDEPENDENT SECTOR reports that nearly 80 percent of people asked agreed that everybody should volunteer to help those less well off, though only about half of those people actually do (Hodgkinson and Weitzman, 1986, p. 7).

Many more people think that caring for the poor is primarily the job of government than think that it is the top philanthropic priority. In Carson's study, twice as many blacks as whites (43 percent versus 24 percent) said that government must assume primary responsibility for the poor (Carson, 1987, p 7). A 1982 Roper poll showed 86 percent of Americans taking this point of view, 50 percent specifying the federal government ("Americans Volunteer," 1982). Joseph (1986, p. 11) states that 77 percent of people think that contributions to private charity

should be higher *and* that government has the basic responsibility
to care for the needy. It has been quite well established that
wealthy people are less likely than those in other income groups
to think that the government should be responsible for services
to the poor. (Joseph, 1986, p. 11).

While the view that government has the major responsibility for the poor might seem to suggest that philanthropy has
less responsibility, this does not seem to be a correct interpretation of these figures, given the real mutual dependence between
government and the voluntary nonprofit sector in social welfare.
This point is discussed further later in this chapter. We will simply
say at this point that there seems to be some support among
the general public for both philanthropy and government to
direct more attention to the issue of poverty.

Private Philanthropy and Poverty: A Cursory Review of History

What can a cursory review of a history well known to scholars
of American philanthropy tell us about why the current proportion of philanthropic effort directed toward poverty is relatively
small? And how can it help us from repeating past mistakes?

The beginning of colonial America's response to those
unable to provide for their own basic needs is based in seven-
teenth-century English poor law. According to Robert Bremner
(1977, p. 95), "All of the English mainland colonies followed
the mother country's example in assigning responsibility for
financing and dispensing poor relief to local authorities. . . .
Before 1820 most communities relied on informal methods [such
as] auctioning off the poor, or arranging for their care by a
private contractor." About the only nongovernmental organizations involved in direct responsibility for the poor at this time
were church-related charities (Katz, 1986, p. 39).

Seeing the failure of local governmental and religious
charitable efforts to help the poor, welfare reformers in the nineteenth century sought to establish "indoor relief" or institu-
tionalized care in public almshouses (Bremner, 1977, p. 96).
Under this plan, government would be responsible for running

institutions for the most desperate poor. Private charity would care for those seen as capable of helping themselves when provided with proper moral uplift. In a dichotomous conceptualization of public and private that continues well into the present, philanthropy and voluntarism came to be seen as superior to government relief. Charity "helped" by seeking self-sufficiency. Public aid "pauperized" by making the poor dependent on others (Bremner, 1977, p. 96; Saveth, 1980, p. 80).

The leaders of private charity formed the Charity Organization Societies (COS) in 1870. These were the precursors to modern organized philanthropy. Their leaders were mostly educated men and a few notable women of the upper classes (Saveth, 1980, p. 82). The Charity Organization Societies did not give material or economic aid. They sought rather to "coordinate, investigate and counsel" in regard to services for the poor (Katz, 1986, p. 75). The Charity Organization Society volunteers (called "friendly visitors") visited the poor in their homes and sought to befriend them and provide moral example, developing a connection between the upper and lower classes based on an assumption of class superiority (Katz, 1986, p. 76; Saveth, 1980, p. 79). The Charity Organization Societies and the men and women who headed them opposed government aid and were successful in eliminating it in at least twelve municipalities (Kramer, 1987, p. 241; Watson, [1922] 1971).

The depressions of 1873 and 1893 proved the downfall of the private Charity Organization Societies (Katz, 1986, p. 82; Huggins, 1971, chap. 6). Despite their failure, they held fast to their methods, continuing to oppose both public relief and the efforts of workers to help themselves through organized labor (Huggins, 1971, p. 154). Early in the twentieth century, one COS leader, Edward T. Devine, confessed failure, saying, "Our use of relief has been most sparing and timid. I am inclined to believe that we have caused more pauperism by our own failure to provide for the necessities of life, for the education and training of children, and for the care and convalescence of the sick, than we have by excessive relief" (Katz, 1986, p. 83).

Despite the failure of the private Charity Organization Societies and local governments to cope with the effects of the late-nineteenth-century economic depressions, efforts to deal with poverty continued to focus almost entirely on these kinds of efforts until the next great depression, in the 1930s. In 1935, the United States established its welfare state with the Social Security Act, well behind most other Western industrialized democracies. The welfare state expanded throughout the 1960s and 1970s, and—though the causes are disputed—poverty rates also declined. By the late 1970s, poverty was again on the rise, and government welfare spending was perceived as being too high. Newly elected president Ronald Reagan promised to cut welfare spending. He also called on private charity to take on responsibility for poverty and posed the old moral agenda. For those who knew the history outlined so briefly here, it was a particularly chilling call.

An alternative history of philanthropy lies in voluntary associations formed by black Americans, beginning with the black benevolent societies of the late eighteenth and early nineteenth centuries. The founding philosophies of the Black United Funds discussed earlier in this chapter emerge out of this history. The focus here was on mutual self-help among equals and self-determination through the creation of voluntary cooperative economic enterprises (Harris, 1979, p. 611). These enterprises were complemented by the educational and literary associations run primarily by black women (Harris, 1979, p. 615). These kinds of organizations tend today to be defined by tax law as noncharitable associations formed for the benefit of members, thus excluding them from our definition of philanthropy (Simon, 1987, p. 69).

The understanding of many leading black Americans that solutions to poverty lie in economics and education as well as moral values and that those solutions need to derive both from peer self-help efforts and from public efforts of government is articulated in a recent influential publication from the Joint Center for Political Studies, which states that currently "more than one third of blacks are trapped in poverty, many with only dim prospects for escape" (Joint Center for Political Studies, 1987, p. 1). The authors articulate a set of principles that moves beyond "polarized debate" about the relative merits of public versus private efforts "that does not clarify the issues" and define "the role of the black community and the role of government in addressing the problems of blacks" (Joint Center for Political Studies, 1987, p. ix).

Out of a history of white upper-class organized charity—distinct from and opposed to public aid, focused on moral solutions to poverty to the exclusion of economic ones, and defined by nonreciprocal giver-recipient relationships of superiority and inferiority—emerged images of private philanthropy that persist to the present day. Though we need to know much more than we do about the history and presence of black philanthropy, we might hypothesize that our current images and theories of philanthropy would be very different if they had been more attentive to this history. Black philanthropy emphasizes material economic help as well as moral standards, and it is based more on mutual cooperation and exchange among peers than on a top-down relationship of charity between class unequals. Black philanthropy also seems to have been more aware of the complementary relation between public and private help.

Images and Theories of Philanthropy and Their Implications for Efforts to Alleviate Poverty

This section argues that persistent mainstream images of philanthropy from political and economic theory are in part responsible for the way in which philanthropy has dealt with poverty. Two major aspects are considered: first, how those views from political theory that dichotomize private philanthropic and public governmental efforts—views in which voluntary philanthropic efforts are implicitly seen as superior to publicly mandated ones—contribute to limiting philanthropic efforts toward poverty and, second, how those economic theories that focus on donor motives perpetuate a nonreciprocal and hierarchical relationship between donors and recipients that is not conducive to or consistent with efforts against poverty. This is followed by a discussion of how philanthropy will need to be reconceptualized if we are to address poverty more effectively.

A dichotomous view of government and the philanthropic sector often implies, whether intentionally or not, a negative view of government. It explains the existence of philanthropy and voluntary nonprofits in terms of carrying out activities that government does not do or does not do well or adequately. Lester Salamon (1987, p. 34) has called this kind of theory "government failure" theory. A prominent political theory sharing certain assumptions with this perspective is the classical liberal pluralist explanation for the voluntary philanthropic sector. Pluralism says that this sector exists to provide a more diverse set of services and to present a wider range of points of view than government provides (Douglas, 1987, p. 47). The implicit, and perhaps unintended, view of voluntary philanthropic activity is that it is superior to government. The nonprofit sector is where people are seen as contributing and doing more and better than they are required to by public mandate.

Several scholars have recently shown that the view of philanthropy and nonprofits as carrying out separate and distinct activities from government is idealized, inaccurate, and incomplete, in terms of both history and the present (Gronbjerg, 1987; Hall, 1987; Salamon, 1987). Nonetheless, the images persist. As social welfare scholar Ralph Kramer (1987, p. 242) summarizes this idealized view, "Government was to provide mass programs for routinized services and to meet economic needs, while voluntary social agencies would experiment, supplement, innovate, and specialize."

It is not difficult to see how this dichotomous image limits the role of philanthropy in regard to poverty. What the poor need most fundamentally is to have basic survival needs met. Meeting the basic needs of people on a daily basis is "routine." It includes substantial attention to economic needs. This view sees both of these direct-service activities as outside of the realm of philanthropy. A reconceptualization of philanthropy that focuses more of our attention on poverty would need to incorporate these activities. This dichotomous view of governmental and philanthropic activity also discourages political advocacy and organizing for social change by private philanthropic groups. Advocacy targeting government is subtly discouraged by such views because government is seen in such negative ways. Political action of any kind is discouraged because philanthropy and charity are defined in such a way as to exclude politics. Others have called attention to this false distinction between philanthropy and politics (Douglas, 1987, p. 51; Jenkins, 1987). A Child Welfare League of America (1981) pamphlet on advocacy suggests that to do direct service without also doing advocacy is rather like rescuing the victims of a bridge collapse without doing anything to repair the bridge. A philanthropy with a priority of alleviating and ending poverty would include political action.

Economists began to pay attention to philanthropic activity only in the 1970s (Phelps, 1975, p. 3). Some have sought to explain the existence of a nonprofit or philanthropic sector by appealing to public-goods theory. This theory argues that nonprofits exist to provide services inadequately supplied by government in what might be called a variation of the "government failure" theory discussed above (Hansmann, 1987). Other economists have focused on donor motives. They have been particularly interested in the Kantian motive for philanthropic activity. In one of the first volumes on the economics of philanthropy, Ireland and Johnson (1970, p. 20) claim this motive as "necessary for philanthropic action." The Kantian motive suggests that "for an individual to commit a good act, he must derive no satisfaction from the end of the act, but do the act only because he attributed the quality of goodness to the act" (p. 21).

Economists are, of course, aware that much philanthropic behavior does not conform to the Kantian motive. Phelps, for example, poses a continuum with altruism as "an investment, a quid with some implicit or conjectured quo," at one pole and "the altruistic act which is an unrequited transfer; the giving provides its own gratification" at the other pole (Phelps, 1975, p. 2). Still, Kantian altruism has been a central point of departure for economic theory, even if used only as a basis for developing alternative motives for donor behavior (Phelps, 1975, p. 7).

What these theories are exclusively concerned with is the philanthropic donor. The recipient is absent from this formulation, and the social relationship between donor and recipient is obscured. Models of philanthropy that focus exclusively on what the donor does or does not want as a condition of giving may divert attention from the recipient's needs and interests. When the focus of attention is on the giver's motives, attention is diverted further from the outcome of giving from the point of view of the recipient. What did the gift actually accomplish in terms of alleviating poverty or working toward social changes that would end poverty? Models of philanthropy that focus exclusively on the donor also perpetuate a nonreciprocal and hierarchical relationship, giving the donor more power and control over what the gift is to be or whether it is given at all and how it is to be used by the donor. The only obvious power the recipient has, according to this model, is to accept or refuse the gift as it is offered. Even the language of ''givers'' and ''receivers'' suggests a one-way relationship in which donees have nothing with which to reciprocate, in which valued goods and services move only in one direction.

This model seems to be at odds with one that would encourage optimal philanthropic efforts to alleviate and end poverty. An effective philanthropy must, as few would dispute, be centrally concerned with meeting the needs of recipients and accomplishing the goals that are set out. A society committed to ending poverty—to creating a nation in which the basic needs of every person are met—is also one in which all people are seen as having a right to control their own lives. Nonreciprocal and hierarchical relationships between donors and recipients are inconsistent with this vision. A reconceptualization of philanthropy that is more consistent with and conducive to alleviating and ending poverty might begin by defining philanthropy as an interactive and reciprocal social relationship between donor and recipient in which the needs of recipients are matched to the interests of donors (Ostrander and Schervish, forthcoming). The final section of this chapter elaborates briefly on this and other reconceptualizations suggested here.

Reconceptualizing Philanthropy: Poverty and Philanthropic Priorities

The historical and theoretical review presented here suggests three broad reconceptualizations of philanthropy that would facilitate a greater focus on alleviating and ending poverty.

We need, first, a view of philanthropy and the nonprofit sector that recognizes the substantial intermingling and interpenetration of the sector with government and that portrays relationships between the two as cooperative and overlapping rather than oppositional and dichotomous. This would encourage philanthropic activity that contributes to meeting the day-to-day basic needs of those who are poor, including their economic needs. The resources of the philanthropic sector are, of course, in no way adequate to this enormous task. The primary responsibility here must be that of government, of a fully developed welfare state. Nonetheless, as poverty researcher Michael Sosin (1986) has shown in his book *Private Benefits,* nongovernmental nonprofit social welfare agencies can and do contribute to the material needs of the poor. Sosin suggests that voluntary agencies can be particularly effective in providing for emergency needs for shelter, food, and clothing, perhaps while clients are awaiting public action (p. 112). Some of the alternative philanthropic organizations discussed earlier in this chapter provide models for how the philanthropic dollar can be directed more toward these kinds of activities.

The second reconceptualization needed is to redefine charity and philanthropy to incorporate political advocacy and organizing for social change. Given the relatively limited resources that are available to philanthropy and the nonprofit sector, probably the most efficient and effective use of these resources is to press institutions in society that have sizable resources to increase their efforts to alleviate and end poverty. While government certainly needs to be the primary target of advocacy and other political action against poverty, the large philanthropic donor organizations, such as the United Way and the major foundations, and the large voluntary social welfare agencies, such as those affiliated with the Family Service Association of America and the Child Welfare League of America, are also appropriate targets. The donee movement discussed here has begun this effort.

The third reconceptualization of philanthropy suggested here is a reconstruction of the relationship between donors and recipients, a democratization of the philanthropic process. This has received relatively little attention in the scholarly literature.

Lester Salamon's "voluntary failure" theory is helpful in initially laying out the undemocratic nature of the current philanthropic process. What he calls "philanthropic paternalism . . . vests most of the influence over the definition of community needs in the hands of those in command of the greatest resources." As a consequence of this influence by those who can and do give at the highest levels, Salamon suggests, "The nature of the philanthropic sector comes to be shaped by the preferences not of the community as a whole, but of its wealthy members. As a consequence, some services favored by the wealthy . . . may be promoted while others desired by the poor are held back" (Salamon, 1987, p. 41).

Salamon's description of how the philanthropic process presently operates supports one of the major points of this chapter. Philanthropy will have great difficulty in effectively addressing issues of poverty until the poor themselves and their representatives—the recipients of philanthropic activity—are at the tables where the decisions are made about where and how to direct the efforts. How philanthropy is organized will need to change. The giving and receiving of philanthropic gifts of money and time will need to be seen as an interactive, reciprocal, and nonhierarchical process of negotiation between donors and recipients. What do poor recipients and the philanthropic groups that work with and for them have to contribute—to bargain with—in a process of negotiation with donors and their representatives? How might the donor-recipient relationship be seen as more mutual, as an exchange of valued goods or services?

Conceptualizing philanthropy in this way requires asking these and other questions to which we do not at present have answers. As a beginning, reconstruction of the relationship between donor and recipient will require an expanded notion of the public interest and the role of philanthropy in promoting it. Some scholars of philanthropy are beginning to define the public interest and public-interest philanthropy not in terms of any specific policy but as expanding the points of view that are represented (Jenkins, 1987, p. 296). This is seen as essential to creating an effective democracy that serves the needs of all who make up the public. A reconstruction of the donor-recipient relationship will also require an image of philanthropy beyond altruism as doing for others. This notion of altruism seems inevitably to dichotomize giver and receiver and to empower the giver at the expense of the receiver. It hearkens a traditional vision of charity that has been largely rejected by contemporary philanthropy, yet an alternative has not really been developed. One alternative to a self-relinquishing altruism is a notion of insurance, a kind of enlightened self-interest that does not assume an impenetrable social barrier between the poor and more affluent socioeconomic classes. One might act philanthropically to protect oneself and those one cares about from becoming poor. One might act to create a society where poverty is not a risk for anyone, including oneself. The validity of this perspective is supported by a University of Michigan study that found large numbers of Americans moving in and out of poverty over time (Duncan, 1984). A reconstruction of the relationship between donor and recipient will also require a strong organized movement of recipient groups, a movement that has already begun.

This chapter has suggested that it is not enough for philanthropy to simply do more to alleviate and end poverty. It has argued rather that to be effective in our efforts, we must also change how we do philanthropy—how we think about it, how we define it, and how philanthropy itself is organized and carried out.

References

American Association of Fund-Raising Counsel. *Giving U.S.A.: Estimates of Philanthropic Giving in 1986 and the Trends That They Show.* New York: AAFRC Trust for Philanthropy, 1987.

"Americans Volunteer: A Profile." *Public Opinion,* Feb.–Mar. 1982, pp. 21–25.

Bremner, R. "Private Philanthropy and Public Needs." In Commission on Private Philanthropy and Public Needs, *Research Papers of the Commission on Private Philanthropy and Public Needs.* Washington, D.C.: U.S. Department of the Treasury, 1977, pp. 89–114.

Carson, E. D. "Black Self-Help and Philanthropy." Unpublished paper, Joint Center for Political Studies, Washington, D.C., 1987.

Child Welfare League of America. *Statement on Child Advocacy.* New York: 1981.

Douglas, J. "Political Theories of Nonprofit Organization." In W. W. Powell (ed.), *The Nonprofit Sector: A Research Handbook.* New Haven, Conn.: Yale University Press, 1987.

Duncan, G. J. *Years of Poverty, Years of Plenty: The Changing Economic Fortunes of American Workers and Families.* Ann Arbor: Institute for Social Research, University of Michigan, 1984.

Eisenberg, P. "In Search of More Responsible Philanthropy." *Foundation News,* Jan.–Feb. 1987, pp. 51–53.

Gronbjerg, K. A. "Private Welfare in the Welfare State." *Social Service Review,* Mar. 1982, pp. 1–26.

Gronbjerg, K. A. "Patterns of Institutional Relations in the Welfare State: Public Mandates and the Nonprofit Sector." In S. A. Ostrander, S. Langton, and J. Van Til (eds.), *Shifting the Debate: Public/Private Sector Relations in the Modern Welfare State.* New Brunswick, N.J.: Transaction Press, 1987.

Hall, P. D. "Abandoning the Rhetoric of Independence: Reflections on the Nonprofit Sector in the Post-Liberal Era." In S. A. Ostrander, S. Langton, and J. Van Til (eds.), *Shifting the Debate: Public/Private Sector Relations in the Modern Welfare State.* New Brunswick, N.J.: Transaction Press, 1987.

Hansmann, H. "Economic Theories of Nonprofit Organizations." In W. W. Powell (ed.), *The Nonprofit Sector: A Research Handbook.* New Haven, Conn.: Yale University Press, 1987.

Harris, R. L., Jr. "Early Black Benevolent Societies, 1780–1830." *Massachusetts Review,* 1979, *20,* 603–625.

Hodgkinson, V. A., and Weitzman, M. S. *The Charitable Behavior of Americans.* Washington, D.C.: INDEPENDENT SECTOR, 1986.

Huggins, N. *Protestants Against Poverty: Boston's Charities, 1870–1900.* Westport, Conn.: Greenwood, 1971.

INDEPENDENT SECTOR. *Daring Goals for a Caring Society.* Washington, D.C.: INDEPENDENT SECTOR Press, 1986.

Ireland, T. R., and Johnson, D. B. *The Economics of Charity.* Blacksburg, Va.: Center for Public Choice, 1970.

Jencks, C. "Who Gives to What." In W. W. Powell (ed.), *The Nonprofit Sector: A Research Handbook.* New Haven, Conn.: Yale University Press, 1987.

Jenkins, J. C. "Nonprofit Organizations and Policy Advocacy." In W. W. Powell (ed.), *The Nonprofit Sector: A Research Handbook*. New Haven, Conn.: Yale University Press, 1987.

Joint Center for Political Studies. *Black Initiative and Governmental Responsibility*. Washington, D.C.: Joint Center for Political Studies, 1987.

Joseph, J. *What Lies Ahead for Philanthropy*. Washington, D.C.: Council on Foundations, 1986.

Katz, M. B. *In the Shadow of the Poorhouse*. New York: Basic Books, 1986.

Kramer, R. "Voluntary Agencies and the Personal Social Services." In W. W. Powell (ed.), *The Nonprofit Sector: A Research Handbook*. New Haven, Conn.: Yale University Press, 1987.

Musselwhite, J. C., Jr., and Salamon, L. M. "Changing Public/Private Roles in the Human Services." Paper presented at the INDEPENDENT SECTOR Spring Research Forum, New York, Mar. 19, 1987.

National Committee for Responsive Philanthropy. *National Committee for Responsive Philanthropy Newsletter*, 1978, *1* (entire issue 1).

National Committee for Responsive Philanthropy. *Charity Begins at Work*. Washington, D.C.: National Committee for Responsive Philanthropy, 1986a.

National Committee for Responsive Philanthropy. *Responsive Philanthropy*. Washington, D.C.: National Committee for Responsive Philanthropy, 1986b.

Ostrander, S. A. "Voluntary Social Welfare Agencies in the United States." *Social Service Review*, 1985, *59*, 434–454.

Ostrander, S. A. "Private Social Services: Obstacles to the Welfare State?" *Nonprofit and Voluntary Sector Quarterly*, 1989, *1* (1).

Ostrander, S. A., and Schervish, P. G. "Giving and Getting: Philanthropy as Social Religion." In J. Van Til (ed.), *Cutting Edge Issues in Philanthropy*. New York: AAFRC Trust, forthcoming.

Phelps, E. S. (ed.). *Altruism, Morality and Economic Theory*. New York: Russell Sage Foundation, 1975.

Piepho, S. *Background Paper*. Washington, D.C.: National Committee for Responsive Philanthropy, 1987.

Salamon, L. "Of Market Failure and Third-Party Government: Toward a Theory of Government-Nonprofit Relations." In S. A. Ostrander, S. Langton, and J. Van Til (eds.), *Shifting the Debate: Public/Private Sector Relations in the Modern Welfare State.* New Brunswick, N.J.: Transaction Press, 1987.

Saveth, E. N. "Patrician Philanthropy in America: The Late Nineteenth and Early Twentieth Centuries." *Social Service Review,* Mar. 1980, pp. 76–91.

Simon, J. G. "The Tax Treatment of Nonprofit Organizations: A Review of Federal and State Policies." In W. W. Powell (ed.), *The Nonprofit Sector: A Research Handbook.* New Haven, Conn.: Yale University Press, 1987.

Sosin, M. *Private Benefits.* Orlando, Fla.: Academic Press, 1986.

Watson, F. D. *The Charity Organization Movement in the United States.* New York, Arno Press, 1971. (Originally published 1922.)

14

JANICE PETROVICH

△ △ △ △ △ △ △ △ △ △ △ △ △ △ △

The Future of Hispanics and Philanthropy

On January 1, 1989, the *Washington Post* declared that Hispanics were "IN" in 1988 ("1988: Who is IN and Who is OUT?," 1989). Although the true meaning of this statement is vague, it is evident that Latinos are receiving much more attention lately. Major publications by the Carnegie Forum on Education and the Economy (Harris and others, 1986), the National Alliance of Business (1987), the National Governors' Association (Center for Policy Research, 1987), the National Education Association (1987), and the Committee for Economic Development (1987), to name just a few, cite the national importance of addressing the needs of Hispanics and other minorities. These reports state that if America does not effectively train the growing minority population, national competitiveness will be negatively affected. A number of Latino organizations are also examining the condition of Latinos in this country with the purpose of pursuing their advocacy function by affecting public policy. However, limited access to resources often restricts the potential effect of these efforts, which are especially important because they represent Hispanics' views of their own needs. All note that the increasing proportion of Hispanics and other minorities in the work force compels the nation's educational system to ensure that these future workers have the skills America needs to compete favorably in the world.

Being "in" or fashionable has paradoxical consequences for Latinos. Organizations want to discuss minority, "at-risk," disadvantaged, and Hispanic populations. Many wish to develop policies to address Latino needs. However, most often Hispanic representation in policy-making bodies is nonexistent, and participation is token. Mainstream nonprofit organizations, foundations, and corporations have few or no Hispanics on their governing bodies or among their senior staff, and more often than not, non-Hispanics define Hispanic needs, develop solutions, and implement the programs.

Recognizing that no lasting improvement in the condition of Hispanics is likely to take place in the absence of a meaningful Latino presence in public policy making, the ASPIRA Association conducted a study to identify the needs and solutions to the problems faced by Latinos in the Northeast (Petrovich, 1987). The study, funded by the NYNEX Foundation, sought to call attention to the critical needs of Hispanics in the region and to assist the government, the independent sector, and the Hispanic community in developing solutions to the problems faced by Latinos. Although the focus of the research is regional, the findings and recommendations appear to be applicable to Hispanic communities around the country. This chapter is based on the results of that research; it focuses on only part of the study: the role of philanthropic institutions in addressing Hispanic needs.

Two issues make this topic particularly significant: the increase in Latino population and the low level of philanthropic support to Hispanic organizations. Nationally, the Hispanic population is growing at a rate five times greater than the white population. It is projected that Latinos will surpass blacks as the largest ethnic minority in the next thirty to forty years. The population of the United States is about 8 percent Hispanic (18.8 million), but research suggests that less that 1 percent of grant funds awarded by foundations go to agencies and projects primarily serving or controlled by Hispanics.

Hispanic Needs

The findings of the ASPIRA study, published in the two-volume report *Northeast Hispanic Needs: A Guide for Action* (Petrovich, 1987), are based on the results of an invitational conference and a survey of more than 400 Latino leaders in five states (Connecticut, Massachusetts, New Jersey, New York, and Rhode Island). The Latino population in these states, estimated to be 2.7 million, is concentrated in large urban areas.

Leaders to be surveyed were identified by reputation or recognition by other Hispanics and included elected and appointed officials, directors of community organizations, educators, and businesspeople. The study included identification and prioritization of needs by state and specific action strategies and recommendations for the public sector, the independent sector, and Latino communities themselves.

Study participants listed more than eighty needs of Latino communities in the Northeast, in areas encompassing education and training, political education and empowerment, health, housing, human services, and community economic development. The following top ten needs were identified:

1. Increase Hispanic school attendance and reduce dropout rates.
2. Increase quality housing for low-income Hispanics.
3. Increase the number of Hispanic voters.
4. Increase the representation of Hispanics in elected and appointed offices.
5. Increase Hispanic representation in administrative and policy-making positions at all levels of the educational system.
6. Promote the development of Hispanic leadership.
7. Increase the availability of training and support programs to facilitate the entry of Hispanic women, youth, and unemployed people into the work force.
8. Improve the delivery of health care in the Hispanic community for all age groups, from prenatal care to gerontology.
9. Increase the Hispanic community's understanding of the political process at the national, state, and local levels.
10. Increase Hispanic representation on housing policy making bodies—planning, zoning, and housing boards.

All of the needs identified were connected by three common themes: *representation, responsiveness,* and *empowerment.*

Representation needs include increasing Latino access to resources, leadership positions, employment, and training opportunities. While expressing a desire for greater levels of representation in the political process and in policy-making bodies, Hispanic leaders also indicated a need to reduce *overrepresentation* among school dropouts, the poor, the unemployed, substance abusers, pregnant teenagers, and AIDS victims.

The second category, *responsiveness,* comprises needs for improving and expanding delivery of social and educational services, effectively combating discrimination, and increasing public awareness of and sensitivity to Hispanic concerns. In short, Latino leaders expressed the opinion that the external social conditions that affect Hispanics should be improved and that the public and private sectors should be more responsive to Hispanic needs.

The third set of needs deals with issues of *empowerment.* With the conviction that knowledge is power, Hispanic leaders indicated that their communities frequently lack information and skills to make decisions such as those concerning their participation in the electoral process or those necessary to secure good jobs. The empowerment category encompasses needs related to the internal conditions of Latinos and their communities, such as developing the leadership skills of Latinos and increasing the involvement of the community in the solution of its own problems.

A Guide for Action

The leaders who participated in the study recognized that the complex nature and wide range of problems confronting Latinos do not lend themselves to simple solutions. There are no quick answers, no ten easy steps for improvement. However, six key principles were identified that can serve as guides for philanthropic institutions in promoting the social and economic advancement of Hispanics in the United States.

Principle One: Focus on Strengthening Self-Help. The Hispanic
communities have many effective organizations and programs
and many skilled individuals. New initiatives should tap these
talents, build on these strengths, and endeavor to transform
the traditional welfare approach to one of skill building and
employment generation. Participants suggested that funders
should recognize that Hispanic community-based organizations
provide highly effective complementary services to schools and
social service agencies—services that other, non-Latino organizations generally are unable to offer. Latino agencies play
a vital role in the Hispanic community. Indeed, investing in
the community's own problem-solving energies is a wise and
cost-effective approach. Hispanic leaders recommend that funders support the efforts of Hispanic community-based organizations by:

- Contributing general operating funds to strengthen their
  infrastructure. Community-based organizations need to
  develop their infrastructures to ensure stability. This requires general support funds, but most funding institutions
  prefer to fund defined projects. While project overhead provides some unrestricted funds, it is too piecemeal and inadequate to promote sustained organizational development
  activities.
- Supporting activities that would improve the ability of community-based organizations to raise funds, such as documenting the effectiveness of their programs or increasing membership.
- Providing both funding and technical-assistance personnel
  for activities that will strengthen the organizations' infrastructures and improve the professionalism of their staffs,
  especially in such areas as budgeting, strategic planning,
  fund raising, and proposal writing.
- Ensuring continuation of nonprogram activities, such as
  public relations, which are essential for public recognition
  of an organization's activities and which, in turn, make the
  organization more attractive to funding sources.

- Assisting with cash-flow problems. There often are funding gaps between the end of a project year and the award letter from a government agency that require organizations to reduce staff and cease all work on a project or go into debt.
- Providing technical assistance through mechanisms such as executives on loan.
- Making in-kind contributions of equipment and supplies.
- Making surplus space available to community organizations.

Principle Two: Emphasize Prevention. Investing in the development of the young has been shown to avoid costly interventions later on. Children derive great benefits from an early start. Programs that motivate and build the self-confidence of Latino youth and programs that ensure adequate health and housing should be supported. Latino leaders urge the philanthropic community to:

- Increase support for programs proved effective for Latinos, especially the youth.
- Help create a greater awareness of the increasing impact of Hispanics as consumers and workers.
- Establish funding of Hispanic initiatives as a priority area.
- Finance the development of creative, culturally relevant day-care programs at employment sites and in local communities.
- Fund training for Hispanic workers, especially women, who are currently offering informal and formal child care so that they are better able to care for Hispanic children.
- Assist in the development of literature and other information sources to aid in evaluating child-care services.
- Provide incentives to employees to work as volunteers and mentors for Latino youth.

Principle Three: Strengthen Latino Leadership. Greater Hispanic representation at all levels of decision making will promote greater responsiveness to Latino needs. Youth should be encouraged and supported in developing their leadership potential. Participants recommend that efforts be made to:

- Increase the number of Hispanic administrators on policy-making and resource-allocation bodies within philanthropic organizations.
- Support organizations that promote community awareness of the importance of participating in the political process and those that promote voter registration.
- Collaborate with community organizations in creating leadership development programs, including internship and mentoring opportunities for Latino adults and youth. Participants agreed that planning for leadership succession and continuity is vital. Staff training and leadership development programs for middle-level managers and other employees of community agencies could help ensure the availability of new leaders in community organizations.
- Create support networks and mentoring opportunities within mainstream organizations to assist in the professional growth of Hispanic employees.

Principle Four: Promote Information Exchange. Disseminating information about successful programs and experiences and about local, regional, and national data on Hispanics stimulates discussion of similarities and differences and encourages better planning to meet Latino needs. Convening Latinos on a regular basis is essential for developing active networks and encouraging articulation and coordination. Leaders indicate that the philanthropic community should:

- Support efforts to regularly convene Latinos for information exchange and planning.
- Disseminate information on corporate and foundation donation patterns to Hispanic organizations.
- Help identify and publicize successful program models that exist in the Hispanic community and models that can be replicated by Latino organizations.

- Disseminate information regarding opportunities for Latinos to provide services and products to large corporations.
- Finance hot lines that will offer bilingual information to Hispanics about emergency services and programs in health, housing, and human services.
- Support research and policy analysis and dissemination from the perspective of culturally and linguistically diverse groups.

Principle Five: Be Holistic and Comprehensive. When dealing with individuals, effective policies and practices should focus on their broad range of needs. Just as programs to improve the educational achievement of children cannot ignore their health and living conditions, improving the condition of Latinos must not be viewed as dependent on the solution of one isolated set of problems. The inherent interrelationship of Latino needs requires comprehensive and integrated efforts. Latino leaders urge the philanthropic community to:

- Support programs that address a broad range of Hispanic needs.
- Promote links between programs serving the needs of Latinos to encourage comprehensive approaches.
- Broaden employee benefit programs to include family health care and day-care plans.

Principle Six: Encourage Collaboration. Hispanic organizations, federal, state, and local governments, private employers, and universities should join in the effort to address Latino needs. Building on the strengths of Hispanic communities, a combination of public and private efforts and resources must tackle the task of addressing emerging and lingering needs of the Latino communities. Participants advise philanthropic organizations to:

- Provide incentives for their own personnel with skills in such areas as budgeting, strategic planning, and fund raising to serve on the boards of directors and advisory boards of community-based organizations.

- Ensure that resources allocated to traditional non-Hispanic organizations are providing services to Hispanics in proportion to their representation in the local population.
- Play a major role in convening community-based groups to develop communitywide plans and strategies. This kind of meeting should take place in a retreat setting, away from the day-to-day pressures of the office. Sufficient time is required to delve into the issues in depth and to develop workable strategies.
- Develop programs to provide small Hispanic businesses with access to training in financial management techniques and credit consultation and advisement.
- Provide challenge grants for projects that involve collaboration between community organizations, private enterprises, and local, state, or national government agencies.
- Seek the counsel of Latino leaders and community spokespeople on how to collaborate in the solution of problems facing the local communities and the nation.
- Develop awareness of the benefits of collaborating with government agencies and community organizations to promote the social, economic, and educational advancement of Latinos. Participants indicated that funding sources should assist Latino communities not only out of a sense of responsibility but also because it is in their best interest to help ensure the progress of tomorrow's workers and consumers. The Hispanic market is growing in importance and its buying power is increasing, yet problems such as the high dropout rate are taxing corporate dollars. Moreover, many of the needs of Latinos—although often more aggravated among them—are shared by the entire population.

Conclusion

Hispanic leaders conclude that there are no quick and easy solutions to the problems faced by Hispanics. Their recommendations outlined in this chapter present key features of effective programs and action strategies. But to remain responsive to emerging needs, local groups must continue to be a major force in efforts to address Latinos' most pressing problems. Harnessing community energy, forming working partnerships, and mobilizing talent and resources require a sustained and concerted effort on the part of community organizations, the independent sector, and local, state, and federal governments. The needs are great, and so must be the joint effort to address them.

References

Center for Policy Research, National Governors' Association. *Making America Work: Productive People, Productive Policies.* Washington, D.C.: National Governors' Association, 1987.

Committee for Economic Development, Research and Policy Committee. *Children in Need: Investment Strategies for the Educationally Disadvantaged.* New York: Committee for Economic Development, 1987.

Cortes, M. *Hispanics and Grantmakers: New Approaches to Growing Hispanic Communities.* San Francisco: Hispanics in Philanthropy, 1987a.

Cortes, M. *Philanthropy and Hispanics: A Research Agenda.* San Francisco: Hispanics in Philanthropy, 1987b.

Council on Foundations. *Hispanics and Grantmakers.* Washington, D.C.: Council on Foundations, 1981.

Facundo, B. *U.S. Foundations' Responsiveness to Puerto Rican Needs and Concerns, Foundation Giving to Puerto Rican Organizations, 1979–1981.* Alexandria, Va.: National Puerto Rican Coalition, 1982.

Harris, L., and others. *The Public Speaks: Redesigning America's Schools.* New York: Carnegie Forum on Education and the Economy, 1986.

Latino Institute. *Strangers in the Philanthropic World: The Limited Latino Share of Chicago Grants.* Chicago: Latino Institute, 1986.

National Alliance of Business. *The Fourth R: Workforce Readiness.* Washington, D.C.: National Alliance of Business, 1987.

National Education Association Executive Committee. *. . . And Justice for All.* Washington, D.C.: National Education Association, 1987.

National Puerto Rican Coalition. *Community Foundations' Support to Puerto Rican Organizations in the United States: An Assessment.* Washington, D.C.: National Puerto Rican Coalition, 1987.

"1988: Who is IN and Who is OUT?" *Washington Post,* Jan. 1, 1989, p. C1.

Petrovich, J. *Northeast Hispanic Needs: A Guide for Action.* 2 vols. Washington, D.C.: ASPIRA Association, 1987.

15

△ △ △ △ △ △ △ △ △ △ △ △ △ △ △

Helping the Underserved Abroad: The Case of Famine Relief

The news report was of famine in Ethiopia. From the first seconds it was clear this was a horror on a monumental scale. The pictures were of people who were so shrunken by starvation that they looked like beings from another planet. . . . The camera wandered amidst them like a mesmerized observer, occasionally dwelling on one person so that he looked directly at me, sitting in my comfortable living room surrounded by the fripperies of modern living which we were pleased to regard as necessities. . . .

Right from the first few seconds it was clear that this was a tragedy which the world had somehow contrived not to notice until it had reached a scale which constituted an international scandal. . . .

The images played and replayed in my mind. What could I do? I could send some money. Of course I could send some money. But that did not seem enough. . . . To expiate yourself truly of any complicity in this evil meant you had to give something of yourself [Geldof, 1986].

This chapter is a commentary on that passage from the autobiography of British rock musician Bob Geldof. Stripped to its essentials, Geldof's experience offers a model of the modern philanthropic mind at work (in my words, now, not his):

- This news affects me, personally.
- These images are unbearable.

- This terrible thing has been going on, and I've been so preoccupied with myself that I didn't even know it was happening. I am comfortable and secure while these people are in agony and near death.
- I can do something about it. I can give money—but giving money isn't enough. I have to become involved.

Bob Geldof is a professional musician. His thoughts carried him along this path of reasoning (again, in my summary):

- Other people are like me. We can work together. We can organize something and use our talent and skills to generate more money than any of us could give individually. We'll use every professional trick we know. We'll work with others who don't feel the same way we do, if we have to. We'll raise money quickly, before Christmas, when people will be more generous. And we'll get the money directly to the people who need it.
- We'll give our talent and our money, and we won't ask anything in return.
- We'll do this with or without permission. This is going to be our show.
- We'll feed those starving people. I will. My friends and I.

The same images that Bob Geldof watched on BBC in October 1984 were later carried by NBC television in the nightly news from New York. The film had been taken by an African, Muhammad Amin, working with narrator Michael Burke, both employed by VisNews on assignment from BBC. Amin had been the catalyst and had managed to win permission from the Ethiopian government to take pictures at the refugee camp at Korem. The report had the same stunning impact in the United States that it had had in England a few hours earlier. The NBC news telephone lines were jammed with calls. By the next morning, there were people lined up outside the offices of international relief agencies waiting to make contributions. Geldof's personal reaction was replicated literally millions of times in the United States and Europe.

Two questions arise immediately: Why was the news so late in coming? Why was the response so great?

The first question is off the mark. There had in fact been news reports of an approaching African famine; the early-warning system had detected the first signs as much as a year earlier (and, on a fragmentary basis, as early as 1982). As relief expert Nan Borton (1983) of International Voluntary Services put it, "It isn't early warning we need; it's early *attention.*"

The NBC executive who was in charge of the London bureau when the BBC report first appeared was Joseph Angotti. His response was professional as well as personal. He responded as Geldof (and Tom Brokaw and millions of others) had responded, but in almost the same moment he made the professional decision that *this* report was different. It was more powerful somehow. Angotti's insistence that Brokaw and his producer in New York look at the film caused them to change their plans for the evening news telecast and include the BBC report.

Why were these pictures different? Why did so many people respond with gifts and other offers of help? No one seems to know. There had been other films of famine in Africa carried by NBC earlier. The photographic subjects at that time were the victims of famine and civil war in Chad. These news reports generated not a single telephone call to NBC news. Is there a lower level of human interest in suffering in Chad than in Ethiopia? Or is the difference in response explicable only on esthetic grounds? (Amin and Burke returned to Ethiopia in 1985 to photograph the camps a year later; those pictures—commissioned by NBC this time—were never used. The professional judgment was that the second film was less powerful than the first. There had been a little rain; there was some green grass in the background.)

Whatever the cause, tends of thousands of contributions flowed into the offices of private voluntary organizations all across the United States (and Canada and western Europe). The initial wave of response caught the organizations off guard. Only four American organizations had relief programs in Ethiopia; within a few months, there were two dozen. News coverage blossomed. *Newsday* had sent a team before the NBC story appeared, and its Pulitzer Prize–winning series by Josh Friedman appeared in November. Well-known public figures began to travel to Ethiopia along with journalists; Senator Edward Kennedy's visits to the refugee camps were covered by *People Magazine*. Bob Geldof organized Band Aid, which recorded a song that became an instant success and inspired the American recording of "We Are the World," which met with similar success here.

Between October 1984 and midsummer 1985, America and Europe were engaged with public and private efforts on a vast scale to relieve the suffering of the estimated fourteen million people at risk in Ethiopia alone. Public enthusiasm overwhelmed the political obstacles: at first, the Mengitsu government in Ethiopia denied that there was a famine, and then it blamed it on the United States. The government of Ethiopia styles itself "Marxist-Leninist," suggesting to some observers that aid of any kind would merely entrench an oppressive regime. The secessionist rebellion in Eritraea in the north was also Marxist, and the long struggle against the regime in Addis Ababa continued unabated despite the famine.

The political dimension became more instrusive when *Reader's Digest* (Brauman, 1986) reported charges by the head of the French medical relief organization Medecins sans Frontieres that relief funds and supplies were being used by the Ethiopian government in its effort to force the relocation of large numbers of people to camps outside the troubled areas of the north.

The position of almost all relief organizations, American and European, was the same: ignore the politics and help the people. If it was necessary to cooperate with the Ethiopian government in order to bring aid to its own starving people, then cooperation was called for. The intricate and sensitive negotiations that made the relief effort possible appear to have been facilitated by the United Nations coordinator in Addis Ababa, working closely with the director of the Ethiopian governmental relief and rehabilitation agency. (The Ethiopian administrator later defected to the United States, adding his voice to the denunciation of the Mengitsu regime.)

The logistical problems of shipping the food, unloading it, reloading it onto trucks, and transporting it to refugee camps and other locations were enormous. According to assessments of relief operations, the Ethiopian government did not interfere with food distribution once it began.

Outsiders often failed to notice or simply brushed aside signs of the Ethiopian government's concern for its dignity and public image. At the very moment when the famine was entering the crisis stage, the Ethiopian government spent more than $100 million for facilities to host the meeting of the Organization of African Unity. At the very moment when news reports appeared about the desperate circumstances in the countryside, the government was trying to present itself to the world as a model of Marxist-Leninist leadership in the Third World. No government is proud of a disaster of such magnitude when its own policies might be part of the cause. In a way, Ethiopia was treated by well-meaning outsiders as unfortunates are usually treated: with little concern for the self-respect of the victim. (Compare the resentment of ''friendly visitors'' to the homes of the poor in nineteenth-century England; compare the condescension shown toward those whose problems seem to be of their own making.)

International relief activity seeks to bring help directly to those in critical need of food, shelter, and medical supplies. In the wake of those first efforts follow steps toward rehabilitation: getting the people out of the camps and back to their homes. That process gradually turns into the third stage: the efforts to change conditions so that the families become self-supporting and better prepared when the next drought occurs. To move through those three stages in the midst of civil disorder and open warfare, attempting to work with a government whose own proposed solutions to its problems seem doomed to failure, is to expect more than is likely to be achieved even under less difficult conditions.

What tentative conclusions might be reached about the political dimensions of the response to the famine?

- Relief efforts are said to have saved the lives of seven million people at risk in Ethiopia. The relief effort was more powerful than the political obstacles, whatever their source.

- Relief efforts are impotent to change things; the Ethiopian people remain victims of their own bad government. No one has a plan to do anything about that.
- The continuation in power of the Ethiopian government, with its apparently unresolvable civil war and its collectivistic agricultural policies, greatly increases the likelihood of the recurrence of the famine.

None of those complications appear in the appeals issued by Geldof, those issued by USA for Africa, or most of the fund-raising literature produced by the private voluntary organizations. News reports carried word of the political conflicts, but even allegations that 100,000 people were the victims of Ethiopian oppression under its relocation and resettlement plans failed to stop the effort to provide assistance. The main thrust of the philanthropic effort was to bring immediate relief to the starving and homeless. Every other complicating issue was brushed aside. The unspoken goal seemed to be: Get food to them. Period.

Geldof said that he wanted to get food to them. He reflected a familiar skepticism about governments of all kinds when he said that he wanted to get the help directly to the people. The image of relief efforts appears to be that of permitting people to starve while bureaucrats make designs of red tape. There appears to be some truth to it: the United States' General Accounting Office reported that there was a delay of five months between the first requests for food aid and the actual delivery of food to the docks in Ethiopia. Geldof and his Band Aid Trust directed their first funds to the purchase of trucks for the delivery of food. Volunteers put a high value on being effective; their goals are precise and simple and immediate, and they have little patience with established procedures. The new actors on the scene showed little respect for the established organizations; they wanted to create their own. They would hold down the costs by enlisting the help of other volunteers; they would get the food directly to the people by negotiating more effectively with the officials along the way; they would target their assistance to high-priority needs, such as trucks; they would deal directly with the people. (Later on, they would make grants to indigenous organizations rather than to international ones.)

The high point of public consciousness was reached with the Live Aid concert simultaneously staged at Wembley Stadium in London and at John F. Kennedy Stadium in Philadelphia on July 13, 1985. The consensus is that the all-day telecast reached the largest audience in history. Estimates of the money raised reached $80 million. (Ireland made the highest per capita contribution.) The U.S. effort added a domestic need to its agenda: USA for Africa would devote part of the funds raised to the needs of the poor in the United States as well as the famine victims in Africa. The European versions remained focused on the African famine. By the time that Hands Across America occurred, the divided agenda was further complicated by competition among the performers. The Hands Across America event was scheduled on the same day as the international run for famine relief, organized by Geldof, that was held in Europe and elsewhere.

Several observations may be in order:

- Coalitions brought together by an emergency do not seem to hold together well over time. Other priorities divide attention and cause conflict.
- A rock promoter in California commented that with an array of performers like that assembled for the Live Aid concert, he could produce an audience of that size *without a famine.* The cause did not generate the audience; the entertainers did.
- Those who made the Ethiopian famine their first priority overlooked the people in need at home. The domestic claims for help are closer and more persistent as well as better organized. The distant problem seemed fated to lose place to the more immediate one.
- No one seems to know whether spectacular benefits recruit new contributors, especially among the young. The young lady who said, at the Live Aid concert, that "It's fun to have fun and do good at the same time" may not make another gift unless she is entertained royally for doing so.
- The most common question among professional fund raisers is whether Live Aid and its long list of imitators have in-

troduced a lasting change in the way funds are raised. The history of Farm Aid, now ended, may indicate that a life span of three or four years is the most that one should expect. (Others did not even succeed the first time.)

Those who were there before the world discovered the Ethiopian famine and who will remain there through the next one are the private voluntary organizations (PVOs). More than a hundred of them belong to the coordinating organization InterAction. From InterAction's self-study, it appears that most PVOs want to be *development* rather than *relief* organizations. They are in the relief business because they have to be—because their contributors want them to be. Only a few PVOs resolutely stay out of the relief field for policy reasons.

PVOs are also in the relief business (most of them) because the U.S. government provides them with large amounts of food supplies, using them as intermediaries in situations where one-to-one government relations are awkward or worse. This is true of religious as well as secular PVOs. Catholic Relief Services, Lutheran World Relief, and Church World Service are leaders among the mainstream religious organizations in the field; Jehovah's Witnesses and the Seventh Day Adventists also have aggressive programs. The new competitors are autonomous organizations; World Vision is the largest and was the most active in Ethiopia until forced to leave.

In Europe, the PVOs are called nongovernmental organizations (NGOs); Oxfam and Medecins sans Frontieres are among the best known. The African famine reached the NGOs as it did the PVOs, but there were eleven NGOs in Ethiopia when the troubles became known worldwide (compared to four PVOs). The Europeans had less trouble with the Ethiopian government, and—according to comments made by the U.S. executive in charge—were more cooperative than were the Americans. Evaluations of PVO and NGO performance in Ethiopia and elsewhere during the famine of 1984–85 fault the Americans for being too caught up in posturing for fund-raising purposes as well as for not working as well together as they should. One central figure, however—Kenneth Hackett of Catholic Charities services—felt that the agencies worked better together in Ethiopia than they had anywhere else during his long experience.

The relief mandate forces PVOs to be where the action is. Some rushed with unseemly haste into Ethiopia. PVOs were often forced to transfer staff from other crisis areas to be able to staff programs in the more visible and better-publicized crisis in Africa. As one PVO administrator said, "Our whole concept of where need is depends on where the cameras are aimed" (Personal correspondence, 1985a). In summary:

- The sense of crisis and emergency and acute suffering seem to be the incentives for philanthropic response that work best.
- Appeals to pity tend to focus almost exclusively on children or on children and their mothers. (There is almost an implication that men should be able to *do* something.)
- There is a low threshold of audience willingness to stay with such images. Audience fatigue comes quickly, and it is followed by donor fatigue.
- The PVO dependence on relief crises to raise money may not work in the long run: "We can't expect to attract donors through guilt and then expect them to get excited about development."
- There is a shortage of experienced relief workers who are trained in handling emergency situations. Few people make their career in relief work.
- On the other side of the desk, too few grant makers, private or public, have a personal knowledge of what goes on in a refugee relief camp or in a village struggling to recover from a famine.

The response to the Ethiopian famine in 1984–85 was a success. Millions of lives were saved. The response to the famine was also a failure; the famine has recurred. As pessimists argued during the first famine, relief efforts only postpone the change that must take place. Bad governments remain in power, their policies continue. Those who pursue military objectives look

upon the sufferings of the innocent as part of the consequences
of the war—and the war is the other party's fault. The war goes
on. People shift their attention to other things: by midsummer
1985, the famine had lost place to the struggle against apartheid
in South Africa. People find themselves able to think of other
things, including more pressing problems. There is a sense that
the intensity of the response to the Ethiopian famine was mis-
placed—why did we think that it was so important?

The famine is back. By late summer 1987, newspapers
carried regular reports and even features about the approach
of famine in Mozambique, Angola, Sudan, and Ethiopia. Government action to make food supplies available was taken early,
but without the intense public pressure brought to bear in 1984.
The public assessment of Ethiopia is mixed with its opinion of
affairs in Africa generally: probably beyond help, possibly
beyond hope.

The first response, that of Bob Geldof and so many of the
rest of us, set records. The relief agencies were pushed to the
limit. Many of them became overcommitted and suffered badly
when contributions faltered and declined by late 1985. None of
the appeals since then has approached the high levels of those
inspired in the eight months between October 1984 and July 1985.

In a seminar on the Ethiopian famine, one of the participants had grown weary of the issue after eighteen months.
''I've come to this decision with regret because I always enjoy
being with you for discussion of any subject. The fact is, however, that I am very busy and I am really not very interested
in Ethiopia, or I should say, I think I've had enough of Ethiopia''
(Personal correspondence, 1985b). Weighed against my friend's
fatigue is the determination of all those people who continue to
work for agencies that bring aid to the suffering wherever they
are. They call on us for help. Sometimes we respond with great
enthusiasm, even generosity. But we cannot be depended on.

If there is a lesson here, it is that one. The weakness of
philanthropy is that it cannot see things through. The challenge
to philanthropy is to find a way to convert the irregular energy
of relief into the sustained dynamic of development.

References

Borton, N. Personal correspondence, 1983.

Brauman, R. "Famine Aid: Were We Duped?" *Reader's Digest,* 1986, *129,* 65–72.

Geldof, B. *Is That It?* New York: Weidenfeld & Nicholson, 1986.

Personal correspondence, 1985a.

Personal correspondence, 1985b.

PART FOUR

△ △ △ △ △ △ △ △ △ △ △ △ △ △ △ △

Managing and Financing
Nonprofit Organizations

The functions and roles of nonprofits came to the forefront in public-policy debate with the major cutbacks in federal funding during the early part of this decade. Part Four focuses on the traditional sources of financial support for nonprofits rather than the new trend toward commercialization. The chapters in this part discuss the fundamental moral issues that concern nonprofit managers, the traditional sources of financing from government and individual giving, and a new proposal for low-interest loans.

The authors examine the limitations on nonprofit organizations that work in the public interest and point out that managers need to be fundamentally concerned with moral practice, not simply honest practice. They review how government-nonprofit partnerships can become effective and efficient and how businesses and foundations can provide low-interest loans to nonprofits engaged in programs to serve the public, loans that will not compete with either business or donations in the form of grants yet will be effective investments. Finally, they offer alternative plans for tax deductions for all contributors to maintain incentives and support for individual giving while not resulting in revenue losses for government. In sum, the contributors to this part provide arguments for the expansion of more traditional sources of funding of nonprofits and offer alternatives to commercial trends.

16

MICHAEL O'NEILL

△ △ △ △ △ △ △ △ △ △ △ △ △ △ △

Responsible Management in the Nonprofit Sector

Like the man who tried to study philosophy but found that humor kept breaking through, Americans sincerely try to practice business and politics as usual but are smitten at regular intervals with an attack of ethics. Now seems such a moment. In politics, Gary Hart, who followed a little too closely the example of John F. Kennedy, is held up for blame. In business, Ivan Boesky and others trudge off to country-club prisons. In religion, Jim Bakker and Jimmy Swaggart earn the scarlet letter. In the movie *Wall Street,* bad guy Gordon Gekko preaches and practices greed, while in *Broadcast News,* good girl Jane Craig refuses to come out and play with the handsome anchorman because he shed an artificial tear on camera. Ethics is bursting out all over.

The study of business ethics alone is clearly a growth industry. A recent bibliography (Bond, 1988) listed more than 2,000 references on the subject. Publications and panels on government ethics abound. Governor Mario Cuomo recently put at the top of his legislative agenda the ethics-in-government issue, always an interesting topic in New York State. But what about the nonprofit sector? Are we once again running a distant third? Don't we have scandals as juicy as their scandals? Doesn't corporate social responsibility also apply to nonprofit corporations? Or is the third sector also the *moral* sector, so that we do not particularly have a problem?

261

While much attention has been given to ethical issues in medicine, education, religion, social work, and other professions represented in the nonprofit sector, there has been a curious silence regarding the ethical characteristics of the sector as a whole. This chapter focuses on one part of that broader question, the ethical dimensions of management in the nonprofit sector. Central to the discussion is the concept of *responsibility,* which has a long and rich tradition in philosophical and religious as well as management literature (as only two examples, see Frankena, 1963, and Niebuhr, 1962). The word itself is etymologically very significant in this context: *responsibility* comes from the Latin verb *spondere,* which means "to promise solemnly, to pledge, to vow." This Latin verb is also the root of the English *spouse.* The word *responsibility* connotes more than an administrative or technical relationship; it suggests some element of the relationship commonly associated with families, friends, clubs, kinship groups, political causes, and religious organizations. The basic argument of this chapter is that "responsibility" exists in all forms of management, that this responsibility has both technical and moral aspects, and that nonprofit management may well include more complex forms of moral responsibility than do other types of management.

It is important to place this discussion in the context of the general literature on management and organizations as well as philosophical and ethical literature on responsibility. Although nonprofits are often seen as a special case because of their frequent ideological, moral, and religious goals, separating them too sharply from other organizations can blind us to the fact that there is a moral dimension of management and organizations *generally.* Far from strengthening the case for management responsibility in the nonprofit sector, treating nonprofits as totally different actually makes the sector weaker. Nonprofit managers do not have moral responsibility primarily because their organizations are religious or humane; they have moral responsibility primarily because they are managers.

Perhaps still the best articulation of this point is Chester Barnard's classic chapter on "The Nature of Executive Responsibility" in his *Functions of the Executive* (Barnard, 1938; see also

Strother, 1976). Barnard, who was the head of a large corporation and was writing primarily though not by any means exclusively about business management, made a remarkable statement about executive leadership: "This general executive process is not intellectual in its important aspect; it is aesthetic and moral" (p. 257). He saw leadership as "the power of individuals to inspire coöperative personal decision by creating faith" (p. 259) and said that leadership had two dimensions: "individual superiority," which is "the technical aspect of leadership" (p. 250), and "responsibility," which is "the capacity . . . of being firmly governed by moral codes" in the presence of strong contrary impulses, desires, or interests (p. 274).

Even in a for-profit organization, cooperative action depends on a complex of "moral" factors, including not only the classical prohibitions against lying, stealing, drunkenness, and adultery (a modern application might be sexual harassment) but also such simple and basic "moral" imperatives as doing something well for the sake of doing it well. "Doing things the 'right' way is a dominant *moral* code in the specialized work of many fine mechanics, musicians, artists, accountants, engineers" (p. 266). Barnard gives the following example: "Mr. A, a citizen of Massachusetts, a member of the Baptist Church, having a father and mother living, and a wife and two children, is an expert machinist employed at a pump station of an important water system. For simplicity's sake, we omit further description. We impute to him several moral codes: Christian ethics, the patriotic code of the citizen, a code of family obligations, a code as an expert machinist, a code derived from the organization engaged in the operation of the water system. . . . He is . . . a very responsible man. It not only takes extraordinary pressure to make him violate any of his codes, but when faced with such pressure he makes great effort to find some solution that is compatible with all of them" (pp. 257–258). Far from being irrelevant to ordinary work, moral codes and responsibility are central to it.

Further, since the chief function of the executive is to inspire and guide cooperative action, understanding the moral aspects of work is essential to the management task. Throughout his book, Barnard argues that certain functions, such as planning and decision making, permeate an organization and that the executive *specializes* in these functions rather than performing them alone. Likewise, moral codes and responsibility permeate an organization. The essence of the executive role, according to Barnard, consists of exercising the function of responsibility. Since, as Barnard argues in his chapter on the nature of authority, the effectiveness of an executive depends critically on the extent to which subordinates accept his or her authority, and since that acceptance and the resultant cooperative action rest on, among other things, a complex set of moral codes, an executive who is unaware of or unresponsive to these moral codes cannot ultimately be effective.

Barnard holds that the leader must not only recognize and respond to but also create morality within an organization: "The distinguishing mark of the executive's responsibility is that it requires not merely conformance to a complex code of morals but also the creation of moral codes for others" (1938, p. 279). This includes building "morale," fostering loyalty, creating conviction, and establishing "the morality of standards of workmanship" (p. 279). This creative function is critical: "the creation of organization morality is the spirit that overcomes the centrifugal forces of individual interests or motives" (p. 283).

In a later paper, Barnard (1958) reflected on the significance of this idea. Discussing the "two leading ideas" of *Functions of the Executive,* he said, "The second idea is that to a large extent management decisions are concerned with moral issues. . . . Recognition of the fact that coöperation among men, through formal organizations of their activities, creates moralities was to me, in 1938, a startling conception" (1958, p. 2). Moralists and theologians did not seem able to apply moral principles realistically to business and government affairs, and business and government leaders could not express the realities they daily managed: "Whenever an attempt was made to apply a moral precept, it semed to me substantially irrelevant; and what seemed to me the essential moral dilemmas of business and public affairs were evidently not contemplated at all" (p. 3). He called for "empirical studies of behavior in business and affairs, of organizations, and of the moralities they create'' (p. 3) and suggested the need for developing a language that would break down some of the communication barriers between the managers and the moralists. Thirty years later, these suggestions still go unheeded.

Other business leaders and theorists have made the same connection between management and morality. Philip Selznick, for instance, wrote: ''The institutional leader . . . *is primarily an expert in the promotion and protection of values''* (Selznick, 1957, p. 28). Thomas Watson, former chair of IBM, said, ''Consider any great organization—one that has lasted over the years—I think you will find that it owes its resiliency, not to its form of organization or administrative skills, but to the power of what we call *beliefs* and the appeal these beliefs have for its people. This, then, is my thesis: I firmly believe that any organization, in order to survive and achieve success, must have a sound set of beliefs on which it premises all its policies and actions'' (Watson, 1963, p. 5).

We instinctively recognize and comprehend this organizational principle in practice. Richard Nixon resigned from the most powerful executive position in the world not for legal or financial or technical reasons but because he had lost moral authority. The nation he led was no longer willing to follow him. He was no longer ''responsible''; he had betrayed the sacred trust. Recent events in all three sectors have given us examples of people whose executive careers came crashing down because they got failing grades in ''responsibility.'' They failed not in the technical but in the moral dimension of leadership. The case of Apple Computer is an especially intriguing one. Steve Jobs had persuaded John Sculley to take the CEO position largely on ''moral'' grounds: the opportunity to change the world by playing a leading role in the societal renaissance of the personal computer movement, as compared with the prospect of selling sugared, colored water (Pepsi-Cola) the rest of his life. Then, with the inexorability of a Greek drama, Jobs himself lost his position because of a failure in moral leadership: arrogance, frequent tirades, and—not insignificantly— treating the Macintosh people better than the Apple II people; that is, not being fair.

Even the Mafia is an organization whose leaders are motivated by responsibility as well as technical proficiency. This was brilliantly illustrated in the film *Godfather II,* in which the young godfather Michael Corleone was so responsible to the Mafia's moral code and to "the family" that he had his own brother murdered. As Barnard noted, "High responsibility there must be even in the lowest, the most immoral, organizations" (Barnard, 1938, pp. 282–283).

The human relations aspects of management theory corroborate Barnard's point about management and morality. The classic and wonderfully funny example is, of course, the experiment at Western Electric's Hawthorne plant, where the experimenters found to their amazement that productivity went up when lighting intensity was increased and then went up *again* when lighting intensity was lowered. Their final conclusion was that productivity had nothing whatever to do with raising or lowering the lights but had everything to with how much the workers were noticed, fussed over, and valued. This conclusion "electrified" the world of management theory and led us out of the darkness of "scientific management" into the light of the "human relations" school. A new definition of management responsibility, a new moral code, had emerged: managers were to attend to the personal goals of the workers as well as to organizational goals. The stated reason was higher productivity, but as Barnard and others saw, the deeper reason was that the moral dimension was central to the administrative role: one could not fully understand either management or organizations without understanding their moral dynamics.

What, then, can one say about management and responsibility in the nonprofit sector? First, managers in the private nonprofit sector must, like all other managers, be aware of and sensitive to the moral codes and responsibility that permeate any organization. They must also "create moralities," create a system of values and beliefs by articulating the chief codes implicit in the organization. They must create a climate that supports the responsible, moral decisions of people within the organization whose cooperative action makes the organization work.

Second, like the musicians and machinists with their moral codes of work quality, nonprofit managers must meet the goals of the organization with efficiency and effectiveness. Sometimes there is a temptation to excuse nonprofits from this basic precept of management. Particularly subject to temptation are smaller nonprofits, heavily "do-good" nonprofits, and nonprofits with strongly religious or moral goals. Many people view such organizations with more leniency than they would a hospital or university or research institute, to say nothing of a trade association or union. But special dispensations are not in order. For all organizations, the basic managerial morality is essentially the same. The manager must make sure that the objectives of the organization are satisfactorily achieved. That is not simply a technical issue; it is an issue of moral responsibility. Morally responsible nonprofit managers are not primarily those who avoid fooling around with the church secretary but those who lead the organization to accomplishing its goals, whether those goals are to provide shelter for the homeless or to make courageous excursions into modern dance. The "promise, pledge, and vow" of responsibility is above all to do well what one is supposed to do as the leader of a particular organization.

It is only when we get beyond this point that management responsibility in the nonprofit sector starts to emerge as a somewhat distinct form. All moral and ethical considerations derive from the characteristics of the realities and relationships being considered. We do not impute an ethical dimension to snowstorms, lightning, or other events in the purely physical world. We impute much less of an ethical dimension to the behavior of small children than we do to the behavior of adults. Even within the adult world, we make ethical distinctions on the basis of knowledge, roles, types of relationships, and the probable effects of actions. Thus, a psychiatrist's work would normally be seen as more open to ethical considerations than the work of a janitor. While there is some overlap between the nonprofit, for-profit, and government sectors with respect to work (psychiatric work being one example), nonprofit organizations are in general more likely than for-profit or government organizations to be involved in work with prominent and complex ethical characteristics: teaching, counseling, healing, preaching, consoling, advocating, caring for the poor, and so on. In this they are significantly different from other service industries, such as fast-food restaurants or auto-insurance companies, different from typical manufacturing industries, and different from many government organizations. There are many exceptions and qualifications that need to be made. The work of some nonprofits (such as organizations to promote birdwatching and many mutual benefit organizations) has no particular relationship to ethical issues, and the work of some government and for-profit organizations (for instance, police work, medical and legal firms) has very important ethical dimensions. Still, there is an observable difference *in general* between the work of the nonprofit sector and the work of the other two sectors. The characteristics of nonprofit work create and shape what Barnard called the moral codes of the organization, and these in turn create the special responsibility that managers of such organizations have. David Mamet's play *Glengarry Glen Ross* dealt with the ethics of a hard-sell real estate office in Chicago. Realtors are probably no more comfortable with this play than ministers are with *Elmer Gantry*, but it hopefully will not be too offensive to realtors to suggest that managing a real estate operation does not demand the same type of moral responsibility that managing a religious institution does. Certainly the reason why the Jim Bakker and Jimmy Swaggart affairs were so shocking or ludicrous, depending on one's point of view, was precisely the fact that these men had freely taken upon themselves a certain level and type of responsibility, that of ordained ministers, television preachers, and managers of large religious organizations. We expect certain things of such people, and rightly so. The mission and work of the organization shape managerial responsibility.

A closely related point is that nonprofit organizations are different from other organizations with respect to the types of paid and unpaid workers in these organizations. Most nonprofit organizations, because of their work, are inhabited largely by professional and quasi-professional staff members and volunteers. Nonprofit employees are on the average significantly more educated and far more likely to be professionals than workers in the other two sectors (Mirvis and Hackett, 1983). The characteristics of workers in the nonprofit field would seem to call for unique types of management responsibility. Barnard (1938, p. 276) noted that different *levels* of management create moral issues of different complexity: "an executive position is exposed to more and more moral conflicts the higher it is, and the process of decision becomes morally and often technically more and more complex." It is similarly reasonable to assume that different *types* of managerial roles—for instance, in organizations with different worker characteristics—would create different moral challenges for managers. The leader of a typical nonprofit organization faces more complex managerial responsibility partly because he or she must lead staff and volunteers who are themselves capable of and daily called on to exercise more complex forms of morally responsible behavior.

Also closely related to the points about nonprofit work and worker characteristics is the matter of organizational mission. One can argue that many nonprofits have missions so directly and intimately involved with ethical, moral, and social purposes that the management of these organizations necessarily demands a more explicit form of responsibility than is the case in other organizations. Advocacy organizations illustrate this point well. As many historians have noted, abolition was the first great secular religious movement in the American experience. Slavery was a burning moral, ethical, and societal issue, one in which the churches were little involved, and when they were, it was usually on the wrong side. The movement was carried by moralists, as was the child welfare movement, the labor movement, the mental health care movement, and the women's suffrage movement, all events of the enormous social creativity of the nineteenth century. The counterparts today are the civil rights movement, the environmental movement, the women's movement, the peace movement, and so on. INDEPENDENT SECTOR president Brian O'Connell has argued that cause organizations are the heart and soul of the nonprofit world, that they more than any other type of nonprofit exemplify the role that the independent sector plays in the society. If this is true, and to the extent that it is true, there is a moral dynamic in the nonprofit sector that keeps moving it toward the ethical, social, and humane aspects of our lives; and if *that* is true, nonprofit management is significantly more likely than for-profit or government management to encounter complex and demanding moral leadership issues emanating from organizational mission.

It is in this context that those concerned with the issue of management ethics in the nonprofit sector have something to learn from, of all people, Milton Friedman (1970). Discussions of social responsibility are particularly vulnerable to the fashions of the moment. Clearly, many of the business and public administration school ethics courses came in response to events such as Watergate, the Vietnam War, the environmental movement, and more recently the Iran-Contra scandal, insider trading, apartheid, and a wealth of happenings in the Reagan administration. But reactions to events and highly visible people will not answer hard questions about ethical behavior in corporations, government, or nonprofit organizations. Those answers will be found only in careful analysis of the essential characteristics and functions of those organizations and their societal context and mandate. Thus, Friedman is at least arguing in the right way, whether or not one agrees with his conclusion, when he says that the only responsibility of the corporation is to make a profit for its stockholders (Friedman, 1970). What he is essentially saying is that a corporation is *not that type of thing,* it is not a reality to which qualities such as responsibility or morality can be meaningfully applied; it makes as much sense to talk about the social responsibility of Mahler's Second Symphony or the Rocky Mountains as to talk about the social responsibility of a corporation.

It also seems clear that the characteristics of the clients served by many nonprofit organizations create special dimensions of responsibility for the managers of these organizations. The primary clients of the for-profit world are adult buyers, most of whom are able to make reasonably intelligent decisions about what they buy. Economic activity among nonadults, though large in absolute terms, is still a relatively minor part of the economy and is indirectly controlled to some extent by adults. The clients of government services are more mixed, since government is much more likely than business to deal extensively

with children and with people of limited faculties. When government does become involved with these more dependent populations (such as children and youth and the physically and mentally handicapped), clearly it has a different type of responsibility
from what it has when it deals with, for instance, taxpayers,
soldiers, and speeding motorists. The nonprofit sector seems
to specialize in providing services to clients who do not have
strong positions in the society: children, young people, women
and minority groups in situations of discrimination, abused
women and children, people with limited legal or political resources, the physically and mentally ill, workers in harmful working conditions, people grieving over loved ones, immigrants,
and so forth. This is not to say that all the clients of the nonprofit sector are in weak positions: many clients of private universities, churches, and mutual benefit organizations are anything
but weak and needy. Nevertheless, it is easily observable that
the nonprofit sector has a far higher percentage of "weak" clients
than does either the business sector or the government sector.
This clearly creates a special type of responsibility for those who
manage and direct these institutions.

At this point, one might wonder, who in his or her right
mind would accept a nonprofit management position, with all
that responsibility? This question suggests a somewhat balancing consideration about management responsibility in the nonprofit sector. One of the principal tasks facing nonprofit theorists
and researchers is the analysis of nonprofit management and
organizations from the point of view of self-interest. It has long
been accepted that "money money money makes the world go
around," at least in the for-profit sector. Nobel laureate James
Buchanan has recently led us to think more about government
officials' behavior as exemplifying the principle of self-interest
first and the public interest second. We need to use the powerful concept of self-interest to examine management behavior in
the nonprofit sector as well. This could enrich nonprofit-sector
theory and research by placing it within broader theories of individual and group behavior and could also delineate more clearly
some of the ethical challenges and problems of the nonprofit
sector. Some of the most truly immoral behavior in the sector

occurs when the legitimate self-interest of people in the sector is ignored. The salaries, benefits, and working conditions of activists and community organizers, for instance, are often appalling; yet their work may be considered some of the most important that goes on in the nonprofit sector. While few people work in the nonprofit sector to get rich, and while ''psychic income'' is certainly an important part of the sector's reality, some advocacy organizations present a stark example of the contrast between the morality of a cause and the legitimate self-interest of workers for that cause.

Applying self-interest theory to the nonprofit sector may be initially unsettling, but we may find that, correctly understood, self-interest actually provides much of the energy that drives the sector. While this point has often been made with regard to wealthy philanthropists and corporate funders, its application is much broader. There may ultimately be little or no contradiction between self-interest and altruistic theories of nonprofit-sector behavior; many studies of ''altruism'' among humans and in the animal and insect kingdoms suggest that altruism and self-interest are less opposites than points on a spectrum, different aspects of the same unity of individual and group behavior. Ironically, complete or extreme altruism is a very poor basis for morality, because it ignores the most fundamental needs of the organism. To paraphrase Aristotle, ''One must eat in order to philosophize.'' Any serious attempt to understand the nature of managerial responsibility in the nonprofit sector must consider not only what the manager owes the organization but also what the organization—and the sector and the society— owe the manager. To go back to the etymology of *responsibility*, we are talking about a pledge, a promise, a moral pact; and the pact goes both ways.

This chapter has argued that (1) any organization and any management process involves ''responsibility,'' the moral dimension of leadership without which any leader is insufficiently effective; (2) nonprofits, because of the somewhat unique characteristics of their work and their workers, seem to present managers with more complex responsibility; (3) nonprofits, because of their relatively unique social, ethical, humane, and religious missions, demand a certain type and level of responsibility from their managers; (4) nonprofits have a significantly higher percentage of relatively "weak" clients than either business or government, with clear consequences for the nature and type of managerial responsibility involved; and (5) nonprofit managerial responsibility cannot be fully understood unless we take into account the managers' legitimate self-interest, as part of a more general inquiry into the application of the principle of self-interest in the nonprofit sector.

More generally and fundamentally, understanding management and responsibility in the nonprofit sector (or any other sector) necessitates analysis of the basic characteristics of the organizations and management roles involved. Morality and responsibility pertain to an organization not to the extent that there have been recent scandals in that organization but to the extent that the nature of the organization demands that such scandals not occur, which is after all why we made such a fuss about the scandals in the first place.

References

Barnard, C. I. *The Functions of the Executive.* Cambridge, Mass.: Harvard University Press, 1938.

Barnard, C. I. "Elementary Conditions of Business Morals." *California Management Review,* 1958, *1* (1), 1–13.

Barnard, C. I. *Organization and Management.* Cambridge, Mass.: Harvard University Press, 1962.

Bond, K. M. *Bibliography of Business Ethics and Business Moral Values.* Omaha, Neb.: K. M. Bond, 1988. (Computer diskette.)

Frankena, W. *Ethics.* Englewood Cliffs, N.J.: Prentice-Hall, 1963.

Friedman, M. "The Social Responsibility of Business Is to Increase Its Profits." *New York Times Magazine,* Sept. 13, 1970, pp. 122–126.

Mirvis, P. H., and Hackett, E. J. "Work and Work Force Characteristics in the Nonprofit Sector." *Monthly Labor Review,* 1983, *106,* 3–12.

Niebuhr, H. R. *The Responsible Self.* New York: Harper & Row, 1962.

Selznick, P. *Leadership in Administration: A Sociological Interpretation.* New York: Harper & Row, 1957.

Strother, G. "The Moral Codes of Executives: A Watergate-Inspired Look at Barnard's Theory of Executive Responsibility." *Academy of Management Review,* 1976, *1* (2), 13–22.

Watson, T. J., Jr. *A Business and Its Beliefs: The Ideas That Helped Build IBM.* New York: McGraw-Hill, 1963.

17 JACK MOSKOWITZ

△ △ △ △ △ △ △ △ △ △ △ △ △ △ △

Increasing Government Support for Nonprofits: Is it Worth the Cost?

In considering its future relationship with federal, state, and local governments, the private nonprofit sector must recognize two important realities: (1) the extent to which carrying out its activities is dependent on government funding, and (2) the fact that the amount of private funds is limited and that, consequently, any substantial growth in services will require more government funds. The evidence is clear. In their study *The Federal Budget and the Nonprofit Sector,* Lester M. Salamon and Alan J. Abramson (1982) found that in 1980 private philanthropic giving totaled $47.7 billion. Of this total, $22.2 billion went to churches, synagogues, mosques, and other religious congregations mostly for sacramental religious purposes, which left $25.5 billion for other types of nonprofit organizations. In that same year these other types of nonprofit organizations had a total expenditure of approximately $116 billion. Of this sum the Federal Government contributed $40 billion.

Salamon and Abramson's findings are supported by a survey conducted by the United Way of America (1987), which showed that more than 41 percent of United Way agencies' income came from government—almost twice the amount that came from the next largest source, fees and dues (21.9 percent), and four times the amount from the agencies' own fund-raising efforts (10.3 percent). United Way agencies provide services to and act as advocates for the poor, minorities, the underprivileged, and the disabled. Many of these agencies receive more than half of their funding from government: day-care centers, 52 percent; drug-abuse agencies, 64 percent; legal aid agencies, 59 percent; mental health agencies, 65 percent; social welfare planning organizations, 71 percent; programs for retarded citizens, 68 percent; settlement housing and neighborhood centers, 51 percent; Urban League affiliates, 56 percent; and women's crisis agencies, 51 percent.

One can draw only one conclusion: without substantial government support, many essential services for those in need would suffer; even given the most optimistic appraisal of private fund-raising efforts, there is no way that the private sector could fully replace government support. Even such efforts as United Way's Second Century Initiative to double resources in five years would fall short. As Salamon and Abramson (1982) point out, the result is an elaborate system of 'government-nonprofit partnership' that takes a variety of different forms and spans virtually every program area.

Yet, if one listened to most spokespeople for the nonprofits, one would never guess the pervasiveness of government involvement in the sector's activities. It is easy to understand the reluctance to trumpet the amount of tax dollars in the system. There is the long history of charities extolling their accomplishments and the belief in the importance of their ability to function efficiently and independently. Also, fund-raising drives obviously are not going to be helped by advertising that a major funder in many cases is Uncle Sam. The accomplishments and promotion of an organization take place in a fund-raising environment where the natural tendency would be to highlight the private effort and downplay government's role. So the growth and success of this effective partnership have been the secret of the agency professionals, their program planners, and those who lobby to maintain or increase funding in Congress, state capitols, county buildings, and city halls.

Unfortunately, the years of suppressing the government funding role and touting private-sector accomplishments created an erroneous impression that, given a chance, the private sector alone could maintain a high level of service. The consequence was a climate in which it was politically easy to make large cuts in federal support for a vast array of programs administered by local nonprofit agencies. Another study by Salamon and Abramson (1986, p. 103) reports that the inflation-adjusted value of federal support to private nonprofit organizations, outside of Medicare and Medicaid, was 28 percent lower in 1986 than it had been in 1980. An example is the cuts made in the Title XX Social Services Block Grant, the major federal source of funds for a wide range of essential social services, such as day care, counseling, homemaker and chore services for older adults, protective and health services, and home-delivered meals and community-based services for the disabled. All of these services are provided by nonprofit agencies. The 1981 Omnibus Budget Reconciliation Act, the key budget-cutting vehicle for the Reagan administration, reduced funding for this program by 20 percent; thereafter, its funding was frozen at 1984 levels until a modest increase was enacted for 1988. The need for these and other services provided primarily by the nonprofit sector is evident. Obviously, this need will not be fully met without more tax dollars.

The questions that nonprofits must face are whether they are willing to openly acknowledge that, although they are in a unique position to deliver quality services, greater government funding will be necessary in order to expand these services and whether they are willing to openly wage a public relations and political battle for increased government funds. The answers to these questions may pose serious political implications that should not be taken lightly. Any attempts to obtain increased funding are sure to be controversial and have some negative impact on fund raising and volunteer involvement. For one thing, they will require a change in the generally noncontroversial nature of many charities, a key departure for organizations that rely on broad support for their endeavors. More tax dollars also mean more regulation and supervision by government, as illustrated by recent attempts on the part of the Office of Management and Budget to require more stringent accounting of nonprofit lobbying activities.

What is needed is a campaign similar to that waged for tax deductions for charitable contributions by nonitemizers. Increased charitable tax incentives, however, had almost unanimous support. Unanimity is sure to be a difficult attainment for budget battles. But, where there is strong public support and the need is evident, consensus is possible. The United Way of America board of governors, for example, supports increased funding for the Social Services Block Grant and elements of welfare reform that would include transitional health care benefits, training and day care for recipients who take jobs, and welfare eligibility for two-parent families. Expanded government–private-sector partnerships could provide greater and more innovative services targeted to those in need. The question for the 1990s is whether the private sector is willing to burden itself with the problems that such partnerships would entail.

The Emergency Food and Shelter Program is a case study of the dramatic potential of government-nonprofit partnerships to help those in need, as well as the problems this partnership brings. Since March 1983, United Way of America and five other national charitable organizations—the American Red Cross, the Council of Jewish Federations, the Salvation Army, Catholic Charities, and the National Council of Churches—have been partners with the federal government in an emergency program to deliver food and shelter services. Under the program, the government designed a distribution system and appropriated money that reached the intended beneficiaries through the charitable organizations involved. This program provided a test of a new system and partnership with private charities. Clearly, Congress feels that it succeeded. It has appropriated money for the program each year since; in its 1987 session, Congress authorized $125 million for the program.

With hindsight, it is easy to see how this unprecedented partnership program came into existence. During the winter of 1982, for political as well as humanitarian reasons, members of Congress were seeking ways to deal with the increasing needs of a larger and larger number of people. With unemployment figures greater than 10 percent, the news media were reporting thousands of people applying for every job opening. From every part of America came stories about people who had never been without a paycheck suddenly having to deal with finding services that could help them keep their homes, feed their children, and pay their medical bills when insurance ran out. At the same time, President Reagan was sounding the theme of voluntarism, of Americans helping each other, as a way to solve social problems. The federal government should not be the answer to all needs, he said. Instead, there should be a return to the time when people looked to one another for help. In March 1983, a combination of these factors led Congress to create a federally funded program that would be administered by charitable organizations to help alleviate emergency demands for food and shelter.

The idea of federal funds being handed over for private distribution was a relatively new one. It had been tried only once before, in 1980, when the government collected a windfall profits tax from energy companies because they had overcharged American consumers. The Carter administration had decided to allocate this money to private charities to help people who could not pay their utility bills. The sum was small and quickly distributed. Remembering the success of this experience, the House Democratic leadership returned to this delivery system in putting together a bill that addressed unemployment and other social problems. However, the new program involved a much larger amount of money than the previous one and focused on the mechanism by which an immediate need could be met, rather than the best way of carrying out a legal obligation. The final bill, passed in March 1983, created the Emergency Food and Shelter Program, with a provision for $100 million to be distributed through two channels: half through an often-used service delivery approach, by which the states would allocate the funds through distribution systems of their own design, and the other half through a new design for delivering federal funds, whereby the federal government would provide the money but a national board made up of private and nonprofit organizations would decide how to spend it.

Congress had purposely left it to this national board to decide how to distribute the funds, largely because of the strong political pressures that would be exerted on Congress if it allocated the funds itself. But this surrender of government control over federally provided funds created some concern that the funds would not reach their intended goal quickly and equitably. In response to this concern, Congress decided to include a federal representative, the Federal Emergency Management Agency (FEMA), on the national board. FEMA convened and chaired the board, which also included the United Way of America, the American Red Cross, the Salvation Army, the National Conference of Catholic Charities, the National Council of Churches, and the Council of Jewish Welfare Federations. These organizations had worked with Congress in designing this delivery system and promised that their expertise and resources would result in a speedy and fair delivery of the federal funds to people in need.

FEMA had never been involved in a program like this before, and the nonprofit organizations had never jointly administered a program of this magnitude. But the members of the board had the flexibility and vision to realize that they could all help each other in organizing the program. The strength of the committee process is that shared resources are greater than those of any one individual. The weakness of the process is the tendency to bog down in detail. Perhaps because of its deadline and perhaps because of its particular mission, the board functioned close to ideally. It became immediately clear to FEMA that the charitable organizations did have valuable expertise in the details of delivering human services. It became clear to the charitable organizations that FEMA was invaluable in helping anticipate the problems of administering a federal program.

Under the terms of the legislation, by April 23, 1983, FEMA was to release the $50 million allocation to United Way of America, which had been chosen as the board's fiscal agent and secretariat. The customary pattern for federal grants is that the funds are released in a letter of credit, which the recipient can draw on as the need arises. This process enables the federal government to continue to receive interest on the unspent part of the grant. In this case, however, because of the character of the grant, the charitable organizations were able to persuade

FEMA to take an unusual step. FEMA released the full $50 million, in two installments, to United Way of America; with the interest raised on these funds, the final amount distributed by the program for emergency food and shelter was $50,776,532.

The experience of the program confirmed the idea that private charities, unfettered by political considerations, would be better able than government agencies to allocate funds on a needs basis. In an attempt to ensure that their states would get a fair share of the appropriations for jobs, senators and representatives from the high-unemployment midwestern states had included an allocation formula in the jobs portion of the bill weighted toward their states. But when senators Carl Levin of Michigan and Arlen Specter of Pennsylvania examined the program's progress, they found that the formula developed by the board was much more effectively targeted than that devised by Congress. Under the board's plan, communities receiving funds set up local boards made up of local government officials, nonprofit organizations, and others in the community familiar with emergency food and shelter distribution. These local boards were given two weeks in which to plan their allocations to the agencies in their communities. The money was appropriated in March; by the end of May, the first checks were being distributed to the agencies providing food and shelter. By the end of September, 80% of the nonprofit funding had been spent. The state program, however, was not as successful. By the end of the fiscal year, the states had distributed only a small amount of the funds allocated directly to them. In the next year's appropriations, therefore, Congress dropped the state program and provided only for the nonprofit program.

The Emergency Food and Shelter Program was by no means meant to solve the problem of the homeless; it was meant to meet an emergency situation. And it did help many people in need. But although the purpose of the program was to feed and shelter the needy, in the long run this may have been one of its most transitory benefits. Everyone involved in the program learned that the federal government can play an effective role in successfully addressing community problems. Most important of all were the alliances and relationships built up among charitable organizations and between those organizations and local elected officials. In one case, for example, the government of a city involved in the program asked the local board to continue to serve in order to help deal with other community needs. Members of the national board, too, received a valuable education in how private and public organizations can work together.

Of course, the program was not an unqualified success. When the Emergency Food and Shelter program was originally proposed, many in the nonprofit sector were concerned that the program would take on the look of a bureaucratic public welfare agency. In large part, they were right. The program is now highly organized, has a staff of its own, and functions much like any other bureaucratic organization. A major problem has been the restrictions imposed on the amounts that the nonprofits involved could use to cover the costs of administering the program. Congress and the nonprofits had initially agreed to a low (2 percent) allowance for administrative costs (most other programs of this type have administrative costs of 10 percent or higher). In fact, at the outset, United Way of America, acting as fiscal agent for the board, waived reimbursement for considerable costs, as did many provider agencies. As the program progressed, however, the low cost allowance caused severe strains on agency personnel and resources. The agencies involved undertook a low-key, almost embarrassed lobbying effort for authorizing legislation to raise the cost cap to 5 percent for 1988. The new appropriation, however, raised the provision to only 3.5 percent. The agencies were reluctant to press for more costs; they felt that such lobbying was unseemly.

Another problem confronting the program is the legal status of the national and local boards that administer and distribute government funds. In this case, the Justice Department issued an opinion that, under the appointments and establishment clauses of the First Amendment to the Constitution, the board is vested with a significant governmental duty, and that its members must therefore be officers of the United States. The opinion also stated that, because of the participation of religious groups, the program may entail unconstitutional government involvement with religion. President Reagan noted this problem when he signed the legislation authorizing appropriations for the Emergency Food and Shelter Program, stating, "in order to void this constitutional infirmity I direct the director of FEMA to construe this provision as granting him complete discretionary authority to determine who should be appointed to the national board." As a result, the board members have been required to take an oath and file conflict-of-interest statements as would any other federal employees—a requirement that has rightfully made the participants uncomfortable. In addition, the director of FEMA could change the membership or size of the board or impose other restrictions that could be detrimental to the agencies. These requirements have subtly altered the relationship between FEMA and the charitable members of the board.

In spite of these drawbacks, the nonprofit-government partnership structure of the Emergency Food and Shelter Program is a model for success. There is no practical reason why such a structure could not be used to provide summer-camp experiences for underprivileged youth, job training, and literacy programs. But if the program is to be expanded and the nonprofit sector is to promote more experimental program partnerships with government, a number of hurdles will have to be overcome. Such participation tends to run against the grain of long-held philosophies and may be seen to infringe on the nonprofit sector's independence. The sector must recognize that a visible, intense lobbying effort will be required to maintain and keep the programs going. The essential constitutional questions are going to have to be dealt with and solved. The question of government involvement with religion has been raised not only in regard to this program but also in regard to other programs for the homeless and programs concerned with senior citizens' housing and community meals. New structures may be required to ensure that there is a separation of church and state while still permitting government funding of religious social service agencies that have valuable experience in this area and are major providers of services to the needy.

There is no question that the nonprofit sector contributes greatly to those in need or that it has the capacity to do much more if funds are made available. But the amount of private funds is limited. Maximum expansion and experimentation will not be realized without more federal funding. And to secure additional funding, the nonprofit sector will have to engage in public debate about the extent of government funding of charitable programs and deal with the possible backlash against both government and charities. Going into partnership with government brings risks, responsibilities, controls, controversy, and interference. It is up to the private nonprofit sector to decide whether it wants to take on this challenge.

References

Salamon, L. M., and Abramson, A. J. *The Federal Budget and the Nonprofit Sector*. Washington, D.C.: Urban Institute Press, 1982.

Salamon, L. M., and Abramson, A. J. *The Nonprofit Sector and the New Federal Budget*. Washington, D.C.: Urban Institute Press, 1986.

United Way of America. *1986 Local United Way Fund Distribution Results by Agency, by Program*. Alexandria, Va.: Research Division, United Way of America, 1987.

18
STEVEN A. WALDHORN
JAMES O. GOLLUB
JOYCE A. KLEIN

△ △ △ △ △ △ △ △ △ △ △ △ △ △ △

New Approaches to Financing Nonprofit Organizations: The Role of Lending

This chapter reviews the possibility of extending the use of program-related investments, until now used primarily in the areas of housing and economic development, into human services. It addresses a number of key questions: How useful would it be to designate special funds to be loaned to nonprofit agencies to assist them in developing new or restructured human service programs? Could borrowed funds feasibly be repaid either from existing cash flows or from new financial packages that could be put together? Would loans help organizations establish more innovative and effective programs? Would they provide incentives for more businesslike performance by the nonprofit sector? Would such programs require establishing special financial intermediary mechanisms in which foundations and corporations could invest? Answers to these questions can help to provide important new directions for the human service system and those who help finance it.

The Changing Human Service System

Both for-profit and nonprofit service providers have important roles in the U.S. human service system. Over the past twenty years, the role of the nonprofit sector has broadened substantially as new areas of special need have been identified and new sources of funding made available. At the same time, the boundaries between the nonprofit and for-profit sectors have begun to blur. Traditionally, nonprofit organizations have operated in fields where ethical and financial considerations constrain private firms, such as family planning and the provision of emergency shelters for abused spouses and children. Nonprofit operations historically have been formed in response to needs of a sensitive or controversial nature and have depended largely on local public funding and charitable contributions rather than government reimbursement. However, recent shifts in sources of financing have allowed the for-profit sector to develop a market in some areas where the nonprofit sector was once dominant. In addition, economic pressures have encouraged nonprofit organizations to adopt more businesslike and enterprise-oriented practices.

Health care services illustrate the growing mix of non-profit and for-profit providers in human services. Since 1965, Medicare has played a central role in transforming the nonprofit, charity-based hospital system into a profitable market, and for-profit hospitals have competed with nonprofit organizations for the publicly financed and fee-for-service market. Although debate continues over which sector provides the best care at the best price, there is no longer much doubt that as long as Medicare or private health insurance exists, there will be both for-profit and nonprofit health care providers, with the nonprofit sector focusing on low-income patients. In education and training, the broadening mix of individual, corporate, and public reimbursement has maintained a mix of nonprofit and for-profit providers for all segments. The market is likely to remain mixed indefinitely, as public and private needs and programs (such as the Job Training Partnership Act) evolve, although nonprofit organizations may gradually be pushed into serving those least able to help themselves.

Need to Finance Design Change

Changes in the structure of the economy and in the demographics of communities have created new needs and opportunities for human service providers over the past decade. In addition to the blurring of boundaries between nonprofit and for-profit operations, new understandings have created pressure for redesign in the nonprofit sector to keep it competitive with the for-profit human service system. Some of the most striking examples of how these forces are operating can be found in the area of health care. Federal and state government concerns over escalating medical costs, combined with employer and insurer cost-containment concerns, have led to a dual assault on the hospital-based health care system. The introduction of the diagnosis-related-group Medicare reimbursement system and the private sector's pursuit of preferred provider organization agreements have led hospitals to undergo substantial reorganization. Beds have been eliminated, lengths of stay have been shortened, and employees have been laid off. This process, however ungraceful, has led to further redesign of the general health care system. Both for-profit and nonprofit hospitals are now competing on prices and services and are diversifying to expand market share. It is not clear whether the best health care is being provided and whether the poor are being served. Nevertheless, less expensive forms of outpatient care, prepaid health care, and community-based long-term care are becoming more widely available. Similar forces are affecting other human services on a smaller scale.

In the field of education and training, economic restructuring has created skill gaps that will have to be filled—from the basic literacy-numeracy level through graduate studies and specialized vocational training. New employer-based, proprietary, vocational, and public school/community college–based education and training programs are emerging or are being sought by business and government to ensure that the labor force required by economic recovery is available. At the same time, the chronically unemployed and long-term displaced workers are being left out of many programs. Thus, there is a clear need to redesign education and training systems, both to meet changing requirements and to ensure equity for those who need help most.

Redesign of the *nonprofit* human service sector is essential for three reasons. First, there may be some forms of human service for which the lack of market makes nonprofit organizations the only feasible providers. Second, there are areas of human services in which participation by profit-motivated providers may never be ethically justifiable (for example, organ banks for transplants). How can such nonprofit providers be assisted to continue operation and to upgrade their programs to meet changing needs? Many will need assistance in redesigning the ways they do business if they are to survive. Third, new human service businesses to meet expanding needs may need to be fostered in some areas, such as child care.

As the above examples show, the pressure to change the systems of human service provision is mounting. Today the question of preserving the nonprofit sector for its own sake matters less than the need to foster adaptation of existing nonprofit services to the new environment or to help establish new nonprofit organizations to meet needs that the market does not address.

Program-Related Investments

Program-related investments (PRIs) are a relatively new mechanism for financing projects or new program initiatives by nonprofit organizations. A program-related investment is a capital investment by a general-purpose or corporate foundation that is made for philanthropic purposes rather than income generation but that requires repayment. This financial innovation was developed in the late 1960s to provide a more efficient way of funding community programs. Some important social and community-development initiatives, while they may not require complete subsidization by a government or foundation, cannot generate the market rate of return required to obtain bank financing. The PRI represents a middle ground—a loan provided at concessional rates for charitable purposes.

The IRS developed special regulations for the treatment of program-related investments in 1969. Investments that qualify as PRIs and the administration costs involved in making them can be counted as part of a foundation's qualifying mandated distribution of funds required of foundations under federal law. Since their inception, the number of PRIs made annually has been increasing, with a marked acceleration in the past few years. PRIs are typically seen by funders as a type of funding completely different from the traditional grant. They are expected to fill two purposes: providing financing for needed projects and promoting new and stronger management capacity among nonprofit agencies.

As PRIs are essentially loans made at concessional rates, receiving agencies are expected to meet many of the same criteria that a bank would expect. Recipients must show a prospective cash flow that can cover the cost of the loan repayments. For a nonprofit agency, this cash flow might come from rents, fees, or third-party reimbursements. Receiving agencies are also expected to put up some collateral for the loan, in the form of a building, equipment, or some other asset. Although investors (foundations and intermediaries) will, of course, consider their overall program goals in selecting which agencies to lend to, loans are typically not made unless there is a reasonable chance of repayment.

Of course, because the "lenders" in this case are foundations or nonprofit intermediaries, they often do not apply these criteria as strictly as a bank would. In cases where financing is needed to cover up-front costs that will not generate revenues, such as feasibility studies or start-up costs, foundations or intermediaries will often pair a PRI with an initial grant, the grant to cover one-time costs and the loan to cover capital costs or provide working capital. While borrowers are expected to put up some type of security for the loan, the collateral is sometimes in practice "softer" than the collateral required by the typical bank. And because these lenders are not interested in repossession, projects that are not able to repay are often refinanced. In other cases, the loan is forgiven or the program or property is turned over to another agency. However, to avoid the prospect of "repossessing," most lenders are very careful to ensure that the projects they finance will generate revenues to cover the required payments.

A number of organizations have examined the potential for using program-related investments as a new source of financing for the nonprofit sector (Council on Foundations, 1984; Ford

Foundation, 1974; Hilbert and Kaufman, 1985). These evaluations focus in part on the experience of foundations and nonprofit intermediaries, such as the Local Initiatives Support Corporation, that have made PRIs. For the most part, however, PRIs have been used to support initiatives in the areas of housing and economic development; so far there has been relatively little experience in using PRIs to support human service programs. Yet research has evaluated the need for financial innovation at the local level in specific service fields, such as child care (SRI International, 1984), adult day health care (SRI International, 1983), and development of health care insurance for the underinsured and uninsured (SRI International, 1986). Other studies have evaluated emerging business opportunities that would serve specific need populations, such as older adults (Gollub, 1984, 1985).

One study that addressed both of these issues was a feasibility study for a "corporation for social investment," a national intermediary that would make program-related investments in nonprofit health and human service agencies. The study, carried out in 1987, was conducted under the aegis of a national steering committee of local United Way executives and managed through the United Way of America, with assistance from a project study team consisting of representatives from the local United Way organizations in the test cities of San Francisco and Cleveland, the United Way of America, SRI International, and Mitchell Sviridoff Associates (see SRI International, 1987). The findings of the feasibility study are the basis for the conclusions drawn in the remainder of this chapter. Since the completion of the study, the United Way of America has made substantial progress toward the establishment of a national intermediary.

The research conducted as part of the feasibility study examined four critical questions that must be answered in determining the feasibility of using lending in the area of human services: Could the development of human service lending programs result in a new source of capital that can promote innovation and adaptation in the human service sector? Could human service agencies develop programs that would generate sufficient revenues to repay loans? Would the foundation and corporate philanthropic community support initiatives in this area? What would be the benefits and drawbacks of establishing new intermediaries to promote investment in human services? The answers to these questions came from experiences in communities across the United States, as well as through interviews with foundations and corporations.

Program-Related Investment
and Innovation in Service Delivery

Examinations of an array of nonprofit service enterprises—conducted in the feasibility study as well as in other research efforts—have revealed three key findings concerning the potential impact of social investments on the delivery of human services. The first is that the use of a loan mechanism can be instrumental in creating a new management perspective among human service agencies (SRI International, 1987; Triesman, 1987). Many agencies have the internal administrative capacity—in terms of financial and planning expertise and management systems—required to take on a loan. However, the use of loans would require that human service agencies take a more market-oriented approach to the services that they provide. For example, in providing case-management services for the mentally ill or establishing an adult day health care center, an agency must be able to estimate how many clients will be Medicaid eligible, what percentage of costs will be reimbursable, how many clients can afford to pay the fees themselves (if any), and how many need to be subsidized through some alternative source. Such businesslike approaches are critical in developing a loan project, because agencies must have firm projections of their costs and revenues to develop a cash-flow analysis that can demonstrate their capacity to repay a loan.

The readiness of an agency to think about its client population as a highly varied market and to recognize that there may be a diverse array of possible revenue sources is central to both innovation in design of programs and the ability to repay a loan. In the case of an adult day health care facility, for example, a program may need to define the different components of its market. Clients might include frail low-income older adults, older workers with occupational rehabilitation needs, dependents of working adults, and independent but recuperating older adults. Potential reimbursement sources include Medicaid, Medicare, private insurance, and contracts with other health care agencies (hospitals, health maintenance organizations), as well as fees for services based on a sliding scale. It is in this area of developing marketing and feasibility studies that a financial intermediary will most likely need to provide technical assistance and grants to nonprofit corporations.

In summary, SRI's research findings suggest that there is increasing sophistication among providers in targeting client markets and in defining reimbursement streams that enable programs to break even while meeting their service mission. Competitive pressures have encouraged improved management and innovation in the design of human services. The availability of loan money as an additional financing source would help to reinforce these trends.

A second key finding of recent research is that loan funds would be able to meet the capital needs of some but not all nonprofit human service agencies. In some cases, the dynamics of the reimbursement system for a particular service will not allow for repayment of a loan. In others, the notion of borrowing money simply does not fit within an agency's organizational culture.

The final key finding is that the availability of loan dollars could result in important benefits in communities where loans are made by enabling the development of innovative service-delivery programs and businesses that both meet existing human needs and provide a new revenue source to the agencies that operate the programs. Such programs might include nonprofit businesses that offer financial management services for frail older adults living in the community to prevent them from becoming custodial or public guardian cases, home equity conversion programs that receive fees from banks for serving as a neutral party in screening and preparing equity conversion loans, and insurance cooperatives that provide health insurance for employees of small businesses.

Clearly, providers are showing increased sophistication in recognizing alternative ways of delivering human services that might be suitable for program-related investment. This emerging human service entrepreneurship could be encouraged by the availability of what could be called "social venture capital" to finance start-ups or diversification by human service agencies.

Foundation and Corporate Support

Another fundamental question addressed by research on the feasibility of mechanisms for making loans to nonprofit organizations is whether foundations, corporations, governments, and other funders would be willing to invest in providing such loans. Each type of potential funder will have different motivations for lending to human service agencies. For example, the use of loans can provide foundations with a means of supplying funding that will allow a program or agency to become self-supporting without resulting in a continuing drain on the foundation's budget. In addition, loans can make a foundation's dollars go further, can potentially leverage other sources of funding, and can help to build new management capacity in the agencies that the foundation supports.

However, it is important to note that, although smaller local foundations are also interested, few of them have had experience with the concept of the program-related investment. This lack of experience is due largely to the complexity of these investments, both in terms of understanding their benefits to the foundation and in terms of the staff expertise required to make a program-related investment. The following list presents some of the barriers and incentives that foundations generally face in making program-related investments (SRI International, 1987; Hilbert and Kaufman, 1985).

Corporations will have slightly different incentives for lending to human service agencies. Firms in industries such as insurance and banking often have access to large amounts of funds that can be loaned out but not given away. These funds are separate from those that might be set aside for corporate

Incentives	*Barriers*
Recyclability—Because loaned funds come back to the investor, they can be invested again.	*Lack of expertise*—Many foundations and corporations are not large enough to develop the needed staff capacity.
Leverage—By providing a portion of the needed financing, program-related investments can often leverage additional corporate or foundation funding.	*Income generation*—Some foundations are uncomfortable with the idea of making money on their charitable giving.
Tax Benefits—Program-related investments and their associated costs are counted toward the qualifying distribution but not as part of a foundation's asset base.	*Performance*—Many foundations are concerned about the impact that a low-interest, high-risk loan will have on their investment performance.
Flexibility—The investments can be funded out of a community or corporate foundation's corpus or its grant budget and can be used in place of or in conjunction with a grant.	*Legality*—Although Internal Revenue Service regulations provide a specific exemption, some foundations fear that the use of program-related investments will violate the prudent man rule.
Capacity building—Program-related investments can help to increase the capacity of recipient organizations by stimulating the development of new planning, managerial, and financial skills.	*Perceived lack of financial strength*—In some cases, foundations assume that only the largest foundations have the financial capacity required to make program-related investments.

contributions. In some cases, these corporations count the interest forgone in making a social investment at concessional rates toward their internal budget for corporate contributions. However, regardless of how these loans are treated internally, the use of loans can allow corporations to support their social and public relations goals of assisting the human service sector in their community without significant costs. In addition, the fact that the use of loans can promote a more businesslike approach to service delivery will be very attractive to corporate lenders.

Finally, the government also has an interest in promoting innovation, fiscal accountability, and a new management perspective in the human service sector, which it is largely responsible for supporting. Federal and state programs such as the Community Development Block Grants have increasingly been using loan mechanisms.

Need for New Financial Intermediaries

An important issue is the extent to which new mechanisms need to be created to serve as financial intermediaries between funders and recipient agencies. Intermediaries not only can allow funders to achieve their programmatic goals of supporting innovation in the human service sector but can allow investors to eliminate some of the administrative and information costs and the risk that they face in making an investment. However, the development and use of an intermediary have also raised certain concerns among potential investors; these must be understood in designing an effective and attractive intermediary.

Overall, the use of a financial intermediary could result in two important benefits to investors. The first is more efficient achievement of program-related investment objectives. Because the financial intermediaries could have a highly skilled and specialized staff that would provide technical assistance as well as financing to recipient agencies, they would be better able to promote innovation and a new management perspective than would a foundation itself. The second is reduced barriers to investing through program-related investments. Financial intermediaries can reduce the administrative costs and staff requirements needed to make a program-related investment, because investors need only make one loan to the intermediary rather than several, more risky loans to individual agencies. On the other hand, the use of financial intermediaries for program-related investments may have drawbacks. Some potential investors have been concerned that, rather than opening up a new stream of funding, new financial intermediaries might simply displace grant funds with loan funds, thereby diverting money from the most needy organizations to those that could sustain a loan. It is important to note, however, that experts in the field strongly believe that the great majority of program-related investments represent new rather than already existing charitable funding. In addition, some foundations are concerned that they would lose control over the types of programs that they assist if they invested in an intermediary rather than directly in agencies. Financial intermediaries are likely to develop unique portfolios and specialties in lending to specific human service providers. As they gain experience, they may broaden their capabilities and ability to lend effectively. Financial intermediaries could, as do banks and investment organizations, have specific concentrations that reflect their sponsors' interests. However, successful financial intermediaries are more likely to have pluralistic lending practices that reflect the quality and capabilities of the human service agencies themselves—including their ability to define a market that needs to be served, rather than specific themes. These concerns can be successfully addressed if the financial mechanisms are properly structured and understood.

Prospects for the Future

Studies by SRI and others have found that the establishment of financial intermediaries to provide pools of loan money at below-market rates could improve both service delivery and management in the human service sector. This work has also found that, although few foundations have as yet made program-related investments in human service agencies, there are growing incentives for them to make these investments as public resources for human services diminish, competition between providers increases, and the need for innovation to meet special needs expands.

The prospects for creation of new financial intermediaries to provide loans to nonprofit organizations appear good, both because potential investors are discovering the value of program-related investment and because human service providers are

entering a period of enhanced entrepreneurship. Social investment mechanisms will be an important force in bringing program-related investments to the human service sector. Efforts
to study the potential of these mechanisms have aroused interest
on the part of national foundations and the federal government,
as well as local foundations and corporations nationwide.

Moving ahead toward the establishment of new financial
approaches for providing loans to nonprofit human service organizations would seem to be worthwhile. The availability of
loan funds can affect both the ability of human service agencies
to meet needs and their management capacity. At the same time,
program-related investments represent a growing yet largely untapped resource that could be drawn out through the establishment of a financial intermediary. Lending to nonprofit organizations as a new business practice will enhance the evolution
of human service providers toward more innovative, entrepreneurial organizations that better serve their clients. However, the
social investment concept is still relatively new. There is a need
for leadership from foundations, corporations, and the nonprofit
organizations in bringing this new stream of funding into the
human service sector.

References

Council on Foundations. " 'Social Investments' Suggested by
    Council." *Public/Private,* 1984, *2* (2), 61–71.
Ford Foundation. "Program-Related Investments: A Different
    Approach to Philanthropy." New York: Ford Foundation,
    1974.
Gollub, J. O. *Business Opportunities Among the Aging Population:
    Unexpected Diversity in a Growing Market.* Business Intelligence
    Program report no. 706. Menlo Park, Calif.: SRI Interna-
    tional, 1984.
Gollub, J. O. *Not the Same Old Story: Values and Diversity Among
    the Aging and Effects on Consumer Behavior.* Menlo Park, Calif.:
    Values and Lifestyles Program, SRI International, 1985.
Hilbert, R., and Kaufman, G. "Program-Related Investments
    for Foundations." In Council on Foundations, *Alternative In-
    vestment Strategies: Selected and Edited Proceedings of the Conference*

on *"Alternative Investment Strategies for Institutions: Combining Financial Return and Social Goals."* Lou Knowles, ed. Washington, D.C: Council on Foundations, 1985.

SRI International. *Supportive Ways Business Can Assist San Francisco's Adult Day Health Care Centers.* Report of the San Francisco Business Leadership Task Force. Menlo Park, Calif.: SRI International, 1983.

SRI International. *Child Care and Corporate Resources: Strategic Directions for Bay Area Corporations.* Report of the Child Care Committee, San Francisco Bay Area Business Leadership Task Force. Menlo Park, Calif.: SRI International, 1984.

SRI International. *Report to the San Francisco Community: The Impact of Competition on Access to Health Care.* Report prepared for the Bay Area Health Task Force. Menlo Park, Calif.: SRI International, 1986.

SRI International. *Establishing a Corporation for Social Investment: Feasibility and Organizational Development.* Report prepared for the Social Investment Steering Committee, United Way of America. Menlo Park, Calif.: SRI International, 1987.

Triesman, J. ''Program-Related Investments: The Investors' Perspectives.'' Unpublished report prepared for the United Way of the Bay Area, June 1987.

19

LAWRENCE B. LINDSEY

△ △ △ △ △ △ △ △ △ △ △ △ △ △ △

Charitable Giving Options That Do Not Affect Government Revenue

The 1980s have proved to be the worst decade on record for providing tax incentives to promote charitable giving. Numerous changes in the tax law, principally in the Economic Recovery Tax Act of 1981 and the Tax Reform Act of 1986, have sharply reduced the incentives for taxpayers to make charitable gifts. In addition, the federal budget situation has created both an increased need for charitable giving and a decreased ability to provide charitable incentives.

This chapter considers alternatives to the present tax treatment of charitable giving that are designed to increase incentives for giving without having any net effect on the federal budget. These options work by offsetting any revenue lost in providing charitable incentives with distributionally similar revenue increases. The first section briefly reviews the changes that reduced incentives for charitable giving in the 1980s. The second section provides the budgetary case for revenue-neutral changes in the tax treatment of donations. In the third section, various revenue-neutral options are presented, with separate estimates of the cost of various incentives and the ways to pay for those incentives.

Declining Incentives for Charitable Giving

Tax incentives for charitable giving are as old as the income tax. Shortly after the enactment of the income tax in 1913, it was acknowledged that charitable gifts should not be part of the income tax base, as the money involved benefited not the donor but the charitable recipient. As the ultimate recipient was not subject to tax, it was decided that no tax should be levied on income that was contributed to charity. Charitable gifts thus became an early adjustment to income.

Recent analysis of charitable giving by the "tax expenditure" approach has neglected this original, and ultimate, justification for excluding charitable giving from the tax base. Presently, a majority of American taxpayers are denied any deduction for their charitable gifts. Equally important, the amount of "tax expenditure" on charitable giving was sharply curtailed during the 1980s, from $11.3 billion in 1981, or 0.45 percent of personal income, to an estimated $9.0 billion in 1988, a mere 0.23 percent of personal income—half the level of seven years earlier. This decline in the tax expenditure budget for charitable giving sharply increased the after-tax cost of making a charitable donation, which is the relevant measure of incentive from the point of view of the donor.

Much of the rise in the cost of charitable giving has little to do with direct legislative action regarding charitable giving. Rather, it is the result of changes in other provisions of the tax law that have an indirect effect on the after-tax cost of making a charitable gift. Most notable is the sharp reduction in marginal tax rates during the 1980s. The average marginal tax rate facing itemizers was 29.5 percent in 1981 and under old law would have risen to 30.7 percent in 1984 and 34.1 percent in 1988. The Economic Recovery Act of 1984 cut this rate to 23.7 percent, and the Tax Reform Act of 1986 cut the 1988 marginal rate to an estimated 21.3 percent.

The price, or after-tax cost, of making a charitable gift is the change in the donor's after-tax income as a result of making the gift. For example, if someone makes a gift of $1 and is in the 20 percent tax bracket, his or her taxes go down 20 cents, producing a net price of 80 cents. As a result of these rate reductions, the after-tax cost of making an additional contribution of $1 for the typical itemizer was increased from 69.3 cents to 76.3 cents in 1984 and from 65.9 cents to 78.7 cents in 1988.

The second major change in the tax law during the 1980s was a change in the number of taxpayers eligible for a tax incentive for their charitable gifts. In most cases, taxpayers were required to itemize their charitable contributions in order to receive a deduction. The number of taxpayers eligible for such treatment depends on what other itemized deductions are allowed and on the level of the threshold for itemizing, called the standard deduction or zero-bracket amount.

The Economic Recovery Tax Act of 1981 was quite beneficial to charities with respect to eligibility. First, the act maintained the zero-bracket amount at the same nominal level as in the year of enactment. As a result of inflation and real economic growth, the percentage of taxpayers with deductions over this threshold rose steadily, from 33.1 percent in 1981 to 39.2 percent in 1986. Thus, increasing numbers of taxpayers were eligible for the deduction. The Economic Recovery Tax Act also gradually extended the deduction of charitable gifts to nonitemizers. During the period 1982–1984, taxpayers were allowed to deduct a share of gifts up to a ceiling amount. By 1985, the ceiling was removed, and in 1986, full deductibility of all charitable gifts was allowed for all taxpayers. Although the extension of full deductibility was a major positive step in the tax code, the intermediate-year provisions were poorly designed to promote charitable giving. The vast majority of all gifts by nonitemizers are given by taxpayers who gave more than the ceiling amounts in place during 1982–1984. Thus, no marginal incentive for extra giving was provided to the donors of the vast majority of all gifts. Nonetheless, the inframarginal incentive of partial deductibility cost the treasury money. Opponents of charitable giving incentives point to these years to make a case against more generous treatment of charitable giving. In fact, very little extra incentive to give was provided during these years. The poor design of the charitable giving incentive was the reason for its ineffective results.

The Tax Reform Act of 1986 reversed the extension of charitable giving incentives to nonitemizers and sharply curtailed the number of itemizers. As Table 19.1 shows, the number of taxpayers enjoying a charitable incentive fell dramatically as a result of the 1986 act. The new law removed the charitable

Table 19.1. Effect of New Tax Bill on Itemizer Status in 1988.

New Adjusted Gross Income Class (in Thousands)	Number of Taxpayers (in Millions)	Percentage That Remained Itemizers	Percentage That Became Nonitemizers	Percentage That Remained Nonitemizers
0–10	27.9	1	1	98
10–20	25.1	7	13	80
20–30	19.4	20	29	51
30–40	14.5	41	33	26
40–50	9.5	61	24	15
50–75	9.2	74	16	10
75–100	2.3	82	8	10
100–200	1.8	86	6	8
Over 200	0.6	91	3	6
Total	110.7	26	16	58

Source: NBER TAXSIM Model. (This is a computerized representation of the actual tax code and a random sample of actual tax returns. The model was developed by Daniel Feenberg, Martin Feldstein, Lawrence Lindsey, and Andrew Metrusi and is widely used.)

incentive for nonitemizers. This eliminated the benefits of the old law for 58 percent of the taxpayer population. In addition, by narrowing the scope of other deductions and by raising the standard deduction, the new law caused a switch in the status of some 16 percent of taxpayers from being itemizers to being nonitemizers. These "switchers" are particularly important in the key $20,000–$50,000 income group, where they constitute between a quarter and a third of all taxpayers. The overall effect of the new law was to limit the tax incentive for charitable giving to only about one quarter of all taxpayers.

A third major change in the 1986 tax law was the inclusion of the appreciated portion of gifts of property in the minimum tax base. The minimum tax is a special tax that increases the burden of taxpayers who engage in certain tax-favored activities, including making large charitable contributions. By including the appreciated portion of gifts of property—the rise in value between the time the property was acquired and the time it was given away by the donor—in the minimum tax equation, the new law effectively raises the price of giving to high-income donors who make large contributions. In 1988, some 70,000 taxpayers with incomes over $200,000 will be subject to the minimum tax. These taxpayers will face a price of 79 cents on both their gifts of cash and their gifts of property. Although they constitute only about 12 percent of taxpayers earning more than $200,000, these minimum taxpayers contribute more than 40 percent of the $7.4 billion given annually by upper-income taxpayers, or more than $3 billion a year. The impact of the minimum tax on the price of giving by high-income taxpayers is therefore quite dramatic. Some 10.4 cents of a total 25 cent increase in the price of giving by upper-income taxpayers is due to the price increase faced by taxpayers in the minimum tax. The overwhelming majority of the value of the gifts by these taxpayers are large contributions (over $100,000) of appreciated assets. Groups that rely on these gifts are likely to face a particularly difficult situation.

The combined effect of these provisions is a dramatic increase in the price of making a charitable gift, from an average of about 72 cents on the dollar to more than 85 cents, as shown in Table 19.2. Stated differently, nearly half the 28 cent "tax expenditure" made per dollar of charitable giving was eliminated by the 1986 tax law changes. While some of these changes had the effect of increasing the disposable income of taxpayers, the available econometric evidence indicates that only a very small fraction of that extra income will be contributed to charity. By all estimates, the adverse effect of a higher price of giving will far overcome any positive effects on giving of the tax cuts.

Budgetary Effects of Tax Incentives

While the effect of tax changes during the 1980s was to sharply cut the tax incentives to make charitable contributions, an enormous amount of econometric evidence suggests that providing generous incentives for charitable giving is sound budget policy. When the price of making gifts is lower, donors tend to give

Table 19.2. Weighted Average Price of Charitable
Giving, 1988 (in Cents per Dollar Contributed).

New Adjusted Gross Income Class (in Thousands)	Itemizers		All Taxpayers	
	Old Law	New Law	Old Law	New Law
0–10	.965	.950	.920	.987
10–20	.850	.879	.847	.977
20–30	.793	.815	.800	.931
30–40	.748	.806	.750	.889
40–50	.716	.765	.714	.828
50–75	.656	.707	.655	.753
75–100	.591	.702	.596	.736
100–200	.536	.686	.538	.702
Over 200	.448	.696	.450	.700
Total	.657	.748	.718	.854

Source: NBER TAXSIM Model.

more to charity. The level of response to a lower price is known as "price elasticity," which is expressed as the percentage of increase in charitable giving for 1 percent decrease in the price of making a gift. Clotfelter (1986) provides an outstanding review of the literature on this matter, which is also summarized by Lindsey (1987). The evidence is overwhelming that a 1 percent cut in the price of giving will increase giving by more than 1 percent. Therefore, each dollar expended by the federal government on increased incentives for charitable giving will increase charitable giving by more than one dollar. There are very few avenues of government expenditure that do more than a dollar's worth of good for every dollar expended.

In fact, careful design of the charitable giving incentive can increase the ratio of charitable gain per dollar expended. Feldstein and Lindsey (1983) show that the appropriate use of floors on charitable giving deductions for nonitemizers can increase the budgetary efficiency of such provisions by up to 50 percent. Setting a floor on the charitable giving provision means that donors receive a full incentive to increase their contributions but do not receive tax reductions for contributions they were likely to make anyway. This makes it possible to use each government dollar as efficiently as possible in increasing the total amount of charitable donations.

There are two principal ways that government can increase incentives for individuals to make charitable contributions. The first is to increase the incentives for the donors who already receive some tax incentives (itemizers). Such an incentive could take the form of an "add-on" credit or of a "multiple deduction." With an add-on credit, in addition to the itemized deduction allowed under current law, taxpayers making charitable contributions would also be allowed credits against their tax liability. For example, a 10 percent add-on credit would lower the price of giving for someone in the 28 percent bracket from 72 to 62 cents on the dollar. The credit could be extended to all contributions or, to increase the budgetary efficiency of the plan, apply only to contributions above a certain amount. A multiple deduction would allow the taxpayer to deduct more than the cost of the gift. A 150 percent deduction, for example, would permit someone who gave $100 to take a tax deduction of $150. For someone in the 28 percent tax bracket, the effective price of giving would be reduced from 72 to 58 cents on the dollar. As in the case of the add-on credit, the multiple deduction could apply either to all donations or to only donations above a certain floor.

The budgetary efficiency of either an add-on credit or a multiple deduction would be roughly equal to the price elasticity of charitable giving. That is, for every dollar the government expends on increasing the incentive for giving, charities will gain more than one dollar. The imposition of a floor on the incremental incentive has two effects. First, it lowers the revenue cost of the incentive for each taxpayer who gives at least as much as the floor. The amount of revenue saved is the taxpayer's marginal tax rate times the dollar amount of the floor. Second, the floor eliminates the incremental incentive to contribute for all taxpayers who give less than the floor. This second effect lowers the incremental amount of giving induced by the incentive.

The budgetary efficiency of imposing the floor depends on the offsetting effects of these two factors. At low levels, the floor affects the incentives of few taxpayers and only a small share of the amount contributed. On the other hand, the floor

lowers the revenue cost of the incentive for a great many taxpayers. This means a large overall savings. Thus, a low floor
will greatly enhance the budgetary efficiency of an incremental
incentive. However, as the floor rises, fewer taxpayers are eligible for the incentive, so that its effect on contributions decreases,
and the incremental revenue gain will also tend to decrease. The
actual budgetary efficiency of a floor depends on the distribution of charitable giving among the population receiving the
incentive.

An add-on credit or multiple deduction to itemizers is
unlikely to be adopted, largely for political reasons. Since upper-
income taxpayers are more likely to be itemizers than are lower-
income taxpayers, and since contributions tend to rise with income, most of the tax incentive from such provisions would accrue
to taxpayers at the top of the income distribution. In addition,
it may seem inappropriate to give an additional incentive to the
quarter of taxpayers who itemize while three-quarters of all taxpayers receive no incentive at all. Therefore, the focus of the
analysis must turn to providing incentives to contribute to the
nonitemizing population.

The budgetary analysis of incentives for charitable giving for nonitemizers is similar to that for itemizers. Absent a
floor, the budgetary efficiency of such a provision is approximately equal to the price elasticity of charitable giving. With
a floor, the budgetary efficiency depends on the distribution of
giving among the population receiving an incentive. Table 19.3
shows that, for nonitemizers, the distribution of donors by level
of donation is quite different from the distribution of total donations by level of donation. On the one hand, the vast majority
of all nonitemizers, 64.7 percent, reported gifts of less than $100
on their tax returns in 1988. Although this group included the
vast majority of donors, their total giving amounted to only 3.2
percent of the total amount contributed by nonitemizers. On
the other hand, only 12 percent of nonitemizers contributed more
than $500, but their gifts amounted to two-thirds of nonitemizer
giving. These figures clearly show that setting a floor entails a
trade-off. On the one hand, a high floor would permit a generous
incentive for those donors who contribute the vast majority of

Table 19.3. Distribution of Giving by Nonitemizers in 1988.

Amount of Donation	Percentage of Nonitemizers Contributing	Percentage of Total Nonitemizer Giving
Zero	52.1	0.0
Less than $50	6.9	1.0
$50–$100	5.7	2.2
$100–$150	5.7	3.7
$150–$200	4.5	4.1
$200–$250	3.3	3.9
$250–$300	2.7	3.9
$300–$400	3.9	7.1
$400–$500	3.1	7.1
More than $500	12.0	66.9

Source: NBER TAXSIM Model.

all gifts. On the other hand, such a floor would exclude the vast majority of all donors from receiving any incentive. Imposition of a floor on nonitemizer giving presents a sharp trade-off between the universality of an incentive and its generosity.

Analysis shows an important difference between the budgetary efficiency of an incentive for nonitemizers and that of an additional incentive for itemizers. Provision of a charitable incentive for nonitemizers might cause itemizers to change their tax status, resulting in a loss of revenue for the government without increasing the incentive for the taxpayer to contribute. Consider the following example. A taxpayer makes charitable contributions of $3,000 and has other deductions of $3,000. If there is no charitable deduction for nonitemizers, then this taxpayer chooses itemizer status, as his or her total deductions of $6,000 exceed the $5,000 standard deduction. However, if there is a charitable deduction for nonitemizers, then it is in this taxpayer's interest to become a nonitemizer. In that case, the taxpayer would be entitled to the $5,000 standard deduction and the $3,000 charitable deduction, for a total deduction of $8,000. Taxpayers who thus switch itemizer status lower the budgetary efficiency of providing charitable incentives for nonitemizers. Each dollar expended providing an incentive for nonitemizers to contribute will therefore bring in fewer dollars to charity than dollars expended to increase the incentive for itemizers to contribute. Nonetheless, distributional considerations make the provision of an incentive for nonitemizers more likely than an increase in incentives for itemizers. In either case, the increased giving to charitable organizations is likely to be greater than the revenue cost to the government of providing the incentive.

Budget-Neutral Charitable Incentives

Although charitable incentives are budgetarily efficient in that the gains they provide to charities are greater than the costs to the government, they still result in a decrease in government revenue. Given the current large deficits, provisions that cause those deficits to increase are likely to be politically difficult to implement. Therefore, particular attention should be paid to proposals that include a way to "pay" for the charitable incentive. It should be made clear that, even if the entire cost of the charitable incentive is borne by funds currently received by the charitable community, such incentive programs would still be of net benefit to charities because of their budgetary efficiency.

There are three ways to provide funds for a charitable incentive program. The first is in the form of direct spending cuts on payments to support certain social welfare activities coupled with an earmarking of funds to support additional incentives for contributions to these areas. Many social services, including higher education, medical research, and community programs, are jointly provided by the government and private philanthropic efforts. Such a program would increase the total level of funds supporting these social services without increasing the budget deficit. It is likely that any such budgetary program would have to be targeted to a particular area of government spending in order to ensure that funds cut from that area would not be reallocated to support other types of philanthropic endeavor.

The second way to "pay" for increasing charitable incentives for some taxpayers is to decrease the charitable incentive for other taxpayers. In particular, the charitable deduction could be extended to nonitemizers while a floor is placed on the deductibility of charitable gifts by both itemizers and nonitemizers.

Table 19.4. Effect of a Floor on Charitable Giving.

Level of Floor	Change in Taxes			Change in Giving		
	Itemizers	Nonitemizers	Total	Itemizers	Nonitemizers	Total
$200	+0.07	−2.25	−2.18	−0.23	+3.66	+3.43
$300	+0.58	−1.90	−1.32	−0.34	+3.35	+3.01
$400	+1.04	−1.64	−0.60	−0.52	+3.08	+2.56
$500	+1.46	−1.41	+0.05	−0.72	+2.78	+2.06

Source: NBER TAXSIM Model.

Table 19.4 shows the budgetary and giving trade-offs involved in such a proposal. The table shows clearly that only a floor of about $500 on both itemizers and nonitemizers would achieve a revenue-neutral result. While under old law, revenue neutrality could be obtained with a floor of around $200, the higher standard deduction provided by the new tax law, $5,000 for a married couple, means that there are fewer itemizers. As imposing the floor on itemizers is the revenue-producing part of this approach, less revenue is raised when there are more nonitemizers.

Compounding this problem is the fact that the high standard deduction produces a very large number of "switchers." Recall that these switchers receive a tax break but no increase in their incentive to give. Under the new law, an estimated 4,910,000 taxpayers will switch from itemizer to nonitemizer status. Their total annual giving amounts to $13.1 billion, or roughly 30 percent of total giving by itemizers. The revenue lost as a result of this switching is roughly $1.2 billion a year.

The effect of a $500 floor would be to exclude a large number of both itemizers and nonitemizers from receiving a charitable deduction. As noted earlier, only 12 percent of nonitemizers gave more than $500 in 1988, although their gifts accounted for two-thirds of total nonitemizer giving. Only 55 percent of itemizers gave more than $500, although their gifts accounted for 95 percent of all itemizer giving. A $500 floor would limit the charitable incentive to the quarter of the population who give more than that amount.

The third method of paying for extending the charitable deduction to nonitemizers is to lower the standard deduction. The justification for this is that a portion of the standard deduction is intended to represent a "standard" level of charitable contributions. Thus, extending the deduction to nonitemizers would make up for the reduction in the level of the standard deduction. Table 19.5 shows the effect that this would have on taxes and giving. These numbers indicate that a revenue-neutral proposal would involve extension of the charitable deduction to nonitemizers coupled with a $400 reduction in the zero-bracket amount. It should be noted that such a scheme would still cause a "switcher" effect, although it would be smaller than other methods would entail. This effect would cause the taxes paid by itemizers to fall, while nonitemizers would pay more because of the lower zero-bracket amount.

**Table 19.5. Predicted Effect of Lower
Standard Deduction on Charitable Giving.**

Amount of Reduction	Change in Taxes			Change in Giving		
	Itemizers	Nonitemizers	Total	Itemizers	Nonitemizers	Total
$200	− 0.93	− 1.27	− 2.20	− 0.14	+ 4.11	+ 3.97
$300	− 0.86	− 0.30	− 1.16	− 0.12	+ 4.14	+ 4.02
$400	− 0.79	+ 0.67	− 0.13	− 0.12	+ 4.16	+ 4.04
$500	− 0.73	+ 1.65	+ 0.92	− 0.12	+ 4.18	+ 4.06

Source: NBER TAXSIM Model.

This approach has two major advantages over the imposition of a floor on giving by itemizers ad nonitemizers. The first advantage is that it would be universal. All donors would be eligible for a charitable deduction, whereas the floor approach would permit a deduction for only about a quarter of all taxpayers. The second advantage is the gain in charitable giving. The net increase in giving would be roughly $4 billion under the lower standard deduction approach but only about $2 billion under the floor approach. Of course, these effects are interrelated. Analysis seems to indicate that a reduction in the standard deduction offers the best method of obtaining an increase in the level of giving without causing adverse effects on tax revenue.

While it is beyond the scope of this chapter to comment in detail on the political feasibility of tax law changes, this analysis of budget-neutral possibilities for providing charitable giving incentives provides three important lessons for those concerned with increasing such incentives. First, budget-neutral changes in the tax law can be made that are likely to increase charitable contributions. Second, the imposition of floors on the charitable giving deduction substantially reduces the number of taxpayers eligible for the deduction. This may, in turn, erode the political support for continuing the charitable deduction. Finally, increases in the standard deduction conflict with the objective of providing increased incentives for charitable giving. Such increases not only erode the revenue available for providing charitable incentives but also reduce the number of taxpayers eligible for a charitable giving incentive. While it may not be politically possible to reduce the current standard deduction, those concerned with providing incentives for charitable giving should consider this fact when viewing future tax changes.

References

Auten, G., and Rudney, G. "Charitable Deductions and Tax Reform: New Evidence on Giving Behavior." Washington, D.C.: Brookings Institution, 1983. (Mimeographed.)

Auten, G. and Rudney, G. "Charitable Giving and Tax Reform: Discussion Tables." Washington, D.C.: Brookings Institution, 1985. (Mimeographed.)

Boskin, M., and Feldstein, M. "Effects of the Charitable Deduction on Contributions by Low-Income and Middle-Income Households: Evidence from a National Survey of Philanthropy." *Review of Economics and Statistics,* 1977, *59,* 351–354.

Clotfelter, C. *Federal Tax Policy and Charitable Giving.* Cambridge, Mass.: National Bureau of Economic Research, 1986.

Clotfelter, C., and Steuerle, E. "Charitable Contributions." In H. Aaron and J. Pechman (eds.), *How Taxes Affect Economic Behavior.* Washington, D.C.: Brookings Institution, 1981.

Dennis, B., Rudney, G., and Wyscarver, R. "Charitable Contributions: The Discretionary Income Hypothesis." Working paper no. 63, Institution for Social and Policy Studies, Yale University, 1983.

Dye, R. "Personal Charitable Contributions: Tax Effects and Other Motives." *National Tax Journal,* Sept. 1977, 311–318.

Feenberg, D. "Are Tax-Price Models Really Identified: The Case of Charitable Giving." *National Tax Journal,* 1987, *40,* 629–633.

Feldstein, M. "The Income Tax and Charitable Contributions: Tax Effects and Other Motives." *National Tax Journal,* Sept. 1975, 311–318.

Feldstein, M., and Clotfelter, C. "Tax Incentives and Charitable Contributions in the United States." *Journal of Public Economics,* 1976, *5,* 1–26.

Feldstein, M., and Lindsey, L. B. "Simulating Nonlinear Tax Rules and Nonstandard Behavior: An Application to the Tax Treatment of Charitable Contributions." In M. Feldstein (ed.), *Behavioral Simulation Methods in Tax Policy Analysis.* Cambridge, Mass.: National Bureau of Economic Research, 1983.

Feldstein, M., and Taylor, A. "The Income Tax and Charitable Contributions." *Econometrica,* 1976, *44,* 1201–1222.

Hausman, J. A. "Exact Consumer Surplus." Cambridge, Mass.: Massachusetts Institute of Technology, 1979. (Mimeographed.)

Lindsey, L. B. "The Effect of the Treasury Proposal on Charitable Giving: A Comparison of Constant and Variable Elasticity Models." Working paper no. 1592, National Bureau of Economic Research, 1985.

Lindsey, L. B. "The Effect of the President's Proposal on Charitable Giving." *National Tax Journal,* 1986, *39,* 1–12.

Lindsey, L. B. "Gifts of Appreciated Property: More to Consider." *Tax Notes,* 1987, *34,* 67–70.

Reece, W. "Charitable Contributions: New Evidence on Household Behavior." *American Economic Review,* 1979, *69,* 142–151.

Reece, W., and Zeischang, K. *Consistent Estimation of the Impact of Tax Deductibility on the Level of Charitable Contributions.* Washington, D.C.: National Tax Institute of America and Bureau of Labor Statistics, 1984.

Taussig, M. "Economic Aspects of the Personal Income Tax Treatment of Charitable Contributions." *National Tax Journal,* 1967, *20,* 1–19.

PART FIVE

△ △ △ △ △ △ △ △ △ △ △ △ △ △ △

Trends in Corporate Giving

While corporate contributions were the fastest growing source of new financing for nonprofits during the 1970s and the early 1980s, major restructuring of the corporate sector resulted in a leveling off in increases in these contributions until, from 1986 to 1987, there was no increase in corporate contributions at all. At the same time, however, a new trend emerged among some corporations to use their contributions as marketing tools. From credit card companies to manufacturers of foodstuffs, corporations tried to increase sales and improve their image by donating a percentage of sales for particular products to selected nonprofit organizations.

The contributors to this part review trends in corporate contributions and assess what is likely for the future. Issues examined include the roles, functions, promise, and limitations of socially responsible corporations, whether corporations are sensitive to minority interests, and whether the trend toward cause-related marketing will last. The debate about corporate social responsibility continues; the key question is whether the new philosophy of attending to the business of profits while leaving the giving to others will become the prevalent stance among corporate leaders in the future.

313

20

HAYDEN W. SMITH

△ △ △ △ △ △ △ △ △ △ △ △ △ △ △

Corporate Contributions to the Year 2000: Growth or Decline?

The meteoric growth of corporate charitable contributions in recent years has captured the attention—and the imagination—of the entire philanthropic community. That any private source of funding could, and would, triple its giving in only ten years, as corporations did between 1976 and 1986, has inevitably thrust the subject forward into the limelight. The excitement engendered by the rapid growth of corporate giving after 1975 also generated much interest in the long-term prospects. Could one realistically expect continued growth at annual rates of 10 percent or more indefinitely, or at least to the year 2000? Or would there inevitably be a slowing to a lower rate, and, if so, what rate? The answers to these questions constitute the subject of this chapter. In a nutshell, there are grounds for believing that the growth of corporate contributions in the future is almost certain to be much slower than in the past. This is not to say that corporate giving will decrease, or that it will flatten out, or that it will not show short-run spurts of rapid growth. But, given reasonable assumptions about economic activity, inflation, the tax laws, and similar influences, a decline in the average rate of growth is almost inevitable. Indeed, it may already have begun.

While it will be several months before there will be any real clue as to what happened in 1988, and more than two years before complete figures are available, it has been clear for some time that the growth of corporate contributions has slowed down appreciably since 1985. The average annual increase amounted to 14.0 percent between 1975 and 1985, but the available estimates indicate that growth fell far short of that figure in 1986 and 1987, and there may even have been a slight decrease in giving in 1988. The prospects for 1989 are by no means clear. Some fragmentary information about the intentions of a few of the major corporations suggests that there will be a modest increase, but there is an unusually high degree of uncertainty in the picture, arising primarily from economic and political factors.

The problem, however, is not the immediate future but the long-term future—to the year 2000 and beyond. And the subject is corporate contributions, not corporate philanthropy. Despite the fact that there are several newsletters and books with the title *Corporate Philanthropy,* and despite the fact that the term is widely used in other ways, the reality is that there is no such thing. The question is important. The names by which things are called ought to be descriptive of what they are, they ought not to confuse the issue, and they should convey as accurate an image of what is being talked about as is possible. Even more important is the tendency to attribute something to a phenomenon on the basis of an inaccurate label. This is especially true of a term like *philanthropy.*

Corporate contributions are not altruistic. Unlike private foundations, corporations exist for purposes quite different from giving money to charity. That many (but not all) corporations do give to charity is merely a reflection of the fact that many senior corporate executives believe that doing so serves the self-interests of their companies. Some corporate managers believe that the corporation has a duty and a responsibility to do so. These matters will be discussed in more detail later; for the moment, let it be clearly understood that the subject of this chapter is corporate contributions, not philanthropy.

Now that we have dealt with the matter of terminology, we turn to the central question of this chapter: What does the past have to tell us about the future of corporate giving? The question is not so much quantitative as qualitative. If one were to deal only with the numbers, there would be little to say. The future is always an outgrowth of the past, and this is especially true of all time-series data that measure economic phenomena. For example, total corporate contributions—as measured by the amounts claimed on corporate tax returns—grew from $30 million in 1936 to an estimated $4.6 billion in 1986, indicating a growth rate for this half century of roughly 10.6 percent per year. Assuming that corporate contributions continue to grow in the future at the same average rate per year as in the past, then the figure for the year 2000 would be $18.8 billion. It is possible, of course, to use other pairs of years and obtain different projections; between 1946 and 1986, for instance, the growth rate averaged about 8 percent per year; with these figures, the projection to the year 2000 would be $13.4 billion.

As guideposts to the future, these kinds of projections are only marginally useful, because they beg the question of the forces that caused corporate contributions to grow as they did in past, and they shed no light at all on the influences that are likely to be important in the future. The only sure bet is that between now and year 2000, events will not be quite the same as they were in the past. What can be said about all the things that caused corporate contributions to increase at 10.6 percent per year in the last half century? The question is important as well as interesting, because any useful speculation about the future of corporate giving requires at least some understanding of the history of such giving in the past.

The Historical Record

Figure 20.1 traces the history of corporate contributions from 1936 to 1985, with estimates for 1986, 1987, and 1988. Also shown is the 10.6 percent growth curve connecting 1936 and 1986, with an extrapolation to the year 2000. It should be noted that the chart is semilogarithmic; that is, equal vertical distances represent equal ratios, not equal amounts (which is why the 10.6 percent growth curve is a straight line). The first fact that hits the eye is that the growth of corporate contributions has been episodic; there are clearly evident four distinct periods of growth, the first three of which were followed by a decline and/or plateau:

Figure 20.1. Growth of Corporate Charitable Contributions
(in Millions of Current Dollars).

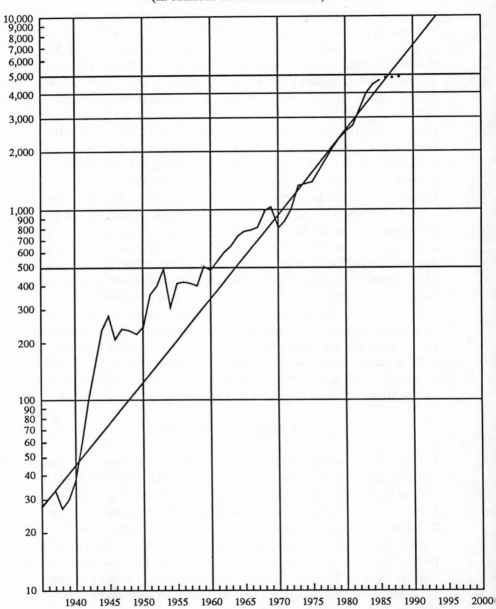

Growth Period	*Decline and Plateau*
1. 1939–1945	1945–1950
2. 1950–1953	1953–1960
3. 1960–1969	1969–1975
4. 1975–1986 (?)	1986–(?)

The timing is fascinating. The first period of growth was coincident with World War II and the second with the Korean War. It seems likely that something associated with these two wartime periods had a positive impact on corporate giving, but it is not at all obvious what it was. Nor is it obvious what caused the third and fourth growth periods. And what about the periods of decline and plateau? Were they merely the aftermaths of conditions that ceased to exist, or were they triggered by negative influences?

The second fact that is evident from the figure is that the average annual rates of growth were typically greater than 10.6 percent for periods ending prior to 1969. While it is not unusual for any series of economic data beginning from a low base to show this kind of pattern, this figure offers evidence that the earlier growth of corporate giving was intrinsically more robust in certain ways than was the later growth. Indeed, 1969 seems to mark a discontinuity between two periods, the major difference between them being the degree of stability. The one prior to 1969 displays a high degree of instability, while the one after 1969 is unusually stable; in fact, the growth of corporate contributions after 1969 conforms to the 1936–1986 curve itself. Is this an accident, or was there something in the picture that was different before 1969 from what it has been since 1970? Some exploration of this is clearly in order.

One final observation about the graphic display of corporate contributions is in order. As to the period 1975–1986, there is some suggestion of two subperiods, 1975–1980 and 1981–1986, with similar characteristics. Both of these subperiods show a typical pattern of diminishing growth after the first three years, but, unlike prior history, there was no decline after 1980, at least through 1985 and probably through 1986 and 1987. It is as though the years after 1980 were given a new burst of energy. This, too, needs to be explored.

The Qualitative Story. While the numbers are interesting and important, it is the story behind the numbers that is the most interesting and the most important. The history of corporate giving is actually a fascinating story, in part because so much was compressed into a comparatively short time and in part because it illustrates the interplay of the many influences at work in this area. In particular, we need to take a close look at the relationship between corporate taxation and corporate giving.

Toward the end of 1935, Congress amended the Internal Revenue Code to include, for the first time, an explicitly allowable deduction for corporate charitable contributions. Before then, some corporations had made gifts that, for tax purposes, they deducted as "ordinary and necessary" business expenses. Such deductions were often challenged by IRS auditors, and many such challenges wound up in the courts. Ultimately, the courts evolved a benefit-based test; if a contribution bestowed a direct benefit on the donor, it was deductible; otherwise, it was not. In other words, if a corporation could demonstrate that a donation was mutually beneficial, it was deductible. The 1935 act put an end to this litigation by making all corporate contributions deductible up to a limit of 5 percent of taxable income.

This change in the tax law initially had little effect on total corporate giving. There are no authoritative figures for 1935 and earlier years, but for the first four years after the passage of this legislation, the amounts reported on corporate tax returns hovered around $30 million, or just under 0.5 percent of corporate profits before taxes. In the circumstances then prevailing, the tax treatment of contributions does not appear to have been a factor. This changed dramatically after the outbreak of World War II. In addition to increased ordinary tax rates, corporations became subject to excess-profits taxes. The result was that the marginal tax rate imposed on many corporations exceeded 80 percent. When faced with rates of this magnitude, added charitable giving became very attractive because the after-tax cost was less than 20 cents per dollar of contribution. Given this incentive, and given the appeals of wartime charities, the corporate community increased its giving substantially. The tax picture also gave impetus to the notion of "stockpiling" money in the hands of corporate-sponsored private foundations as a hedge against periods of poor profits. Indeed, many of the largest and best known of today's corporate foundations were created in this era, in large part because of the attractiveness of financing them cheaply.

The end of the war and the end of the excess-profits tax saw an end to the sharp growth of corporate contributions. The pattern, however, was repeated in the early 1950s during the Korean War: another excess-profits tax, another upsurge in total contributions, and another spurt in the formation of corporate foundations. Clearly, the imposition and removal of excess-profits taxes had much to do with the fluctuation in the levels of corporate giving in the years between 1941 and 1954. There were, of course, other factors at work that were specific to the times, such as the appeals of war-related charities and the compelling needs of many nonprofit agencies that focused on social problems peculiar to those periods. In addition, the military conflicts generated increases in corporate profits, both before and after taxes, that were broadly parallel to the changes in corporate giving, and it seems clear that there was at least rough causal connection between them.

Nontax Influences. One can only speculate about what the course of corporate contributions would have been in the absence of wartime conditions and excess-profits taxes. There is, however, a clue in the behavior of contributions expressed as a percentage of profits before taxes in the peacetime years. Between 1936 and 1941, this figure was typically less than 0.50 percent. From 1947 to 1950, it averaged just under 0.70 percent, and from 1954 to 1960, it averaged close to 0.90 percent. Assuming these to be "normal" years, it is clear that there was a slow upward trend in the importance of charitable giving relative to profits. What forces caused this upward trend? The most satisfactory analysis concerns the evolution of the climate of opinion prior to the late 1960s.

Three Obstacles and How They Disappeared. There is much evidence that during the 1930s it was not considered proper for corporations to be involved in eleemosynary activities of any kind. The business of business was business, not charity and not action in the social sphere. Moreover, there were three fairly distinct obstacles to the willingness and ability of corporations to undertake any involvement in social matters (Brown, 1969). The first was legal. A judicial dictum handed down from one of the British courts stated that ''charity has no seat at the Board table'' (*Hutton* v. *West Cork Railway Co.,* 23 Ch. D. 654 (C.A. 1883), at 672). As the managers of corporations had become increasingly divorced from ownership, they were more and more regarded as the custodians of the property and other resources belonging to corporate stockholders, with no right or authority to distribute funds that they did not own themselves for the support of charitable enterprises. Indeed, the powers derived from corporate charters did not include charitable giving, and, prior to the 1930s, only a few states had amended their corporate statutes to include contributions as a legitimate activity.

The second obstacle arose from the principles of classical economics. In this view, the ability of a corporation to make gifts to charity was clear evidence that the corporation was at least a quasi monopoly. In the theory of perfect competition, each of the factors of production (land, labor, capital) would be paid only what was required to get the amount that would be needed for the enterprise, no more. If the corporation had any surplus for charitable giving, it was confessing to a certain exploitative influence over prices that it was not entitled to have. Corporate management must have felt especially uncomfortable on this score when Congress set up the Temporary National Economic Commission in the late 1930s to investigate the market structure of the leading industries.

Finally, there was another reason why it was felt that corporations should not indulge in eleemosynary kinds of activity, one that involved the concept of welfare. Whether it was education or any other field of charity, social involvement was thought to be the function of individuals, churches, and government, not business. In theory at least, corporations could be accused of encroaching on the prerogatives of government and other sectors if they moved into any welfare activities.

While they continued to characterize some corporate thinking for many years, the force of these three obstacles eroded steadily. By the early 1960s, the dominant view in all three areas was exactly the reverse of what had been the case only a quarter of a century earlier. On the legal front, the circumstances had changed completely. By 1960, nearly all the states had adopted statutes expressly empowering corporations to make charitable contributions. And the issue had been tried successfully in the courts, with the result that legality was no longer an obstacle at all. Indeed, in the landmark case in the early 1950s, the court ruled that corporations not only had the right to make contributions, they also had a duty to do so as a matter of social responsibility (*A. P. Smith Manufacturing Co.* v. *Barlow,* 13 N.J. 145, 98 A.2d 581, appeal dismissed, 346 U.S. 861 [1953]).

Likewise, the classical economists' model of perfect competition gave way to a more sophisticated view of the proper structure of business. Some degree of monopoly power seemed an acceptable price to pay if business would better serve the interests of society through large-scale production, mass marketing, and mass consumption. Modifications of perfect competition became accepted as a means of stimulating the development of new ways of doing things and rewarding initiative and enterprise.

As to business participation in welfare activities, the older view gradually disappeared, and in its place there grew an awareness that the business community is perhaps the most effective device in our society to get things done. The inability of government and other sectors to accomplish everything that society wanted done led more and more to the notion that the help of corporations should be sought in areas that were formerly off limits to business. Today we hear of the creative interface between business corporations and the rest of society, of partnerships between business and government, and of community initiatives involving corporations.

In retrospect, it seems clear that these changes were the dominant forces behind the growth of corporate contributions prior to 1970. The two wartime periods with their associated changes in the tax law were merely a kind of overlay to the fundamental trends. Corporate giving as a percentage of corporate profits was clearly increasing. In the ten years after 1960, it averaged nearly 1.07 percent and was below 1.0 percent in only two of the ten years; prior to 1960, it was as high as 1.0 percent in only three years, and they were all in wartime.

Taxation and Corporate Contributions

While there is now an impressive body of evidence that tax policy does have an influence on the propensity of individuals, especially those in the upper income groups, to give to charity, no one has ever investigated the relationship between taxes and corporate contributions. Yet it is apparent that the imposition of excess-profits taxes did have an important influence on corporate giving on the two occasions mentioned above. The likelihood that tax policy does play a significant role in corporate giving is reinforced by two episodes in more recent years.

A glance at Figure 20.1 indicates clearly that 1968 and 1969 were unusual years; there was an increase in corporate contributions of more than 21 percent in 1968 and an additional small increase in 1969, followed by a 24.4 percent decrease in 1970. Relative to corporate profits before taxes, contributions increased from 1.04 percent in 1967 to 1.13 percent in 1968 and then to 1.22 percent in 1969, the highest level since 1945. In 1970, the figure fell back to 1.06 percent. The only factor that can conceivably account for this aberration in the growth pattern is the change in federal taxation in those years. In 1967, Congress added a temporary 10 percent surcharge to both individual and corporate tax rates for 1968 and 1969; the surcharge fell to 5 percent in 1970 and was eliminated thereafter. Again, as in the two wartime periods, there was not only an upsurge in corporate giving but also a spurt in the rate of formation of corporate foundations. The latter phenomenon was followed by a significant drop in 1970 and later years as a result of the Tax Reform Act of 1969, which, among other things, imposed stringent rules on, and a tax on the net investment income of, all private foundations, thus making such entities less attractive as vehicles for corporate giving.

The second episode is of current vintage, and it bears on the question raised earlier about the 1981–1986 subperiod. Prior to 1970, corporations could make contributions of company products (inventory) and claim a tax deduction based on fair market value. The basis for valuation was reduced to cost by the Tax Reform Act of 1969. Although there are virtually no data available regarding the total amount of these kinds of contributions before 1982, it is believed that such giving decreased sharply in 1970 and stayed low until after 1981.

The tax treatment of gifts of company products has been changed twice since 1969, in both instances to permit a much more generous deduction, but only in special cases. The first change, in 1976, was designed to encourage giving to agencies providing care to "the ill, the needy, and infants." The second change, in 1981, was aimed at encouraging contributions of scientific property used in research. In both cases, the new incentive for making contributions of inventory was effective. While it is clear that there was some growth in giving aimed at "the ill, the needy, and infants" after 1976, the amounts appear to have been small in comparison to total corporate contributions. The effect of the 1981 act was much more dramatic, although valuation problems make it difficult to measure precisely. For example, gifts of company products reported by 1,194 colleges and universities in academic year 1985–86 amounted to $231 million (Council for Aid to Education, 1987), and this figure understates the actual amount: $205 million was reported by only 69 companies in 1986 (Council for Aid to Education, 1988). Hence, a significant share, perhaps as much as 10 percent, of total corporate giving is now made up of gifts of company products.

The Economic Recovery Tax Act of 1981 also raised the limit on the charitable deduction for corporations from 5 to 10 percent of taxable income. The long-term effect of this change has yet to be determined, but it clearly had a significant impact in 1982. In that year, there was a 22.4 percent increase in the number of companies reporting contributions equal to 5 percent or more of "net" income (a tax concept) and a 38.4 percent increase in the average amount of their contributions. The total contributions of companies reporting 5 percent or more increased from 25.5 percent of total giving reported by all corporations in 1981 to 37.7 percent in 1982 (Smith, 1989). There are technical reasons why the amounts reported for tax purposes may not be the same as the amounts actually given, but these figures suggest very strongly that this change in the tax law did have a positive impact on corporate giving.

To a very large degree, therefore, the reacceleration of the rate of growth of corporate giving after 1981 was induced by these two changes in the tax law. This episode highlights the importance of taxes as an influence on corporate contributions. There is likely to be some further influence as a result of the Tax Reform Act of 1986, but the provisions of that act are still not yet fully effective, and there will be a time lag in the availability of data with which to appraise its impact.

The Climate for Corporate Giving

However important taxation may be as an influence on corporate contributions, its primary effect is to induce increases or decreases in the amounts given. Taxes alone do not appear to be a determinant of the decision whether to give. That decision is very clearly a function of the attitudes of corporate managers and the prevailing climate of opinion. We have seen how that climate and those attitudes changed between the late 1930s and the late 1960s; what can be said about them after the early 1970s and on into the future? Three important factors are relevant here: the incidence of corporate contributions (the distribution of the corporate population with respect to charitable giving), the effect of inflation on corporate contributions, and the influence of corporate profits.

The Incidence of Corporate Contributions. The corporate universe is anything but static. Between 1970 and 1982, the number of firms filing federal tax returns increased from 1.7 million to more than 2.9 million. Some of the increase in corporate contributions was due to this growth of the corporate population rather than to increases in average levels of giving per company. How much that population will grow between now and the year 2000 is unpredictable in the absence of any analytical framework, but any growth at all will continue to be a plus factor in the future growth of corporate giving. However, only a small fraction of the corporate community reports any charitable giving for tax purposes. In 1970, the first year for which there are any data on this subject, just under 20 percent of all corporations filing tax returns in that year reported any contributions whatever (Vasquez, 1977). By 1977, this figure had increased to 23.4 percent, but in 1982, it had fallen back to only 20.8 percent (Smith, 1983, 1989). One may infer from these data that the rapid growth of corporate contributions between 1970 and 1982 was attributable to only about one-fifth of the expanding corporate universe.

That such a small fraction of all corporations report any contributions for tax purposes is not surprising. Among the firms not reporting any contributions, well over half are net-loss companies, and virtually all of the others are very tiny enterprises. Since the tax law limits the charitable deduction to a percentage of taxable income, a net-loss corporation may not legally report any contributions as a deduction for tax purposes. The small firms with taxable incomes that report no contributions are really proprietorships or partnerships, not the kind of public corporations usually thought of in connection with charitable giving, and their owners usually give as individuals rather than through the companies they own.

It seems very unlikely that there will be much of an increase in the incidence of corporate giving in the future. There is likely, however, to be some increase in corporate population, a corresponding increase in the number of companies reporting contributions, and a continued increase in the average amount of contributions per company. The period for which we have this kind of data is relatively short, but it is worth examining as a possible clue to the future. In the years between 1970 and 1982, there was an 83.9 percent increase in the number of contributing companies and an increase of 98.4 percent in their average contributions (Smith, 1989). These factors underlie an increase of nearly 265 percent in total corporate contributions, as shown in Table 20.1.

Table 20.1. Corporate Contributions, 1970–1982 (in Thousands of Dollars).

	Total Contributions	Companies Reporting Contributions	Average Contribution
1970	$ 797,029	330,532	$2,411
1977	1,791,244	525,122	3,411
1982	2,906,463	607,700	4,783
Percentage increase	264.7	83.9	98.4

Similar data for the years after 1982 are not yet available, but the continued growth of total contributions undoubtedly involved further increases in both the number of contributing companies and the average amounts reported for tax purposes. If the rates of growth for 1970–1982 were to continue to the year 2000, the number of companies would increase to 1.5 million, their average contribution would be $13,350, and total corporate contributions would reach $20 billion. It is, however, very unlikely that the 1970–1982 rates of growth will continue to the year 2000, especially for the average contribution per company. The 1970–1982 increase took place during a period of high inflation; with the figures adjusted for inflation, the average contribution per company *decreased* 20.2 percent in this period. Therefore, we next take a look at how inflation impinges on contribution figures.

The Effect of Inflation. The growth of average contributions for companies that reported contributions for tax purposes was 5.9 percent annually between 1970 and 1982; the rate of inflation during this period was 7.9 percent. It thus appears that *real* average contributions declined by about 2.0 percent a year. This does not necessarily mean that average contributions would have decreased by this much if there had not been any inflation; it is simply not known what would have happened to corporate giving in the absence of inflation. Nor does this mean that individual companies, on the average, reduced their giving in real terms between 1970 and 1982; this result may well be due, at least in part, to a shift in the distribution of large and small corporate givers. But it does suggest that much of the long-run growth of corporate contributions has been exaggerated by the upward movement of general price levels during these years. It is, therefore, useful to look at the data with an adjustment for rising prices.

There exists no price index that is well suited for the kind of adjustment that is required. There is no price index that measures the purchasing power of the corporate profits from which contributions are made, and there is no price index that measures the purchasing power of funds put to charitable uses. However, the Consumer Price Index (CPI), though it is only a surrogate, does measure in a very rough way the degree of inflation over a period as long as fifty years. For the period from 1936 to 1986, the CPI increased at an average annual rate of 4.2 percent. This means that total corporate contributions increased not at the 10.6 percent rate that the unadjusted figures show but at 6.1 percent per year in real terms. When compared to other indices of real economic activity, this is an impressive rate of growth. For example, the gross national product (GNP), in constant prices, grew only 3.6 percent per year, and corporate profits before taxes grew only 3.1 percent per year, in this period.

When the CPI is used to deflate the data to dollars of 1967 purchasing power, the historical picture of corporate contributions takes on a somewhat different complexion. Figure 20.2 shows the data for the period from 1941 to 1985, with estimates for 1986, 1987, and 1988. All of the data points for years prior to 1943 lie so clearly outside the pattern that they are irrelevant to further analysis. For the years from 1943 onward, the data appear to conform to a well-defined trend, one that has an implicit growth rate of 3.4 percent per year (as against 2.9 percent per year for the GNP). An extrapolation to the future yields a figure of nearly $2.2 billion for the year 2000. If this number is translated from 1967 prices to 1988 prices, the result is $7.4 billion. This may be interpreted as a projection of corporate giving to the year 2000 based on the historical trend and the assumption of zero inflation. The actual number will undoubtedly be larger than this, depending on the degree of inflation during the remainder of this century. In passing, it should be noted that, with a projection of 3.4 percent per year real growth, corporate

Figure 20.2. Growth of Corporate Charitable Contributions
(in Millions of 1967 Dollars).

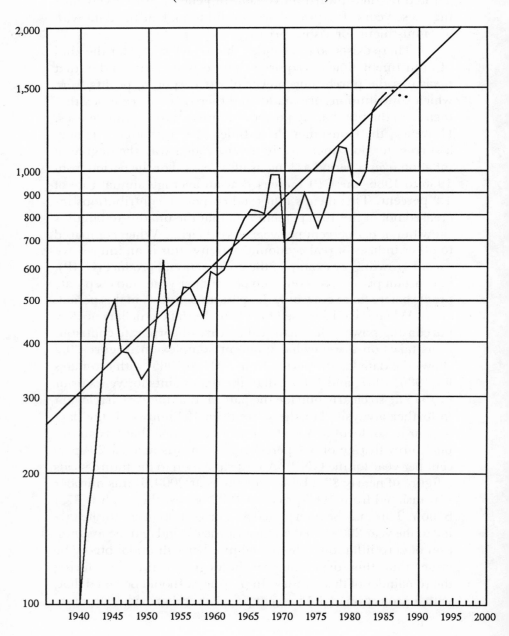

contributions can continue to grow at 10.6 percent per year in current prices only if inflation should average about 7 percent per year in future years. Whether that will happen and, if it does, what its effect will be on corporate giving are purely matters for speculation.

The constant-dollar plot of corporate contributions accentuates the instability of corporate giving throughout the period shown. It also provides new insight into the developments since 1970. These data show, for instance, that corporate giving, in real terms, actually declined in 1974–1975 and in 1979–1981, something that one might have expected in view of the business cycle developments of those periods. These data also show that corporate contributions made a significant recovery after 1981, one that is most surprising in view of the sluggishness of corporate profits before taxes in recent years.

The Influence of Corporate Profits. Since 1979, the relationship between corporate contributions and corporate profits before taxes has taken an unprecedented turn. In all previous periods for which there are data, corporate giving mirrored in some degree the ups and downs of corporate earnings. The relationship has often shown a lag of a year or more, but by and large it has been remarkably stable, at least from the early 1950s to the early 1980s. Throughout the period 1952–1980 (with the exception of 1953, 1968, and 1969, for reasons indicated above), corporate contributions never amounted to less than 0.81 percent or more than 1.10 percent of profits before taxes. As noted earlier, there was an upward long-run trend within this range.

Beginning in 1980, however, the historical relationship changed significantly. Corporate profits before taxes declined in 1980 and remained well below the 1979 level for seven years; that is, through 1986. Contributions, by contrast, rose in every year and by 1986 were roughly double their 1979 level. As a result, contributions rose from 0.89 percent of pretax profits in 1979 to an estimated 1.94 percent in 1986. Government estimates show that there was a sharp rise in pretax profits in 1987 and 1988, while contributions were relatively stable, with the result that the percentage fell to about 1.60. This is still substantially higher than for any year prior to 1982.

The relationship between corporate contributions and pretax profits for the last few years represents such a significant discontinuity in the historical trend and has such important implications for the future that it merits a close examination. An inspection of Table 20.2 indicates clearly that the discontinuity took place in 1982 and reflected both a large increase in contributions and a sharp fall in profits before taxes in that year. In 1983 and 1984, there was a recovery in profits but a parallel further increase in contributions, with the result that the percentage did not change very much. A small slump in profits in 1985, accompanied by another double-digit percentage rise in giving, caused the percentage to reach an all-time high of 1.99. Although the data for 1986–1988 are estimates based on sample surveys and other information, the percentages are believed to be within a reasonable range of their true values. Corporate contributions are now on a plateau, and while the percentage has receded from its 1985 high, it remains well above all pre-1982 levels.

There has been considerable interest in this development. What are its underlying causes? Why should there be a sudden discontinuity in a relationship that had been so stable for so

Table 20.2. Corporate Contributions as Percentage of Pretax Profits.

	Corporate Contributions (in Millions of Dollars)[a]	Corporate Profits Before Taxes (in Billions of Dollars)[b]	Contributions as Percentage of Profits Before Taxes
1979	$2,288	$257.2	0.89
1980	2,359	237.1	0.99
1981	2,514	226.5	1.11
1982	2,906	169.6	1.71
1983	3,627	207.6	1.75
1984	4,057	240.0	1.69
1985	4,472	224.3	1.99
1986	4,600[c]	236.4	1.94
1987	4,600[c]	276.7	1.66
1988	4,700[c]	307.0[c]	1.53

[a]Internal Revenue Service figures. These figures are amounts claimed as deductions on corporate tax returns; hence, they include amounts given to corporate foundations and exclude grants made by these foundations.

[b]U.S. Department of Commerce figures.

[c]Estimate of the Council for Aid to Education.

long a period of time? And, more importantly, what are the implications for the future? Will the relationship remain in the 1.5–2.0
percent range? Will it drift back to its prior levels? Or might it
increase further in the years to come? Adequate answers to these
questions can be only conjectural. Yet there are several known
developments in these years to which one can point as contributing factors. None of these by itself provides a sufficient explanation of this extraordinary upsurge in corporate giving in the face
of sluggish corporate earnings. Taken together, however, they
suggest that to a very large degree, the 1979–1986 ''explosion''
in corporate contributions was accidental in that several nonrecur-
ring developments took place at about the same time.

One such development was changes in the tax law in regard to corporate contributions. As discussed above, the Economic Recovery Tax Act of 1981 (ERTA) raised the allowable
deduction for corporate contributions from 5 to 10 percent of
taxable income, effective in 1982, and provided an enhanced
deduction for certain gifts of company products. The increased
percentage limit has resulted in increased amounts of contributions reported by thousands of small, privately owned corporations, in part because ERTA also lowered the marginal tax rates
for individuals so that in many instances it became more advantageous for the owners of small businesses to make their contributions through their companies than to do so as individuals.
The upsurge in gifts of company products is now well known,
and the available measurements indicate that the amounts are
significant. Taken together, these two changes in the tax law
may well have accounted for more than a third of the increment
in corporate giving between 1981 and 1986.

Another factor is gifts of surplus corporate assets. From
time to time over the years, corporations have given surplus
property—land, buildings, equipment—to charitable organizations, and the tax law provides a charitable deduction for such
gifts. The valuation rules are complex, but essentially they allow
a deduction based on fair market value with an offset for recapture of depreciation. This formula provides important incentives
for the contribution of such property to charity once it is determined to be surplus to corporate needs, and it provides an attractive way of funding corporate foundations. By definition, these

gifts occur randomly, and large gifts of this type—say, $5 million or more—were infrequent prior to 1981. Since then, however, and in large measure as a result of the massive restructuring of American business, more than ten such gifts in the range of $10 to $110 million are known to have been made. Taken together, these large, nonrecurring gifts account for a significant share of the 1981–1987 increment in corporate giving.

A third factor is reduced government spending on social programs. One of the hallmarks of the Reagan administration was a policy of trying to shift responsibility in the social sphere from the federal government to the private sector. In his 1981 budget message, for example, the president proposed cutbacks of several billions of dollars in federal social programs, encouraging corporations and foundations to take up the slack. The policy also manifested itself through the continued encouragement of local, private initiatives involving partnership arrangements in many of which corporations were expected to play a major role.

One of the consequences of this policy was a significant rise in the degree of attention given to corporations as funding sources by charitable organizations. Most of the larger public corporations and their sponsored foundations experienced very significant increases in the number of requests for funding, a large part of which came from organizations outside the areas to which corporations had traditionally made their contributions. And most charities, new and old, became more sophisticated in their approaches to the business world. Although it would be difficult to measure the extent to which this pressure caused an increase in corporate contributions, there is little doubt that the business community became more aware of and responsive to the increased needs of the charitable community. Some of the 1981–1987 increment in corporate giving is undoubtedly attributable to this development.

Accompanying the above developments were a series of changes in attitudes toward corporate giving, both internally and externally. Concurrently with the disappearance of the three obstacles to corporate giving between the late 1930s and 1970, there emerged two positive influences that slowly diffused through most of the corporate community: the concept of "enlightened self-interest" and the notion of "corporate social responsibility."

The first involved the idea that corporate charitable giving is a *permissible* activity because it advances the company's own welfare; the second went further by saying that the corporation has a *duty* to participate in efforts to solve social problems and to advance the welfare of the nation by making money, facilities, and employees' time available to the charitable community.

By the end of the 1970s, the business world had begun to respond to these forces by moving contributions and related functions from an obscure corner of corporate life to a position of visibility, from an incidental activity on the part of people whose principal duties lay in other areas to a very businesslike operation. The techniques that had proved so successful in other areas of the corporation were applied to contributions and other facets of corporate social responsibility, and the people involved brought increasing professionalism to their work. Managerial philosophy also changed; instead of merely giving in reaction to the appeals for charitable grants,the process became proactive, with sets of objectives, budgetary priorities, program planning, coordination, and accountability.

Externally, there was a growing awareness of corporate contributions and a rising tide of public expectations. In the early 1980s, corporate giving was suddenly "discovered" as a new and untapped source of private-sector money. Almost overnight, corporate contributions became the focus of interest in the philanthropic community, in the media, and among public officials. For example, the Council on Foundations, the INDEPENDENT SECTOR, and other organizations turned their attention to this area and began to devote a substantial part of their program activities to it. The White House sponsored a Task Force on Private Sector Initiatives, and the Business Roundtable established a Task Force on Social Responsibility, both of which urged higher levels of corporate giving. One response to this was the establishment of "2 percent clubs" in various cities, movements on the part of businesspeople to encourage increased corporate support of charitable endeavors. In addition, regional "grant-makers' " groups, which acted as information and service mechanisms, opened their doors to corporate members. This change in the climate for corporate giving was undoubtedly responsible for some of the increase in corporate contributions between 1979 and 1986. While a doubling of contribution amounts and percentages was a notable achievement, it was also a disappointment to those who expected an even larger growth in corporate giving.

Self-Interest, Not Philanthropy

Prior to 1981, when Congress raised the allowable deduction from 5 to 10 percent of taxable income, it was common to hear something like the following: "corporate giving [which was then slightly more than $2 billion] amounts to only 1 percent of corporate profits before taxes; the tax law, however, allows corporations to give up to 5 percent; therefore, since corporations have the capacity to give five times as much, they should increase their giving up to what the tax law allows." That this was spurious reasoning and that these expectations were grossly unrealistic is obvious. But it does illustrate the awakening of interest on the part of many who had previously had only a dim awareness of corporate contributions. The error of reasoning was compounded in many instances by a tendency to equate corporate giving with foundation grants, an understandable confusion in light of the fact that many major corporations sponsored foundations. Hence, the expression "corporate philanthropy" arose and became used frequently as a descriptive phrase for corporate contributions and some other aspects of corporate social responsibility.

But corporations, unlike foundations, do not exist for philanthropic purposes. Business corporations are entities whose purpose in life is far removed from charity. Corporate contributions consist of money and other property that belongs not to corporations themselves but to their stockholders, who are the legal owners. Corporations do have the power to make charitable contributions, and they are encouraged to do so in a variety of ways, but charitable giving is, at best, an incidental activity in the corporate world. And corporations do have the option not to give at all.

The motivation for charitable giving is rooted not in altruism but in the corporation's own self-interest. Enlightened corporate management explicitly recognizes that some small sacrifice of short-term profits might be necessary if the ultimate self-interest of the corporation is adequately to be served. As one observer put it, "Corporate activity in the social sphere is not, in fact, altruistic. It does not represent a purely voluntary and gratuitous act of generosity. It does not reflect a partial transmutation of the corporation into an instrument of social progress. It reflects a tactical judgment as to the most advantageous manner for the corporation to conduct its business in the light of the climate of opinion in which it must function. Nor is justification of the validity of corporate action in terms of its being 'good business' outmoded. On the contrary, this is the fundamental test of whether the action—even though involving gratuitous expenditures—is intended to fulfill the objectives of the business" (Blumberg, 1970, p. 207). That corporations do make contributions and gifts is simply a reflection of the fact that corporate management now recognizes that the long-run welfare of business depends, among other things, on the health of the society of which they are a part.

No two corporations are alike. Each determines how much to give, and to whom and for what purposes, according to its own assessment of its interests. In making that determination, corporate managers necessarily give weight to a host of factors, some of which are internal to the corporation while others reflect the external "climate of opinion." The most important single factor in the determination of a corporate contributions budget is the company's ability to give, usually measured by its earnings. A company with large profits will tend to give more than a company with small profits, and any one company's giving will tend to rise and fall as its profits increase and decrease. Among companies with similar profit levels, however, there may be a wide range of giving levels; this reflects, among other things, differences in viewpoint among corporate managers as to what is appropriate for their respective companies.

There has been a trend in recent years for management to increase only modestly the size of their contributions budgets relative to corporate earnings. For the most part, this reflects a reaction to the external factors that impinge on corporate giving. Among these are various changes in the tax laws and certain pressures arising from social and political change. All such factors have limited force and limited tenure, but while they are in place and effective, they can be and have been instrumental in bringing about sharp increases in the average amounts of giving per company.

Speculations on the Future

Given the dynamic growth of the corporate population and the probable growth of corporate profitability, it is an odds-on bet that total corporate contributions will continue to grow in the future, at least in current prices. The question is: will it continue to grow as fast in the future as it has in the past? Ultimately, of course, the rapid growth of corporate contributions that has characterized the last half century *must* come to an end unless the rate of growth of corporate profits should increase to levels approximately equal to those of contributions. Otherwise, corporate contributions as a percentage of pretax profits would rise without limit. In the long run, the growth of corporate giving cannot outpace the growth of corporate earnings.

That having been said, it is by no means certain that the slowdown will occur in the next twelve years or, for that matter, within any future period of predetermined length. What actually happens between now and the year 2000 depends on many factors whose future courses are highly uncertain. The following list of such factors is meant to be suggestive, not by any means exhaustive:

- The health of the nation's economy, including the rate of economic growth and the growth of corporate profits before taxes.
- The stability of general price levels.
- Government policies, especially tax policy and the nature of the federal and state involvement in the social arena.
- The views of political leadership with respect to the balance between public and private initiatives in the social sphere.
- The general "climate of opinion" toward corporate giving and corporate social involvement.
- The growth of alternative sources of funding for the nation's charitable organizations.
- The effectiveness and accountability of charities and the skill and sophistication of their fund raisers.
- The attitudes of corporate management with respect to the appropriate levels of corporate giving.

- The willingness of corporate stockholders to allow corporate contributions at any specific levels.
- The relative attractiveness of alternative means of response to the dictum of ''social responsibility.''

Clearly, the ability and willingness of corporations to raise the levels of their giving in the future are in large part a function of developments that are outside the control of corporations themselves. The perception of corporate self-interest will not go away, nor will there likely be any diminution of corporate interest in being socially responsible good citizens. What corporations actually do in the next dozen or so years depends most of all on the kinds of stimuli they receive from the external world. In the absence of continuous stimuli—new incentives for increased levels of giving and new forces leading to larger perceptions of corporate duty—the rate of growth of corporate contributions is virtually certain to be slower in future years than in the past.

The past growth of corporate contributions was certainly unplanned, and much of it was the inadvertent result of actions that had quite different objectives; changes in tax policy, for example. The historical picture painted above reveals a series of influences that were almost accidental in origin, timing, and impact. Together they resulted in an extraordinary era of growth, one that is unlikely to be repeated in the future. This is not to say that corporate giving will stagnate in the years to come. On the contrary, the corporate community has committed itself to underwriting what it considers to be its appropriate share of the nation's charitable endeavors, and there is every likelihood that it will continue to do so. But corporations will continue primarily to be business organizations, and their charitable contributions will continue to be incidental to their principal purposes and objectives. Corporations are, after all, designed to produce and sell goods and services and to earn profits for their stockholders. To the extent that charitable giving is compatible with that design, one may expect it to grow as corporations themselves grow. At the same time, charity must be prepared to share the vicissitudes of corporate fortunes—the business cycle, competitive inroads from abroad, industrial restructuring, and similar dynamic changes—that affect the ability to give. The reality is that it is not philanthropy.

References

Blumberg, P. I. "Corporate Responsibility and the Social Crisis." *Boston University Law Review,* 1970; *50* (2), pp. 157–210.

Brown, C. C. *Corporate Support of Higher Education: History, Needs, and Growing Dimensions.* New York: Council for Aid to Education, 1969.

Council for Aid to Education. *Voluntary Support of Education, 1985–86.* New York: Council for Aid to Education, 1987.

Council for Aid to Education. *Corporate Support of Education, 1986.* New York: Council for Aid to Education, 1988.

Smith, H. W. *A Profile of Corporate Contributions.* New York: Council for Aid to Education, 1983.

Smith, H. W. *A New Profile of Corporate Contributions.* New York: Council for Aid to Education, 1989.

Vasquez, T. "Corporate Giving Measures." In Commission on Private Philanthropy and Public Needs, *Research Papers of the Commission on Private Philanthropy and Public Needs.* Washington, D.C.: U.S. Department of the Treasury, 1977, pp. 1839–1852.

21

PETER GOLDBERG

△ △ △ △ △ △ △ △ △ △ △ △ △ △ △

Corporate Social Responsibility and Public-Private Partnerships

The philosophical underpinnings of this chapter are straight-forward and unambiguous. Ours is a society of interdependent institutions. The business community—one major institution in American society—is not an impregnable island unto itself. Whether we like it or not, the business community has a long-term stake in how this nation addresses the major social issues of our time. Poverty in America stands out as a major social issue of the 1980s. Nonetheless, despite substantial increases in corporate philanthropy and the advent of public-private partnerships, it is still unclear just how committed corporations are to antipoverty efforts and just how seriously they view the problems of poverty in American society. National efforts to alleviate the tragedy of poverty in the richest nation in the world would be considerably strengthened if the business community would voice more active public-policy support for governmentally financed antipoverty programs.

The Extent of Poverty and the Growing Income Gap

Although there are many different interpretations of the nature of poverty in America and many different prescriptions about how to respond, the size of the problem is large by anyone's definition. Poverty in America is a major social concern. The business community has a vital long-term interest in the poverty

341

problem. Poor people have less money with which to buy the products businesses make and the services they offer; poor people need greater levels of public assistance, which in turn means higher tax rates. Poor children, poorly educated, grow up poorly prepared to participate in the labor force. Given current demographics, business may find itself unable to hire all the workers it needs if too many Americans grow up lacking basic skills; at the least it will face unnecessarily high training costs. Finally, the increasing number of people deeply entrenched in poverty raises the specter of a permanent underclass, a form of social and economic dynamite that is in the best interests neither of the business community nor of the larger society.

According to recent Census Bureau data, 32.4 million Americans—13.6 percent of the population—lived below the poverty line in 1986. Moreover, 12.7 million people subsisted on incomes of less than half the official poverty level. The poverty rate for black Americans in 1986 was 31.1 percent, and for Hispanics it was 27.3 percent. The future health and vitality of the United States rests with its children. Yet in 1986, 20.5 percent of all American children lived in conditions of poverty. Among black children, the rate was 43 percent; the childhood poverty rate for Hispanic children was similarly high (Center on Budget and Policy Priorities, 1987). Poverty is commonly associated with many indices of child, youth, and family problems, such as child abuse, juvenile delinquency, infant mortality, and drug abuse. The social and economic costs of poverty-related problems ripple throughout our society, affecting just about every individual and institution in one way or another.

The national poverty rate declined very slightly in 1986 and 1987. Whatever comfort may be derived from this trend, however, is not necessarily shared by those who work closer to the front lines. Since 1982, the U.S. Conference of Mayors has regularly surveyed the extent of hunger, homelessness, and poverty in American cities. Their December 1987 report paints a bleak picture of sustained and serious social and economic conditions (Reyes and Waxman, 1987). Compounding the very high rate of poverty in the 1980s are Census Bureau data showing an ever-widening gap between rich and poor. According to the Center on Budget and Policy Priorities (1987), in 1986 the wealthiest 20 percent of American families received 43.7 percent of the national family income, the highest percentage ever recorded since the Census Bureau began collecting such data in 1947. At the other end of the scale, the poorest 40 percent of American families received 15.4 percent of the national family income, the lowest percentage ever recorded. The large and growing number of people living in deep and entrenched poverty in the 1980s raises serious concerns about the creation of a permanent underclass, a group of American citizens for whom the hope of escaping poverty and pursuing the American dream becomes increasingly remote.

The economic public policies that have exacerbated the dire straits of millions of poor Americans during this decade have been generally more favorable to the business community. Corporate tax rates have gone down. Corporate profits have increased handsomely. The stock market has risen significantly since 1982 (even given the October 1987 "crash"), yielding good returns for those who have invested in it. Public opinion about corporate wealth is molded by other observations as well. The proliferation of high-stakes corporate takeover battles leaves the public uneasy and with a sense that such boardroom drama enriches very few at the expense of many more. Highly publicized insider-trading scandals add further fuel to the public's sense that in this era of government deregulation, greed is overwhelming legitimate business accomplishments and the public interest. The intermixing of widely held impressions with available data shapes a picture of corporate America that stands in sharp contrast to that view of the other America defined by the Census Bureau statistics on poverty. With these pictures in mind, we now turn to a discussion of how corporations have reacted and responded to the problems of poverty in the 1980s.

Corporate Philanthropy and Public-Private Partnerships

The adequacy of the corporate response to the problems of poverty in America is subject to different interpretations, dependent on wholly subjective standards and reference points. It is possible to set low standards that corporations can meet with ease and to great applause. It is also possible to set high standards and watch more critically as corporations approach the challenge with temerity.

From one vantage point, it is quite possible to applaud America's corporations for their commitment to philanthropy during the 1980s. Corporate giving to nonprofit organizations rose from $2.4 billion in 1980 to $4.4 billion in 1985 (Platzer, 1987), although this increase has now apparently leveled out. From a different vantage point, however, one may suspect that the increases in corporate philanthropy are something of a palliative, of uncertain endurance, with uncertain motives, and of limited utility. The skeptic would point out that increases in corporate philanthropy should not be allowed to mask the basic fact that America's corporations benefited from substantial reductions in tax rates as well as other national public policies that have, in effect, made the rich richer and the poor poorer.

From one perspective, it is quite possible to applaud the corporate commitment to social problem solving through public-private partnerships. Encouraged by all levels of government, corporations have produced scores of examples of successful corporate participation in problem solving in fields as diverse as hunger, education, housing, and youth employment. From the other perspective, however, there are those who can point out that the vast majority of America's corporations were woefully silent as the Reagan administration and the Congress trimmed away the so-called "social safety net." From this perspective, corporate philanthropy and participation in public-private partnerships would not have been so important had the federal government not been allowed to redefine and reduce its commitments to domestic antipoverty programs.

In one sense, though, American corporations have exceeded their social and public responsibilities: in point of fact, they are not legally compelled to make any philanthropic contributions at all. Corporations do not have to participate in any public-private partnerships whatsoever. But corporations have voluntarily chosen to be involved. The motivations for this involvement may be fueled by different mixtures of altruism and self-interest. Whether these commitments are of the here-today-and-gone-tomorrow variety or are of more lasting endurance also varies from one company to the next. Regardless, corporations have frequently sought recognition and been widely hailed for their generous willingness to participate in social problem solving. It is neither unreasonable nor unfair to set high standards by which to appraise the aggregate effectiveness of such efforts.

High standards of expectation are also preferable to low standards because (1) the needs of people in poverty are substantial and (2) corporations have a long-term, important stake in how American society addresses the problems of poverty. It is also healthier to search for challenges that extend our efforts and to find ways to improve on them than it is to engage in hearty rounds of backslapping and self-congratulation.

The Limits of Corporate Philanthropy

Despite the impressive growth of corporate philanthropy in the 1980s, the overall dollar value of corporate grant making could hardly make a dent in the constellation of poverty-related problems. The Salamon-Abramson analysis of "Nonprofit Organizations and the FY 1988 Federal Budget" (Salamon and Abramson, 1987) makes clear just how difficult it is for *all* private giving to offset federal spending reductions. It is certainly not unreasonable—indeed, it is probably very conservative—to suggest that we could double, double, and double again the amount of corporate philanthropic giving and it would still be inadequate to meet the needs of poor Americans and still be small in total dollar size compared to a relatively small percentage increase in government commitments.

Moreover, only a fraction of the corporate philanthropic budget is directed toward poverty problems. Corporate foundations make grants to a diversity of organizations for a diversity of reasons. Poverty is not at the head of the priority list for most corporate foundations. While the overall amount of corporate philanthropic funding available for serious antipoverty efforts has never been precisely calculated, it is most assuredly well under $1 billion per year. The actual impact of even this amount is further diluted by legitimate concerns about the general thoughtfulness and quality of effort that characterize even well-intentioned corporate grant making (O'Connell, 1987).

Another factor that limits the effectiveness of corporate philanthropy in addressing problems of poverty is that corporate grant making tends not to be countercyclical. Poverty problems worsen during recessions, and the need for assistance increases. However, recessions require many corporate grant makers to tighten their own belts, because the budgets of many corporate foundations are indexed against pretax income levels. Pretax income does not rise at the same rate during recessions as during periods of growth, and corporate expenses of all types are scrutinized more carefully during recessions. Ironically, just when corporate grant making could be most valuable in addressing the increased needs of growing numbers of poor people, corporate grant makers must hunker down with the rest of corporate America to weather the storms of economic recession.

This scenario could be particularly profound whenever the next recession occurs. In recessions, unemployment and poverty levels are likely to rise, with the increase somewhat correlated to the severity and duration of the recession. Since the last recession, in 1981–82, unemployment levels have dropped considerably, but the poverty rate remains abnormally high. Thus it is possible that the next recession—whatever its overall severity—could hurt poor people disproportionately.

The Limits of Public-Private Partnerships

The potential of public-private partnerships to alleviate poverty is also limited. Such partnerships can help to identify innovative solutions to some problems; they can become the means by which to offer some assistance to some people and some communities. It is a mistake, however, to let such partnerships be magnified and misinterpreted as a comprehensive form of private-sector substitution for public-sector responsibility. Corporate donations of food to the national network of food banks, for example, have risen impressively from a few million pounds in 1979 to 352 million pounds in 1986 (Second Harvest, 1987). But these donations—as welcome as they are—are only a stopgap measure and cannot solve the problems of hunger and inadequate nutrition for millions of Americans. A more effective response would be to ensure that all eligible recipients participated in the federal food stamp program and received benefits sufficient to maintain adequate nutritional levels.

School-business partnerships are also limited. This type of partnership has become exceedingly popular in the corporate community. Many schools and many schoolchildren have benefited from school-business partnerships. The policy problem with focusing on the successful examples of school-business partnerships is that they overlook the overwhelming majority of schools and schoolchildren who are *not* affected by them. In contrast to the corporate commitment to school-business partnerships, corporate executives have been far less outspoken in their support of greater public-sector expenditures for successful educational programs such as Head Start and Chapter One, effective programs that should be made available to all disadvantaged school children.

Public-private partnerships have provided corporations and corporate executives with valuable learning experiences. Three lessons stand out. First, these partnerships offer a window to the world in which less fortunate Americans must struggle to survive. Senior corporate executives are often touched by their personal experiences. They see conditions of poverty firsthand. They witness valiant efforts to escape the traps of poverty. They have renewed appreciation of the value of programs to help poor people. Second, private-sector partnership programs with government agencies offer penetrating insights into the extraordinary problems of administering effective, large public-sector programs. Corporate executives may emerge from their partnership experiences with equal or even more withering criticisms of the public-sector bureaucracy, but they also frequently gain a new appreciation of the scope, complexity, and difficulty of running large public-sector programs. Finally, corporate-sector leaders have to be impressed by the limits of the private sector to respond to the overwhelming size of poverty-related problems without the involvement of the public sector. It far exceeds anyone's definition of corporate social responsibility to try to replicate successful public-private partnership programs at a sustained year-to-year level sufficient to respond to intransigent social problems of a large magnitude.

The Need for Corporate Participation
in Public Policy Making

Should corporate America be satisfied with its antipoverty efforts solely through its own philanthropy and participation in public-private partnerships without also speaking up in vigorous support of effective public-sector programs, particularly underfunded government programs with demonstrated track records of success? Is corporate America so enamored with its own efforts that it has forgotten to look at the problems that prompted those efforts in the first place? Will corporate America continue to be preoccupied with private-sector initiatives that are limited in potential? Or are these efforts the necessary passageway through which most corporate executives must travel before they discover the larger antipoverty resources potentially available through the public sector?

A breakthrough of sorts occurred in March 1986, when five senior executives from five different major American businesses testified together at a joint House-Senate hearing on behalf of the reauthorization of federal aid to public elementary and secondary schools serving high concentrations of disadvantaged children (Woodside and others, 1987). It was the first time in the twenty-year history of the Chapter One program (formerly known as Title One) that any American businesspeople directly communicated their concern and support to Congress for this important antipoverty and education program. Representative Augustus Hawkins, a long-time champion of the program, referred to the business executives' testimony as an important element in the recent reauthorization process ("A Business Lobby for Public Education," 1987). The additional funds now authorized for this federal program will exceed the annual dollar value of all school-business partnerships nationwide.

In another example of the willingness of the business community to involve itself in the public-policy making process, the Committee for Economic Development (1987) recently issued a report expressing strong support for the federal government's Head Start program. However, these examples stand in relative isolation and thus far are confined primarily to issues of public education. There has been very little outspoken corporate support for most public-sector antipoverty efforts.

In 1985, Fred Hechinger of the *New York Times* issued a stern warning about possible corporate duplicity with respect to its support for public education: "In the end, all these cooperative ventures [school-business partnerships] will amount to little more than public relations unless the business community abandons its frequently schizophrenic posture; supporting the local schools while simultaneously instructing, or at least permitting, its lobbyists to support cuts in state and federal expenditures for public education and such legislation as tax credits for parents whose children attend private schools. Common sense should show the futility of any corporate policy that gives to the local schools with one hand and yet takes away funds with the other" (Hechinger, 1985, p. 143). Hechinger's words can be applied to a broader range of corporate involvement in the pressing social problems of the day.

Not every governmentally funded antipoverty program is an unqualified success; nor is every one an abject failure. Corporations and corporate executives ought to be both encouraged and prodded to speak out on behalf of effective programs such as Head Start, the Special Supplemental Program for Women, Infants, and Children (WIC), and Child Immunization; they ought to lend their talents and energies to help strengthen marginally effective programs. And business leaders ought to participate in the development of new public policies and programs to attack poverty in America. After all, public policy and the priorities expressed through government budget making will be significant determinants of the nature, extent, and severity of poverty in America.

What Does the Future Hold?

For those who set high standards of expectation for corporate contributons to national antipoverty efforts, the aggregate effectiveness of current programs falls short of the mark. Disappointment may conceivably be tempered by belief in progress— such as growing sophistication of partnership and philanthropic efforts and occasional glimmers of hope that some corporations and corporate executives are willing to speak out forcefully, even passionately, on the important social and economic public-policy decisions that affect poverty in the United States. But beyond the fact that this progress is not fast enough to produce any measurable dent in poverty, business may be on the way to paying a price in the public's perceptions of it. According to a recent issue of *Time* magazine, for example, "If Big Government was the villain of the Reagan cycle of American history, the *bete noire* of the new may be Big Business" (Morrow, 1987). *Time* goes on to cite surveys from pollster Lou Harris that showed 69 percent of the American public giving corporate America a favorable rating in 1979, while the comparable 1986 figure was 35 percent. Harris concludes that "the mood about business has turned negative on a massive scale" (Morrow, 1987).

What will happen to the corporate commitment to philanthropy and public-private partnerships if Harris is right? Will business undertake to do more about poverty in order to redeem itself in the public's eye? Or will the corporate sector display less sensitivity to poverty in America when government is regulating it more and applauding it less? What will happen to the corporate commitment to corporate philanthropy and social responsibility if corporate tax rates go up? In many ways, these are litmus-type questions for the corporate community. The answers will shed much light on what corporate America believes about poverty; whether corporate efforts to address poverty problems are short-term, paper thin, and of questionable motivation or whether they are the modest beginnings of a longer-term commitment; whether corporate America believes that the problems of poverty affect its long-term health and vitality or whether corporations hold to the "impregnable island" concept.

The answers to these questions are also important to many poor citizens. It is possible to make substantial inroads against poverty without active corporate support in the public policy-making and government budget-setting processes. These inroads, however, could be made more swiftly, more effectively, and more deeply if the business community moves into an active and visible advocacy posture.

Conclusion

In the final analysis, the adequacy of the corporate response to poverty in America depends on the measures one chooses to employ. Measured against themselves over time, corporate philanthropy and public-private partnerships have grown in size and sophistication. In a social vacuum, blind to the problems against which they are applied, it is relatively easy to construct an argument for great praise. But if we look at the impact of current efforts on the problems to which they are directed, the aggregate effectiveness and success and the speed of progress are discouragingly small.

References

"A Business Lobby for Public Education." *New York Times,* Oct. 26, 1987, p. A-18.

Center on Budget and Policy Priorities. "Gap Between Rich and Poor Widest Ever Recorded." Working paper dated July 30, 1987 (rev. Aug. 17, 1987).

Committee for Economic Development. *Children in Need.* New York: Committee for Economic Development, 1987.

Hechinger, F. M. "Turnaround for the Public Schools?" *Harvard Business Review,* Jan.–Feb. 1985, pp. 136–144.

Morrow, L. "A Change in the Weather." *Time,* Mar. 30, 1987, pp. 28–37.

O'Connell, B. "Corporate Philanthropy: Getting Bigger, Broader and Tougher to Manage." *Corporate Philanthropy,* 1987, *7* (4), entire issue.

Platzer, L. C. *Annual Survey of Corporate Contributions, 1987 Edition.* Research report no. 896. New York: Conference Board, 1987.

Reyes, L. M., and Waxman, L. *The Continuing Growth of Hunger, Homelessness and Poverty in America's Cities: 1987.* Washington, D.C.: U.S. Conference of Mayors, 1987.

Salamon, L. M., and Abramson, A. J. "Nonprofit Organizations and the FY 1988 Federal Budget." Report prepared for the INDEPENDENT SECTOR and the 501(c)(3) Group, Aug. 1987.

Second Harvest. *The Benefits of Donating.* Chicago: Second Harvest, 1987.

Woodside, W. S., and others. "Reauthorization of Chapter I." Testimony presented to the Senate Subcommittee on Education, Arts and Humanities and the House of Representatives Subcommittee on Elementary, Secondary and Vocational Education, Mar. 16, 1987.

22

ROBERT O. BOTHWELL
ELIZABETH WIENER

△ △ △ △ △ △ △ △ △ △ △ △ △ △ △

Trends in Corporate Reporting on Philanthropic Efforts

Today, for all its importance, corporate philanthropy is basically shrouded in secrecy. Whether we consider its finances, its governance, its giving priorities, its application procedures, its non-cash contributions, or even the identity of its grantees, corporate philanthropy is essentially a mystery. Those receiving the corporate largesse obviously know the passwords to gain entrance to the corporate coffers. But the many who are not now corporate grant recipients but who want to be are given few clues as to whom to approach, how, when, for what, and for how much. Lack of information also bedevils those seeking to understand more of the nexus between corporations and charities—whether Olasky and the Capital Research Center (Olasky, 1987), the Council on Economic Priorities (Lydenberg and others, 1986), the *Los Angeles Times,* the *Wall Street Journal,* or other interested media.

During the early 1980s, corporate contributions increased substantially each year and in 1983 they surpassed foundation contributions for the first time ever. Equally significant has been the growth of corporate donations from the 1 percent of pretax profits that had been virtually constant for several decades up to 1.64 percent in 1987 (American Association of Fund-Raising Counsel, 1988). However, as international competition has overtaken many American industries, as merger

mania has turned corporate boardroom tables upside down, and
as American businesses are making wholesale staff and other
cuts to adjust, corporate philanthropy has slackened its pace.
During the period 1981 through 1985, the average annual
growth rate was 13.5 percent. But in 1986 it was only 2.3 percent. And according to the American Association of Fund-
Raising Counsel (1988), corporate giving registered no increase
in 1987.

Nevertheless, corporate philanthropy, while currently
undergoing great change, appears to be here to stay as an important part of the philanthropic landscape. United Ways depend on it for a quarter of their revenues (United Ways also
obtain another 50 percent of their income from corporate employees through annual business charity campaigns). Educational institutions, as the largest recipient category of corporate
philanthropy, depend on it. Arts organizations have found
diverse ways to increase their dependence on it. Untold numbers
of other local community institutions also depend on it. And,
if Marvin Olasky (1987) is to be believed, public-policy groups
of the left depend on it far more than those of the right.

Signs of Change

Despite its importance, corporate philanthropy remains a mys-
terious phenomenon. Three recent events, however, stand out
as indicators that this status quo may not be allowed to continue. In June 1987, for the first time ever, the media met the
charity world in a civilized confrontation. Twenty-five representatives each of the media and charities met in Chicago's Tribune
Tower in a conference arranged by Nicholas Goodban, executive
director of the Tribune Foundation and Craig Smith, editor of
the insightful *Corporate Philanthropy Report* with the goal of increased understanding of each other. The climate of the meeting
was initially confrontational. The charities wanted better media
coverage of their good works, of course. The media representatives said that they covered charitable activities when the latter
were newsworthy, but they would not be used as a free public relations agency. Nevertheless, what emerged were clear indications

that this event signified a trend toward increasing interest in each other on the part of charities and the media.

The second event, which took place in Washington, D.C. in September 1987, was a meeting arranged by the Council on Foundations. The participants included several eminent members of the foundation world (Merrimon Cuninggim, Paul Ylvisaker, and Homer Wadsworth, among others), as well as other foundation representatives and a few representatives from both progressive and right-wing groups interested in public policy. After a day and a half of discussions, this group reached agreement that the promotion of private philanthropy, particularly foundation philanthropy, would be best accomplished in two ways: through more independent, not necessarily academic, studies of the field, particularly of public and private policies that affect it, and through more investigation and analysis of abuses in the field. Whether action will be taken to make these things happen remains to be seen. Nevertheless, given the foundation world's previous distaste for self-examination and public interaction, it is significant that this mostly establishment group came to such a consensus about how best to improve the field.

The third event took place on Capitol Hill. This was the passage at the end of 1987 of H.R. 2942, a bill introduced by Representative J. J. Pickle of Texas that imposed new disclosure requirements on most charities. The bill was a result of Pickle's anger at the actions of Carl (Spitz) Connell, who set up a nonprofit organization and made use of 501(c)(3) advantages to fund the Contras, Oliver North's lecture circuit, and scathing political advertisements against members of Congress, such as Pickle, who did not support the Contras. Although Connell's organization was patently illegal, the IRS did not prosecute it because the only tool at their disposal was to revoke its tax-exempt status, which is a huge penalty; there were no penalties that could be immediately applied and were of appropriate scope. To introduce such penalties and to force the disclosure of activities were the focus of Pickle's subsequent legislation.

H.R. 2942 was drafted after only two days of hearings on the lobbying and political activities of tax-exempt organizations by Pickle's Oversight Subcommittee of the Committee on Ways and Means. Pickle introduced the bill on the floor of the House of Representatives, and it was attached to the 1987 Budget Reconciliation Act and sent to the Conference Committee with no House floor vote. It prevailed in conference with the Senate Finance Committee. Although the members of the Finance Committee did not agree on the necessity of the bill, they included it as part of the Budget Reconciliation Act because H.R. 2942 was only a tiny part of the Act.

This new law will affect all organizations defined as charities by Internal Revenue Code Section 501(c)(3), as well as other tax-exempt organizations. In some respects, greater disclosure will now be required of public charities than of private foundations. The legislation also includes a series of tax penalties designed to discourage violation of the new disclosure provisions. The important lesson of this event is the shocking rapidity with which this legislation, given its historical importance and magnitude, proceeded—there were no hearings on the bill itself along the way. And while the Pickle bill includes some new law concerning what is and is not prohibited to 501(c)(3) organizations, its essence is to require substantially more disclosure.

These three events—the media-charity confrontation, the foundation representatives' consensus on priority action to promote the field, and the bill imposing unprecedented new disclosure requirements on charitable organizations—suggest that the era of openness and disclosure that dawned in the 1960s and grew substantially in the 1970s but was reported near death in the 1980s is indeed very much alive and well and growing in strange new places. In the words of Dave Johnston, the *Los Angeles Times'* ubiquitous reporter on the world of philanthropy, there is "a growing national movement . . . challenging foundations to be more open about their policies and finances" (Johnston, 1986).

Corporate philanthropy's existence behind the veil of secrecy cannot continue indefinitely. Indeed, the right-wing Capital Research Center's study of corporate philanthropy (Olasky, 1987) and the progressive Council on Economic Priorities' study of the "corporate conscience" (Lydenberg and others, 1986) indicate fresh interest in this subject, in which only grant seekers and corporate contributions officials had previously shown interest.

The Current State of Corporate Philanthropy and Public Information

What then is the state of public reporting by corporate philanthropy? What proportion of corporations are publishing anything about their contributions programs? Are any corporations doing superior jobs? How many? Which ones? What information is most often provided? What least often? What information should be provided—for grant seekers, for the public at large (media, interested public-policy centers, legislators, public officials, private nonprofit leaders)? In order to answer these questions, the National Committee for Responsive Philanthropy undertook a study of the 200 largest profit-making corporations (using the *Forbes* magazine list in 1985). The committee examined the printed information that these corporations provided voluntarily and routinely to grant seekers and the general public. The study encompassed both corporate foundations and direct corporate giving programs.

This was not a study of corporate giving to public affairs organizations, as was Olasky's (1987) study, or of the size and nature of corporate contributions, as was the Council on Economic Priorities' effort (Lydenberg and others, 1986). The committee's study sought to make no judgments on the worthiness of grants or grantees. The simple goal was to ascertain the availability of information itself and the quality or usefulness of that information from the standpoint of both grantees and the general public.

Study Methodology. The researchers began by identifying the contributions officer in each of the 200 largest profit-making companies and, if the company had a foundation run separately from a direct giving program, the foundation contributions officer as well. With advice from five corporate executives and a corporate consultant, they prepared a letter explaining the background and purpose of the study and requesting all printed information on the corporate foundation and/or direct giving program. Up to three written requests were sent to each business, and up to three follow-up phone calls were made if necessary. By summer 1986, all 200 corporations had responded, either in writing (172 responses) or by telephone, even if only to say that they had no information to send. None said that they had no contribution program. As a control, a cooperating nonprofit organization made similar requests for information of most of the same corporations, seeking the information as if it were a grant seeker rather than a public-interest group embarking on a study (as the committee projected itself). In the twelve cases where this organization received more information than the committee, these responses were incorporated into the study.

Meanwhile, criteria were developed to evaluate the quality of information made available. Starting with the same criteria that the committee had used to evaluate foundations' responses to a similar study in 1980 (Bothwell and others, 1980), nineteen people working directly in corporate social responsibility were asked to identify items that it was inappropriate or unfair to expect from corporations and to suggest additional useful criteria. They were also asked to comment on the original scheme of differently weighting different types of information. The final criteria and weighting scheme selected by the committee do not represent a consensus of those consulted, though it is fair to say that they incorporate suggestions from a wide range of corporate officials and critics. The twenty-seven final criteria encompass six different areas: (1) information on kinds of grants possible (including overall purpose and funding policies); (2) procedures for proposal application and evaluation; (3) a recent listing of specific grants awarded; (4) governance of the corporate giving program; (5) finances; and (6) noncash or in-kind contributions.

With one exception, each of the twenty-seven criteria was given a weight of either 3 or 6, depending on its relative importance. For instance, if the material contained the "purpose of the corporate giving program," 3 points were scored. But if a "statement of program/funding interests/priorities" was provided, 6 points were given, since this was seen as more important information. Sometimes, information submitted was less than complete, in which case a lower score was given. The exception to the basic 3/6 weighting scheme was providing a complete grants list for one or more years, which counted 12. A total score of 129 was theoretically possible on this "disclosure scale."

After all the materials had been gathered from each corporation, they were read and a rating form was filled out. In order to make this process as objective as possible, two different staff people prepared a rating form for each corporation. When all materials had been reviewed, the two forms for each corporation were compared. If they contained discrepancies, the materials were reexamined and an attempt made to reconcile the differences. If the two staff people could not reach agreement, a third staff member was called in to arbitrate. There were few instances where it was difficult to resolve a difference. If a difference about a particular item persisted, the corporation always got the benefit of the doubt.

Once all the items had been rated for each corporation, each staff person then independently marked down the scores, and the two sets of forms were compared to make sure that the correct scores had been assigned for each particular item. Section scores and total scores were then calculated, both manually and by computer. Results were compared and differences corrected by referring to the individual rating forms.

Summary of Findings. Roughly one-quarter (46) of the nation's 200 largest profit-making corporations make absolutely no contributions information available to grant seekers or the public, even after repeated requests for such information. On the Committee's scale to measure the quality of disclosure, only one corporation scored higher than 75 percent of the maximum possible, and only 27 of the 200 corporations studied scored better than 50 percent. If better than 50 percent is considered a "high" score, then few (13 percent) of the country's major corporations meet high standards for disclosure. The median score of the 200 businesses studied was 29, equivalent to 22 percent of the maximum possible score of 129.

For each of the twenty-seven information items included on the disclosure scale, at least 4 of the 200 corporations studied provided some information. For fifteen items, at least 19 percent of the corporations provided some data. A corporation providing information on these fifteen items and no more would have received a "high" score in this assessment. This means that the scoring system is based on the reality of what corporations are already providing to grant seekers and the public.

Findings by Subject Area. More than 60 percent of the 200 corporations surveyed provided no information on grants made, finances, or noncash (in-kind) contributions, and nearly half (44 percent) provided no information on governance of their giving programs. Of the 200 corporations, 16 percent made the maximum score on application and proposal evaluation procedures. But only 1 percent or fewer made maximum scores in the other five areas: kinds of grants possible, grants made, governance, finances, and noncash contributions. More than half the corporations scored "high" in providing information on grants possible and application and proposal evaluation procedures. One-quarter scored "high" on finances and noncash contributions information.

Overall, the 157 corporations providing any information made some types of data available more readily than others. The order of corporate preference for the six subject areas covered in this study was (1) application and proposal evaluation procedures, (2) kinds of grants possible, (3) governance of giving programs, (4) grants made, (5) finances, and (6) noncash contributions.

Findings: Significant Factors. Corporations with a foundation and a special annual report on their giving program consistently scored highest. This means that they provided the most comprehensive information. Of the 47 businesses in this category, none scored zero (that is, provided no information), and 49 percent scored "high" (that is, provided twice as much information as the median corporation). Corporations with no foundation and no annual contributions report generally scored lowest.

This means that they provided the least amount of information. Of the 93 corporations in this category, 35 (38 percent) scored zero, and only 1 percent scored "high." Corporations with either a foundation or an annual giving report generally provide more information than corporations with neither and less information than those with both. But of the two factors, as might be expected, publishing a contributions report is much more likely to lead to a "high" score than simply having a foundation, although having a foundation greatly increased the likelihood of a "high" score.

Conclusion

The current state of public reporting by corporate philanthropy is deplorable. Nearly one-fourth of our largest profit-making corporations refuse to provide any information on their contributions programs when repeatedly requested. And more than 30 percent of those that do provide information score on the low end of the "disclosure scale" developed by the National Committee for Responsive Philanthropy to assess the quality of information provided. Clearly, this scale contains committee bias (although much corporate input was sought in devising it). It is, however, solidly based in corporate reality. Four or more corporations provided data on every one of the twenty-seven items used in the scale, and 38 or more of the 200 businesses studied made available data on fifteen of the items. (The same corporations did not provide information on each and every item, however.) Any corporation providing complete information on these fifteen items would have scored "high" on our disclosure scale. In fact, 27 corporations (13 percent) did score "high." They show what is possible for all corporations in communicating with grant seekers and the public about their contributions programs.

While the era of openness and disclosure has frequently been declared dead since the Reagan years in the White House, there are important things happening in the nonprofit and public-policy world that suggest otherwise: for instance, the models and experience of the high-scoring corporations in our study and the Johnson & Johnson approach to public relations (after seven deaths due to poisoned Tylenol capsules, Johnson & Johsnon immediately publicized a nationwide recall of the capsules and introduced a new tamper-resistant product). Will traditions of secrecy about research and development efforts, product development, and marketing continue to hold corporate philanthropic communications in their bear hug? Or will the continuing trend toward openness and disclosure ultimately succeed in transforming corporate philanthropy into philanthropy accessible to all, and not just the favored few?

References

American Association of Fund-Raising Counsel. *Giving U.S.A.: The Annual Report on Philanthropy for the Year 1987.* New York: AAFRC Trust for Philanthropy, 1988.

Bothwell, R. O., and others. *Foundations and Public Information: Sunshine or Shadow?* Washington, D.C.: National Committee for Responsive Philanthropy, 1980.

Johnston, D. "Foundation Reports: To Publish . . . or Not." *Los Angeles Times,* Jan. 10, 1986, part V, pp. 1–5.

Lydenberg, S. D., and others. *Rating America's Corporate Conscience.* Reading, Mass.: Addison-Wesley, 1986.

Olasky, M. *Patterns of Corporate Philanthropy.* Washington, D.C.: Capital Research Center, 1987.

23

KATHLEEN A. KRENTLER

△ △ △ △ △ △ △ △ △ △ △ △ △ △ △

Cause-Related Marketing: Advantages and Pitfalls for Nonprofits

The term *cause-related marketing* is a hot buzzword currently being bandied about the public and nonprofit sectors as well as the corporate world. It can be defined as the set of activities engaged in by a private, for-profit firm designed to help the firm meet its own profitability objectives while simultaneously benefiting a chosen social or charitable cause. The phenomenon seems to have been receiving its current attention only for about the last five years. The term itself appears to have originated with the American Express Corporation, which coined it to describe a number of activities that firm had undertaken that were designed to benefit both itself and an assortment of social and philanthropic causes. The concept of cause-related marketing has grown beyond the scope of this single corporation, however, and is today being hailed or criticized (depending on the source) as a new form of marketing that brings the activities of the public and private sectors closer together.

This chapter examines the phenomenon of cause-related marketing and the debate surrounding it. Its proponents and opponents appear equally vociferous in defending it as the long-awaited messiah for both the public and private sectors or, conversely, criticizing it as the devil incarnate of commercialism, tainting both sectors equally. The truth most probably lies in the

363

region between these two extreme positions. Consideration of several pertinent issues will help address the benefits as well as the hazards of this new concept and thus provide for an informed assessment of whether it is indeed a passing fad.

Distinguishing Cause-Related Marketing

Cause-related marketing is not simply a new name given to the social and philanthropic activities of private-sector corporations. Some companies have long felt that they have a moral obligation to put something back into the community (both locally and on larger scales) from which their profits come. This activity in most instances is at least partially inspired by the firm's desire to be socially responsible. Beyond this desire, however, it cannot be denied that such activities are typically seen as benefiting corporate image and resulting in some long-run general benefit to the firm. This benefit may or may not be directly related to increased revenues for the firm. Corporate image, however, is generally enhanced through philanthropic activities that typically take the form of direct donations to a nonprofit organization.

Cause-related marketing, however, is not "image-oriented" as basic corporate philanthropy is. It is distinguishable from such traditional approaches in that it is "bottom-line-oriented" for the firm. This bottom-line orientation entails several new approaches for the firm involved in cause-related marketing, two of them particularly significant. First, from a practical standpoint, funds to support this type of activity should (and typically do) come from the firm's marketing budget. The firm that draws on its corporate foundation to support cause-related marketing activities is indicating a basic misunderstanding of the concept and intent of such activities. The impact that such resource allocation may have on the overall charitable activities of the firm is a questionable issue to those on both sides of the cause-related marketing fence.

Second, a bottom-line orientation should alter the way in which cause-related marketing's success (or failure) is judged. Its purpose is not solely to improve a company's corporate image (a rather nebulous objective that has proved difficult to measure for firms engaged in philanthropic activities through the years). Rather, cause-related marketing is designed with specific objectives related to increasing business for the firm (however that increased business is measured: sales revenues, number of customers, profits). With this perspective, it is easier to judge success, since specific, quantifiable measures can be applied, but it also puts greater pressure on the cause-related marketing activity to prove itself. As Higgins (1986) points out, activities that do not have specific measurement criteria built in, activities whose objectives are to produce ''warm and fuzzy'' feelings toward the firm, are not cause-related marketing. Firms branding them thus are confusing marketing with publicity.

Now that we have distinguished cause-related marketing to some extent in terms of how it differs from philanthropy and the basic charitable activities of a firm, it would be helpful to define it in terms of what it is, rather than only what it is not. As noted at the beginning of this chapter, cause-related marketing activities are activities of a private firm that directly benefit its business while simultaneously benefiting a chosen social or charitable cause. For such activities to be judged successful, both parties (the firm and the cause) must profit. A cause-related marketing effort that provides support to the chosen cause but does not benefit the firm by meeting the business objective specified for it must, by this definition, be deemed a failure. American Express, for example, promoted a program called Project Hometown America. Each time a new American Express card was issued or an existing one used, a specified dollar amount went to a fund that provided support to a variety of grass-roots social programs throughout the country. In terms of charitable support, the $4 million donated to social programs would certainly indicate that the program was a success. From a business perspective, however, since American Express reported only marginal increases in card use and applications, the activity was a failure.

Cause-related marketing can be further defined by looking at its relationship not only to the firm and the nonprofit or social cause but to the consumer as well. The concept, after all, involves an intricate triangle among these three parties. Wiegner (1985) describes the role of the consumer by stating, ''give consumers an easy way to fill [their] altruistic desires by buying your product and you have 'cause-related marketing.' '' Cause-related marketing may indeed solve the age-old problem of nonprofits who find that a ''good feeling'' is simply not enough to offer in exchange for a tangible contribution. When consumers participate in a cause-related marketing activity, they can feel good about the contribution they are making to a cause while at the same time acquiring goods or services that provide them with a direct, tangible benefit.

As here defined, cause-related marketing is an activity distinguishable from the charitable and philanthropic activities of a firm. Thus, when critics such as Maurice Gurin (1987) maintain that the basic concept of cause-related marketing is flawed because it fails to recognize the rationale for a philanthropic sector, they themselves are failing to recognize the distinction between philanthropy and cause-related marketing. The latter does not (and probably should not) replace the former; rather, the two can and do coexist, complementing each other, in many firms.

Benefiting the Public Sector?

The first issue of critical importance in judging the efficacy of cause-related marketing is its effect on the nonprofit organization or social cause that is to profit from the effort. To meet the criteria defined earlier, both the nonprofit and the company must profit. If the nonprofit cause does not profit, the cause-related marketing effort is not a success. Does cause-related marketing help or hinder the nonprofit organization that is its target? At first, this would appear rather obvious. How can the organization help but benefit from efforts undertaken by a corporation in its behalf? Any amount of money raised for the cause is a ''profit'' from the organization's viewpoint. But monetary gain may not be the only issue of consequence here. The nonprofit might fairly raise the question of whether there will be ''strings attached'' to the efforts and contributions of the corporation. At a minimum, most corporations expect their names to be prominently displayed in materials associated with the cause. Nonprofits, for the most part, appear comfortable with this agreement. An organization such as the Tampa Symphony Orchestra no doubt feels that naming its pop concert series the Citicorp Super Pops is a small price to pay for sponsorship of the program by Citicorp (Mescon and Tilson, 1987). As such recognition grows more common, however, the public-sector partner may feel increasing pressure not only to recognize the source of its support but to give it an increasingly prominent role in its promotions and activities. There may be no turning back as the nonprofit continues to accept dollars from the firm, which in turn continues to overtake and overshadow the cause-based organization. While profiting monetarily, at some point the nonprofit may feel that the cost outweighs the benefit and yet be unable to extricate itself.

On the other hand, it would be wise to question whether the nonprofit organization could be mistakenly lulled into believing that more is forthcoming from the organization than actually is the case. A sense of complacency may overtake the nonprofit that has established a symbiotic relationship with a corporation. Since the cause benefits at the pleasure of the corporation, such a false sense of security could spell problems for the organization. A company that encounters problems cannot be counted on to continue its cause-related activities. The recent volatility of the stock market provides a dramatic example of uncontrollable factors that could have a chain effect on the cause being targeted.

While such indirectly nonmonetary issues as the two just discussed must be considered in assessing the benefit of cause-related marketing to the nonprofit organization, the effect of such activities on the monetary position of the cause cannot be overlooked. It may seem nonsensical to question whether the $1.7 million generated for the Statue of Liberty by American Express or the $1 million raised by General Foods Corporation for the Muscular Dystrophy Association is beneficial to the causes in question. In looking at the larger issue of fund raising, however, the wise organization should question the impact that cause-related marketing activities may have on its overall ability to raise funds. Two specific issues are of particular importance here.

First, can the sponsoring corporations be counted on to clearly differentiate between their basic philanthropic activities and their cause-related marketing programs? As discussed previously, the two are not the same. They should complement each other, not substitute for one another. Furthermore, monies to support the two should come from two entirely separate places (charitable giving coming from foundations or other funds earmarked for community giving, cause-related funds coming from corporate marketing budgets). The corporation that views its cause-related activities as alternatives to generalized corporate giving may in actuality be reducing its total contribution. This is, in fact, the basis of Gurin's (1987) fear that "if cause-related marketing became widespread, it could undermine the very basis of philanthropy."

The second question the nonprofit should face is whether cause-related efforts could hinder its own abilities to raise funds and other types of support. Corporate fund-raising activities may meet with less and less success as the cause becomes increasingly associated with another firm. Furthermore, individual fund-raising efforts could be hampered in two ways. First, there is what Caesar (1986) refers to as the "taint of commercialism." Donors, both companies and individuals, may feel uncomfortable giving directly to a private-sector corporation. Many potential donors no doubt believe that nonprofit organizations and the public sector in general somehow remain "pure" and above the "dirty work" of the private, for-profit sector by maintaining a distance. Since cause-related marketing, by necessity, directly links the nonprofit with the corporation, such distance cannot be maintained. Could this discourage a potential donor from an act of direct giving? Potential donors may feel that the nonprofit's image is in some way "sullied" through its association with the products of a private firm. The nonprofit may be viewed as selling the products of the firm in some way, thus raising the question of integrity. When General Foods raised money for school athletic equipment by sponsoring "Fun 'n'

Fitness'' events linked to couponing efforts, it was criticized for turning schoolchildren into sales representatives for its products (Haugh, 1981).

Second, the risk exists that the cause may appear ''well cared for'' by the partner corporation. Potential donors may perceive that a cause is in less need of their support when it has been taken under the sheltering wing of a corporation engaged in a cause-related marketing activity. When Coca-Cola supported ''Hands Across America,'' for example, with several million dollars generated through sales revenue, one can only guess at how many potential individual donors chose not to send a more modest contribution. After all, ''my $10 can't be very important compared to what the cause is getting from Coke.''

If any of these circumstances result in sufficient reductions in total fund-raising dollars as to offset the funds generated from cause-related marketing, the nonprofit is not benefiting. Thus, while cause-related efforts clearly have the potential to benefit the nonprofit, it cannot be automatically assumed that that is the only possible outcome.

Benefiting the Private Sector?

Since our definition of cause-related marketing suggests benefit to the company as well as the cause, consideration of its efficacy must include attention to its effects on the firm. Furthermore, the extent to which cause-related activities benefit the corporation is clearly a key determinant of whether they are likely to endure, since marketing activities that do not meet the business objectives set forth for them are destined to pass on quickly.

With any marketing activity, the biggest danger to the firm lies in the simple possibility that it may not work. Beyond questions of ethicality and appropriateness lies this acid test of any bottom-line-oriented activity. Cause-related marketing may sound noble and altruistic, but since its objectives are meant to reach beyond the ''warm and fuzzy'' feelings inspired by image-oriented efforts, its efficacy can be judged more specifically. If the profit or revenue objectives set for the effort are not met, it must be judged a failure. If continued cause-related efforts are deemed failures for a corporation, it would make good business sense to question the value of continued efforts of a similar nature.

The potential dangers to the firm associated with cause-related marketing, however, go beyond just the acid test of its profit potential for the firm. Beyond failing to generate the desired revenues or profits, could cause-related marketing efforts actually hurt the corporation, either in terms of its image or in even more concrete terms? Choice of an inconsistent, inappropriate, or overly controversial cause could damage the corporation. It is important for a firm to carefully consider its target market, both demographically and psychographically, when considering the causes it chooses to support. Sports sponsorship or cultural events may be appropriate for firms whose target markets are so oriented. A blue-collar television watcher, on the other hand, may actually be demotivated to purchase a product when part of the proceeds are going to support the opera or ballet. Likewise, the firm that supports AIDS patients with proceeds related to its revenues may find objections from certain target markets.

Causes with more generalized appeals (Coca Cola's association with "Hands Across America" or American Express's support of the Statue of Liberty, for example) may be less of a problem for a firm concerned with the choice of a cause inconsistent with the interests of its target market. Scott Paper Company, for example, currently supports six national health agencies, all involved in helping children with special needs, with the amount of contributions based on the sales of its paper products. Scott's project, entitled "Helping Hand," is likely to generate only positive feelings from consumers, in addition to increased revenues and profits. A controversial cause, however, may produce negative feelings that cause problems for the corporation. The company that supports high school family planning clinics with proceeds from sales revenues may soon find that it has little to go to the cause and even less to meet its own profit objectives.

To allay this potential problem, some corporations have turned to creating their own causes. American Express's "Project

Hometown America'' was just such an approach. It was a generalized fund designed to provide support to deserving local nonprofits around the nation. Any such organization could apply for funds, which were meted out at the discretion of American Express. To protect itself from criticisms regarding choice of causes to fund, the company appointed a board of volunteers from assorted nonprofit organizations to make funding decisions. Still, American Express was backing the decisions, and as Wiegner (1985, p. 245) asks, "Isn't there a risk that rejected grassroots groups will blame American Express if there's not enough money to go around?"

This need for corporations to choose their causes with care will, of course, ultimately affect the nonprofit and public sectors. If support is restricted to noncontroversial, middle-of-the-road causes, will more controversial but equally needy ones not suffer? Will this selectivity in support, which can certainly be understood from the firm's perspective, ultimately change the public sector as organizations and causes seek to downplay potentially controversial issues in their bids for corporate attention?

Here to Stay or a Passing Fad?

As we move toward the year 2000, the face of corporate philanthropy is changing. While still desiring to be socially responsible corporate citizens, firms are finding it increasingly difficult amid the realities of today's financial market to remain strictly charity-oriented in all their giving programs. This is the environment that has paved the way for cause-related marketing. To the extent that the independent sector can aid corporations in adjusting their philanthropic endeavors to this changing environment, all parties involved stand to benefit, and cause-related marketing could be predicted to root itself firmly in the corporate repertoire of marketing activities. As can be seen from the discussion in this chapter, however, the issue of the continuing efficacy of cause-related marketing is more complex than this. While on the face of it, such activities are clearly beneficial for the nonprofit sector, organizations in this sector must be warned to dig below the surface in analyzing the total impact such programs could have on them. It is easy to be dazzled by corporate promises of large sums of money, but the cause must be cautious. Consideration of the nature of the commitment and its likely long-term consequences on the cause is critical. The nonprofit should consider all potential consequences of the program as the first step in assessing an offer of such aid from a corporation. While there is always a temptation to say ''yes'' when money is offered, in-depth analysis will no doubt uncover occasional instances of cause-related activities that do not clearly benefit the nonprofit sector. Such programs should be unhesitatingly rejected by the cause-based organization.

Despite this advice, it is likely that organizations in the nonprofit sector will frequently find it difficult to reject the offers of assistance that cause-related marketing programs dangle before them. It will be left, therefore, to the private sector to ultimately determine whether cause-related marketing is here to stay. Beyond all other considerations, the overriding issue for this sector will be, does it work? If it meets the goals of the firm, both its revenue and profit objectives and its social responsibility aims, it appears here to stay. While the final answer to this will come only with the test of time, it would appear that a concept with the clear-cut potential to benefit all parties involved (the corporation, the nonprofit sector, and the consumer) while dealing progressively with a changing environment stands an excellent chance of being here to stay.

References

Caesar, P. ''Cause-Related Marketing: The New Face of Corporate Philanthropy.'' *Business and Society Review,* 1986, *59,* 15–19.

''The Changing Face of Philanthropy.'' *Public Relations Journal,* 1984, *40,* 24.

Doyle, M. ''Cause Marketing Wins 3–1.'' *Ad Week,* 1986, *27,* 24.

Gurin, M. G. ''Do Marketers Understand Philanthropy?'' *Nonprofit Times,* Oct. 1987, p. 23.

Haugh, L. J. ''Coupons, Charities Team Up.'' *Advertising Age,* Aug. 31, 1981, p. 32.

Higgins, K. T. "Cause-Related Marketing': Does It Pass the Bottom-Line Test?" *Marketing News,* 1986, *20,* 1.

"Marketing Links Up with Causes." *Ad Forum,* 1982, *3,* 29.

Mescon, T. S., and Tilson, D. J. "Corporate Philanthropy: A Strategic Approach to the Bottom-Line." *California Management Review,* 1987, *24,* 49–61.

Rodney, B. "A New Spirit of Partnership." *Public Relations Journal,* 1984, *40,* 21.

"Verdict Is Not Yet In on Charity Tie-Ins as a Promotional Tool." *Marketing News,* 1984, *18,* 9.

Wiegner, K. K. "A Cause on Every Carton?" *Forbes,* Nov. 18, 1985, pp. 248–249.

PART SIX

△ △ △ △ △ △ △ △ △ △ △ △ △ △ △ △

Trends in Individual Giving and Volunteering

At the heart of the nonprofit sector are individual participation and service to organizations, the community, and the nation. One way of estimating future health of nonprofits is to take the pulse of the people. Lower participation in organizations and community, it is posited, will result in less giving and volunteering. This assumption is addressed by the contributors in this part. These chapters also consider the relationship between individual giving and community sustenance and services, whether volunteering can continue to grow in an aging society, and whether wealthy Americans can be expected to support institutions serving the poor. Finally, the relationship between civic education and volunteering is explored.

It becomes clear in this part that individuals and communities are not organized into a large movement called voluntarism; rather, voluntary action and nonprofit organizations flourish in communities with particular characteristics, giving by individuals to certain charities and causes is influenced by the individuals' background, experience, and personal interests, and the habit of individual participation and philanthropy and its importance to democratic traditions are an important component of civic education. In other words, voluntary responsibility is a learned behavior, and if it is not taught, the tradition can be substantially weakened or even forgotten. These contributors demonstrate the extent to which individuals, communities, government policy, education, and traditions are integral to an understanding of individual giving and volunteering in the United States.

375

24

JULIAN WOLPERT

△ △ △ △ △ △ △ △ △ △ △ △ △ △ △

Key Indicators of Generosity in Communities

We generally think of generosity as an attribute of individuals or groups, but the focus here is on places—the generosity of communities. Generous communities are those that make substantial public and private efforts within their means and cultural preferences to provide a wide range and high quality of affordable services. Generous communities are somehow able to resolve their "free-rider" problems by arousing altruistic feelings or civic pride or by creating services of direct or indirect benefit to donors and taxpayers. Their residents manage to donate part of their income or wealth and/or tax themselves to expand amenities and make them available to those who would otherwise be excluded.

Some American communities have a marvelous set of accessible and affordable cultural, social, health, and educational services that contribute to the well-being and quality of life of residents. Some communities have well-stocked free libraries, low-cost day care, natural history museums, and good salaries for teachers. In other communities, there are few if any of these services, or they are not affordable by low-income people. There may be no local live theater, few services for mentally handicapped

Note: The research described here was supported by Guggenheim and Wilson Center fellowships. Grateful acknowledgment is made to the United Way, Catholic Charities, and the Council of Jewish Federations for making this data available and to James Heel for his able research assistance.

people, and hospitals that discourage Medicaid patients. The private market cannot provide all the services that residents are likely to want, can use beneficially, or wish to make available to others at affordable prices.

Why should some places be significantly more generous than others in providing services to their residents, and why should such distributional patterns have some stability over time (see Reiner and Wolpert, 1985)? Furthermore, how can private generosity, charity, and philanthropy, which are often altruistically motivated and voluntarily given, be equated with public-sector expenditures for transfers and services that are supported through a coercive system of taxation?

With such a nationally integrated community of values in the United States, one should expect a homogenizing process that would eliminate over time regional or local differences in civic virtue and commitment. Why do interest groups differ significantly between communities in their advocacy, skills, or access to capital for development of such amenities and services? Why is it that preferences for varieties and levels of service do not diffuse nationally, as does professionalism in fund raising and management of service-providing organizations? How is persistence of regional patterns sustained with the continuing migration of people and jobs, the strong pressures toward national homogenization of social values, and the almost universal civic rivalry between places to improve their reputation for quality of life? After all, since communities are forced to compete for highest ranking on the national "mental map" of amenity places and to erase stigmatizing social gaps, won't the absence of services requiring subsidy (for example, ballet or major research hospitals) in Metropole spoil its opportunity to attract income and job growth (Boyer and Savageau, 1987; Cutter, 1985)?

Are the inequalities and disparities between American communities then simply a function of stages in life cycles of growth and development that will bring ballet and hospitals to all communities when they reach the requisite size, wealth, and market access? Shouldn't our standard urban theories of supply and demand of services and amenities adequately explain why

Gotham is better served by libraries or social services than Metropole? If disparities persist after making allowances for resources and centrality, could they not be attributed to differences in regional and cultural tastes? Metropole may simply prefer to invest in hockey and movie theaters (which are commercially viable) rather than ballet and art museums (which require subsidy) because residents have no affinity for "high culture."

The primary thesis to be examined in this chapter is that regional differences in generosity and civic virtue persist even after allowing for variations in resources and tastes. It is assumed that generosity can be measured in terms of charitable donations and support for those civic and amenity services that must be subsidized to be accessible to all those who can benefit. A related thesis is that both private and local public generosity work in tandem rather than competing for support. Both private and public forms of generosity are presumably maintained structurally through political and economic institutions that reflect underlying distinctions and diversity in local cultural heritage and social philosophy. The opposing thesis would deny the validity of national quality-of-life indicators and comparative analysis of amenities. This perspective would deny the assumptions of a national integrating culture, social philosophy, and commonality of civic responsiveness that are manifested in support for local service institutions and their programs.

The major elements and assumptions of this regional approach need to be tested. We begin by assuming, for example, that generosity can be measured and assessed comparatively after making proper allowance for differences in community resources and distress; that patterns of regional generosity exist and have some stability; and that public and private expressions of generosity, at least at state and local levels, are likely to be consistent and work in tandem rather than displacing one another. The opposing thesis would suggest that the level and variety of service provision simply reflect the resources, distress, and centrality of places; that generosity as a voluntary moral gesture should not be distinguishable from the cultural expression of tastes (for example, Gotham has no ballet and lacks community mental health facilities because of local preferences and not because of lack of generosity); that community differences could be a reflection not of generosity but merely of tastes that vary between regions or between the cultural, ethnic, or religious groups represented in these communities; and that the scarcity of any particular service could mean simply that local residents do not value its provision or have an adequate substitute.

Private and Public Generosity

The term *generosity* implies giving behavior prompted by mixed rather than solely altruistic motives (Collard, 1978). Recipients (for example, users of subsidized services) are likely to benefit, while donors may or may not benefit either directly or indirectly from the donation. In contrast, a *true gift* implies asymmetry and no reciprocity, as exemplified by an activity that benefits only future generations or places or social groups too distant to reciprocate (see Ball, 1986). *Charity* generally refers to gifts that span a considerable social gap, while *philanthropy* involves substantial support for institutions that provide worthy services or work toward solving significant societal problems (Katz, 1984).

Private Generosity. We do not have the proper data to distinguish among true gifts, charity, and philanthropy; we can measure only the flow of funds (and some volunteer labor) to nonprofit organizations that provide services and are eligible to receive tax-deductible donations (Jencks, 1987). Generosity, then, is utilitarian and functional. Decisions to give are sparked by solicitations as well as information about needs and are intended to support services perceived as beneficial. The donor, it is assumed, solves a complex and interdependent problem in responding to the solicitation, according to the service need and merit of the potential recipients, trust in the institution to provide the service efficiently and humanely, knowledge of the donations of others toward the fund-raising goal, the donor's own discretionary income or wealth, and competing demands for giving.

Donations targeted for social and welfare services are likely to be somewhat more "giftlike" and asymmetrical than those supporting cultural, hospital, and educational institutions (Weisbrod, 1977). Little detailed study has been done, however, about reciprocity or redistributive effects of various types of donations in different locales. Furthermore, virtually nothing is known about donor-beneficiary links in religious giving, which constitutes almost half of all donations. Disaggregated information is also lacking about funds raised in the national "disease" campaigns and for overseas and emergency relief, some portion of which must be classified as true gifts.

Ample national evidence shows, however, that a rather substantial proportion of giving behavior can be readily explained by our traditional economic models of rational self-interest, with only a small residual (but a large variance) for pure altruism (Jencks, 1987). We know, for example, that a rather stable 2 percent of our household income is donated in good times and bad, and virtually all donations support local institutions from which donors benefit directly or at least indirectly. Furthermore, little generosity spans social, cultural, or class boundaries. Even the modest 2 percent level is supported by tax deductions that reduce the cost of giving and subsidize differentially the targeting preferences of the more affluent donors. The 2 percent equilibrium would seem to suggest, at least from the national perspective, a degree of satisfaction and consensus regarding the share of collective goods and services to be provided by nonprofit organizations, as opposed to federal, state, and local government.

Private generosity has found its niche as a predominantly local activity providing chiefly amenity (rather than basic) services and virtually no income transfers. The role of assisting the poor and the handicapped has largely been surrendered by local municipalities and nonprofit organizations to state and federal government. Nevertheless, private generosity has been quite successful in creating and supporting a wide range of service institutions and making their activities somewhat more accessible. It is uncertain, however, whether more funds could be raised to augment local service levels or to extend assistance to distant communities over an extended time.

Private and public forms of generosity, then, perform increasingly different functions that cannot adequately substitute
for one another. A division of functions and specialized responsibilities has evolved for both private and public generosity at
each level of the local to national hierarchy that appears to satisfy
both donors and the electorate. Interdependencies and linkages
have developed that minimize competition and duplication of
functions and services.

Private generosity is, therefore, the more inclusive term for
the composite of donations that support services and extend their
provision with some subsidy to those the community agrees can
benefit. Since the overwhelming proportion of giving is extended
within the community where the donors live for current service
use by the donors themselves or others similar in social class,
such generosity is not primarily a true gift or even charity or
philanthropy but largely a contribution to civic or community
quality of life or improvement (that is, amenity supporting.)

Public Generosity. Local public-sector generosity also involves
subsidy to support amenities and extend their relative scope and
quality beyond the "usual" public-service levels to be expected
in a community of similar size and resources. The pluralist
American tradition, however, is to regard federal or national
efforts at social justice and reduction of disparities as coercive,
to view the payment of local taxes as a form of membership dues
or generosity, and to assign a flexible and shifting role to state
government (see Dahl, 1982). We are apparently willing to
regard the redistribution of income and provision of access to
basic services through federal social welfare programs as a national public good to be supported principally by taxes on income. But we appear to be reluctant (though more so in some
places than others) to support such transfers through taxes on
property, the main base of support for municipal government.
Our decentralized and pluralist system gives local communities
and states the dominant control over the provision of both public
and amenity services. The practice, therefore, of separating
residents into communities by social level may reinforce differences not only in resources and tastes but in levels of generosity
as well. Thus, an expanded (or contracted) federal presence

should have a differential role in displacing (or restoring) local public and private generosity depending on local initiatives and division of functions (Salamon, 1987; Steinberg, 1987).

The increasing public-sector role in the activities traditionally performed by charitable organizations and the growing professionalization of the nonprofit sector have sparked greater integration between public and private generosity. The partnership efforts benefit from the comparative advantage of each sector. Places generous in their private support for amenities will have worked out mechanisms for local public support for the same or complementary services (Salamon, 1987). The same benefactors are likely to be influential in both sectors and would regard the two support streams as parallel and supplementary. The share of private versus local public support is likely to be neither very relevant nor significant to the level and variety of services provided.

The public-nonprofit partnership has resulted in a quite well-integrated system of service provision that has endured without major upheavals even the federalism movements of the past several decades. The system can even accommodate the occasional disequilibriating forces that have raised the cost of giving through tax changes or required some reallocation of support to target newly defined needs at local, national, or international levels. From a functionalist and national perspective, the stability in division of activities and in giving and taxing levels suggests a finely tuned evolution of an intentionally rational strategy. The integration of public and nonprofit sectors taps support for a diversity of services preferred by various large and small, federal and local constituencies. Despite the best efforts of fund raisers, therefore, one should not expect the rate of giving to expand substantially for any significant time period or the balance between private and public generosity to be altered.

Competing Approaches

Theory based primarily on social choice motives for giving would lead us to expect that private and local public generosity levels would be higher in the smaller, more affluent, and more homogeneous metropolitan areas with relatively low levels of distress (Buchanan, 1967; Becker, 1974). Giving rates and support for amenities, according to this approach, should be predictable from community size and diversity and from income and wealth distribution. Generosity should, therefore, be consistent with the representation in communities of socioeconomic cohorts who would contribute at the same level and target their giving similarly wherever located. Predictably, rich, middle-aged, and religious residents of smaller communities donate a greater proportion of their income than do the young and the old and the more secular residents of large cities. Differences in giving can then be attributed, according to this approach, to implied motivations of civic commitment, self-interest, and free-rider tendencies that would minimize the role of altruism or impulse giving.

In contrast, theory based on an extended framework of the type proposed by Tiebout (1956) would suggest that residents and firms sort themselves differentially by community according to preferences for levels of services and amenities and willingness to tax themselves (privately and) publicly to underwrite their costs, holding other factors constant, of course. Those strongly favoring lower taxes and more modest public expenditures for services than the prevailing community preferences would favor places with like-minded residents. Decisions by households and firms as to where to locate reflect at least partially the attraction of amenities and their "tacit agreement to be taxed" for public as well as charitable and civic services to be used not only by themselves but for the benefit of others in their community. According to this extended Tiebout approach, areas similar in social and economic composition could differ considerably in generosity and amenity levels. Regional and community diversity in values and preferences for services should be reflected in the amenities and quality of life that residents are committed to supporting.

Local giving targeted to social services could be vulnerable to displacement by federal contributions and potentially offset by the competing solicitations from local health, education, and arts institutions. The decision problem for donors is analogous to the crowding-out framework of Stouffer's (1960) "intervening opportunity'' and ''competing migrant'' models. Donors are confronted by an array of alternative opportunities for targeting their contributions (for example, the new art museum rather than the homeless shelter). The pluralism (regional-values) framework would lead us to expect that the targeting of generosity would be consistent—that is, that places generous in their support of health and cultural facilities would also be generous in supporting educational and social services.

Competing federal generosity in the form of cash transfers to the needy or in-kind support for local services may completely or partially substitute for and crowd out local private or public efforts. Federal substitution effects, especially in cash transfers, will have long since been absorbed. The relatively more generous places will make greater effort (within their means) to branch out and supplement federal efforts and compensate for federal retrenchment (Salamon, 1987). Few places may be able or willing, however, to assume the ''safety net'' transfer functions and support of basic health, welfare, and housing services that citizens expect from the federal government. A state and local versus federal and national perspective would be more relevant for examining generosity than a private versus public focus. Support of local government in a reasonably homogeneous community is more analogous to private generosity than is support of the more ''coercive'' and distant federal or state taxing bodies. A comparative analysis needs to test for these intervening opportunity and competing donor influences.

Empirical Analysis

The analysis presented here uses communities as the active behavioral unit that translates residents' social welfare and amenity preferences into a mix of service institutions and a formula for their private and public support. The preference mix reflects both social choice factors and self-selection of residents according to service preferences and civic commitment. Communities are motivated, therefore, primarily to maintain existing services that have continuing value, a reinforcing process that favors places with residents dependent on a rich variety of services and an older, more established, and larger inventory of service institutions. Shifts in the service complement and its support can adjust, however, to substantial community growth or decline and broad changes in social composition, such as in the Sunbelt cities. "Catch-up" efforts involve investment in amenities to reduce the lag between community growth and development of cultural, educational, health, and social services "befitting" the new image.

The Metropolitan Unit of Analysis

How can the comparative generosity of places be measured, and what would be an appropriate local unit of analysis? The metropolitan level should be a suitable compromise unit for our study. States are internally too heterogeneous for a meaningful comparative analysis of community differences, and the municipal level would be affected more by city versus suburban factors than by the regional pluralism that is the object of study here. The primary local health, educational, social, and cultural institutions are supported through the taxes and contributions of residents from throughout the metropolitan area. American metropolitan areas differ considerably (although not, of course, as much as cities, suburbs, and exurbs) in their complements of services.

Metropolitan-level analysis also makes sense because almost all private contributions are both raised and expended in the same communities or regions. Relatively little leaks outside to the rest of the nation or abroad. Communities would likely not donate or tax themselves as highly if allocation and targeting decisions were made nationally. The metropolitan area is the primary marketplace for the solicitation of contributions, the optimum locale for purchasing corporate "goodwill" and for contributing to the service amenities that corporations' own employees can enjoy. The fortunes that established foundations were typically made in single metropolitan areas and are characteristically drawn to the support of local institutions. Individual contributions are used principally to support local institutions that the donors use themselves and that they can observe others using.

Comparative Analysis

The generosity of places is examined here by looking at both the direct charitable contributions of their residents to support services and the level and variety of local amenities requiring private and/or public subsidization. The objective of this empirical analysis is to examine the theses outlined above: generosity differs significantly by region; local private and public generosity is consistent and moves in tandem; and place-to-place differences in generosity should persist after allowance is made for the effect of resource factors (community size, homogeneity, stability, wealth, and so on), community needs or level of distress, the potential displacement effect of federal and state support for services, and the competing solicitations for cultural, health, and educational institutions and their services.

Cash Contributions. Two alternative ways are used here to assess generosity cross-sectionally among America's largest eighty-five metropolitan areas—those that have more than half a million people and are able to support a full complement of services. The list of these areas and some of the measures are presented in Table 24.1. These areas differ significantly in affluence, distress, and the level of federal, state, and municipal support targeted to local services. The poorest areas (as measured by median household income and population below the poverty threshold) are in the South and the Rustbelt region (including Birmingham, Greenville, Knoxville, Memphis, Scranton, and Toledo), and the most affluent are the metropolitan areas surrounding New York, San Francisco, Washington, Minneapolis, and Denver. Furthermore, the disparities are being intensified through differential job and income growth.

The first set of generosity measures reflects direct cash contributions to local "umbrella" organizations, represented here by the United Way, the Catholic Campaign for Human Development, and the Jewish Federations. These contributions cover only a portion of household giving, emphasizing support primarily for social and welfare services in the home community for 1986. United Way contributions are solicited in the workplace

Table 24.1. Metropolitan Area Measures of State and Local Generosity Levels.

Metropolitan Area	Cash Contributions[a]	State Business Climate[b]	State Welfare Share[c]	Local Welfare Share[c]	State Environmental Rank[d]	ACA Score[e]	State AFDC Maximum Share[f]
Akron, Ohio	3	23.3	48	8	18	15	8.65
Albany–Schenectady–Troy, N.Y.	2	33.7	12	26	7	45	13.04
Allentown–Bethlehem, Pa.	2	32.2	47	0	23	89	9.69
Anaheim–Santa Ana, Calif.	NA	42.9	46	2	2	95	14.40
Atlanta, Ga.	3	65.0	27	1	29	32	7.24
Austin, Tex.	2	68.8	35	3	39	40	7.22
Baltimore, Md.	3	48.6	48	0	7	0	10.94
Bergen–Passaic, N.J.	1	47.2	38	7	3	33	11.56
Birmingham, Ala.	5	57.4	24	1	50	70	4.59
Boston, Mass.	3	40.7	47	2	4	3	12.64
Buffalo, N.Y.	3	33.7	12	26	7	44	13.04
Charlotte–Gastonia–Rock Hill, N.C.	4	65.9	13	14	29	NA	6.86
Chicago, Ill.	3	29.3	50	3	23	21	10.66
Cincinnati, Ohio	5	23.3	48	8	18	53	8.65
Cleveland, Ohio	5	23.3	48	8	18	18	8.65
Columbus, Ohio	5	23.3	48	8	18	67	8.65
Dallas, Tex.	3	68.8	35	3	39	48	7.22
Dayton–Springfield, Ohio	4	23.3	48	8	18	30	8.65
Denver, Colo.	2	58.2	52	0	27	24	10.60
Detroit, Mich.	3	11.8	50	4	18	19	11.13
Fort Lauderdale–Hollywood–Pompano, Fla.	3	79.4	38	6	17	53	8.52
Fort Worth–Arlington, Tex.	3	68.8	35	3	39	37	7.22
Fresno, Calif.	NA	42.9	46	2	2	15	14.40
Gary–Hammond, Ind.	2	49.8	27	13	11	NA	7.42
Grand Rapids, Mich.	1	11.8	50	4	18	NA	11.13

City							
Greensboro–Winston-Salem, N.C.	4	65.9	13	14	29	43	6.86
Greenville–Spartanburg, S.C.	2	60.5	NA	NA	29	85	5.72
Harrisburg–Lebanon–Carlisle, Pa.	3	32.2	47	0	23	75	9.69
Hartford, Conn.	5	38.6	49	4	14	10	14.02
Honolulu, Hawaii	3	NA	38	1	12	25	14.99
Houston, Tex.	3	68.8	35	3	39	54	7.22
Indianapolis, Ind.	3	49.8	27	13	11	69	7.42
Jacksonville, Fla.	1	79.4	38	6	17	76	8.52
Jersey City, N.J.	2	47.2	38	7	3	16	11.56
Kansas City, Kans.	4	65.6	47	2	33	NA	11.15
Kansas City, Mo.	3	56.6	36	1	49	29	8.07
Knoxville, Tenn.	2	60.6	32	5	33	80	5.25
Los Angeles–Long Beach, Calif.	3	42.9	46	2	2	37	14.40
Louisville, Ky.	4	50.1	35	2	12	33	5.81
Memphis, Tenn.	3	60.6	32	5	17	5	5.25
Miami–Hialeah, Fla.	3	79.4	38	6	17	12	8.52
Middlesex–Somerset–Hunter, N.J.	3	47.2	38	7	3	24	11.56
Milwaukee, Wis.	3	32.1	32	11	7	19	11.62
Minneapolis–St. Paul, Minn.	4	29.4	34	19	1	5	12.46
Monmouth–Ocean, N.J.	1	47.2	38	7	3	6	11.56
Nashville, Tenn.	4	60.6	35	5	33	47	5.25
Nassau–Suffolk, N.Y.	NA	33.7	12	26	3	57	14.50
New Haven–Meriden, Conn.	2	38.6	49	4	14	10	14.02
New Orleans, La.	3	59.0	35	2	43	54	6.14
New York, N.Y.	3	33.7	12	26	7	15	13.04
Newark, N.J.	3	47.2	38	7	3	50	11.56
Norfolk–Virginia Beach–Newport News, Va.	3	65.1	32	8	23	85	10.34
Oakland, Calif.	NA	42.9	46	2	2	13	14.40
Oklahoma City, Okla.	2	56.9	42	0	45	80	8.44

Table 24.1. Metropolitan Area Measures of State and Local Generosity Levels, Cont'd.

Metropolitan Area	Cash Contributions[a]	State Business Climate[b]	State Welfare Share[c]	Local Welfare Share[c]	State Environmental Rank[d]	ACA Score[e]	State AFDC Maximum Share[f]
Omaha, Nebr.	4	71.1	30	12	39	90	9.18
Orlando, Fla.	NA	79.4	38	6	17	83	8.52
Oxnard–Ventura, Calif.	1	42.9	46	2	2	90	14.40
Philadelphia, Pa.	3	32.2	47	0	23	19	9.69
Phoenix, Ariz.	2	70.8	41	31	32	84	7.93
Pittsburgh, Pa.	3	32.2	47	0	23	19	9.69
Portland, Oreg.	3	21.3	26	7	5	10	9.62
Providence, R.I.	3	26.3	45	1	27	7	12.24
Raleigh–Durham, N.C.	3	65.9	14	13	23	NA	6.86
Richmond–Petersburg, Va.	4	65.1	32	8	23	43	10.34
Riverside–San Bernardino, Calif.	1	42.9	46	2	2	62	14.40
Rochester, N.Y.	5	33.7	12	26	7	33	13.04
Sacramento, Calif.	2	42.9	46	2	2	5	14.40
St. Louis, Mo.	4	56.6	36	1	49	15	8.07
Salt Lake City–Ogden, Utah	1	66.3	29	2	33	NA	7.53
San Antonio, Tex.	5	68.8	35	3	39	19	7.22
San Diego, Calif.	3	42.9	46	2	2	55	14.40
San Francisco, Calif.	3	42.9	46	2	2	5	14.40
San Jose, Calif.	2	42.9	46	2	2	5	14.40
Scranton–Wilkes Barre, Pa.	3	32.2	47	0	23	45	9.58
Seattle, Wash.	4	34.5	60	0	6	NA	12.30
Springfield, Mass.	3	40.7	47	2	4	10	12.64
Syracuse, N.Y.	2	33.7	12	26	7	90	13.04
Tampa–St. Petersburg–Clearwater, Fla.	3	79.4	38	6	17	61	8.52
Toledo, Ohio	4	23.3	48	8	18	29	8.65

Tucson, Ariz.	5	70.8	41	31	32	10	7.93
Tulsa, Okla.	5	56.9	42	0	45	55	8.44
Washington, D.C.	NA	NA	0	44	6	37	10.86
West Palm Beach–Boca Raton–Delray Beach, Fla.	3	79.4	38	6	17	37	8.52
Wilmington, Del.	5	37.7	43	0	21	67	8.52
Youngstown–Warren, Ohio	2	23.3	48	8	18	30	10.10

[a]Quintiles of cash contributions to United Way, Catholic Campaign for Human Development, and Jewish Federations. 5 = highest giving level.

[b]An index of state labor costs, productivity, unionization, taxes, and welfare and environmental regulations. Figures from *General Manufacturing and Business Climate Survey*, 1984.

[c]State (or local) share of finances for public welfare. Figures from Advisory Council on Intergovernmental Relations (ACIR), 1986.

[d]State rank (1 = best, 50 = worst) for environmental effort. Ranking taken from Conservation Foundation, 1983.

[e]Americans for Constitutional Action (conservative) score of voting records of metropolitan area congressional members (averaged).

[f]Maximum AFDC payment in states divided by the federal matching rate—a measure of generosity in state supplements. Figures from ACIR, *Significant Features of Fiscal Federalism*, 1987.

and tend, therefore, to be biased in favor of places with larger labor forces and a higher percentage of workers employed in large companies (Rose-Ackerman, 1980). The data are clearly not a sufficient indicator of local generosity, but they become more revealing when examined for common patterns of Catholic and Jewish donations.

Whether examined on a per employee or per capita basis or relative to disposable income, the United Way contributions show a tenfold difference between the most and the least generous metropolitan areas. The Catholic Campaign for Human Development and the Jewish Federation fund drives for the same 1986 period show a sevenfold and a twentyfold difference, respectively, in the generosity extremes (Shields and others, 1987; Silberstein and others, 1987). Furthermore, the United Way 1986 distribution over the eighty-five areas is entirely consistent with the 1972 pattern, and the Jewish Federation 1986 giving is consistent with that in 1981. The patterns are not only separately stable over time but also consistent with one another across the metropolitan areas; United Way giving is in tandem with Catholic and Jewish generosity.

The Effects of Resource Capacity. Are contributions highest in the most affluent or in the most distressed communities, where federal expenditures are highest or where they are lowest, and where the competition of other service sectors is greatest or where it is least? The regression equation used for Tables 24.2 and 24.3 includes variables that index each of the four factors—capacity, distress, public generosity, and philanthropy alternatives—presumed to account for the variations in cash contributions to United Way across the eighty-five areas. Models A and B follow the same regression format but explore different sets of variables. The resulting analyses show higher giving rates in the moderate-income and less distressed, smaller metropolitan areas with more of a manufacturing than service economy and only modest growth in jobs and income. Giving is higher in the more accessible than in the more remote metropolitan areas and where there are fewer aged people and members of minority groups. Areas with much higher giving rates than expected on

Table 24.2. The Relationship of Cash Contributions
to Metropolitan Resources, Distress, Public Generosity,
and Alternative Targets for Giving: Model A.

	AFDC Maximum Share	Local Welfare Expenditures	United Way Total Contributions
Business climate (state)	-.01	.48[b]	-.24[c]
Arts	-.33[c]	-.46[a]	.24[c]
Education	.18[b]	.40[b]	-.06
Health	.11	-.16	.11[a]
Percentage of births to women under 20 years	-.45[c]	-.44[b]	.11[b]
Federal expenditures	.08	-.05	.01
Income growth 1974–1986	.24[b]	.08	-.07
Job growth 1974–1986	-.14	-.34	.08
Local expenditures—welfare	.11[a]	---	.06[a]
Environment (state rank)	-.47[c]	-.53[b]	.21[c]
City-suburban income disparity	.12[a]	.11	-.09[b]
United Way contributions per employee	.06	.40[b]	---
Percentage drop in AFDC 1974–1986 (state)	-.15[b]	-.08	.11[c]
AFDC maximum share (state)	---	-.50[a]	.09
Metropolitan area population	.21[b]	.38[b]	-1.28[c]
Number of United Way employees in area	---	---	1.98[c]

Note: Figures represent standard regression coefficients.
[a]Significant at the 90% level.
[b]Significant at the 95% level.
[c]Significant at the 99% level.

the basis of resources and size are Cleveland, Detroit, and Rochester; those with much lower than expected rates are Los Angeles, Salt Lake City, and the Florida metropolitan areas.

The Effects of Distress Levels. Theory suggests somewhat greater generosity in the presence of need or distress, but the United Way, Jewish Federation, and Catholic donations generally show the opposite effect. Higher poverty and crime rates and larger minority population are reflected in lower rates of giving after allowing for the effects of population size, median income, and public-sector funding support (Carson, 1987). The only distress variables directly related to giving levels are such measures of heterogeneity as center-city/suburban income disparities and the proportion of children born to women younger than twenty (see column 3 in Tables 24.2 and 24.3). A reasonable interpretation

Table 24.3. The Relationship of Cash Contributions
to Metropolitan Resources, Distress, Public Generosity,
and Alternative Targets for Giving: Model B.

	AFDC Maximum Share	Local Welfare Expenditures	United Way Contribution Per Employee
Business climate (state)	-.18[a]	.05	-.43[b]
Percentage in poverty	-.32[c]	.29	-.33[a]
AFDC per capita	.50[c]	-.33	-.05
Percentage of births to women under 20 years	-.35[c]	-.24	.27
Federal expenditures	.13[a]	-.08	.03
Income growth 1974–1986	.33[c]	-.20	.25[a]
Local expenditures—welfare	.06	---	.22[a]
Migration change 1970–1980	.22[b]	.01	-.22
Percentage minority	.13	-.05	.03
Percentage aged	.10	.16	-.18
United Way contributions per employee	-.09	.27[a]	---
Percentage drop in AFDC 1974–1986 (state)	-.10	.04	-.04
AFDC maximum share (state)	---	.26	-.31

Note: Figures represent standard regression coefficients.
[a]Significant at the 90% level.
[b]Significant at the 95% level.
[c]Significant at the 99% level.

of these findings is that donors tend to be more generous when they can assume that the recipients of services will be much like themselves, an assumption difficult to maintain in a metropolitan area with strong cultural, social, and racial differences.

Metropolitan areas with much higher giving rates than expected on the basis of distress levels are Cleveland, Detroit, Seattle, and Minneapolis; much lower than expected rates were found in Los Angeles, the New Jersey suburbs of New York City, Grand Rapids, and Phoenix. When allowances are made for the cash contributions to the three umbrella groups as well as both resource and distress levels in the metropolitan areas, the giving levels are much higher than predicted in Hartford, Rochester, Wilmington, Cincinnati, Cleveland, and Columbus and much lower in the New York and Los Angeles suburbs, among other places (see Table 24.4).

The Effects of Public Generosity. Private contributions should theoretically be displaced or "crowded out" by public expenditures

Table 24.4. Generosity Outliers—States and Metropolitan Areas.

More Generous States	*Less Generous States*
Most generous metropolitan areas	
Cincinnati	Birmingham
Cleveland	Charlotte–Gastonia–Rock Hill
Columbus	Greensboro–Winston-Salem
Dayton–Springfield	Kansas City, Mo.
Hartford	Memphis
Minneapolis–St. Paul	Nashville
Richmond–Petersburg	Omaha
Rochester	St. Louis
Seattle	San Antonio
Toledo	Tucson
Wilmington	Tulsa
Least generous metropolitan areas	
Albany–Schenectady–Troy	Austin
Allentown–Bethlehem	Gary–Hammond
Bergen–Passaic	Greenville–Spartanburg
Denver	Oklahoma City
Grand Rapids	Phoenix
Jersey City	Salt Lake City-Ogden
Kansas City, Kans.	
Los Angeles–Long Beach	
Monmouth–Ocean	
New Haven–Meriden	
Oxnard–Ventura	
Riverside–San Bernardino	
Sacramento	
San Jose	
Syracuse	

that provide true substitute support for community and social services. According to the "crowd-out" theory, contributions should be relatively low in those metropolitan areas that are recipients of generous public funding from federal, state, and local sources. Private donations should be higher in communities receiving little public funding. As noted earlier, however, displacement interdependencies are complex, because complete substitution would be relatively rare. The most likely prospect of crowd-out would be in the relation of federal to state expenditures. Since local private and public generosity is expected to be consistent and applied to different uses than federal transfers and grants, we should not expect to find federal crowd-out or joint crowd-out of local efforts. Area differences should be reflected in the degrees of local effort and displacement.

Local and state indicators of public support for low-income residents and amenity services include an index of state business climate (as a measure of free-rider behavior); state and local shares of AFDC match (to measure generosity to dependent populations); state ranking on the severity of environmental management; the voting record of area congressional members according to the conservative Americans for Constitutional Action (to index local predisposition to publicly funded support); and the state ratio of maximum AFDC payments relative to the federal matching rate (a measure of AFDC generosity) (refer to the scores in Table 24.1).

The analyses (holding the other factors constant) show a modest but not significant crowd-out effect of federal expenditures on private contribution levels but a direct relationship between donations and state and especially municipal assistance (see the alternative models in Tables 24.2 and 24.3). Local public generosity appears to move in tandem with private contributions. On the other hand, the variable indexing state and municipal supplements to AFDC payments is related directly to the numbers of residents on AFDC and the minority and aged population and inversely to local private generosity. Private and local public support of amenities is more prevalent in the less populous and moderate-income areas, while income transfers are more generous (predominantly by state government) in bigger metropolitan areas with larger low-income minority populations. These findings are in general agreement with other analyses of the joint crowd-out of charitable and local public financing of services by federal programs (Steinberg, 1987). Rochester, Hartford, Cleveland, and Cincinnati, among others, show much higher contributions and the New Jersey and California metropolitan areas and Phoenix show much lower rates than would be expected from the local public-sector assistance and transfers.

The Effects of Alternative Targets for Generosity. If one assumes that donors contribute a fixed proportion of income each year, then potential recipients must compete for their share. The opposing view is that since such a small share (about 2 percent) of disposable income is donated, donors can easily augment their contributions if "properly solicited" without reducing their level of consumption or quality of life.

Do the metropolitan areas differ in availability and access to amenity services? Unlike the case with basic and public services, for amenity services to be made available to all who could benefit, some partial subsidy support is typically required. The variables index the variety, magnitude, and quality of services in the educational, cultural, and health sectors. The education index, for example, combines university ratings, college attendance, pupil-teacher ratios in elementary school, and expenditures per high school student. The health measure indexes health care costs, doctors per capita, specialized hospital departments, and area air pollution and fluoridation. The arts index includes libraries, museums, symphonies, theaters, and opera and dance companies and measures the number of facilities, budgets, and number of performances, among other factors.

The education scores are especially high in New England metropolitan areas but are also high in Rochester, Albany, Washington, and Raleigh-Durham. The scores are lowest in Sunbelt and Rustbelt places. The health index is best in some of the largest cities and relatively weakest in the smaller Rustbelt places. The cultural amenities are strongest, of course, in the largest centers of New York, Los Angeles, San Francisco, Philadelphia, and Boston.

In general, one must conclude from the indicators that amenity differences even between metropolitan areas of more than half a million people are quite significant. Some of the places have access to a wide variety of high-quality services in all three sectors, while others consistently rank low or have quite mixed scores. The measures are gross, but they point to persistence of regional differences not only in access to services but also in the public and private generosity that supports their provision. Residents of Boston and Minneapolis, at one extreme, are much better served than those of San Antonio and Birmingham.

The analysis of United Way contributions shows them to be consistent by area with support for cultural and health and hospital institutions and inversely related to support for educational facilities (Table 24.2). Umbrella-group contributions are much higher than expected from the support for arts, educational, and health organizations in Cleveland and Cincinnati and much lower than expected in Los Angeles and Salt Lake City. One might expect to find a higher level of service amenities in larger cities because of the threshold population numbers needed to fill concert halls and to listen to public radio. Agglomeration economies would also help to explain why ballet, opera, and university ratings should coincide by area.

Does local public generosity, measured by the community share of welfare expenditures, show consistency with local support for educational, health, and cultural institutions? The findings indicate a close positive relationship to educational support, reflecting greater generosity in teacher salaries and pupil-teacher ratios (Table 24.2). The same is true for state welfare supplements. Communities whose states are relatively more generous with welfare recipients spend more per pupil on their schools and other educational institutions. Arts and cultural support (and health services to a lesser degree) suffer, however, in climates generous in their welfare transfers.

Is support for educational, health, and cultural services simply a function of population size and community wealth? Separate analyses test the effect on service levels of metropolitan area population, median income, and a variable measuring locational centrality or accessibility. The findings tend to confirm our expectations: population numbers are most important in fostering a high level of cultural and health services; educational amenities are affected more by income levels; and the access measure is important in all three sectors (suggesting that these services are likely to have regional use extending beyond single metropolitan areas). The addition of the variables indexing distress and poverty levels confirms their expected negative but not very significant influence on service availability.

A simple two-by-two classification of the forty-three outlier metropolitan areas (Table 24.4) according to highest or lowest level of local as opposed to state support of services provides four meaningful categories of places (after allowing for differences in income and distress levels): the most generous communities in the more and less generous states and the least generous communities in the more and less generous states. The Ohio industrial metropolitan areas are prominent in the most generous dual category as are Minneapolis–St. Paul, Seattle, and certain eastern industrial cities. The southern and Sunbelt metropolitan areas are a good deal more generous than their respective states, while New Jersey and California communities are among those relying more heavily on state generosity; and metropolitan areas such as Oklahoma City, Phoenix, and Salt Lake City appear to have relatively little private or public, local or state support for their social, educational, health, or cultural services relative to their affluence levels. The remaining forty-two areas have state and local patterns of support that are more consistent with their median socioeconomic characteristics.

Summary

The analyses portray a more complex pattern of generosity than either a strict social choice or a Tiebout-type process would predict. Some of the complexity that has been revealed is undoubtedly a function of measuring generosity at metropolitan and state rather than at the more homogeneous municipal levels and the limitations of the data. Even with these more aggregate units, however, differences occur that can be attributed to the two processes acting in combination. Population attributes such as income, race, and age do become expressed in local preferences for both public and private support for services and transfers at community and state levels. Yet characteristics based solely on conventional socioeconomic indicators do not provide a sufficient explanation for the generosity patterns and their dispersion. For the outlier more and less generous metropolitan areas and states, additional factors are at work that point to a Tiebout-like self-selection process of higher or lower civic support and commitment. A complex set of interdependent place variables yields different environments for private and public support for different types of services. The outlier places are ideal sites for comparative case studies of regional (and place) values and institutions.

Will greater decentralization (from the federal government to states and localities) of responsibility for supporting cultural, health, educational, and social services result in wide regional disparities in well-being and quality of life? This chapter has examined the diversity of generosity patterns in America's states and largest metropolitan areas. The findings indicate that generosity levels differ significantly among the areas; local private and public generosity is consistent rather than competitive but is expressed more in civic improvement and support for amenities and services than in charitable transfers; and support for social services is also consistent rather than competitive with support for local cultural and health (but not educational) institutions.

Generosity levels are higher in moderate-income communities than in the highest-income communities without much distress and with a relatively smaller proportion of minority and aged residents. Some of the generous communities and/or their states also provide substantial income and service supplements to their AFDC residents, while other communities provide neither generous local amenities nor significant supplementary aid to their dependent populations. The analyses point to a dual pattern of generosity: local private and public efforts, especially in the smaller metropolitan areas, aimed at improving services and providing amenities and a second system shared between the federal government and the better-off states and largest communities that assists the poor and the handicapped. Decentralization of responsibility for transfers and support for services from the federal government to states and localities could be effective in some places but would likely be hazardous in others without an ample safety net.

References

Advisory Council on Intergovernmental Relations (ACIR). *Significant Features of Fiscal Federalism.* Washington, D.C.: ACIR, 1987.

Ball, T. "The Incoherence of Intergenerational Justice." *Inquiry,* 1986, *28,* 321–337.

Becker, G. S. "A Theory of Social Interaction." *Journal of Political Economy,* 1974, *82,* 1068–1093.

Boyer, R., and Savageau, D. *Places Rated Almanac.* Chicago: Rand McNally, 1987.

Buchanan, J. M. "Cooperation and Conflict in Public Goods Provision." *Western Economic Journal,* 1967, *5,* 109–121.

Carson, E. D. "The Charitable Giving and Voluntarism of Black Americans." In V. A. Hodgkinson, ed. *1987 Spring Research Forum Working Papers.* Washington, D.C.: INDEPENDENT SECTOR, 1987.

Collard, D. *Altruism and Economy.* Oxford, England: Robertson, 1978.

Conservation Foundation, Washington, D.C., 1983.

Cutter, S. C. *Rating Places.* Washington, D.C.: Association of American Geographers, 1985.

Dahl, R. A. *Dilemmas of Pluralist Democracy: Autonomy vs. Control.* New Haven, Conn.: Yale University Press, 1982.

General Manufacturing and Business Climate Survey. New York: Alexander Grant & Company, 1984.

Jencks, C. "Who Gives to What?" In W. W. Powell (ed.) *The Nonprofit Sector: A Research Handbook.* New Haven, Conn.: Yale University Press, 1987.

Katz, S. N. "Influences on Public Policies in the United States." In W. McN. Lowry (ed.), *The Arts and Public Policy in the United States.* Englewood Cliffs, N.J.: Prentice-Hall, 1984.

Reiner, T. A., and Wolpert, J. "The Not-for-Profit Sector in Stable and Growing Metropolitan Areas." *Urban Affairs Quarterly,* 1985, *20,* 487–510.

Rose-Ackerman, S. "United Charities: An Economic Analysis." *Public Policy,* 1980, *28,* 323–350.

Salamon, L. M. "Partners in Public Service: The Scope and Theory of Government-Nonprofit Relations." In W. W. Powell (ed.), *The Nonprofit Sector: A Research Handbook.* New Haven, Conn.: Yale University Press, 1987.

Shields, J. J., and others. *An Analysis of the Campaign for Human Development Annual Collection.* Washington, D.C.: Department of Sociology, Catholic University, 1987.

Silberstein, R., and others. "Giving to Jewish Philanthropic

Causes." In V. A. Hodgkinson, ed. *1987 Spring Research Forum Working Papers.* Washington, D.C.: INDEPENDENT SECTOR, 1987.

Steinberg, R. "Voluntary Donations and Public Expenditures in a Federalist System." *American Economic Review,* 1987, *77,* 24–36.

Stouffer, S. "Intervening Opportunities and Competing Migrants." *Journal of Regional Science,* 1960, *2,* 1–26.

Tiebout, C. M. "A Pure Theory of Local Expenditures." *Journal of Political Economy,* 1956, *64,* 416–424.

Weisbrod, B. *The Voluntary Nonprofit Sector: An Economic Analysis.* Lexington, Mass.: Heath, 1977.

Wolch, J., and Geiger, R. K. "The Distribution of Urban Voluntary Resources." *Environment and Planning A,* 1983, *15,* 1067–1082.

Wolpert, J. "Social Income and the Voluntary Sector." *Papers, Regional Science Association,* 1977, *39,* 217–229.

Wolpert, J., and Reiner, T. A. "The Philanthropy Marketplace." *Economic Geography,* 1984, *60,* 197–209.

25

ROBERT J. O'CONNOR
REBECCA S. JOHNSON

△ △ △ △ △ △ △ △ △ △ △ △ △ △ △

Volunteer Demographics and Future Prospects for Volunteering

Nonprofit organizations are highly dependent on attracting, utilizing, and motivating volunteers to accomplish their goals. Volunteers are, in fact, a valuable financial resource to the organizations they serve. Using 1985 data to estimate the monetary value of the time donated by volunteers in the course of a year, INDEPENDENT SECTOR (1986) found that the time donated just to charitable organizations was worth $84 billion. In addition, data from a recent national survey conducted for United Way and other nonprofits indicate that 52 percent of volunteers are involved in fund-raising activities (Gallup Organization, 1987), an essential process for charitable organizations to meet their financial goals. Third, virtually every study examining the subject finds that those who volunteer to any charitable cause are more likely than others to donate money to charity (Hodgkinson and Weitzman, 1986; O'Connor, 1985; Morgan, Dye, and Hybels, 1977). Whether giving precedes volunteering or the other way around does not matter very much. It is enough to say that involvement breeds further involvement, with positive impacts on fund raising.

This chapter examines the prospects for volunteering over the next five to twelve years. To do so, we will look at the current number of volunteers to charitable organizations, the variables that tend to influence volunteering, and the ways in which charitable organizations may be able to increase the number of volunteers. Finally, we discuss the importance of attentiveness on the part of charitable organizations to the wants and needs of volunteers, a vital issue if the organizations are to dramatically increase and retain volunteers.

Estimating the Number of Volunteers

In a study carried out in September 1987 for United Way of America and other charitable organizations, the Gallup Organization (1987) conducted personal, in-home interviews with a nationally representative sample of 1,033 adults, eighteen years of age or older. Respondents were asked whether they had volunteered to a "religious, charitable, not-for-profit or fundraising organization" in the past twelve months; 16 percent of those interviewed reported that they had. Projected against the number of Americans eighteen years of age or older, about 176,269,000 in 1985, this would indicate a total of 28.2 million volunteers.

This estimate is noticeably lower than that reported by INDEPENDENT SECTOR (1986), probably because of differences in the interview sample and question wording. INDEPENDENT SECTOR's sample included fourteen- to seventeen-year-olds. Its definition of volunteering included informal volunteering, as well as volunteering for for-profit and governmental organizations (21 percent of the volunteers in the study). The Gallup study excluded both these types of volunteering.

Demographic Variables Influencing Volunteering

Both the INDEPENDENT SECTOR (1986) study and the Gallup Organization (1987) studies show some consistent relationships between certain demographic variables and what can be called "organized volunteering" (that is, excluding those who volunteer informally, without a tie to a particular organization).

Volunteering is related to age in a somewhat curvilinear fashion; the proportion volunteering is highest among those in the twenty-five to thirty-four and thirty-five to forty-nine age groups but is somewhat lower among those over fifty and those eighteen to twenty-four. The twenty-four to forty-nine age bracket is of particular interest, as it includes most of the baby boom generation born between 1946 and 1964, a very sizable demographic group. Figure 25.1 shows the data on this obtained by the INDEPENDENT SECTOR (1986) study; the results of the Gallup Organization (1987) study are consistent with these data.

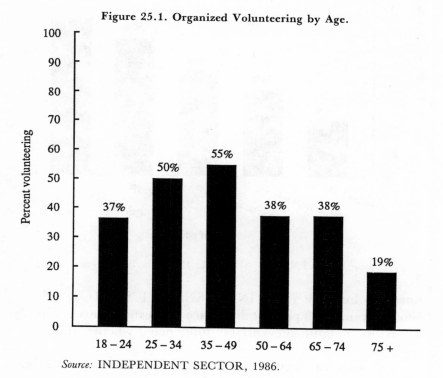

Figure 25.1. Organized Volunteering by Age.

Source: INDEPENDENT SECTOR, 1986.

As shown in Figure 25.2, education has a strong consistent effect; both studies found that formal volunteering increases as education increases. As one would expect, income is also related to volunteering, but not as consistently as is education. People who are married are more likely to volunteer than those who are not; the presence of children also increases the chances that one will volunteer. In the Gallup Organization's survey, 15 percent of the men and 18 percent of the women responding re-

Figure 25.2. Organized Volunteering by Education Level.

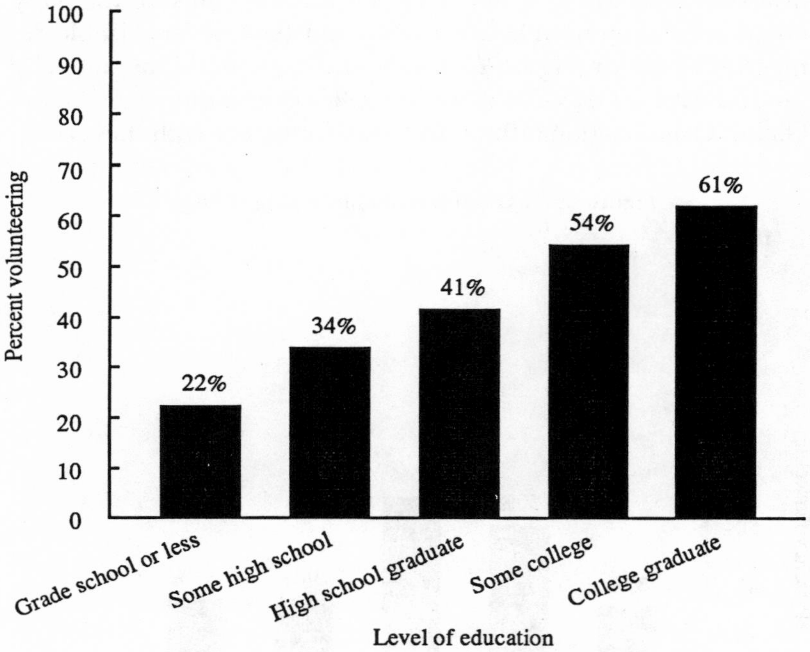

Source: INDEPENDENT SECTOR, 1986.

ported volunteering; the INDEPENDENT SECTOR's data showed a similar 3 percent difference between the sexes. Thus, sex is not a significant variable influencing whether one volunteers.

The overall picture that emerges from this review of the demographics of volunteering is that the volunteer tends to be a person of above-average income and education who is middle-aged or slightly younger and domestically settled with a spouse and child. One way to evaluate the prospects for increasing the number of volunteers over the next five to twelve years, then, is to examine census projections for the key demographic groups to see whether the number of people in these prime demographic categories is likely to increase or decrease.

Projections for Key Demographic Groups

What are the prospects that the key age groups for volunteering (those twenty-five to thirty-four and those thirty-five to forty-four years old) will grow in numbers over the next five to twelve years? As Table 25.1 shows, the younger age group will actually increase only slightly between now and 1990 and thereafter will decline, according to the projection of the Census Bureau. The thirty-five- to forty-four-year-old group will increase substantially over the next five years, continue to show impressive growth through 1995, and then decline in numbers between 1995 and 2000. When both age groups are taken together, the prospects are for a 10 percent growth of the prime volunteer market up to 1990, with growth leveling out through 1995 and the numbers decreasing between 1995 and 2000.

Income projections reported in a 1984 issue of *American Demographics* ("Households and Income in 1995," 1984) indicate that the proportion of households with relatively high incomes ($40,000 and over) will increase from 16 percent in 1980 to 24 percent in 1995. The proportion of people married, an important variable influencing volunteering, has been stable over the past four or five years and will probably continue to remain stable (U.S. Bureau of the Census, 1986). The proportion of women between twenty-five and fifty-four years old in the labor force is projected to increase from about 71 percent to 81 percent by the year 2000, a much slower rate of increase than in previous years (U.S.

Table 25.1. Projected Populations of Key
Age Groups, 1990 to 2000 (in Thousands).

Age	1990	1995	2000
25–34	43,529	40,520	36,415
Percentage change	+3%	−7%	−10%
35–44	37,847	41,997	43,743
Percentage change	+19%	+11%	+4%
25–44	81,376	82,517	80,158
Percentage change	+10%	+1%	−3%

Source: U.S. Bureau of the Census, 1987.

Bureau of Labor Statistics, 1987). The growing number of women entering the labor force has already had an effect in decreasing the pool of available volunteers.

In sum, it appears that, with the exception of age groups, demographic patterns will not materially alter over the next few years. Clearly, strenuous efforts will have to be made to recruit and retain volunteers if volunteerism is to increase by more than 10 percent over the next five years; riding the demographic tides with a business-as-usual approach will not be enough.

Recruitment of Volunteers

While nonprofit organizations have little control over the demographic changes in the population, they can do something about their recruitment practices. In most instances, people volunteer because they are personally asked to. It seems logical, then, to focus on the proportion of people that are actually asked to volunteer each year.

In the Gallup Organization's (1987) study of awareness and involvement, 21 percent of the public indicated that they had been asked to volunteer for a religious or charitable organization in the past twelve months; seventy-four percent indicated that they had not been asked. Obviously, one clear path to increasing the number of volunteers is to increase the proportion asked. There are some indications that this would be successful. According to the INDEPENDENT SECTOR (1986) study, 78 percent of those asked to volunteer accepted, and only 20 percent declined. Even if allowances are made for overreporting among those who wish to appear altruistic, this is a very good acceptance rate.

What kinds of people are asked to volunteer? To a considerable extent, they resemble the profile drawn earlier of the volunteer. Most of those asked are between thirty-five and forty-nine years of age, are college educated, and have relatively high incomes. Married people are more likely to be asked than those who are single. Even among these groups, the proportion asked is no higher than 31 percent, so there is ample room for improvement in these key segments. Furthermore, given the resemblance between the types of people asked and those actually serving, perhaps nonprofit organizations should consider "democratizing the ask." Given the large proportion who are not asked to volunteer, there is certainly room to extend the opportunity to volunteer to those with more modest incomes and educational attainments and those who are older or younger than the typical volunteer.

Modes of Recruitment. How are volunteers actually recruited? The recruitment process seems to be tied to people's existing organizational and social affiliations. When the Gallup Organization (1987) asked people how they were recruited, the most frequent response was "by someone in an organization" to which they already belonged (59 percent). The next most frequent response was being asked by a friend or neighbor (22 percent), followed by being asked at the workplace (14 percent). Interestingly, only 14 percent of the volunteers cited mass media approaches (including television, radio, and print).

There are some differences by demographics in how volunteers are recruited. For example, men are 10 percent more likely than women to have been recruited through an organization to which they already belong and about 10 percent more likely to have been asked at their workplace. Those in the prime age group for volunteering (thirty-five to forty-nine) are more likely to have been asked by a friend or neighbor than are those who are younger or older.

Given that mass media approaches do not seem to be an effective means for recruiting volunteers, nonprofits need to develop a more effective means of mobilizing people through the organizations to which they belong or through their workplaces. In addition, they could devote more attention to another potential source of volunteers: the users of nonprofit services and their families.

Service Usage and Volunteering. In an analysis of United Way of America's workplace survey data base, O'Connor (1985) found that one of the variables most strongly related to volunteering is whether the respondent or a family member has used the services of a nonprofit or charitable organization in the past twelve months. Of the people surveyed, those who had volunteered for charitable organization were much more likely to have been service users (23 percent) than were nonvolunteers (9 percent). This suggests that one very effective way of recruiting volunteers, and perhaps of "democratizing the ask," is to routinely ask clients or family members of clients to volunteer.

These analyses suggest a fourfold strategy: (1) recruitment and membership drives to expand the total number of people who are members of some standing of a voluntary or nonprofit organization; (2) working through existing organizations to better mobilize their members and to better provide them with opportunities to volunteer; (3) providing opportunities to volunteer in the workplace; and (4) providing service recipients and their families with the opportunity to volunteer.

Volunteer Satisfaction

An issue often neglected is the danger that a dramatic increase in the number of volunteers could overwhelm many nonprofit organizations' ability to absorb and effectively use volunteers. New volunteers mean additional training, supervision, and matching of abilities, interests, and talents to the needs of the organizations. If many new volunteers are recruited but are not put to good use, their experience could have a negative effect on their attitudes toward and perceptions of the nonprofit sector generally. Once we have attracted volunteers, then, how do we increase the chances that they will be satisfied with their experience? A related question is how do we keep the volunteer involved? The answers to these questions require that we look at the volunteer as a customer and be attentive to his or her needs and wants. What are the needs and wants of the volunteer, and what are the implications for how we absorb and handle volunteers?

Wants and Needs of Volunteers. One of the best sources of national data on the wants and needs of volunteers is the INDEPENDENT SECTOR (1986) study. In that study, respondents were asked to indicate the reasons they had first become involved in a volunteer activity (see Figure 25.3). The most frequently chosen reason has to do unequivocally with altruism: "Do something useful to help others." However, the second reason, "Had an interest in the work or activity," may combine altruism with an interest in the activity itself. The third most frequently chosen reason was "enjoy doing the work." It very much appears that, while volunteers become involved partly because they have altruistic needs, a contributing motivator is the intrinsic worth of the volunteer job. This hypothesis gains further support if we look at the reasons people give for continuing to be involved with volunteer activity. While the altruistic motivation remains the most frequently chosen and even increases in importance, enjoying the work also gains importance as a motivation. While

Figure 25.3. Reasons for Involvement in Volunteer Activity.

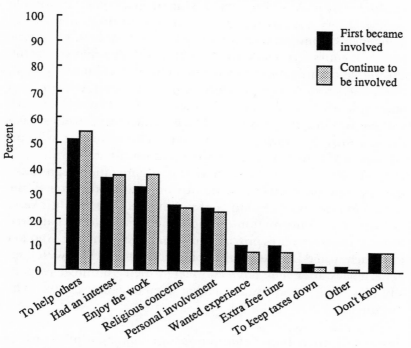

Source: INDEPENDENT SECTOR, 1986.

the evidence is indirect, it appears that a drive to attract new volunteers needs to address the very real need to help others but at the same time must offer work for the volunteer that is enjoyable and interesting. In other words, the volunteer job itself must have intrinsic value to the volunteer, as well as altruistic value.

Adding to the challenge is evidence of another need of the volunteer or prospective volunteer. Respondents to the Gallup Organization's (1987) survey were asked whether they had been asked to volunteer and had refused and, if so, why they had refused. The predominant reason, overshadowing all others, was "lack of time/too busy." Lack of time can be seen as an excuse or rationalization, and for many respondents it probably is. However, there undoubtedly remains a substantial proportion of people for whom time is in fact their scarcest resource. Time may be particularly scarce for the growing number of households with children in which both parents work (United Way of America, 1987). This suggests that if charitable organizations were to reduce the amount of time they expect from each volunteer, they might be able to attract more volunteers. Of course, this sets up a classic trade-off situation for the charitable organization: can it restructure its volunteer jobs to require less time without neglecting the need for interesting and enjoyable work? Can it provide interesting and enjoyable work without training the volunteer? Once a volunteer is trained, can the organization recover its investment in training without demanding a more extensive time commitment?

It is hard to see how charitable organizations can make the appropriate trade-offs without some basic attention to the wants and needs of the kinds of volunteers they would like to attract. Some information on these matters could be gathered through questionnaires provided to incoming volunteers. Another approach would be to examine volunteers' satisfaction with their experiences after they have completed their volunteer responsibilities. This second approach has been taken by United Way of America.

Survey of United Way Volunteer Satisfaction. In a pilot project carried out in cooperation with one of its local chapters, the United Way mailed a questionnaire to 384 volunteers involved in a wide range of activities, including planning and allocations committee work as well as fund raising. The questionnaire included items on how the volunteers felt about their experience and training and how satisfied they were. The response rate was a very respectable 46 percent. The study found quite a high level of satisfaction among the respondents. For example, 57 percent were very satisfied with their volunteer experience, and 92 percent said that they would volunteer for United Way again. (For the most part, data analysis was limited to whether respondents felt very satisfied or merely somewhat satisfied.)

Several key variables in this pilot study of volunteer satisfaction are associated with higher levels of volunteer satisfaction. For example, volunteers who felt that the time demanded of them was "just about right" or "too little" were more likely to be very satisfied with their experience; those who felt that too much time was demanded were less satisfied. One reason for involvement was consistently related to satisfaction: respondents who indicated that a reason for their involvement was enjoyment of the work were more likely to be highly satisfied with the experience than those who did not choose that reason.

These results further underline the need to establish the appropriate time commitment for volunteers, to provide realistic training (rather than just an orientation to the organization), and to offer meaningful recognition for volunteer work, as well as to offer volunteers an opportunity to do work that they enjoy. Combined with the indirect evidence from the Gallup Organization's (1987) data, the results indicate that if charitable organizations are able to attract a significantly higher number of volunteers, they will have to pay considerable attention to the issues of how to structure volunteer tasks and training. This in turn may well require volunteer-intensive organizations to invest more heavily than ever before in staff and other resources required to train, supervise, and support volunteers in carrying out their responsibilities.

Conclusion: The Prospects for Volunteering

Volunteers are important to charitable organizations not only for the wide range of activities they perform and the monetary value of the time they donate but because volunteers are "cheer-ful givers." It is vital to the health of the nonprofit organiza-tions that voluntarism continue to grow. But, as we have shown, the demographic trends over the next five years favor only a modest expansion in the pool of likely volunteers, and thereafter the tides will begin to run against increasing numbers of volunteers.

One effective way to increase the number of new volun-teers is to do a better job of recruitment. Since only 21 percent of the public nationwide is asked to volunteer in a given year, there is obviously ample room for improvement. In the short run, increased recruitment efforts can best be done through or-ganizational membership, the workplace, and service contacts. It appears that the mass media play a minimal role in this pro-cess. But there is also ample room for widening the base of those who are asked to volunteer. It appears that those who are asked have a distinctly upper-socioeconomic-level profile, as do those who actually volunteer. One way to incease the number of vol-unteers is to "democratize the ask" and provide more people at middle and lower socioeconomic levels with the opportunity to volunteer.

Finally, as we have noted, attention to the wants and needs of volunteers is crucial; charitable organizations cannot risk alien-ating those who contribute their time by not using that time ef-fectively. But attending to these wants and needs can pose a dif-ficult trade-off situation for the charitable organization that wishes to maximize the number of its volunteers: maintaining or im-proving the quality of the job itself while being responsive to the needs of some volunteers for a less demanding time commitment.

Since so few people are asked to volunteer each year, and so few actually decline when asked, it appears that the prospects for substantial growth in volunteers are excellent, particularly over the next five years. This success will generate another challenge: making the volunteer experience a satisfying one.

References

Gallup Organization. *The Gallup Study of Public Awareness and In-volvement with Non-Profit Organizations.* Princeton, N.J.: Gallup Organization, 1987.

Hodgkinson, V. A., and Weitzman, M. S. *The Charitable Behavior of Americans.* Washington, D.C.: INDEPENDENT SECTOR, 1986.

"Households and Income in 1995." *American Demographics,* 1984, *6* (4), 50.

INDEPENDENT SECTOR. *Americans Volunteer 1985.* Washington, D.C.: INDEPENDENT SECTOR, 1986.

Morgan, J. N., Dye, R. F., and Hybels, J. H. "Results from Two National Surveys of Philanthropic Activity." Unpublished paper, Commission on Private Philanthropy and Public Needs, 1977.

O'Connor, R. J. "Giving and Volunteering at the Workplace." In Virginia A. Hodgkinson, ed. *1985 Spring Research Forum Working Papers.* Washington, D.C.: INDEPENDENT SECTOR/United Way Institute, 1985.

U.S. Bureau of Labor Statistics. *Monthly Labor Review,* Sept. 1987 (entire issue).

U.S. Bureau of the Census. *Statistical Abstract of the United States, 1987.* Washington, D.C.: U.S. Government Printing Office, 1986.

United Way of America. *What Lies Ahead: Looking Toward the '90s.* Alexandria, Va.: United Way of America, 1987.

26

TERESA J. ODENDAHL

△ △ △ △ △ △ △ △ △ △ △ △ △ △ △

Charitable Giving Patterns by Elites in the United States

The philanthropic wealthy believe that private contributions and nongovernmental charitable organizations are integral to the American way of life. They contrast individual giving to charity with the taxation policies of European welfare states; they want to be the ones who make decisions about where their surplus money goes, rather than the government doing so. They think that their funding is better than the state's, and they believe that services are provided most effectively and efficiently by non-profit agencies. This ideology is the basis of wealthy people's involvement in voluntary organizations.

Philanthropy has recently served as a justification for minimizing the welfare role of government. Yet charitable giving by the wealthy supports primarily upper-class institutions, such as Ivy League universities, that reproduce a "power elite" (Mills, 1959). The political economy of giving allows moneyed elites, rather than elected representatives, to exercise substantial leadership within and control over many nonprofit endeavors. This chapter explores the ideology and rhetoric of the charitable wealthy, as well as the power they exercise as a group. When sociologist C. Wright Mills described the power elite, he focused

Note: This chapter contains material from a manuscript by Teresa J. Odendahl, *The Culture of Philanthropy,* to be published by Basic Books. The author is grateful to Michael Bernstein, Elizabeth Boris, Peter Hall, Richard Lyman, Eric Odendahl, and Mary Odendahl for comments on previous drafts.

on the common backgrounds and interests of leaders in finance, industry, the military, and politics. In a preliminary attempt to extend Mills's analysis to the leaders of philanthropy, I examine the charitable pursuits of the wealthy. Other scholars have suggested this line of inquiry (Domhoff, 1971, 1983; Ostrander, 1984), although it has not been the primary focus of their work. Of course, because philanthropy interacts with business and government, it cannot be fully understood without examination of both.

A team of collaborative researchers conducted 136 confidential, in-depth interviews with millionaires from across the United States as part of a joint study by Yale University's Program on Nonprofit Organizations and the Council on Foundations (Odendahl, 1987). The researchers interviewed eighty-two men and fifty-four women of wealth who were active in local and national networks of philanthropists. The vast majority are married and have children. This elite group is mostly white, Protestant, and over forty years old. Fewer than ten of the informants are not college graduates. More than half of those for whom data are available attended Ivy League universities. A third of the wealthy people (forty-three) are self-made, first-generation millionaires. The rest inherited at least some of their money or married into rich families. There are forty-five second-generation heirs, and declining numbers in subsequent generations, with ten who are in at least the fourth generation from the original fortune. Before proceeding, it should be emphasized that this chapter employs anthropological rather than statistical methods in order to understand the political economy of charitable giving by elites.

Philanthropic Ideology

As one informant put it, "If there were not a nonprofit community out there, two things would have happened. I do not think we would still be a democratic country. This may be exaggerated, but the public demand for the government to do this, that and the other would be to such a degree because of their needs . . . we would probably be a huge big government doing all these things, socialistic.'' Rich philanthropists equate their ability to make individual decisions about dispersing their wealth with capitalism and democracy. Most are opposed to the politics of the welfare state. Like other Americans, they are subject to a prevailing fear of socialism, which they assume is the opposite of democracy. Or rather, as in the case of the millionaire just quoted, their view of the appropriate role of the state is narrow in scope. They hold that, while the masses may have the vote, the elected government should be limited in its power. The ''public'' should not ''demand'' too much, whatever ''their needs'' might be.

A middle-aged northeastern woman of wealth expressed her views: ''We get closer and closer to an undemocratic society if we shift all the responsibility onto government. And that is what is going to happen if private philanthropy is discouraged.'' Once again, a peculiar idea about democracy is voiced, wherein it is undemocratic for the state to have major responsibility. There is little recognition here of the extent to which government contributions already fund nonprofit organizations in the United States (Hodgkinson and Weitzman, 1986; Salamon, 1987), but there is a notion that private charity can counteract or balance economic and state power. This rich woman continued: ''Somebody has got to take over or we are all going to be ciphers in some government-sponsored social agency. I think it would be disastrous.'' She has an unabashed view about where control should rest. ''Somebody,'' presumably an individual philanthropist and not the government, should seize power.

Wealthy people of every political persuasion made remarks about the importance of private nonprofit endeavors. Informants proudly referred to the history of charitable giving in this country, as well as their desire to fund projects that perpetuate traditional ''American'' values. Several different interpretations of what actually constitutes that tradition emerged, although an ethic of individualism and ethnocentrism pervaded many people's remarks. When referring to his family and company giving, a conservative western grantmaker stated, ''We are defenders of the American Way. We believe that it is in danger. So organizations that address themselves to the preservation of the traditional rights, the traditional freedoms, and particularly the traditional responsibility of the great American citizen we favor." His interests are "primarily in education. I support things like the boys' club . . . and universities that appeal to me."

A liberal easterner said that she thinks people give "because of a very strong Judeo-Christian, American principle. I think de Tocqueville observed it, and it is true. We do believe, as American people, that we can change life for other people and for ourselves, and make it better. We really do believe that. Other societies, I don't think, have that belief." She said she funds "high-risk, interesting ventures." These include the ballet, education, and religious organizations. From her descriptions of these projects, only the private schools that she supports are risky. They seem to be on financially shaky ground, in part, she implies, because they are ethnically and racially integrated and provide scholarships for poor students. This liberal philanthropist might appear at odds with the conservative quoted before her, but their basic, underlying philosophies are similar. Apparently, they both think that it is up to the individual philanthropist to determine what makes life "better." They do not want to leave this responsibility to the majority of citizens, public officials, or the state.

Another example sharply highlights inconsistencies between political views, perspectives on charity, and practice. A young funder who inherited his money and described himself as a leftist stated, "I think the philanthropic tradition in the United States is very important. It is different from Europe. . . . Europe does not give tax deductions for charitable giving. . . . Individuals are not encouraged to give money there. So when they do, they give less. . . . The needy organizations fall under the government and the attendant bureaucracies. I think those societies move more slowly, and individual initiative is not rewarded as fully. There is a rigid structure that has to do with this interweaving of politics, bureaucracy, and the existing order." He has been involved with other young rich people in an alternative foundation that has made grants to small local groups such as the La Raza Legal Center and the Medical Coalition for the Rights of Women. In spite of this young man's avowed politics, his outlook is totally consistent with philanthropic ideology, including what amounts to a kind of bald nationalism. He did not concur with many of the positions of the Reagan, and now the Bush, administration, but he supports the American system, especially individualism in philanthropy.

Conservatives, liberals, and radicals who give to charity may not consciously understand the ways in which much of philanthropy maintains the status quo and can even perpetuate inequities. They may be critical of aspects of the political economy, but at the same time they are ardent supporters of nonprofit activity in the United States. In the final analysis, because of their contributions, philanthropists hold power over the projects they choose to fund or not to fund.

Business and Charity

Economics and charity are interrelated. For the wealthy, business and investments provide the profits for their philanthropy. Most charitably minded elites believe that a free-market system fosters a giving environment because it provides a surplus that may be privately used for the public good. An Atlanta philanthropist claimed that giving is strong because "There is more money around." He continued, "it is a matter of leadership. There is a pattern in the community that you can follow.[One woman] gave $50,000. She is worth $50 million. Somebody else makes six gifts of a million dollars each. [She's] worth $50 to $100 million."

Business people donate personal money to charity, and they often view such disbursements as work-related. Many companies, both small and large, are family controlled, and family members may use profits for philanthropy. In addition, corporate giving committees or company-sponsored foundations award grants with funds donated by parent corporations. Business executives generally serve on corporate grant making committees. It is difficult to separate business and personal interests, for they often overlap. A midwestern businessman explained that philanthropy is vital in his community because "We have a relatively small number of very wonderful families on the one hand, and the leadership of the business community on the other hand." In his town, the leading families own the leading companies. The mix of corporate and individual wealth varies by location, but all wealthy people have business interests. Historically and presently, business leaders are philanthropic leaders (Hall, forthcoming).

Companies and the wealthy are unlikely to fund projects that might jeopardize their profits. One millionaire admitted, "We pretty much give to the same things, the safe things." He said, "It is a club. What is the phone company giving? What is the bank giving? What is the other bank giving? And everybody else falls into line, in proportion." Corporations not only fund safe projects but systematically keep certain organizations from getting funds. This man continued, "If one guy [head of a company] has a problem with a neighborhood group, more than likely other corporations will have problems with the same neighborhood group—like neighborhood groups that go after banks for not making loans ["redlining"]. . . . Well, suddenly, everybody's badmouthing this neighborhood group. I would guess that they have never taken the time to personally visit the people about their concerns."

The predominant opinion is that business comes before charity. In a temporal sense, this is obviously true, but once the money is made, it might be used in any number of ways: reinvested to generate more income and profit, spent on consumer items, or contributed to charity. A California entrepreneur stated, "The prevalent view is that a corporation's job is to make the shareholders' net worth grow. Then it is the shareholders' function to decide what they want to do with their money. In this company we take a very narrow view of what our philanthropic obligation is. If it does not relate fairly directly to the interests of the company or to our employees, we pass it by." Company giving programs reflect corporate interests, or the personal opinions of the chief executive, other officers, and owners. Corporate gifts may be clear-cut contributions to charity or in the gray area of advertising, public relations, or marketing (Knauft, 1986; White and Bartolomeo, 1982).

"Philanthropy is not a question of commitment, but one of economics," said one straightforward eastern businessman. When asked about the process by which he makes his individual charitable decisions, he claimed, "It is what is good for the business. An example of that would be that somebody we are in business with is really strongly advocating their favorite charity. Or, we do it because of the connection of the individual, or because the charity is so linked with some business activity we are doing. A good example of that would be [a private university], which is a large client of the firm. We do a lot of business with them, and therefore we give to the university." Private nonprofit universities are good cases in point. They may undertake substantial building and maintenance projects that they contract out to for-profit firms. In fact, most big higher education institutions are very similar to large businesses.

A well-known philanthropist claimed, "There is only one excuse for American business and it is to serve society. Profit is our reward. . . . When business does not do its job, then we get punished with adverse legislation, stringent regulations, pressure groups of all kinds. . . . It is business' and the nation's best interest to have a large proportion of the demand for services, whether it be social, cultural, educational, medical or whatever, filled in the private sector." Here is one of the clearest explanations of the business component of philanthropic ideology. If the business community takes the lead and funds "for the public good," then its other activities are less constrained. In this straightforward way, philanthropy serves capitalism, but is this the appropriate way to "serve society"? Or should redistribution be primarily a government role determined through the political process?

Politics

Whether right-wing, conservative, moderate, liberal, or left-wing, many of the charitably wealthy are involved in politics. This activity is a tangible link between philanthropy and the political economy. One millionaire said, "I have always been on [philanthropic] boards, even in my political years." Some have held or run for public office. Many have been appointed to high posts, such as cabinet seats. Others serve in Congress, the Senate, and state government.

The giving practices of most philanthropists are related to their political beliefs and involvement. Except for tax purposes, no distinction is usually made between these activities. When asked about charity, a funder from the mid-Atlantic region said, "I give money to conservative causes." Another said, "My original fund raising and giving away money was really encouraged in the political arena. I was head of [a committee] for George McGovern's presidential candidacy." In a few cases, the primary commitment is recognized as political, rather than charitable. A young man admitted that his motives for charitable giving are "almost purely political." Another funder stated, "I decided that I wanted to have an impact politically, and that one of the things people in politics listen to is money." Most philanthropists are like the middle-aged eastern woman with moderate politics who suggested, "You cannot get away from politics, agendas for people. . . . I am a Republican, and I have always enjoyed public affairs. I pay a lot of attention."

A fairly representative philanthropist indicated, "I have always been politically active, if you define politically broadly, not just electoral politics." Most charitable elites are committed to promoting particular causes through their philanthropy. One individual said, "If you have something that you believe in that ought to be done, and you believe it is not being adequately addressed by an existing agency, then you have a powerful incentive to try to do whatever you can. Sometimes there is no way except to put up the money. You can . . . try to enlist the help of other people, and convince them of the merit of your idea. But if you get right down to it in the final analysis, some things just take money." In contemporary America, money equals power.

Political activity involves more than individual or small-group efforts, candidacies, and funds. Ideas, policy formulation, and the organization of political agendas are increasingly apt to come out of nonprofit higher education institutions and private research institutes. These organizations usually take the stance of being impartial experts outside of government. As a recent example, the Heritage Foundation, a right-wing nonprofit think tank, gained prominence in the early 1980s with its financial support of conservative philanthropists. Less than a week after Ronald Reagan was elected president, Heritage released a book (Heritage Foundation, 1980) outlining its recommended policy programs and was sending résumés to the White House transition team. The foundation had been formed ten years earlier with the express purpose of serving conservative members of Congress in need of intellectual support for their positions.

The shift to the political right and expert marketing and public relations, as well as substantial charitable contributions, help explain the success of the Heritage Foundation and similar organizations. Historian James Smith, who has been studying public-policy research institutions, documents their "techniques of advocacy" in a forthcoming book, *The Policy Elite*. But Heritage is only one case. Smith estimates that there are over 1,000 policy think tanks in the United States and Canada. They include the American Enterprise Institute, the Brookings Institution, the Hoover Institution, and the Rand Corporation. Each has been accused of leaning one way or another on the political spectrum. While this diversity of policy approaches might promote pluralism, significant segments of the population who do not have the means to fund think tanks or other intellectual activity may not be heard.

Tax Policy

Charitable tax policy in the United States encourages private citizens to give to the causes of their choice but does not provide for equity. Because they are able to make larger donations, wealthy people have disproportionate power within nonprofit organizations. Whether philanthropists have a particular interest in the arts or in welfare, often their voices, rather than the voices of those served, are the ones heard. For example, according to the Internal Revenue Service, in 1984 the 16,295 individuals or couples with annual adjusted gross incomes of $1 million or more claimed an average charitable contribution of $139,291 on their tax returns. The overall average deduction taken by all 57.5 million itemizers was based on an average of $1,223 in gifts, slightly above the average $1,133 that taxpayers in the

$30,000 to $50,000 bracket donated and well over the $672 average claim of people who had made between $5,000 and $10,000 that year. In addition, nearly 23 million nonitemizers showed an average $51 charitable donation (American Association of Fund-Raising Counsel, 1987). In proportion to their income, the poor and middle class are generous, especially to religious organizations. But they have less to give and therefore have less influence.

The hypothetical millionaire who gave $140,000 to charity might have made ten gifts of $10,000 each to her favorite organizations—or two gifts of $50,000 each—and divided the remaining $40,000 among several nonprofits. A middle-class person probably wrote checks of $100 or less to each of ten or twelve causes. The $10,000 contribution and almost certainly the $50,000 donation would put the wealthy person in a position of influence with from two to ten charities. The $100 contribution, which for most of us is sizable, would have gone into a pot of money over which the middle-class person has little control.

The real story is slightly more complicated. There is evidence that major philanthropists are the very wealthiest people in the country, those whom Ferdinand Lundberg (1968) labeled the "super-rich." A recent economic study on the charitable contributions of the wealthy, based on a stratified random sample of income tax returns filed between 1971 and 1975, found great variability in levels of giving, especially for those with the highest incomes. Researchers Gerald Auten and Gabriel Rudney suggest that "the reputation of the wealthy for generosity is largely the result of exceptional generosity on the part of a minority of high income givers rather than widespread generosity among the wealthy" (Auten and Rudney, 1987, p. 9). They also indicate that "the proportion of generous givers rises with income" (p. 31). In the early 1970s, wealthier donors who gave more to charity made annual median contributions of about $435,000. Let us assume, along with the economists, but discounting inflation, that this figure is more accurate than the average $140,000 that includes millionaires who are not very charitable.

The hypothetical multimillionaire philanthropist has contributed $400,000 to the causes of his choice. He can dominate one organization, or he can have substantial leverage by donating $100,000 each to four organizations. Or he may give $40,000 each to ten groups and still have a great deal of influence. He probably gave two or three large grants and several smaller ones in the range of $10,000 which would offer him a significant voice in several organizations. The giving is not usually to small nonprofit enterprises, but rather to larger institutions where it might permit the millionaire to join governing boards and gain status and visibility. As a group, elites help determine policies at, for example, arts organizations, private schools, and colleges. In addition, they often contribute $1,000 to $5,000 to other organizations at the request of friends and relatives. They also raise money from them for their favorite causes. And wealthy people, their friends and relatives, and their companies and foundations are making contributions to each other's preferred charities.

Taxes do not have a direct effect on the amounts that the wealthy give to nonprofit organizations. But, as one typical philanthropist explained, "The government makes it pretty attractive to you [to make charitable donations] in two ways: giving you a deduction for what you put into philanthropic purposes, and also taxing you at a very high rate if you do not." Charitable tax incentives are of greater benefit to the wealthy than to those in lower income tax brackets, because the rich are able to substantially reduce the taxable portion of their income through their philanthropic contributions. The larger the gifts, the more they save in taxes and the greater the influence they wield with nonprofit organizations. Furthermore, provisions in estate law allow the wealthy to set up charitable trusts that are virtually tax free. Interest income benefits nonprofit organizations that the donor chooses and may even control, but eventually the corpus of the trust reverts to the donor's heirs.

In the last 30 years, top individual income tax rates have declined from 92 percent to 28 percent. The 1986 Tax Reform Act dramatically changed the top rate from 50 percent to 28 percent. This means that there will be a greater direct economic cost for giving by individuals than in the past, but rich philanthropists will still receive a deduction. The current price of giving is 72 cents for every dollar donated to charity. In other words, when a wealthy person makes a $10,000 gift, it is really costing only $7,200, because of savings in taxes. It also means lost revenue to the government but probably increased funds to non-profits. But the charitable deduction for low-income taxpayers (nonitemizers) has been repealed. They receive no tax benefit.

The comments of a millionaire help clarify the consequences of this policy. "I am sure I give away more because it is deductible than if it was not because I am sharing it with Uncle Sam. Instead of a congressman telling me where my dollars are going to go, I am telling them where their dollars can go." He understands that money given to charity is an alternative form of taxation over which individual donors, rather than the legislature or civil service, make decisions. Add to this the statement of another wealthy philanthropist: "There is a feeling of power that goes along with all this, and a feeling of being able to hand it out."

Conclusion

This chapter has examined the philanthropic ideology of American elites, as well as the interconnections between business, charity, and government. Wealthy givers sincerely believe that they are "doing good" by contributing to nonprofit organizations. Elites want to determine where "their" excess money goes rather than having the state redistribute through taxation and government programs. In addition, the philanthropic rich often prefer private to public provision of services. But the nonprofit organizations that the wealthy fund tend to be institutions that benefit the upper class to a greater extent than the lower or middle class. In 136 interviews, educational funding was referred to by far the most often—186 times. There were 160 specific mentions of the arts and culture, followed by 136 instances of human service grants, 49 references to religious funding, and 48 to health.

Tax policy in the United States is not equitable, and in the last three decades it has become increasingly less redistributive. The charitable deduction is available only to the affluent who itemize. In addition to this tax break, wealthy philanthropists have the potential to control the nonprofit organizations they fund or limit the effectiveness of causes they do not endorse or support. A large donation often leads to an appointment to the board of trustees of the recipient group and substantial influence in policy making at the institution.

A sizable portion of revenue to nonprofits comes from the government. Many services are not produced by the state but are partially financed by the government and provided through private organizations. This means that philanthropic elites often have authority over both public and private funds. The charitable wealthy are not always making decisions about "their" money alone.

One could conceive of a different public-policy environment that could alter the role of philanthropy in this society. If, for example, the tax system were modified to allow for a more systematic redistribution of income, it is plausible that the state could fund efforts to sustain minimum standards with respect to nutrition, health care, and housing for the population at large. Philanthropy could then be what advocates claim that it already is, an arena for the development of new ideas—even of experimentation with model programs and vanguard charities. Privately funded educational institutions would, for example, be free to pursue initiatives in large part "chosen" by wealthy donors. At the same time the maintenance of an adequate public schooling and higher education system need not be jeopardized. And obviously, in this context, an equitable charitable tax deduction would allow people of all classes and backgrounds the freedom to donate to their favorite nonprofit organizations and causes.

References

American Association of Fund-Raising Counsel. *Giving U.S.A.: Estimates of Philanthropic Giving in 1986 and the Trends They Show.* New York: AAFRC Trust for Philanthropy, 1987.

Auten, G. and Rudney, G. *The Variability of the Charitable Giving of the Wealthy.* Working paper no. 126. New Haven, Conn.: Program on Nonprofit Organizations, Yale University, 1987.

Domhoff, G. W. *The Higher Circles: The Governing Class in America.* New York: Vintage Books, 1971.

Domhoff, G. W. *Who Rules America Now? A View for the 80's.* Englewood Cliffs, N.J.: Prentice-Hall, 1983.

Hall, P. D. *The Invention of the Nonprofit Sector.* New York: Basic Books, forthcoming.

Heritage Foundation. *Mandate for Leadership: Policy Management in a Conservative Administration.* Washington, D.C.: Heritage Foundation, 1980.

Hodgkinson, V. A., and Weitzman, M. S. *Dimensions of the Independent Sector.* Washington, D.C.: INDEPENDENT SECTOR, 1986.

Knauft, E. B. *The Management of Corporate Giving Programs.* Working paper no. 114. New Haven, Conn.: Program on Nonprofit Organizations, Yale University, 1986.

Lundberg, F. *The Rich and the Super-Rich: A Study of the Power of Money Today.* New York: Lyle Stuart, 1968.

Mills, C. W. *The Power Elite.* New York: Oxford University Press, 1959.

Odendahl, T. (ed.). *America's Wealthy and the Future of Foundations.* New York: Foundation Center, 1987.

Ostrander, S. A. *Women of the Upper Class.* Philadelphia: Temple University Press, 1984.

Salamon, L. M. "Partners in Public Service: The Scope and Theory of Government-Nonprofit Relations." In W. W. Powell (ed.), *The Nonprofit Sector: A Research Handbook.* New Haven, Conn.: Yale University Press, 1987.

Smith, J. *The Policy Elite.* New York: Free Press, forthcoming.

White, A. H., and Bartolomeo, H. *Corporate Giving: The Views of Chief Executive Officers of Major American Corporations.* Washington, D.C.: Council on Foundations, 1982.

MARGOT STERN STROM
ALAN L. STOSKOPF

27

△ △ △ △ △ △ △ △ △ △ △ △ △ △ △

Fostering Philanthropic Values in a Modern Democracy

If we are relying on our educational institutions at the secondary level to prepare students for informed participation in American society, then we may be sadly disappointed. A recent survey of eighteen textbooks by the People for the American Way found that "Eighty pecent of the civics books and half of the government books minimize conflict and compromise. The dynamic sense of government and politics—fierce debates, colorful characters, triumphs and tragedies—is lost. . . . Voter turnout among young people is abysmal. Textbooks about our democracy should inspire students to become active, involved citizens. Instead, these books prepare students to be bystanders in history" (Cohen, 1987a, p. 20). Learning the history of American philanthropy and voluntary associations can help meet this challenge and in turn enrich our students' understanding of their own citizenship responsibilities and choices today. This chapter will suggest how the nonprofit sector's future is connected to the citizenry's understanding of the role it has played in our democracy.

A number of scholars have expressed concerns about the current state of civic education. Gilbert Sewall, a researcher at Teachers College of Columbia University, believes that "American history textbooks often forsake good storytelling, energetic writing and even honest history to comply with adoption procedures, group pressures, the social studies approach, readability

430

formulas and other market forces'' (Cohen, 1987b, p. 11). A recent study of college students done by Alexander Astin and cited by David Mathews in an article on civic intelligence stated that ''only about 40 percent, far less than half of the next generation are interested in public affairs or the great issues of the day. Only 20 percent, one out of five are likely to become involved in helping other people in some form of community activity. On-campus speakers who discuss how to play the stock market or become 'computer literate' draw crowds; those who discuss social issues speak to empty houses'' (Mathews, 1985, p. 678).

There is no quick fix or formulaic response to this problem. But there are alternative paths that can be pursued in order to develop viable models for citizenship education. Through its approach to curriculum development and teacher training, the Choosing to Participate project of the Facing History and Ourselves National Education Foundation is pursuing another direction in this area. This effort is an attempt not to overturn centuries of educational theory but rather to highlight some of the individuals and groups that have often been left out of the textbooks but that have nonetheless helped shape our democratic inheritance today.

Throughout American history, educators have debated ways to define and improve civic education. Progressive educators in the 1930s advocated social participation for all students. Paul Hanna's curriculum solutions for the Depression years are echoed today by those who believe that children learn to be socially responsible by practicing democracy and by experiences in governing themselves. Hanna argued ''that children had an obligation to contribute to the solution of the great social and economic problems of the nation, not by merely understanding them, but through social participation (Ravitch, 1987, p. 2). In the 1940s, a Harvard committee of educators emphasized the study of history through philosophy and literature as necessary for bringing goodness to our society. Albert Einstein extended this thinking in the 1950s when he said, ''A good education will teach young men and women the importance of independent, critical thinking. . . . It is essential that the student acquire an understanding of and a lively feeling for values.

He must acquire a vivid sense of the beautiful and of the morally good. . . . He must learn to understand the motives of human beings, their illusions and their sufferings in order to acquire the proper relationship to individual fellow men and to the community. . . . This is what I have in mind when I recommend the 'humanities' as important, not just dry specialized knowledge in the fields of history and philosophy. Overemphasis on the competitive system and premature specialization on the ground of immediate usefulness kill the spirit on which all cultural life depends, specialized knowledge included" (Fine, 1952, p. 37). Yet we hear from some today that philosophy and the humanities should best be left to the few, the "elite," in special university settings, who will contemplate inwardness away from the problems of the world.

While the debate about who is best suited to study philosophy is usually reserved for the college level, secondary schools are responding to those who call for vocational or preprofessional training for most secondary students. Harry Boyte, director of the Public Philosophy Project at the Humphrey Institute, criticizes this trend as limited: "the language of civic commitment and virtue has been largely replaced by a narrow, technical and careerist vocabulary of education" ("A Symposium on Renewing the Commonwealth," 1987, p. 12). Though the debate about extremes draws some attention to the role of education in America, the more thoughtful outcomes will probably come from the innovative educator who recognizes and tries to balance the need to understand and think about one's life as a citizen in a community and the need to prepare the labor force. Hannah Arendt (1984) a twentieth-century philosopher, has spoken to this challenge; her idea has been restated by Leon Botstein, president of Bard College: "Unlike labor, which is an alienating process, work is compatible with her desired ideal of the active life. The ideal *vita activa* calls for speech and action in the public realm, for the virtuous display of freedom by individuals on behalf of the human community" (Botstein, 1978, p. 34). It is clear that she expresses the importance of work as well as emphasizing the active participation of each citizen to ensure the health of the community.

Even with these efforts to recognize the failings of civic education, the efforts to improve it have not been encouraging. Fred Newman, director of the National Center on Effective Secondary Schools, offers these ideas on the problem: "Both mainstream and reform programs have failed for three reasons: first, compared to other goals of education, our society refuses, in practice, to place citizen education as a high priority; second, the curriculum offers inadequate attention to issues central to democratic citizenship in a mass modern society, and it denies students the opportunity to confront these issues through experience; and finally, reforms that have addressed these issues have been impotent because they have issued pronouncements, programs, and texts without developing a sense of ownership among teachers, who shoulder the major educational responsibilities. . . . Most evidence indicates that numbers of citizens lack the implied commitment, understanding, and skill. If, by definition, democracy demands a citizenry educated along these lines, then citizen education must be improved" (Newman, 1987, p. 281).

Recognizing that most teachers will use the inadequate textbooks and that thoughtful in-service education for teachers is not likely to happen across this nation, reformers are looking for new avenues for enhancing the education of teachers and their students. One such avenue could be the study of America's unsung traditions of volunteerism and philanthropy. This sector should have a place alongside government and the business economy when students think about how the key arenas of American society operate. The study of voluntary and nonprofit service and advocacy will not only enhance people's notions of citizen participation but also enable them to rediscover the groups and individuals, often blacks and women, that have practiced self-help, advocated change, and used the protections of the First Amendment to challenge and claim the promise of America's democratic society.

Few people in the field of education besides those engaged in research or advocacy for the independent sector have deemed that sector important enough to be included in social studies courses or textbooks. The same market forces that drive many textbook publishers to "dumb down" or eliminate in-depth investigation of historical case studies have contributed to the dearth of information on the nonprofit sector. Also, little if any attention has been given to identifying the sector as a distinct avenue of involvement by the citizenry throughout our history. Unless a textbook writer or teacher is making a deliberate attempt to track the sector and uncover its role in key social, economic, and political developments, he or she will not find it; or, as the authors of this chapter have discovered, its role in poverty reform or the civil rights movement will be ignored because the writer has no analytical framework or even language for recognizing its unique function in the period being studied and the evolution of our social institutions.

The Choosing to Participate project has developed a resource manual for teachers and students that uses case studies from the third sector as an alternative model for civic education. Through its approach to curriculum development and teacher training, the project highlights some of the individuals and groups that have helped shape our democracy but often have been left out of textbooks. The project shows how people—as students, citizens, volunteers, and paid workers—can reach beyond themselves to develop goals and consider their shared responsibilities. It is a serious inquiry into the role that voluntary associations and philanthropic activity have played in American society, allowing students to see how some of our basic democratic ideals have evolved over time and how they affect their lives today. Harry Boyte, director of the Public Policy Center at the Humphrey Institute in Minneapolis, underscores the importance of examining the third sector in promoting civic awareness in our students today. He says, "Voluntary associations have not only taught a deepened regard for the common good of communities, as de Tocqueville argued. They have also proven a vital meeting ground where people of diverse background, viewpoints and outlooks could become acquainted and learn an ethos of mutual accountability and practices of cooperation" ("A Symposium on Renewing the Commonwealth," 1987, p. 12). When students can study these kinds of examples, it is hoped, they will develop a better understanding of how they can participate more fully in our society and balance the needs of self and others.

This sentiment really gets to a central question that has concerned Facing History and Ourselves and is intrinsic to the study of citizen participation: the relationship of the individual to society. This kind of thinking about self and others is an aspect of what David Mathews refers to as civic intelligence. ''Being civically intelligent means having the capacity to find out what the facts are and what the facts mean to others'' (Mathews, 1985, p. 680).

An understanding of the democratic institutions and protections that help us grapple with the proper balance between individual rights and our responsibility to others will help push students into thinking about issues beyond their private concerns. Examples of twentieth-century genocide, such as the Holocaust, remind us that democracy must be nurtured and practiced so that neighbor does not turn against neighbor. Research in this area by Facing History and Ourselves has led to creation of educational materials that encourage students to consider their citizenship responsibilities in today's democracy. This consideration is properly rooted in philosophy, where ethical questions guide our thinking about choice and action, and can be best learned through an examination of the stories of men and women who have acted as historical characters. Case studies illuminating the everyday heroes and heroines who are part of the under-valued associations of individuals that make up the history of American democratic citizenship help students understand their role as productive citizens in a democratic society. In essence, students have to take themselves seriously historically. In a 1986 interview with the executive director of Facing History and Ourselves, Bill Moyers said,

> The problem of democracy is the problem of the individual citizen who takes himself or herself lightly historically, no matter how bloatedly one might take oneself personally. By that I mean if you do not believe that you can make a difference, that you matter, you're not going to try to make a dif-

ference, you're not going to try to matter, and you
will leave it to someone else who may or may not
do what is in the best interest of your values or of
democracy's values.

I find increasingly frustrating the student who
comes to me and says, "Well, I just don't really
believe anyone does matter," and I say, "Shame
on you for taking yourself so lightly historically."
You have to realize how, brick by brick, . . . a nation is built, a city is built or a society is sustained.

Unless students today realize that the school,
the church, the synagogue, the library, the street, the
park, the television screen, that everything we have
comes to us through the contribution of others over
time from the past, then how is the student going
to realize, "I have to help build the next school or
the next church or synagogue or the next library,
or the next book on the shelf or the next television
broadcast" [interview with author, 1986].

Through its experience of working with adolescents learning history, Facing History and Ourselves has found that there
is an untapped potential for them to extend their thinking toward
more mature notions of what it means to be a responsible citizen in a democracy. As Mathews tells us, "the word 'public'
is rooted in *pubes,* the word for maturity, implying a people
with the capacity to understand the consequences of individual
actions on others, the capacity to see beyond the personal"
(Mathews, 1987, pp. 1–2). The authors agree with Mathews
and Moyers: maturity or citizenship is not something to be taken
for granted. It requires constant work.

Because adolescence is a time of heightened moral awareness, the ethical content of certain questions attracts the attention of high school students. The questions of who gives and
who gets in our society echo teenagers' concerns about who is
in and who is out, power and helplessness, care and indifference.
If students are to participate in answering the questions that
face our society, then we must hear, confirm, and develop that

sense of justice and care. By focusing on American traditions of participation, students can learn that individual and group involvement can influence their schools, communities, and larger democratic society. The Choosing to Participate project aims to help students learn how people choose to become involved and why participation is important. It encourages students to reach beyond themselves to consider the needs of others and their own responsibilities for imagining and creating the future.

In pushing students to think beyond their own immediate concerns, the project prepares students to tolerate ambiguity, because there are not always clear-cut and simple answers to the complex questions confronting us in society. The lessons being developed for the Choosing to Participate resource manual encourage students to critically reflect on situations before making quick judgments. Students need that opportunity to engage in what Hannah Arendt (1984, p. 12) has termed the "soundless dialogue" in our own mind, where we question our preconceived notions about a situation. This is to be, as Socrates stated it, "perplexed," purging ourselves of "unexamined prejudgments which prevent thinking" (Arendt, 1984, p. 12). Once students examine their own thinking and have time for personal reflection about a subject, they are better able to critically listen to other viewpoints. Students need practice in this art of listening to others and weighing different perspectives before making their judgments on an issue. These are the basic elements that help lay the foundation for critical thinking. A sound civic education provides students with the tools by which they can personally reflect on and sort through the ideas of others so that they can make choices to act responsibly.

Toward this end, the resource manual uses the case studies and examples from the voluntary tradition and nonprofit activity in American history to stretch students' notions of self and other and hence deepen their thinking about what constitutes civic responsibility. To help frame this thinking, students are introduced to a new vocabulary, which includes such words as *altruism, charity,* and *philanthropy*. These terms continue to be revisited throughout the resource manual as a way of getting students used to the idea that they have a place in how we examine fundamental aspects of human behavior. Working on what these terms mean helps form the rudiments for what can be called a language of caring. The absence of such a language can handicap the student as learner and as citizen. William Sullivan, one of the authors of *Habits of the Heart* (Bellah and others, 1985), comments on this point: "The limitation for millions of Americans who remain stuck in the duality of one or another form of individualism is that they are deprived of a language and a moral vision genuinely able to mediate between self and society, a moral vision that can enable them to make sense of the reasons for these tensions in their lives, as well as taking collective action to remedy them" (Sullivan, 1988, pp. 6–7).

Once students have a working vocabulary and are engaged in thinking about questions of motivation, the manual builds on the language of caring by providing a philosophical and historical context for how philanthropy has evolved in American society. It asks, for example, how have we as a society developed notions of responsibility from colonial times to the present? Students learn how early efforts at poverty relief were prompted by a reluctance of governmental bodies to provide public assistance to most of those in need. The relationship between local and state relief agencies and the many private benevolent and reform groups is emphasized as an important dynamic in the way we have historically confronted poverty. Attitudes and policies toward the poor are traced from colonial times through the nineteenth century and examined in the context of today's debates about welfare reform. Students begin to see that both the problem of homelessness and the way we understand it are not new but are part of an evolving heritage. They also recognize that philanthropy and other nonprofit activities have consistently been involved in the debates about and approaches to social welfare problems in every era of our nation's history. The sector takes on legitimacy in the minds of the students as a place where new ideas are formulated and alternate avenues, beyond government and business, are explored.

These readings are built around the ideas and actions of men and women grappling with challenges without romanticizing the voluntary tradition. All too often, textbooks practice what

Michael Kamen, a historian at Cornell University, calls "the heritage nostalgia [which] freezes history into a vague golden time, and the tension, paradox, and triumph that are the truth of the past become lost" (Marquand, 1986, p. 21). The personal failings and biases of many of the reformers, such as Cotton Mather and Jane Addams, are presented along with the sacrifices and risks that various philanthropists and volunteers have endured. Students begin to understand that tensions within the sector and between it and government and business form a necessary part of participation in American democracy.

The notion of history and change also figures prominently in the manual. One of the case studies examined is the early civil rights movement. Students are first introduced to the story of Ida B. Wells and the antilynching movement of the 1880s. This kind of example from the voluntary tradition exposes students to the role that gender and race have played in the history of this country, an area that is often underrepresented in traditional textbooks. By reading about the frustrations and setbacks that this woman encountered in combating some of the social evils in the age of Jim Crow, students realize that change does not come overnight but is based on the work of those who came before and requires the work of those who will follow in the future. This idea is emphasized in an account of the efforts of the abolition societies decades before Wells helped begin the antilynching movement; students see how she built on the traditions and associations of the earlier abolitionists. Students also read about the role that philanthropists played in aiding the movement she helped lead. They see how many of the key philanthropists and activists from this movement continued to struggle for social justice into the twentieth century through their contributions of money and time to the National Association for the Advancement of Colored People. Students begin to appreciate how these individuals and associations laid the moral foundation for what eventually would become law and government policy.

When students examine case studies such as the antilynching campaign and the settlement-house experiments of the Progressive Era, they see the vital and dynamic role that independent associations have played in helping this country better realize its democratic ideals. In this way, the resource book addresses a problem that Gilbert Sewall has noticed in the teaching of American history: "Textbooks should face historical conflicts and tensions squarely, outlining them in strong and dramatic prose, not shrinking from class, religious, racial or gender controversies for fear of giving offense to potential book buyers" (Cohen, 1987b, p. 11). They read about the development of the modern foundation and its importance in sustaining and initiating projects that address the social and economic needs of this country. These examples underscore how our basic freedoms as outlined in the Bill of Rights have been kept alive by the persistent efforts of individuals and groups working outside the environs of government and business activity.

Finally, students are presented with examples and models for participation in their lives today; applying the lessons on motivation, responsibility, and change. In a chapter on political participation, students are asked to consider the civic dimensions of political activity when they analyze case studies on the property tax revolt and nuclear waste disposal. Through these examples and others, they realize that the First Amendment allows individuals and associations to express viewpoints that sometimes are at variance with most of society's notions of what constitutes good civic behavior, underscoring the inherent tension in our democracy that allows refuge for ideas that are unpopular yet visionary as well as those that are regressive and filled with hate. This polarity is evidenced in the protections accorded to both civil rights advocates and the Ku Klux Klan. If the Klan is outlawed, are the floodgates opened for censoring other nonprofit associations now protected by the First Amendment? This kind of difficult dilemma presses students to think about the social costs we pay for protecting the vast majority of independent associations working to enrich the human condition along with the few that seek to diminish it.

Students also look at forms of involvement beyond mere voting or learning to describe the branches of government. They examine the role of community associations and nonprofit organizations in mobilizing people to act on issues. They read about young people helping set up shelters for the homeless, working in community service clubs, and putting their energies into global concerns by joining Amnesty International or working on world hunger. In these readings, students confront the earlier questions about why one should act, how one chooses where to act, and how one knows whether one is making a difference, but now within a historical framework provided by examples from the history of their own nation. The case studies from both the past and the present offer students a way of thinking about civic responsibility and lead them to a better understanding of the choices available to them.

As important as it is to provide students with reading material that complicates their notion of civic life, there is another important dimension for reinvigorating citizenship education. As Paul Gagnon writes in the report *Democracy's Untold Story*, "We understand that such a major reform of the curriculum will require more effective textbooks and auxiliary materials, aimed less at 'coverage' than at comprehension of what is most worth learning. It will require continuing collaboration between faculty members from the schools and universities, where both work together as equals to clarify what is most worth teaching in their subjects and to devise ways to convey the material to diverse clienteles. And it requires new approaches to teacher education, both pre-service and in-service, to help teachers present the revamped and strengthened curriculum" (Gagnon, 1987, p. 24).

The Facing History and Ourselves National Education Foundation attempts to act as a liaison between scholarly research and adult learners (most of whom are schoolteachers), particularly through its Choosing to Participate project. An advisory board including representatives from a cross section of the nonprofit and philanthropic community has contributed to the project's vision and direction. For example, the ideas of Kathleen McCarthy on noblesse oblige (McCarthy, 1982) provided an important foundation for the presentation of the history of charity and philanthropy in the resource book. Brian O'Connell of INDEPENDENT SECTOR, Lester Salamon of the Urban Institute, and John Simon of the Program on Nonprofit Organizations at Yale University are among those who have contributed their expertise to the project. The authors of this chapter have also participated in symposia such as the Humphrey Institute's forum on "Renewing the Commonwealth" that consider the latest thinking and research in the nonprofit field.

The Choosing to Participate project underscores the important connection between learning about the role of the nonprofit sector in our democracy and civic education. Most Americans are not aware of the inextricable link between our nation's democratic experience and the survival and growth of philanthropic activity and voluntary associations. Fostering this awareness among the young provides a deeper understanding of one's citizenship duties as an adult and a realization of the many opportunities available to them to make a difference in society. The real-life stories presented in the manual enable students to discover the types of community service and national philanthropic activities going on around them all the time. This kind of knowledge increases the potential for greater civic involvement in our democracy.

Our challenge is to bring these case studies into the minds of students and help explain how they are part of the history that has shaped our society today. The activities of people who are part of this tradition are inspired by time-honored philosophical ideals. Indeed, for students to feel that they can make a difference, a comprehensive civic education must be rooted in the soil of philosophy and history. This will not be an easy task, because students are easily distracted by other powerful forces in our culture: what Benjamin Barber despairingly labels "the nation's true pedagogues—television, advertising, movies, politics and the celebrity domains they define" (Barber, 1987, p. 23). It will require a concerted effort to interest students in role models from among the ordinary people who have helped shape this nation's history, not the larger-than-life stars of our commercial media industry.

If the young of our nation are not exposed to a rigorous and comprehensive study of the voluntary tradition, the future of the third sector is at risk. Educators and students have to see this exposure as a fundamental element of civic education and not as an "extra" that is briefly mentioned in a textbook paragraph or a classroom discussion. The high school students of today will form the pool of potential donors, volunteers, researchers, and advocates for nonprofit organizations of the future. If the sector is to tap this potential and thus ensure its own survival, these young citizens need to attain a basic understanding of philanthropy's role in American democracy.

References

Arendt, H. "Thinking and Moral Considerations: A Lecture." *Social Research,* 1984, *51,* 7–37.

Barber, B. "What Do 47-Year-Olds Know?" *New York Times,* Dec. 16, 1987, p. 23.

Bellah, R. N., and others. *Habits of the Heart: Individualism and Commitment in American Life.* Berkeley: University of California Press, 1985.

Botstein, L. "Hannah Arendt: The Jewish Question." *New Republic,* 1978, *179* (32), 32–37.

Cohen, M. "School Civics Textbooks Get Yawns in Survey." *Boston Globe,* Apr. 10, 1987a, pp. 1–20.

Cohen, M. "Study Finds Distortions in History Books." *Boston Globe,* Oct. 21, 1987b, p. 11.

Fine, B. "Einstein Stresses Critical Thinking." *New York Times,* Oct. 5, 1952, p. 37.

Gagnon, P. *Democracy's Untold Story.* Washington, D.C.: American Federation of Teachers, 1987.

McCarthy, K. *Noblesse Oblige.* Chicago: University of Chicago Press, 1982.

Marquand, R. "Americans Need History Without Myths and Heritage Nostalgia." *Christian Science Monitor,* Oct. 10, 1986, p. 21.

Mathews, D. "Civic Intelligence." *Social Education,* 1985, *49,* 678–688.

Mathews, D. "The Independent Sector and the Political Responsibilities of the Public." Keynote address presented at the INDEPENDENT SECTOR Spring Research Forum, New York, Mar. 19, 1987.

Newman, F. "Citizenship Education in the United States: A Statement of Needs." *National Civic Review,* 1987, *76* (4), 280-287.

Ravitch, D. "Tot Sociology: What Happens to History in the Grade Schools." *Key Reporter,* 1987, *53* (1), 1-4.

Sullivan, W. "Culture As a Moral Argument: Recasting the Progressive Legacy for Education." *Moral Education Forum,* 1988, *13* (1), 1-9.

"A Symposium on Renewing the Commonwealth." *Antaeus Report,* Spring 1987, pp. 1-12.

PART SEVEN

△ △ △ △ △ △ △ △ △ △ △ △ △ △ △ △

Future Directions
for the Nonprofit Sector

Part of the exercise in predicting the future is examining current trends and practices and projecting what may happen if those trends continue or change. Much prediction turns out to be wrong, because events occur that were not factored into the original analysis. The major use of predicting the future, however, is to help us to understand the present and to work at changing those trends over which we have some control. The purpose of this part is to provide possible scenarios for future research needs and to propose some recommendations for action to practitioners.

The nonprofit sector, comprising nearly one million separate organizations, is primarily local in nature. But out of this local strength have come many national movements. In Chapter Twenty-Eight, Forrest Chisman presents alternative scenarios for the future of the nonprofit sector, based on positive and negative views of the political environments that nonprofits function in. He suggests that, working from their strengths, nonprofits have the capacity to set the future agenda by acting together.

Developing an agenda for the research priorities of the sector is a complicated and somewhat dangerous business. While contributions to this volume recognize some overarching needs, much scholarship is individual in both nature and personal interest. In Chapter Twenty-Nine, John Simon, chairperson of

445

the oldest research program on the study of this sector—the Program on Nonprofit Organizations at Yale University—draws from experience an agenda from the last decade and proposes what kind of research is needed in the future. Much of what he suggests provides a good summary of future research needs, and many contributors to this volume would agree with at least parts of his agenda.

The last chapter is addressed to practitioners. It urges them to become more involved in a few critical issues that have emerged from the research of the contributors to this book. It suggests that public education and attention to mission and practice are issues that can be advanced by those who lead or work in nonprofits. Support for research is a fundamental necessity to provide for the future vitality of the nonprofit sector and its ability to provide public service.

△ △ △ △ △ △ △ △ △ △ △ △ △ △ △

28

Alternative Futures for the Sector

This chapter describes three alternative futures for the relationship between the independent sector and two other major centers of institutional power in the United States, business and government. The first two alternatives are projections based on the way in which these institutions have influenced each other in recent years. The third is a proposal for changing the role that the independent sector has played. In making these sorts of projections, it is hard to avoid merely embroidering on the obvious. And the obvious is that, in the normal course of affairs, the future of nonprofit organizations and activities will depend largely on whether the American economy achieves solid and sustained real growth in productivity and profits and whether government, particularly at the federal level, revives the spirit of activism that in the past has enabled it to come to grips with the nation's major social and economic problems.

There is nothing novel about this forecast. In this century, at least, the independent sector has prospered largely through partnerships with business and government. Business has been crucial as a donor, creator of endowed organizations, and customer for nonprofit services. In addition, the general state of the economy, as reflected in business conditions, directly or indirectly, determines how much real income Americans have available as well as its distribution and, hence, the willingness

447

of individuals to make charitable contributions. The role of government is critical for many of the same reasons. Lester Salamon (1985) and others have documented how dependent most independent-sector organizations are on government grants and contracts for service delivery. And, of course, the areas of the sector that Salamon did not study—many health care services and traditional forms of education—are the most dependent of all.

Finally, the linkage among government, business, and the nonprofit world comes full circle when one considers that a major goal of government at all levels is maintaining economic prosperity. And the rate of economic growth often determines how much Americans are willing to invest in government services, as the influence of economic worries on both the Carter and Reagan administrations most recently has shown.

In short, when government and business grow, the independent sector grows too. When they slow down, it falls on hard times. Given this perennial linkage, three possible scenarios should be of particular interest to those who are concerned about future relationships among the sectors.

An Optimistic Scenario

The first scenario assumes a rosy future. If we can work the present kinks out of our economy, the United States could well experience a period of healthy economic growth well into the next century—at least until the burden of dealing with the retirement of the baby boom generation falls on us, and possibly beyond if we make adequate provision for that pivotal development. If this rosy scenario unfolds, businesses will reinvigorate their programs of corporate philanthropy and public service. Some of their contributions obviously will go to the traditional beneficiaries of corporate largesse: educational, research, cultural, and local improvement efforts in the communities where particular companies have their operations or in areas of endeavor where they perceive at least some indirect self-interest.

But new twists in business support can also be expected. Many large companies are now coming to realize that it is very much in their self-interest to help their employees deal with a wide range of personal problems that have not previously been of concern to corporate America. For example, we are likely to see more corporate investment in day care, long-term care facilities, continuing education, innovative health care experiments, and possibly even affordable rental housing. Most companies know that they are not very good at running enterprises of this sort: it literally is not any of their business. Thus, many are likely to turn to the people who do have a track record: independent-sector organizations. This is already happening in the day-care field, where most of the (admittedly small) corporate investment takes the form of either contracts with nonprofit providers or payments to employees that allow them to buy services on their own, again usually from nonprofits (U.S. Bureau of Labor Statistics, 1988).

So, if the economic future is rosy, independent-sector organizations should gear up for a flood of demand to help corporations with human service projects, and they should begin planning the most effective ways to do so now. One way to proceed is to seek out a few companies that are willing to serve as testing grounds for the development of model programs. "The company store" or early-twentieth-century "welfare capitalism" may well be replaced by the company grant or contract of welfare capitalism in a new form, and if it is, nonprofits would do well to be ready.

To imagine a rosy future on the governmental side, it is necessary only to recall the statements of the large field of presidential candidates during the 1988 election campaign, particularly the Democrats. Most of the candidates appeared to believe that the nation should develop a more adequate system of health insurance: a system that would protect the thirty-seven million people now without coverage, pay the costs of catastrophic illness for the elderly, and lighten the burden of long-term care. Most also believed that we need to improve the quality of our educational system at all levels, convert welfare programs into jobs programs, help poor children get a better start in life, solve the problems of the homeless, do a better job of protecting the environment, and stabilize our shaky financial markets. And opinion polls have repeatedly shown that a majority of voters both share these goals and say that they are willing to pay substantially more in taxes to achieve them. Cognizant of these sentiments, the 100th Congress passed legislation implementing welfare reform, catastrophic health care insurance for the elderly, and other activist measures, and the 101st Congress is attempting to grapple with other issues on the human services agenda.

If Washington gets back into the business of doing these sorts of things, it is obviously going to need partners, as it has in the past. In the first instance, the partners are likely to be state and local governments. But when it actually comes to service delivery, they in turn will work through independent-sector organizations, as they always have. Or at least it should be hoped that they will. It is frightening to imagine most public welfare departments, on their own, trying to develop individualized evaluation, training, placement, and day-care packages for welfare mothers, as the 1988 Family Support Act (welfare reform) calls on them to do. While there are many able people in state and local agencies who understand what is involved in this sort of undertaking, the constraints under which they work will make it very difficult for them to gear up quickly to deliver comprehensive "work-welfare" services on a large scale, as they are required to do, without a great deal of outside help. Likewise, it appears that most government efforts to shelter the homeless have been less effective than more modest voluntary-sector initiatives.

In short, if there is a revival of federal activism, the independent sector should get ready for a truly enormous surge of demand, because the likely directions of new activism will be heavily weighted in the areas of improved human services in which most of the sector specializes. And, importantly, much of that demand will be to deliver services that nobody today fully understands how to provide. Mainstreaming welfare mothers and caring for the homeless have already been mentioned. We can add to that list developing cost-effective, noninstitutional systems of long-term care, establishing more abundant high-quality child nutrition and day-care services, finding mechanisms to provide universal, affordable health care services, and working with government to fight drug abuse, reduce dropout rates, upgrade elementary and secondary education, and develop better environmental strategies.

In all probability, there is no one best way to do any of these things, no "cookie cutter" model for the nation as a whole. Different approaches will be effective in different locales. And that is why the independent sector is particularly important in a rosy future. The sector is everywhere, it takes many different forms, and it often has strong community ties. It should use these advantages to do its homework: to look for ways to accomplish the things that we presently do not know how to accomplish, before the demands of a revived federal government arrive. Otherwise, nonprofits will be caught unprepared and once more face the charge "voluntary-sector failure." More importantly, they will be letting the nation down.

What must the sector do? Make up-front investments. Experiment now with progressive states and communities (and there are a lot of them) to find models for the future. And do not look only at service technology. Look too at new management and financial structures, such as chartering nonprofit corporations in the areas of day care, long-term care, health insurance, and so forth. Finally, develop improved systems of recruitment, so that the very best people will be attracted to newly expanded efforts.

A Pessimistic Scenario

So much for optimism. The independent sector must also face up to another possibility.

Anyone who is paying attention must have very grave doubts about whether this country's economy will, in fact, take off again in the near future and whether the federal government will continue to adopt progressive measures. With regard to the former, the reasons for doubt can be found on the business pages of any major newspaper: the recovery of the mid-1980s was always artificial in a great many ways, productivity has lagged, many sectors are besotted with wasteful speculative activity, foreign competition is stiff, financial markets suffer from borderline schizophrenia, and so forth.

On the political front, we have faced a cruel paradox epitomized by the fate of the candidates who entered the 1988 presidential primaries. Although most of the candidates promised a new wave of activism, and although overwhelming majorities of the public supported their agendas, nobody seemed to believe what they said. The presidential contenders appeared to be suffering from a credibility gap that could well destroy the prospect that the president and Congress we elected will pursue a progressive course. And, strangely, that gap had little to do with either the candidates or their proposals.

The same polls that showed widespread public support for those proposals also showed that the public is highly skeptical about the ability of government to deliver on its promises. In other words, ordinary Americans would like to enjoy the benefits of all the new initiatives discussed, but they have a hard time believing that any of those measures can be implemented, at the federal level, anyway. They apparently find it difficult to imagine an America in which they can count on national government to solve national problems. During the 1988 campaign, this public skepticism meant that the candidates who advocated progressive reforms appeared to be the more unrealistic in the field. The public assumed that the more outspoken candidates could not possibly be serious about the bold ideas they set forth: in their innermost thoughts, they must have been contemplating some diminished version of what they described. As a result, there was a temptation for many of the "smart" people on the campaign trail to pull their punches, to lapse into a rhetoric of half measures and vaguely stated good intentions. There was a lot of talk about "first steps," "trade-offs," and "goals" that would be achieved only at some time in the indefinite future.

But the credibility gap that separated candidates from voters was more than a cruel twist of fate for those who aspired to be president. It was a gutting of the American political process. What should be the essence of politics in this country— responding to public needs and aspirations—became impolitic in much of the presidential campaign. The result was an election without meaning: an election that signified nothing, ratified nothing, sent no message that would guide or constrain either the president or Congress. And the person who can take most credit for these turn of events is none other than Ronald Reagan.

The greatest success of the Reagan presidency was to focus public attention on concerns about the size and scope of government, rather than on questions about its effectiveness in meeting national needs (see Chisman and Pifer, 1987, pp. 85–118). The president who began his term by declaring that "government is the problem" and then ran up a massive federal deficit to prove his point propagated two great myths: that big government is inherently a bad thing and that even if it were not bad, we cannot afford it anyway.

This is old stuff from conservatives, and every few decades the nation rediscovers that it simply is not true. In an increasingly complex and interdependent society, national government must play a large role in securing the general welfare. And big government in the United States has a long string of successes to its credit: greatly reducing poverty among the elderly and other groups, advancing civil rights, making home ownership and higher education possible for tens of millions of people, building and maintaining our national transportation system, promoting science and technology, subsidizing virtually every sector of our economy, and much more. Everyone in the United States benefits enormously from big government, and few Americans would be willing to live without the benefits it confers. Moreover, no one can realistically believe that America will be able to meet the challenges of the future in areas such as health, education, and the environment without the national leadership and resources that only the federal government can provide.

So much for the issue of size. The issue of cost is also illusory. The United States devotes a far smaller portion of its gross national product to social programs than most other developed countries do, and there are few economists who believe that devoting somewhat more would harm our national prosperity. Social spending does not destroy national wealth; it reroutes it to building a stronger society and economy. Federal deficits *are* a problem, but most economists believe that we can afford to pay for the government we have and to buy somewhat more if we need it to solve our national problems. But despite the transparent falsehood of Reaganism's two great myths, most politicians and "experts" these days feel obliged to pay homage to the idea that we live in "an era of limited resources." And the same people portray the federal deficit as a stopper to any serious discussion of large new initiatives.

In short, shrouded in a cloud of misunderstanding and distrust, candidates and voters appear to have spent a great deal of time "faking each other out" in 1988 and since. And there is a very good chance that the result will be a continuation of the do-nothing politics of the Reagan years. That would be a very great national tragedy. The problems that face us today are not just temporary aberrations. They are the results of enormous social and economic changes that are profoundly transforming the lives of each and every one of us (see Chisman and Pifer, 1987, pp. 169–218). Changes in the structure of our economy are creating widespread anxiety about job security, skills, and incomes. Social changes such as the entry of women into the work force are sending families in search of more adequate systems of day care for their children and long-term care for their elderly parents. America has developed an underclass of several million people, and children raised in that environment will make up a large proportion of the workers and citizens of tomorrow. And American society is aging: in the future we will have fewer active workers and more dependent retirees, whose cost to society, particularly in the area of health care, is soaring out of sight (see Pifer and Bronte, 1986).

In sum, in virtually every area of our social and economic life, this country is on a collision course with the future. But because of the political confusion created by eight years of Reaganism, there is a good chance that we will not act to avert that collision very soon. What happens to the independent sector then? What happens to it if a pessimistic scenario on both the economic and political fronts comes true? If past history is any guide, the sector will suffer, diminish, muddle through, try to fill gaps, speak out, and hope, as it has in recent years. And, as in recent years, it will seek partnerships with progressive industries and state and local governments that are trying to fill the void left by federal inaction. That is not a wholly gloomy prognosis, but it is certainly not as attractive as the rosy scenario outlined above. And in light of the national tragedy that would result from continued federal inaction and economic decline, people who care as much about the future of the nation as most people working in the independent sector do can hardly be expected to find it acceptable. They have already seen their numbers dwindle and their influence diminish. They cannot relish more of the same.

The Sector as Movement

If the pessimistic scenario unfolds, and if people working in the independent sector find it unacceptable, there is another approach to the future they should consider adopting. The sector might be mobilized to put the shoe on the other foot: rather than responding to political and economic events, it might take the leadership in bringing about progressive change. This would require more than leadership in small ways. Independent-sector organizations already support progressive institutions and contribute to meeting neglected needs on a case-by-case basis. These efforts are eminently worthwhile, and they should certainly be continued. But leaders of the independent sector should also consider the possibility of using their resources to raise national consciousness and force action on a larger scale.

For example, looking back over the history of voluntary activities in the United States, we see that there is obviously a great difference between the grange movement, the settlement-house movement, the cooperative movement, and the trade-union movement of the late nineteenth and early twentieth centuries and more recent independent-sector activities. They were *movements*. They were everywhere; they mobilized enormous numbers of people; they tried to *solve* problems by voluntary action, not just "make a contribution"; and inevitably they were breeding grounds for reform politics. Of course, they failed to solve the problems entirely, but their large efforts at the very least forced government to get involved. And they created institutions that continue to be of importance of our national life.

Their reform culture also nurtured future activists, and the approaches they developed through trial and error often proved to be critically important experiments for future state-building developments.

If these examples seem too remote from the experience of today, there is a type of movement with which most people in the independent sector are intimately familiar. One of Andrew Carnegie's concerns was for the future of college teachers. In particular, he believed that they deserved a decent income in their retirement years. So he set up the Carnegie Foundation (now the Carnegie Foundation for the Advancement of Teaching) for the purpose of providing pensions to all retired professors. That was truly an ambitious effort to solve a problem by voluntary effort. And it was a failure in its initial form. Carnegie and his advisers soon realized that no endowed foundation could possibly muster the resources required. So they set up the insurance plan now called TIAA-CREF—the Teachers Insurance and Annuity Association and the College Retirement Equities Fund—on which many people in the independent sector now depend for a great part of their retirement income.

Like the grangers, the co-ops, the settlement houses, and the unions, TIAA was also a movement, in the sense that it entailed the active involvement of large numbers of people banding together for their mutual benefit. And, like those other efforts, it was a *self-help* movement: it asked something of its members as well as of its sponsors or the public at large. That was at a time when few companies had private pension plans and long before Social Security. TIAA met a real need. And together with social insurance ideas that another nonprofit institution, the University of Wisconsin, developed in working with state government, it served as a model, experiment, and forcing activity for developments in both the public and private sectors (see Stevens, 1988).

If the economy falters and the Bush administration proves to be a fizzle in terms of social reform, it is at least worth considering whether independent-sector organizations should band together in large-scale efforts of this sort. There are some very hopeful recent precedents. Two of the most noteworthy were initially developed by the Ford Foundation. They are Michael Sviridoff's Local Initiatives Support Corporation (LISC), dealing with low-income housing problems, and the Manpower Demonstration Research Corporation (MDRC), originally headed by Barbara Blum and now ably led by Judith Gueron. It is impossible to exaggerate the importance of MDRC in changing the conventional wisdom in the political world about how welfare programs should be structured and in bringing about welfare reform. And it is impossible to exaggerate the influence of LISC in the area of housing policy, let alone the enormous good it has done for thousands of low-income people and their communities. Although sponsored by foundations, various levels of government, and industry, they, like earlier movements, are based on the idea of self-help: tenant-managed housing in the case of LISC and helping people to become self-supporting in the case of MDRC. They deserve the encouragement of everyone in the independent sector in their continuing efforts to grow and influence thinking.

There is no danger that the success of such groups will create the impression that government action is unnecessary. Unlike earlier movements, they acknowledged at the outset that the problems they are trying to solve are too vast: they are simply trying to do as much as they can. But the more they do, the more pressure they exert on government and business to act by showing skeptical politicians and businesspeople that complex problems really *can* be solved. Government and business come to believe that all they have to do is to replicate what such groups are doing on a larger scale. Even if this is not true, their example at least creates a constituency in government, business, and the general public for a reform agenda.

So, if the worst-case economic and political scenarios come true, independent-sector organizations should consider banding together to launch other large-scale, coordinated movements in areas where they can hope to have some impact. The plight of the homeless is an example of the type of problem that commends itself. This is because of the enormous public concern it has generated, because it is almost everywhere, and because, in any particular location, fairly small numbers of people are affected. To take just one case, it is estimated that there are 5,000 to 6,000 homeless people in the nation's capital, Washington, D.C. It seems criminal that so small a number of distressed people cannot be helped and helped very well. If the cost of providing shelter, food, counseling, treatment, training, and outplacement assistance, as appropriate, for each one of these people is estimated at what would have to be a very high number, poverty-level income, $25 million to $30 million would be required. Given the fact that local government already makes a substantial contribution, the cost of a government–voluntary-sector partnership that would do a first-rate job of coming to grips with the problem in Washington would be far less than that. It would be well within the capacity of a consortium of large and small nonprofits, particularly with a special fund-raising effort. And, of course, the cost would be reduced if there was more emphasis on self-help, rather than just custodial care: if the more able among the homeless were involved in running the shelters and if the major goal of the effort was to help homeless people either return to their families or find better ways to care for themselves.

Admittedly, voluntary organizations already do a lot for the homeless. But they might consider submerging their institutional identities long enough to make this or some other problem *the* priority for a coalition of groups. And the priority should be not just to help but to solve the problem to the greatest extent possible, with involvement by both the general public and the beneficiaries of voluntary-sector action. Of course, the voluntary sector should not take permanent responsibility for caring for the homeless or similar problems. But if it takes up this or some similar challenge and succeeds, or even makes a good showing, there is a good likelihood that government at every level would feel compelled to mount an adequate response. The plight of the homeless is only an example of a great many worthy causes around which the independent sector might organize a movement. It does not matter which is selected. The important thing is to create a strong and visible impression on the public mind and on the minds of politicians that social problems can and must be solved: forcing action by example.

This view of how the sector might function as a movement implies that the conservative theory of the independent
sector is just wrong. Independent-sector activism will not and
should not replace government and business activism. It never
has. The more any one sector leads in addressing major problems, the more likely it is that the others will follow. And government and business are the greatest copy-cats of all when it comes
to human service issues. Conservatives should know this better
than anyone else. The development of the conservative "movement" as an intellectual force in the United States over the last
few decades was to a significant extent funded by donations from
wealthy individuals and conservative foundations. And that funding entailed not only support for research and writing but also
the development of intellectual networks and the dissemination
of ideas. Independent-sector activism on the right fostered a
movement that eventually contributed to a major change of
direction by government at the national level.

Independent-sector organizations that are on the progressive side and primarily committed to supporting ideas rather
than activism can profit from the example of conservatives. Why
do progressive foundations do so little to disseminate progressive
ideas? Too often they are content to fund research and writing
without taking into account the fact that those products must
be aggressively sold in the marketplace of ideas. Most people
who have developed intellectual products—books, reports, and
so forth—that set forth progressive ideas find that there is practically no place they can turn to to get the type of high-powered
assistance required to bring those ideas to public attention, even
if they have the money to pay for it. There is practically nobody
in that business. One way that organizations devoted to ideas
and concerned about the lack of social progress could help to
stage a "movement" would be to establish a full-service public
relations agency capable of providing a complete menu of assistance at reasonable cost to their members and grantees.

But this is only one way to instigate a movement. There
are many other ways, and they are all valid undertakings at all
points on the political spectrum. In fact, many causes, such as
the condition of the homeless, should provide fertile common

ground for independent-sector organizations with widely different perspectives. The conclusion of this chapter is simply the following: if political and economic clouds blot out a bright future for the independent sector, leaders of the sector should consider combining their efforts to change the climate within which they operate. They should consider forcing action by example: showing that major public problems can and must be solved by mounting large-scale efforts to solve them. And if they do, they should make a special effort to involve as many members of the public as they possibly can.

References

Chisman, F., and Pifer, A. *Government for the People: The Federal Social Role: What It Is, What It Should Be.* New York: Norton, 1987.

Pifer, A., and Bronte, D. L. (eds.). *Our Aging Society: Promise and Paradox.* New York: Norton, 1986.

Salamon, L. M. *Partners in Public Service: Toward a Theory of Government-Nonprofit Relations.* Washington, D.C.: Urban Institute Press, 1985.

Stevens, B. "Blurring the Boundaries: How Federal Social Policy Shaped Private Sector Welfare Benefits." In M. Weir, A. S. Orloff, and T. Skocpol (eds.), *The Politics of Social Policy in the United States.* Princeton, N.J.: Princeton University Press, 1988.

U.S. Bureau of Labor Statistics. *Recent Trends in Daycare: A Survey of Corporate Provision.* Washington, D.C.: U.S. Government Printing Office, 1988.

29

△ △ △ △ △ △ △ △ △ △ △ △ △ △ △

Agendas for
Nonprofit Sector Research:
A Personal Account

These pages proffer a report, not a call to action. It is an account, rather skeletal, of how one research center, the Yale University Program on Nonprofit Organizations, has grappled with the problem of agenda setting over the past thirteen years—during the preparatory stages of the program, during its first decade of activity, and, in recent months, as the program prepared for its third five-year phase. It also includes, as a gloss, some of the items that have appeared on my own research "wish lists" from time to time. This report is not tendered—and cannot possibly be treated—as an agenda for the research community as a whole. I make this threshold point not only in a spirit of diffidence but for more important reasons that have to do with the nature of research on the nonprofit sector—and the nature of the sector itself.

The pluralism that is the hallmark—some would say the quintessential virtue—of the nonprofit sector applies to the nonprofit research community as well. Just as the programs, styles, governance systems, and demography of nonprofit organizations range wide and far (displaying what Kingman Brewster (1965) called the "calculated anarchy of dispersed initiative, individuality and variety"), so the research enterprise is heterodox, motley, indeed unruly. The scholarly actors not only bring to this enterprise different disciplines—that is a given—but they employ

461

different research strategies, perspectives, data bases, appetites, and ideologies. Moreover, they examine different subparts of a vastly varied universe; for example, studying voluntary hospitals is a very different business from studying protest groups in South Africa. In the presence of this rampant pluralism, it is quite simply impossible to impose on nonprofit-sector researchers a consensus agenda, a structured and harmonious orchestration.

Nor, I would argue, is such an agenda desirable. Even if we could develop one that was accepted by all participants, it would run the risk of becoming a prevailing orthodoxy that discourages the outliers, the nonconventional players who reasonably fear that their efforts will be disparaged as "out of the mainstream" or "second order," perhaps "odd." If the consensus agenda is coupled to funding decisions, the result for the outliers could be not merely discouragement but exclusion.

The proposition that a consensus agenda for nonprofit research is impossible or unwise does not apply to everything that bears the name of an agenda. It does not apply to truly global agendas, those constructed at the highest levels of generality, abstraction, or inclusiveness. With respect to generality and abstraction, for example, we probably can get agreement that it would be well to study the distinctive features of a voluntary sector, its place in a democratic order, and its place in a market economy. Similarly, one would enounter little quarrel with an open-ended, all-embracing agenda that included everybody's favorite projects without any rank-ordering and with no closing date for new entries. Global agendas have their uses: the highly generalized and abstract agenda can remind us of first principles and values, and the 100 percent inclusionary agenda may provoke or inspire those who encounter it. But these global lists do not give the direction or sense of priority that would be the point of a focused consensus agenda—if it were possible or desirable to develop one.

Apart, then, from global agendas, are we to have no guidance? Yes, we are, but it will have to be our very own, designed by each scholar and each scholarly center, cognizant of and, perhaps, inspired by what others are doing, but basically expressing one's own convictions and instincts and a sense of one's own gifts and limitations. The fact that institutional research centers must do some agenda setting may prompt the question: does not this process present the same perils that haunt agenda setting for the research community as a whole? In other words, when this takes place at the institutional level, is it not just as unfeasible or just as coercive as national agenda setting?

The risks that arise at the institutional level appear to be far less serious. For one thing, the existence of multiple research centers, each with a different focus, means that no one center is engaged in the probably futile task of designing a fits-all-sizes agenda. The corollary is that there will be alternative doors on which scholars may knock; the outlier with respect to one center's agenda may be welcomed by another institution.[1]

A second reason why institutional agenda setting is more feasible and benign than a nationwide process is that a research center has to and does adjust to the available resources—to the funds that can and cannot be obtained for certain projects and, even more important, to the available *human* resources. If a scholar with the right talents and the right interests is not available at the right time for a certain project, the agenda must make way. The institution has to stay in touch with its troops, present or potential, and this interaction shapes and reshapes the agenda. On the other hand, agenda setting at a national level, whether carried out by center directors or by others, cannot have the same nexus with, and sensitivity to the needs and preferences of, the scholarly troops; it is, therefore, likely to lack the plasticity of agenda setting that takes place at the retail level.[2]

I do not suggest that agenda setting at the retail level is not or should not be attentive to policy and management problems facing the sector (or the society) as a whole. Researchers need to look at shifts in the economic, cultural, and regulatory environment and to listen hard to practitioners, donors, beneficiaries, and consumers (and victims)—and to take this looking and listening into account. Inevitably, however, the research centers have to come to terms with the researchers themselves.

The agenda setting that took place at the Yale Program on Nonprofit Organizations reflected this interactive process, even after the early "wide-net" years. Although the following account is too short to provide detailed proof of this point, I ask the readers to accept my assertion that this was the case and that, more generally, availability of human and fiscal resources played an important part in the evolution of the program. That is not, however, the only reason for providing an account of the program's development; I hope also that this brief summary of many of the ideas we have had over the years will be suggestive or otherwise useful to our colleagues at home and abroad.

The first effort to sketch a research agenda for the program was a lengthy prospectus prepared by Kingman Brewster, Charles E. Lindblom, and myself in October 1975. It said that what was then called a "Study of Independent Institutions" (the Yale program was more prosaically renamed later on) would be grouped around two basic inquiries—function and accountability: "1. What are various kinds of 'independent' organizations good for? That is, what social objectives can they achieve (or what social functions can they discharge) and under what circumstances? Similarly, what are their limitations? What can they not do? How can they be modified to achieve greater usefulness? 2. How [can the] various kinds of 'independent' organizations [be] made accountable, responsive, or answerable without destroying their independence?" (Brewster, Lindblom, and Simon, 1975, p. 12). The proposal suggested both "direct" and "indirect" routes to the examination of these questions. The "direct" attacks included studies of these topics:

- Performance of nonprofit organizations compared with corporate or public entities operating in the same field.
- The "political and social intangible values" attributed to the nonprofit sector, such as decentralization and participatory control.
- The tie between accountability mechanisms for nonprofit organizations and democratic theory and practice.
- The mechanisms that reward and measure efficiency and other aspects of success in the nonprofit world.
- The mechanisms that promote and impede change and adaptation by nonprofits.
- The extent to which nonprofits can and do carry out a redis-

tributional function—as to income or power—and the normative question of whether this is an appropriate goal.
* The role that nonprofits play—or ought to be permitted to play—in legislative and electoral politics.

The "indirect" research strategy called for the construction of one or more formal rationales for the nonprofit sector and descriptive models on which such rationales could be based. Three alternative routes were envisioned: building on the concept of "market failure"; building on an analogous concept of "government failure"; and a more "positive" approach—the development of affirmative explanations for reliance on nonprofits and for the main accountability mechanisms.

Finally, the 1975 prospectus called for a number of "supporting studies": historical and international comparative work; case studies of nonprofit "industries" and individual firms; studies of incentives for participation (as donors, managers, employees) in nonprofit organizations, of the decision-making and implementing processes in these organizations, and of the legal environment; and a series of measurement efforts, accompanied by preparation of "a taxonomy of the nonprofit population."

The program, launched in 1977, began working along all these fronts—or those for which funds and scholars were available. (Because of space limitations, I will have to omit, with apologies, references to the scores of scholars who have worked on most of the topics listed below.) Within a couple of years, there were requests for another form of agenda from foundation officers who wanted to know more about the policy implications of our research. In 1979, we prepared a roster of the "real-world" problems that our program was addressing, grouped around five policy and management dilemmas, which I phrased as follows in a speech at the 1979 National Conference on Philanthropy (later reprinted as an INDEPENDENT SECTOR research report):

1. *The Mission Dilemma:* What social, economic, cultural tasks shall the nonprofit sector—alone or in conjunction with business or governmen-

tal entities—be called upon to take up, to retain, or to surrender?

2. *The Financing Dilemma:* Can the financial survival of nonprofit institutions be pursued in a
manner that honors their own institutional purposes, the needs of the business and governmental sectors, and principles of legislative
fairness?

3. *The Power Dilemma:* To what extent can nonprofit organizations exercise—or be permitted
to exercise—power over decision-making in the
governmental and for-profit sectors?

4. *The Effectiveness Dilemma:* How can nonprofit
organizations improve their effectiveness in the
absence of conventional "bottom-line" measures?

5. *The Governance Dilemma:* Can nonprofit organizations improve—or be compelled to improve—
their "accountability" to various constituencies
without impairing their contribution to the
"pluralism of the social order"? [Simon, 1980]

We were able to relate all 104 of what were then the program's current or proposed research projects to one or another
of these five dilemmas. It must be said, however, that, although
some scholars found it a helpful organizational tool, the "dilemmas" list was not itself a research agenda. It did not set forth
tasks to be done or specify research approaches or strategies.

The broad compass of the original 1975 prospectus and
the far-flung nature of the program's research activity during the early years—we deliberately cast a wide net, as explained—led to later efforts on our part to "tame" our research
program while, at the same time, honoring the interests and
commitments of our colleagues. The first of these efforts was
intended simply to tie things together. A memo on "cross-cutting
themes" was circulated to all program participants (Simon,
1981). It stated: "The work of the Program on Nonprofit Organizations is, in substantial part, carried out by individual scholars

investigating particular industries (television, hospitals, arts, education, federated fundraising, etc.) or conducting theoretical or behavioral research from the perspective of a particular discipline (e.g., economics, sociology, political science, law) or examining a particular group of actors within the nonprofit world (entrepreneurs, managers, employees, trustees). One important task that looms before the program is to examine some of the 'cross-cutting themes' that emerge from these separate studies—themes that may have something to tell us about the entire nonprofit sector, or at least major parts of it, and that involve analysis that cuts across industries, disciplinary perspectives, and categories of nonprofit actors.'' Examples of these cross-cutting themes were spelled out; briefly summarized, they included the following:

- ''Constraints on the values of the nonprofit sector''—''factors that prevent nonprofit organizations from living up to some of the attributes that John Gardner has assigned to the nonprofit sector.''
- ''Competition with the for-profit and governmental sectors.''
- ''Incentives for participation in nonprofit organizations''—including the question of the ''incentive systems that condition our behavior'' as participants in a nonprofit.
- ''The impact of government patronage'' on the behavior of nonprofits and their donors, including the impact of the regulation that accompanies such patronage.
- ''The problems of old age and tired blood''—the various modes of organizational response to hard times.
- ''Public perception'' of the role and behavior of nonprofits as compared to governmental and business entities.
- ''Cross-subsidization within nonprofit organizations''—how does it differ from what goes on within proprietary firms, and ''how is it to be evaluated in terms of efficiency and equity?''
- ''Effects on personality'' of participation in nonprofits—effects on ''feelings of self-esteem, autonomy, competence, and on the development of collaborative and altruistic attitudes.''

A year later, in 1982, as the program entered its second five-year phase (under Paul DiMaggio's directorship), an agenda was developed that sought to focus our research in five areas— areas that emerged from the work of our many colleagues during the program's first phase:

1.   Economic and demographic studies—an effort to collect and make available data on the scope and shape of the sector and to estimate the likely effects of various policy alternatives on the financial health of the sector. (Later economic work under this heading focused on charitable giving by the wealthy and on competition between nonprofits and proprietary firms.)
2.   Industry studies, comparing the roles of nonprofit, governmental, and business entities where they coexist. (Approximately a dozen such industries have been studied to date.)
3.   "Intersectoral relations"—the impacts of government and corporate policy and practices on the nature and welfare of the nonprofit sector.
4.   Historical work—on the nonprofit sector in general, on the history of business philanthropy, and on the nonprofit sector in health, the arts, and higher education.
5.   International studies—comparing the American experience with that of other countries and also examining the role of nongovernmental organizations in developing countries and in authoritarian societies. (Recently, we have also started work on the role of organizations that resemble nonprofits in socialist regimes.)

Subsequently, the program added two more areas of emphasis to this list of five. One was the field of "management and governance," starting with studies of planning by nonprofits—when, how, and why they do it and with what results— and studies of trusteeship. The second was the area of "motivations for giving and volunteering," which included a major study of the attitudes of wealthy donors toward use of the foundation vehicle and charitable giving in general; we also initiated psychological studies of the dynamics of the donative process and of how choices are made among a sea of supplicants. It is quite likely that the program's agenda will shift still further during its third five-year cycle, under the directorship of Bradford Gray.

As a supplement, and if my readers can abide another list, I wish to add a personal agenda of items that are less broad-based that the program's primary fields of focus. Some of these items are substantive topics, some are research strategies:

- Changelings. As the political scientist Harold Orlans originally suggested to us, a good window of observation on organizational behavior is the entity that moves from one sector to another. (For example, when Duke University's mental hospital was acquired by a for-profit chain, what happened to the quality and cost of care, to access, to ambiance? When *Ms.* magazine went from for-profit to nonprofit status and back to for-profit, what were the consequences?)
- Phenomenon-focused studies. In discussions about future directions for our program, Paul DiMaggio has suggested that we look at the role of nonprofits through another window by seeing how different types of organizations (nonprofit, proprietary, public) respond to a particular societal crisis or problem. AIDS is one topic on which researchers at Yale University are already working: what light does the AIDS phenomenon throw on different forms of patient-serving institutions and on different forms of research organizations (when they are asked, for example, to share their research findings to accelerate the race for a solution)? Homelessness and the problem of "orphan" pharmaceuticals are other possible phenomena that may lend themselves to this treatment.
- Empirical testing of legislative assumptions. Congress made a host of assumptions about the behavior of private foundations when it passed the 1969 Tax Reform Act, about the behavior of nonprofits when it exempted them from the Social Security tax, about for-profit physical therapy agencies when it limited their participation in the Medicare program, and so on. What were those assumptions, and how well do they stand up to empirical scrutiny?

- Rationales for property tax exemption, income tax exemption, and income and estate tax deductibility. Controversy surrounds each of these tax treatments; each has been subject to some scholarly analysis; each could benefit from (and, in some cases, is receiving) further work.
- New areas of activity for nonprofits. What would happen if we tried to introduce the nonprofit sector to new fields of social importance—such as commuter railroads, liability insurance, the provision of alternative daily newspapers in monopoly towns?
- Hybrids. In much of what we do, and certainly in this chapter, one falls into the easy habit of treating the "sectors" as three watertight categories. That, of course, is not the case; most organizations one encounters in the real world are somewhat hybridized, by reason of support, regulation, governance, or joint-venturing activity. But some are more explicitly hybrids than others—the Smithsonian, for example, or some state universities. The hybrid provides yet another window through which to look at the question: what difference does organizational form make?

Once there was on my wish list another item: the development of an overarching theory of the nonprofit or independent sector—the fully integrative rationale that embraces all the others. I was told that if Josef Schumpeter were alive today, he could have produced it. We have not found Schumpeter's replacement, and, if we did, it is not clear to me that he or she could come up with an overarching theory that could explain a group of organizations as diverse, in so many ways, as the nonprofit population. In any event, has anyone ever come up with a Big Explanatory Theory that does the whole job? Can we really pay such a tribute to Freud, Keynes, Marx, Toynbee, Einstein—or (dare I say it?) the major prophets?

We shall have to settle for less apocalyptic scholarship. As the foregoing agenda lists should demonstrate, there is plenty of this work to do. The nonprofit research enterprise is still in its early days; many opportunities and challenges lie ahead. Our situation evokes the words of Winston Churchill in a very different context. Speaking in 1942 in the House of Commons after the successful outcome of the Battle of Egypt, Churchill said, "This is not the end. It is not even the beginning of the end. It is perhaps the end of the beginning."

Notes

1.   The emergence of several centers is fairly new: in the early years of the Yale program, despite its rather modest size, it was the only multidisciplinary center with the capacity to sponsor a number of research projects in the nonprofit field. Indeed, concern about this status was one factor that led us to be far less rigorous in our own agenda setting than some of our advisers would have preferred. We cast a very wide net, partly in order to enlist scholarly interest and energy across a wide spectrum, but partly also because we did not wish our own agenda decisions—which could have been viewed as approaching "monopoly power"—to have a constraining or excluding effect on research initiatives.

2.   I am indebted to Bradford Gray for this point, although he is not to be held responsible for the way I have expressed it.

References

Brewster, K. "Address to Yale Alumni Fund dinner." New Haven, Conn.: *Yale Alumni Magazine,* 1965, *28,* 10–11.

Brewster, K., Lindblom, C. E., and Simon, J. G. "Proposal for a Study of Independent Institutions." Unpublished memorandum, Oct. 1975, p. 12.

Simon, J. G. *Research on Philanthropy.* Washington, D.C.: INDEPENDENT SECTOR, July 1980, pp. 5, 6, 8, 9, 10.

Simon, J. G. "Thoughts on Some 'Cross-Country Themes.' " Unpublished memorandum, June 11, 1981.

30

RICHARD W. LYMAN
VIRGINIA A. HODGKINSON

△ △ △ △ △ △ △ △ △ △ △ △ △ △ △

Meeting the Challenges
of the Future

This book represents a work in progress. As John Simon notes in Chapter 29, serious research on the nonprofit sector is still in its early stages, having thus far achieved no more than "the end of the beginning." Given that fact, what is the point of urging practitioners of the sector to pay attention to this volume? What benefits does it offer to the volunteer leaders, managers, professionals, and other staff members, as well as the policy makers, who confront daily many of the problems and challenges discussed by our contributors? Is it not premature to offer the lessons of research, let alone a blueprint for action?

It would indeed be premature to do this if one could reasonably expect that the world would stand still and wait for the production of such research. But as practitioners know only too well, the world reels on regardless, and in our own institutional self-interest we must do the best we can to keep up with the trends, favorable and unfavorable, and do what we can to influence the crucial decisions that will be made and thereby determine the fate of our enterprise.

Nonprofit organizations receive tax-exempt status because their purpose is seen as serving the public. To sustain that purpose must be the primary responsibility of boards of trustees and staff leadership, although many of the contributors to this volume have noted signs of wavering from public purposes. There is the trend toward commercialization, often by undertaking revenue-producing activities without paying enough attention to whether these activities are really related to the mission of the organization. There is also a move, understandable to be sure, toward services rendered, and there are flirtations with unrelated business ventures that result in blurring the distinction between nonprofit and for-profit.

This last issue is a serious one for colleges and universities engaged in research that is contracted by corporations: how do they preserve their mission, which includes the free exchange and dissemination of research? The issue is also challenging for social service agencies that charge fees for services that could exclude clients unable to pay. Focusing on "products" as a way to derive additional revenue can also divert organizations from their basic mission.

Another major issue that will be under increasing scrutiny is fund-raising and marketing schemes of nonprofits. Organizations that engage in sweepstakes fund raising or hard-paced commercial marketing will come under increasing scrutiny especially when a substantial proportion of the public contributions garnered from these campaigns is used to cover the costs of fund raising, not to fund the programs for which the contributions were solicited.

The nonprofit sector cannot succeed by trying to exclude the for-profit sector from activities once dominated by the nonprofits. There are and will remain areas in which both are active—hospitals are an obvious example. When this is the case, nonprofits must remain alert to the need for distinctiveness in what they offer. They need to be able to demonstrate that they serve identifiable public purposes not fully served by their for-profit neighbors in the field. Attention to community needs, such as public education about measures that individuals can take to stay healthy, is imperative for nonprofits.

It is important for nonprofits to be clear in their mission and steadfast in their public purpose because the threat to the sector and its organizations from government regulation is ever-present and probably growing. This is the case because of a central dilemma of the philanthropic world: accountability. Everyone agrees that nonprofits must be accountable in some manner to somebody. They are run by human beings, creatures whose fallibility can be assumed, and so they can be run in unethical ways, turned to the self-aggrandizement of their boards or staffs rather than to the public will. Governments exist to protect their citizens, not only from other governments but also from one another and one another's organizations. When nonprofit organizations appear to be a menace to the safety or peace of mind of their employees, their clients, or the general public, we can expect governments to be tempted to intervene and try to alter that behavior.

When they intervene, governments not surprisingly tend to try to shape the regulated institutions in their image of accountability, such as uniform bureaucratic practice or periodic reporting to democratically elected legislative bodies. Thus, the more the third sector is regulated the less it will appear (and *be)* distinct from government. Carried far enough, the process could bring nonprofits in the United States to something not unlike the Norwegian predicament described by Gjems-Onstad (1988), who portrays the nonprofit sector in Norway as overtaxed, overregulated, and judged more than anything else on its "willingness to cooperate with governmental agencies and adjust to governmental plans" (p. 584). This, quite aside from the individual concerns of institutions or groups of institutions about the harm that regulation might do them, is the overriding reason to fear and distrust governmental intervention in nonprofit affairs.

So what can we nonprofits do to be more accountable? We can strive to be virtuous, so as to minimize the number and seriousness of the excuses we give government to move in on us. As has already been suggested, human beings have but limited capacity to accomplish this in a sustained way. We must nevertheless try, and we shall do better if we get informed guidance as to our moral and ethical dilemmas and our responsibilities from the work of scholars who know how to probe such matters, as our friend, colleague, mentor, and benign critic, Bob Payton, from time to time reminds us (Payton, 1988). We can strive to report honestly and accurately about the finances, missions, and outcomes of our organizations. This is our minimum public obligation, because we are given public trust and thus must demonstrate that we are accountable to that trust. This means that 990 tax forms should be filled out accurately because the public has a right to request them. It also means that our organizations should have regular external audits and public annual or biennial reports and we should provide contributors with accurate reports on the finances and use of those finances to achieve our missions. Lack of attention to our public trust will only lead to more governmental scrutiny.

We can learn more about ourselves and government so that we are better able to distinguish real threats from imaginary ones, better able to distinguish our vital interests from our lesser ones, and more skilled at dealing with government at all levels.

But more importantly, we can follow the superb advice so eloquently offered by David Mathews (1987) to recognize and be unafraid of the "essentially political—and politically essential" (p. 61) nature of our work. It is not as if we were no longer needed by a society whose infrastructure is deteriorating, whose sense of community is repeatedly shown to be deficient, whose propensity for seeking satisfaction through the mindless accumulation of material comforts shows no signs of slackening—and whose dissatisfaction with all of these conditions is grimly reflected in its retreat into drug-assisted fantasy that threatens to become a rout.

In the face of such conditions, the "blurring" that so many observers see as characterizing the relations among the sectors may even have its advantages; at least it suggests that we are not on the way to becoming irrelevant. As Harlan Cleveland has suggested, "the blur is where the action is" (Evangelaus, 1987, p. 6). Rather than allowing ourselves to become obsessed with the fear that doom is just around the corner every time one sector manages to steal a little turf from another, we should keep our focus on the overriding considerations of how best to serve a society that needs us as much as, if not more than, ever.

This view is all well and good, but how can practitioners defend themselves against attempts, however misguided, to subsume under government what they do?

We cannot wait for the research on the sector to mature before undertaking the most vigorous efforts at public education. People need to know about the history of philanthropy in this country and its relation to our democracy because there is the ever-present danger of the public taking for granted what is in fact a quite distinct American contribution to the pursuit of the public interest through private sources. It is not that other countries do not have a philanthropic tradition or activity, but rather that such a tradition is more firmly established here and such activity is far more significant in governing our lives and our way of providing for society's needs than elsewhere in the world. Perhaps ironically, while Americans remain ignorant of their own tradition, people in other countries are starting to look with fresh interest at how philanthropy has developed in America. They see it offering constructive alternatives to the provision by centralized government of all kinds of public goods, from cultural events to relief of poverty.

We need to strongly support the traditions of voluntary association and giving not simply because they are important to those who work in nonprofit institutions or because government will harm us if it does not understand our contributions to the public good, but because this sector is responsible for *creating* the public, as David Mathews (1987) has shown. Practitioners, of all people, should know about the tradition they represent, and leaders of nonprofit organizations need to make it possible for staff and volunteers to learn about the tradition as well. Practitioners can also assist the sector by supporting the education of the public through civics and social studies courses throughout the school systems. The lack of attention to the sector, including the role of advocacy groups, in school and college textbooks shows the need and the challenge. The organization INDEPENDENT SECTOR has begun to tackle this problem by organizing meetings with textbook publishers. We can join forces with groups that are working to restore the study of history to the high school curriculum and insure that the history that is taught recognizes the role of the nonprofit sector. A public informed on these matters is far less likely to turn a blind eye and a deaf ear when the threat of government regulation arises.

The textbook effort is but one instance of INDEPEN-
DENT SECTOR's work to expand awareness of philanthropy's
role in society and recognition of its importance to the management of the public's business. The goal of these efforts is for
the sector to emerge from the present sorry situation in which,
each time there is some crisis involving the welfare or even survival of nonprofits, we have to mount a crash program in public
and Congressional education at all levels while simultaneously
lobbying on whatever particular points happen to be at issue.
Thus, for example, the battle in recent years to keep the Office
of Management and Budget or the Internal Revenue Service
(or both) from whittling away the First Amendment rights of
nonprofit organizations by tinkering with the rules that limit
lobbying had to be fought on two fronts: by lobbying directly
against the specific provisions proposed, and, more importantly,
by educating people as to the long, honorable, and, indeed,
essential part played by advocacy groups outside government
throughout our history. The connections between philanthropy,
in the sense of relieving suffering, and philanthropic advocacy
needed to be pointed out, since people are unaccustomed to
thinking of them in the same context.

Of course we are being optimistic when we assume that
the more the public knows about philanthropy the more supportive it will be. That this is INDEPENDENT SECTOR's
view is appropriate, because this is and has been an optimistic
organization from the very beginning. It was optimistic to imagine that we could bring together under one roof the enormous
diversity, even the mutual antagonisms, of the not-for-profit
world, and not have carnage be the principal outcome. And
when one thinks about the assumption that if only the sector
can become better known it will be safer from harm, let alone
destruction, one can scarcely doubt that optimism prevails.
Granted, it is not a particularly rare human trait to think that
if only people really understood us they would love us, but we
do know that even paranoids have real enemies and that mar-
tyrdom has been an occupational hazard among saints—not
because their saintliness was unrecognized, but because it was
understood and found to be intolerable. On a more mundane

level, it was once again demonstrated as recently as Judge Robert Bork's experience in Congress that sometimes the better someone's position is understood the more it is disliked.

Signs of negative outcomes from learning about the sector have been spotted here and there in the chapters included in this volume. For example, several writers note the fact that nonprofit organizations, even in the field of human services, pay only limited attention to the poor. Some conclude from this—mistakenly, in the authors' view—that the sector has been false to its principles, or at least (and this is more defensible) that the sector is not in reality the lineal descendant of nineteenth-century charities aimed entirely at bettering the circumstances of those in poverty, which is what many members of the public think it is.

Henry Hansmann's brilliant chapter, "The Two Nonprofit Sectors" (it is brilliant whether or not one agrees with it), puts another aspect of the matter starkly. Research can solidify the sector by discovering commonalities, but it can also exert pressure in the opposite direction by analyzing fissures and lines of differentiation within the sector. Hansmann's delineation of the two sectors is a centrifugal force. In the end he speculates as to whether it might not "be in the interest of the first nonprofit sector—the philanthropic nonprofits—to protect itself by, as it were, throwing the second nonprofit sector [the commercial nonprofits] to the wolves." He continues, "More particularly, the traditional philanthropies may wish to lobby for the establishment of a clear line between those nonprofits that will continue to benefit from special preferences, such as tax exemption, and those that will not and to place the commercial nonprofit sector on the far side of the line. The alternative could be that preferences will ultimately be lost for *all* nonprofits, including the philanthropic ones."

Practitioners engaged in hand-to-hand combat with ignorance, poverty, and disadvantage may have little patience for such suggestions. Yet this would be shortsighted, because the survival of philanthropy depends on unending vigilance and tireless work toward self-definition. The problems to which Hansmann calls our attention are real and will not disappear by wishing them away; furthermore, opting for ignorance rather than running the risk of unpleasant discoveries is not a real possibility for scholars, however much particular institutions in the third sector may yearn for the good old days when fewer investigators were snooping into their affairs.

On balance, improving our knowledge (and eventually the public's knowledge) of the sector is in our own interest. As long as we are unknown, we run the risk of being hurt or even destroyed unintentionally by government policies and actions. One after another, friendly members of Congress urge us to tell our story on the Hill more often and more effectively. If we fail to respond they are likely to become less friendly—and fewer. We are gradually learning the value of sustained contacts with members of Congress and their staffs, rather than relying on our past strategy of periodic wild dashes to Capitol Hill when our ox is in imminent danger of being gored.

Because research on this sector has been neglected, practitioners hold most of the accumulated knowledge about the history, management, financing, and practice of their institutions and organizations. Practitioners must make an effort to communicate with researchers, and scholars must give more attention to collecting information from practitioners. There is a need to test theory against practice and to develop better definitions and descriptions of the work we do and the causes we serve.

Practitioners are a key resource for promoting the understanding of philanthropy for another reason: they are bound to see the problems confronting the whole sector, because they are not tied to particular academic disciplines or specialties. In academia we extol the virtues of interdisciplinary study because the world we study stubbornly refuses to be compartmentalized. Its problems arrive in forms that are unrecognizable to particular disciplines and, a fortiori, not resolvable by any single discipline. So we all pay homage to the virtues and indeed the necessity of interdisciplinary approaches.

We pay homage, but often that is about all that we do. There are good reasons for this. The forward march of specialization is not the product of wrongheadedness. There is a basic dilemma here. The very complexity that causes us to despair of the specialist's ability ever to command all the significant aspects of a problem is what gives rise to specialization in the first place. Consider the following brief catalogue offered a year ago by a distinguished scholar and a contributor to this volume, Julian Wolpert (1987, p. 8): "I would maintain that our knowledge about philanthropy is so meager because: donative behavior does indeed include a very diverse set of heterogenous contexts; our social science notions of the 'rational actor' are insufficient to capture the diverse motivations for giving; the marketplace of donors and recipients has not been well specified; the issues have been studied at too high a level of aggregation; and the data for rigorous behavioral analysis of individual and organizational giving are woefully inadequate." It is not difficult to see in that quotation suggestions for many useful specialized monographs—not because Wolpert is incapable of thinking broadly (his work, including the chapter prepared for this volume, gives the lie to any such suspicion), but because he knows the difficulties of making bricks without straw. The third sector still needs to produce a lot of straw for its brickyard: we need the "data for rigorous behavioral analysis" not only of "donative behavior" but also of many other little-understood aspects of the nonprofit world.

Practitioners need to participate in this process; they need to help formulate the questions that researchers ask and explore the implications of the research results for public policy, management, and practice. They bring first-hand experience and a lively concern for the welfare of their organizations and programs. One cannot read the chapters that precede this without recognizing the reciprocal needs of researchers and practitioners: each bring to the table qualities and capacities needed by the other.

It is not the purpose of this volume to write "finis" to any aspect of the great subject that our authors are studying. Nor do we pretend that practitioners and scholars will see things in the same way or that they will necessarily reach similar conclusions on the basis of what they learn about the sector, whether by research in the commonly accepted sense of the word or by personal experience. We do see, and we have tried to argue, that philanthropy, broadly defined, is seriously at risk because of the prevailing ignorance, even among its practitioners, of its history and defining characteristics. We hope that this volume makes a start at combatting this shortfall in understanding, and that further research and writing, side by side with the devoted labors of those who work in the sector, will improve the situation significantly, perhaps even dramatically. There is a potential contribution here to the solution of global problems; as we have noted, the rest of the world is awakening to the accomplishments of the nonprofit sector in the United States even if those accomplishments are not always perceived at home.

References

Evangelaus, D. "Line Between Public and Private Institutions Is Blurring in Nations Throughout the World." *Wingspread Journal,* Sept. 1987, p. 6.

Gjems-Onstad, O. "The Role of Nonprofits in a Social-Democratic State: The Relationship Between the State and Private Organizations in Norway." In V. A. Hodgkinson, ed. *Working Papers for the 1988 Spring Research Forum.* Washington, D.C.: INDEPENDENT SECTOR, 1988.

Mathews, D. "Our Shared Life in All Its Forms." *Foundation News,* July–Aug. 1987.

Payton, R. L. *Philanthropy: Voluntary Action for the Public Good.* New York: American Council on Education/Macmillan, 1988.

Wolpert, J. "Philanthropy: A Research Agenda." In C. Clotfelter, ed. *Setting the Research Agenda in Philanthropy and Voluntarism.* Durham, N.C.: Center for the Study of Philanthropy and Voluntarism, Duke University, 1987.

Name Index

△ △ △ △ △ △ △ △ △ △ △ △ △ △ △

Subject Index

△ △ △ △ △ △ △ △ △ △ △ △ △ △ △

A

Abrams v. *United States,* and advocacy, 208, 216

Accountability: analysis of trends in, 75–88; under common law, 75–77; crisis in, 8–13; demands for, 27; developments in, 80–85; issues of, 85–88, 473–475; and state regulation, 78–80, 86; and tax laws, 77–78

Activities, concept of, 185. *See also* Commercial activity

Adoption, advocacy for, 211–212

Adoption Assistance and Child Welfare Act of 1980, 212, 215

Adult day health care, loans for, 290, 291–292

Advisory Council on Intergovernmental Relations (ACIR), 391*n,* 400

Advisory Group on Exempt Organizations, 84

Advocacy: aspects of, 203–218; and child abuse and adoption assistance, 210–212; for children, 207–209; conclusion on, 214–216; function of, 10–11, 12, 17, 201–202, 477; and litigation, 207; and monitoring enforcement, 205–206; and moral issues, 269; organizations for, 212–214; and philanthropy for poverty, 228–229, 231; regulating, 29; and research groups, 66; service related to, 203–207

Africa, famine relief in, 248–258

Aggregation rules, and subsidiary corporations, 177–178, 179

Aid to Families with Dependent Children (AFDC): and community generosity, 388–391, 393, 394, 396, 400; and poverty, 221; and welfare state, 49

AIDS phenomenon, and research agenda, 469

Akron, Ohio, community generosity in, 388

Alabama, community generosity in, 387, 388, 395, 397

Albany, New York, community generosity in, 388, 395, 397

Allentown, Pennsylvania, community generosity in, 388, 395

Allied Stores, and sale-leaseback, 159

Altruism: and community generosity, 381; as donor motive, 229–230, 233; and self-interest, 272; of volunteers, 411

American Academy of Pediatricians, 210

American Association of Fund-Raising Counsel, 233, 353–354, 362, 425, 428

American Bar Association, 211

American Civil Liberties Union, 207

American Council on Education, 131, 132, 138

American Enterprise Institute, 69, 424

American Express Corporation, cause-related marketing by, 363, 365, 367, 370–371

American Hospital Association, 92, 101

American Humane Association, Children's Division of, 210